Bronisław Malinowski and His Legacy in Contemporary Social Sciences and Humanities

As one of the most renowned figures in the history of anthropology, Bronisław Malinowski is recognised as having been central to the development of the discipline, with interpretations of his thought usually drawing attention to his work in founding the approach of functionalism and his innovative method of intensive field research. This book offers a decisive extension of Malinowski's achievement, referring to the accomplishments of present-day social sciences and humanities and the debts that they owe to Malinowksi's oeuvre.

Bringing together eminent scholars in such fields as social anthropology, sociology, law, cultural studies, literary and theatre studies, and art history, this book emphasises the importance of Malinowski's theoretical and methodological insights as a treasure trove of inspiration for contemporary researchers.

A critical commentary on the life, work, and legacy of Bronisław Malinowski, it sheds light on his academic work, while personal documents, many of which are not well known – or are completely unknown – in the Anglophone sphere, prove their fundamental importance for understanding his oeuvre, and the intellectual connections between his work and the work of other most prominent intellectuals of the 20th and 21st centuries. It will therefore appeal to scholars across the social sciences and humanities with interests in the history of anthropology and sociology and fundamental questions of theory and research methodology.

Grażyna Kubica is Professor in Social Science at the Social Anthropology Section in the Institute of Sociology, Jagiellonian University, Kraków.

Dariusz Brzeziński is Assistant Professor at the Institute of Philosophy and Sociology at the Polish Academy of Sciences and Visiting Research Fellow at the School of Sociology and Social Policy at the University of Leeds.

Classical and Contemporary Social Theory
Series Editor
Stjepan G. Mestrovic, Texas A&M University, USA

Classical and Contemporary Social Theory publishes rigorous scholarly work that re-discovers the relevance of social theory for contemporary times, demonstrating the enduring importance of theory for modern social issues. The series covers social theory in a broad sense, inviting contributions on both 'classical' and modern theory, thus encompassing sociology, without being confined to a single discipline. As such, work from across the social sciences is welcome, provided that volumes address the social context of particular issues, subjects, or figures and offer new understandings of social reality and the contribution of a theorist or school to our understanding of it.

The series considers significant new appraisals of established thinkers or schools, comparative works or contributions that discuss a particular social issue or phenomenon in relation to the work of specific theorists or theoretical approaches. Contributions are welcome that assess broad strands of thought within certain schools or across the work of a number of thinkers, but always with an eye toward contributing to contemporary understandings of social issues and contexts.

Titles in this series

Norbert Elias and Sigmund Freud
The Psychoanalytic Foundations of the Civilizing Process
André Oliveira Costa

A Weberian Perspective on Home, Nature and Sport
Michael Symonds

Bronisław Malinowski and His Legacy in Contemporary Social Sciences and Humanities
Edited by Grażyna Kubica and Dariusz Brzeziński

For more information about this series, please visit:https://www.routledge.com/sociology/series/ASHSER1383

Bronisław Malinowski and His Legacy in Contemporary Social Sciences and Humanities

On the Centenary of *Argonauts of the Western Pacific*

Edited by
Grażyna Kubica and Dariusz Brzeziński

LONDON AND NEW YORK

First published 2024
by Routledge
4 Park Square, Milton Park, Abingdon, Oxon OX14 4RN

and by Routledge
605 Third Avenue, New York, NY 10158

Routledge is an imprint of the Taylor & Francis Group, an informa business

© 2024 selection and editorial matter, Grażyna Kubica and Dariusz Brzeziński; individual chapters, the contributors

The right of Grażyna Kubica and Dariusz Brzeziński to be identified as the authors of the editorial material, and of the authors for their individual chapters, has been asserted in accordance with sections 77 and 78 of the Copyright, Designs and Patents Act 1988.

All rights reserved. No part of this book may be reprinted or reproduced or utilised in any form or by any electronic, mechanical, or other means, now known or hereafter invented, including photocopying and recording, or in any information storage or retrieval system, without permission in writing from the publishers.

Trademark notice: Product or corporate names may be trademarks or registered trademarks, and are used only for identification and explanation without intent to infringe.

British Library Cataloguing-in-Publication Data
A catalogue record for this book is available from the British Library

ISBN: 9781032583655 (hbk)
ISBN: 9781032583686 (pbk)
ISBN: 9781003449768 (ebk)

DOI: 10.4324/9781003449768

Typeset in Times New Roman
by codeMantra

Contents

List of illustrations and their description	ix
Notes on contributors	xi
Acknowledgements	xvii

**Revisiting the Life and Work of Bronisław Malinowski:
On the Centenary of *Argonauts of the Western Pacific***   1
GRAŻYNA KUBICA AND DARIUSZ BRZEZIŃSKI

PART I
Bronisław Malinowski: Known and Unknown   17

1 Bronisław Malinowski – The (Somewhat Anglicized and Cosmopolitan) Pole: Biographical-Anthropological Reflections on His Polish Identity   19
GRAŻYNA KUBICA

2 Our Ancestors: Making Sense of Bronisław Malinowski and Elsie Masson   47
PATRICK BURKE

PART II
Revisiting Malinowski's Intellectual Background   59

3 An Argonaut from Kraków: Pre-field Malinowski as a Theorist   61
PETR SKALNÍK

4 Bronisław Malinowski in the Laboratories of Leipzig 78
KRZYSZTOF ŁUKASIEWICZ

5 Malinowski: A Modernist in His Way 92
ADAM KUPER

PART III
Malinowski's Intellectual Relations: New Insights 105

6 'I Am Not Really a Real Character': Malinowski, Witkiewicz
and the Pitfalls of Making Oneself a 'Character' 107
NATALIJA JAKUBOVA

7 Malinowski and the Disciples of Freud: Otto Rank, Ernest
Jones and Wilhelm Reich 124
LENA MAGNONE

8 Under the Wing of the Rockefeller Foundation: On the
Cooperation of Bronisław Malinowski and His Polish
Student Józef Obrębski 140
ANNA ENGELKING

PART IV
Reconsiderations of Interpretive Frameworks 159

9 Bronisław Malinowski: An Icon of a Body-centric Anthropology? 161
ANDREAS LIPOWSKY

10 'The Gardens Are, in a Way, a Work of Art': Bronisław
Malinowski's Social Anthropology as Anthropology of Art 176
ANDRZEJ KISIELEWSKI

11 Exploring the Intersection of Law, Culture, and Biology:
Tensions and Unfulfilled Potential in Malinowski's Legal Thought 189
MATEUSZ STĘPIEŃ

PART V
Malinowski and Anthropology Today 201

12 *Gimwala* and *Kula*: Malinowski's Living Ethnography 203
   LINUS S. DIGIM'RINA

13 What If We Had Followed Malinowski Instead of Staying on
   the Trobriand Islands? Notes on the Anthropological Multiverse 213
   MARTA SONGIN-MOKRZAN

14 Bronisław Malinowski and the Anthropology of Nostalgia 233
   DARIUSZ BRZEZIŃSKI

   Afterword: Malinowski in Context 254
   ALEKSANDAR BOŠKOVIĆ

   Index *261*

Illustrations and their description

1	Portrait of Bronisław Malinowski for "Life Magazine" 1942 photographed by John Philips	x
2	Elsie and Bronisław Malinowski with their daughters: Józefa, Wanda and Helena in Oberbozen in 1926, photographed by Raymond Firth	17
3	Bronisław Malinowski photographed after his doctoral promotion at the Jagiellonian University in Kraków in 1908	59
4	Portrait of Bronisław Malinowski photographed by Stanisław Ignacy Witkiewicz in Zakopane in 1912	105
5	Bronisław Malinowski and a group of Trobrianders, 1916–1918	159
6	Bronisław Malinowski with the sons of the chief Toulouva, 1916–1918	201

We are grateful to Patrick Burke, on behalf of Malinowski's descendants, for permission to publish the photographs.

Illustration 1 Portrait of Bronisław Malinowski for "Life Magazine" 1942 photographed by John Philips.

Notes on contributors

Aleksandar Bošković is a social anthropologist currently working as Professor of Social Anthropology at UFRN, Natal (Brazil). He also taught at the University of St. Andrews (Scotland, UK), Faculty of Social Sciences (FDV), University of Ljubljana (Slovenia), Universidade de Brasília (Brazil), University of the Witwatersrand (Johannesburg), Rhodes University (Grahamstown, South Africa), and University of Belgrade. He is the author and editor of many books, including *William Robertson Smith* (2021), *Mesoamerican Religions and Archaeology: Essays in Pre-Columbian Civilizations* (2017), and *The Anthropological Field on the Margins of Europe* (2013, co-edited with Chris Hann).

Dariusz Brzeziński is Assistant Professor at the Institute of Philosophy and Sociology at the Polish Academy of Sciences (Department of Theoretical Sociology) and Visiting Research Fellow in the School of Sociology and Social Policy at the University of Leeds. He teaches sociology and socio-cultural anthropology at the Jagiellonian University in Kraków as well. His research focuses on contemporary social thought, sociology, anthropology, and the theory of culture. He is the author of *Zygmunt Bauman and the Theory of Culture* (2022) and the co-editor of *Revisiting Modernity and the Holocaust: Heritage, Dilemmas, Extensions* (2022). Dariusz Brzeziński wrote on many aspects of social theory and sociology of culture in such journals as *European Journal of Social Theory*, *Thesis Eleven*, *Studia Litteraria at Historica*, and many others.

Patrick Burke is one of ten grandchildren of Bronislaw Malinowski and Elsie Malinowska. He is Senior Lecturer in the School of Social Sciences at the University of Westminster. His main research interest is the West European peace movements of the 1980s. His most recent publication, 'British and international peace campaigning against the Strategic Defence Initiative', is published in Luc-Andre Brunet, (ed.), *NATO and the Strategic Defence Initiative: A Transatlantic History of the Star Wars Programme* (London and New York, Routledge, 2023).

Anna Engelking is a cultural anthropologist and Professor at the Institute of Slavic Studies of Polish Academy of Sciences in Warsaw. The main fields of her interest are anthropology and memory of Belarusian villages, and history of Polish ethnology. Since the early 1990s, she had conducted field research at the Belarusian-Lithuanian-Polish borderland, Polesia, and Eastern Belarus. She is the author of two monographs: *Kołchoźnicy. Antropologia tożsamości wsi białoruskiej przełomu XX i XXI wieku* (*Kolkhozniks: An Anthropological Study of the Identity of Belarusian Villagers at the turn of the 20th and 21st centuries*, 2012) and *Klątwa. Rzecz o ludowej magii słowa* (*The curse. On folk magic of the word*, 2000, 2nd revised ed. 2010), as well as a scientific editor of several works of an eminent, forgotten Polish anthropologist Józef Obrębski, who researched, i.e., Macedonia and Belarusian-Ukrainian Polesia. She edited and published several works of this scholar and his work, first of all two volumes of his collected writings published in a series 'Studia etnosocjologiczne' ('Ethnosociological Studies'): vol. 1 Polesie (2007) and vol. 2 Macedonia (2022). She is the author of several papers on Obrębski's research, works, and biography in Polish, Belarusian, Macedonian, and English. She is also an author and co-author of articles on several less-known and forgotten pre-WWII Polish and Jewish-Polish anthropologists.

Natalija Jakubova is a historian of literature and theatre. Since her postgraduate studies at the Russian Academy of Theatre Art, she concentrated on the Polish culture dedicating her thesis (1996) to the ambivalent relations between Stanisław Ignacy Witkiewicz and the legacy of "Young Poland" movement. Subsequently, she worked both on the history of Polish culture and on the contemporary Polish theatre. Numerous scholarships in Poland made her possible extensive library and archival research resulting in papers published in such journals as *Didaskalia, Dialog, Pamiętnik literacki* and later included in the book *O Witkacym* (*About Witkiewicz*) published in the series "Polish Studies Abroad" of the Institute of Literary Studies of the Polish Academy of Sciences (Warsaw, IBL: 2010). Affiliated at the same institute in the years 2013–2015, she conducted the gender-linked research on the biography of the actress Irena Solska that recently resulted in a highly acclaimed monograph.

Andrzej Kisielewski is Professor at the University of Bialystok. He is an art historian specialising in the art history of the 20th and 21st centuries, the theory and anthropology of art, as well as contemporary visual culture, member of Art Historians Association in Poland and Polish Association of Cultural Studies. He practised art criticism and essay writing devoted to contemporary art. He is the author of academic articles on contemporary art and modern visual culture. He is also the author of books (all in Polish language): *Karny* (1995), *Art and Advertising. Relations between Art and Culture* (1999), *Primitivism in the Avant-garde Art of the First Half of the 20th century. Mythologies and Images of Primordiality* (2011). He is the editor of the books: *Artists Play with Culture* (2009), *Art and Non-Art. Reflections on Artistic Culture, Popular Culture and Culture in the Broadest Sense. Bialystok Cultural University 2011–2014. Part I* (2015). He is the co-editor of the books: *Culture of Desires and Horizons of Neoliberalism* (together with Wojciech J. Burszta, 2015), *Myths, Legends and Histories. Bialystok Cultural University 2011–2014. Part II* (with Alicja

Kisielewska, 2016), and *The Future of Culture. From Diagnosis to Prognosis* (with Alicja Kisielewska and Monika Kostaszuk-Romanowska, 2017).

Grażyna Kubica is Professor in Social Science and works in the Social Anthropology Section at the Institute of Sociology, Jagiellonian University, Kraków. One of her research areas is the history of anthropology. She co-edited the volume *Malinowski – Between Two Worlds* (Cambridge University Press, 1988). She authored the introduction and annotations of the full version of Malinowski's diaries in their original language, *Dziennik w ścisłym znaczeniu tego wyrazu* (2002) and a spin-off in Polish: *Malinowski's Sisters. Or the Modern Women at the Beginning of the XX century* (2006, Narcyza Żmichowska Award). Kubica has recently published an anthropological biography of another Polish-British anthropologist: *Maria Czaplicka: Gender, Shamanism, Race* (Critical Studies in the History of Anthropology Series, University of Nebraska Press 2020; Kazimierz Dobrowolski Award, and Klio Award for a Polish version, 2015). At present, she is carrying out a project "'Written with the other hand' – literary ethnographic writing and its Polish specificity". Another research area is connected with her fieldwork, historical research, and autoethnography in Polish Teschen Silesia, her home region.

Adam Kuper was most recently Centennial Professor of Anthropology at the London School of Economics and Visiting Professor at Boston University. A Fellow of the British Academy and a recipient of the Huxley Medal of the Royal Anthropological Institute, Kuper has appeared many times on BBC TV and radio and has reviewed regularly for the *London Review of Books*, the *Times Literary Supplement*, and the *Wall Street Journal*. His new book, *The Museum of Other People: From Colonial Acquisition to Cosmopolitan Exhibition*, appeared in 2023.

linus s. digim'Rina is the Head of Anthropology, Sociology & Archaeology in the School of Humanities & Social Sciences, University of Papua New Guinea. His main research interests centre around Melanesian ethnography and development issues among communities. He has written extensively about Melanesian culture in journal articles (e.g. "Canberra Anthropology", "Anthropological Notebooks"), edited books, and reports. Lastly, he co-authored a research report "Dynamics of Informal Customary Land Transactions Between Landowners and Migrants at Taurama Valley, National Capital District" (2023).

Andreas Lipowsky is Magister Artium of "Cultural History and Theory" and Musicology (Humboldt-University of Berlin). After several years as a policy assistant to members of the Berlin House of Representatives and pressure groups in development politics, he joined a Graduate Research Training Group at the University of Konstanz funded by the German Federal Research Foundation (2017–2019). He has been a Visiting Scholar to the University of California, Berkeley (2019), the University of British Columbia (2019), and Cornell University (2021). In 2020, he joined the Leibniz-Zentrum für Literatur- und Kulturforschung, Berlin, as research assistant.

xiv *Notes on contributors*

Krzysztof Łukasiewicz is the Head of the Department of Theory and Critique of Culture, Institute of Cultural Studies, University of Wrocław; member of the Scientific Council of the Polish Society for Cultural Studies; associate of the Contemporary Humanities Laboratory; his main areas of interest are the history of thought about culture, especially at the turn of the 19th and 20th centuries, Lebensphilosophie as philosophy of culture, W. Ostwald's culturology and its reception, qualitative research on culture; an editor and author of many volumes of "Prace Kulturoznawcze"; his essay on the "Leipzig school" is in print – in Polish and English.

Lena Magnone, Ph.D. with habilitation, works at the Carl von Ossietzky University of Oldenburg in Germany. In the 2022/2023 academic year, she was a visiting scholar at the Sorbonne University in Paris, affiliated with the research group Eur'ORBEM – Cultures et sociétés d'Europe orientale, balkanique et médiane. Previously, she worked as assistant professor at the Institute of Polish Literature, University of Warsaw (2007–2020), visiting scholar (Fulbright fellow) at the Center for European and Mediterranean Studies, New York University (2019–2020), and visiting scholar (Humboldt fellow) at the Institute of Slavic Studies, Carl von Ossietzky University of Oldenburg. She is the author of, among others, two monographs: *Maria Konopnicka. Lustra i symptomy* [*Maria Konopnicka. Mirrors and Symptoms*] (słowo/obraz terytoria, Gdańsk, 2011) and *Emisariusze Freuda. Transfer kulturowy psychoanalizy do polskich sfer inteligenckich przed drugą wojną światową* [*Freud's emissaries. The Cultural Transfer of Psychoanalysis to the Polish intelligentsia before World War II*] (Universitas, Kraków 2016; English translation appeared in 2023 with Sdvig Press).

Petr Skalník is Emeritus Extraordinary Professor at the University of Wroclaw, Poland. Previously, he taught at Comenius University, Leiden University, University of Cape Town, Charles University, and the University of Pardubice. He has edited and co-edited over two dozen books over the course of his career, and is the 2006 recipient of the Chevalier dans l'Ordre des Palmes Académiques. From 1992 to 1997, he served as the Ambassador of Czechoslovakia/Czech Republic to Lebanon, and from 2003 to 2013, he was Vice-President of the International Union of Anthropological and Ethnological Sciences.

Marta Songin-Mokrzan is doctor of humanities in the field of ethnology and Assistant Professor in the Laboratory of Practical Anthropology at the Institute of Ethnology and Cultural Anthropology at the Faculty of Philosophy and History of the University of Lodz. Her research interests focus on anthropology of materiality, anthropology of technology, ethnography of production processes, philosophy, and ontology of machines. She is the author of the book entitled *Zwrot ku zaangażowaniu. Strategie konstruowania nowej tożsamości antropologii* (2014).

Mateusz Stępień is Professor of Sociology of Law in the Faculty of Law and Administration at the Jagiellonian University in Kraków, Poland. His research primarily centres on examining the cultural dimension of law. He has authored publications that delve into Bronislaw Malinowski's concept of law, the role of images in judicial opinions, and the concept of power distance within courtrooms. At present, he is actively engaged in research on the topic of judicial empathy and legislative placebo.

Acknowledgements

The chapters collected in this volume are based on the papers presented at the international conference The Legacy of Bronisław Malinowski in Present-Day Social Sciences and Humanities, which took place at the Jagiellonian University in Kraków, his alma mater on 26–27 September 2022. The aim of this event was to reflect on the significance of Bronisław Malinowski's work on the centenary of the publication of his *Argonauts of the Western Pacific*. The conference was attended by scholars from Austria, the Czech Republic, Germany, Italy, Mexico, Papua New Guinea, Poland, Serbia, the United Kingdom, and the United States. The participants represented an array of disciplines, such as sociology, cultural studies, socio-cultural anthropology, history, art history, law, political science, and theatre and literary studies. This multidisciplinarity was a major advantage of the event, which proved a welcoming platform for discussing Bronisław Malinowski's legacy from varied perspectives and theoretical contexts. All conference talks are available at https://www.youtube.com/playlist?list=PL1JoiRNL6NsrhA7IEiIljuKHXxznAi1Vx

As the editors of this collection, we would like to thank all those who supported the organisation of the conference. The event was funded by the Jagiellonian University's Institute of Sociology and the City of Kraków. Professor Jacek Popiel, Rector of the Jagiellonian University, was the Honorary Patron of the conference, and the list of patrons also includes the Polish Sociological Association, the Polish Association for Cultural Studies, the Polish Ethnological Association, and the City of Kraków. The scientific committee was formed by the editors of this volume and Maria Flis, Kaja Gadowska, Ewa Kopczyńska, Marcin Lubaś, Jacek Nowak, Krystyna Romaniszyn, Agata Dziuban, and Agnieszka Trąbka. The organising committee of the conference comprised the editors of this volume and Karol Piotrowski.

We are grateful to Neil Jordan, Gemma Rogers and Helena Parkinson from Routledge for their guidance and cooperation.

Last, but not least, Grażyna Kubica would like to thank her family for their patience, and Dariusz Brzeziński would like to thank his wife Karolina for her love and unfailing support.

Editors' Note

All references to *Argonauts of the Western Pacific* in this volume are to its first edition of 1922: Bronisław Malinowski, *Argonauts of the Western Pacific: An Account of Native Enterprise and Adventure in the Archipelagoes of Melanesian New Guinea* (Routledge: London and Kegan Paul LTD, 1922).

Revisiting the Life and Work of Bronisław Malinowski

On the Centenary of *Argonauts of the Western Pacific*

Grażyna Kubica and Dariusz Brzeziński

Introduction

Bronisław Malinowski (1884–1942) was one of the most renowned anthropologists in the history of the discipline. With his achievements in both methodology and theory, his work has exerted a powerful influence on the development of sociocultural anthropology, and his publications have remained a valid point of reference for its practitioners to this day (e.g. Firth 1957; Kuper 1973, 2015; Clifford 1988; Ellen et al. 1988; Geertz 1988; Kuklick 1991, 2008; Stocking 1992, 1995; Gellner 1998; Eriksen and Nielsen 2001; Deliege 2006; Mills 2008; Tauber, Zinn 2023). Due to the interdisciplinary nature of Malinowski's pursuits, an outcome both of his education and of his functionalist orientation, his research and ideas have also made an impact on other disciplines, particularly on sociology, cultural studies and linguistics (e.g. Sztompka 1988; Senft 2007; Bartmański 2012; Senis 2023).

The knowledge of Malinowski's field research in the Trobriand Islands has become an entrenched part of the canon of the social sciences and the humanities. His major monographs were *Argonauts of the Western Pacific: An Account of Native Enterprise and Adventure in the Archipelagoes of Melanesian New Guinea* (1922), *The Sexual Life of Savages in North-Western Melanesia* (1929) and the two volumes of *Coral Gardens and Their Magic: A Study of the Methods of Tilling the Soil and of Agricultural Rites in the Trobriand Islands* (1935). Malinowski also conducted field research in Central Africa and Mexico, and he wrote extensively on the societies living in these parts of the world (e.g. Malinowski 1945; Malinowski and de la Fuente 1982). His other notable research interests encompassed theory of culture, applied anthropology and the relationship between freedom and civilization (Malinowski 1944a).

Malinowski also wrote an intimate diary, which was posthumously published as *A Diary in the Strict Sense of the Term* (translated into English by Norbert Guterman in 1967), which, partly because of the controversy that it aroused, has become one of the most famous works in the history of anthropology. The controversial issues with which some of Malinowski's statements can be associated, such as colonialism, indirect rule, racism and ethnocentrism, need to be historically and discursively contextualized today (as has been done, for example, by Wax 1972; James 1973; Rapport 1990; Foks 2018; Weston and Djohari 2020; Kubica 2024b),

DOI: 10.4324/9781003449768-1

as Malinowski was not only an anthropological visionary but also a man of his times. Notwithstanding, he may be an example of processes and phenomena that are to be noticed and analysed only today (like reflexivity, internal conversation, or identity migration, as analysed by Kubica in this volume). The first part of his life is masterfully recounted in Michael W. Young's literary biography, *Malinowski: Odyssey of an Anthropologist, 1884–1920* (2004).

Our volume brings together articles that analyse the life and work of Malinowski in the light of recent developments in the social sciences and the humanities. The production of this book was prompted by the centenary of the publication of his most famous work, *Argonauts of the Western Pacific* (Malinowski 1922). Accordingly, the first part of this introduction discusses the unique significance of this book. The following part sketches a timeline of the most important events in Malinowski's life. The subsequent two sections correspond to the two main objectives of this volume. One of those is to present the latest findings on Malinowski's life, including his relationship with his homeland and with his immediate family, his intellectual background and his intellectual exchanges. The other objective is to revise the interpretive framework of his work and to reconsider it from the perspective of the contemporary social sciences and humanities. Crucially, given the extraordinary breadth of Malinowski's research, the contributions to this volume were penned by intellectuals from various academic disciplines. This, we hope, will help our book better showcase the richness, importance and relevance of Malinowski's work.

The Significance of *Argonauts of the Western Pacific*

Argonauts of the Western Pacific was the first report on field research in the Trobriand Islands, during which the most important assumptions of Malinowski's ethnography were formulated and tested, and that got unwavering interest among anthropologists, and not only them. In his famous introduction to the book, Malinowski stated that the goal of field research was to capture the 'body and blood,' that is, the everyday life and ordinary behaviour of the studied community; the 'skeleton,' that is, a clear image of the tribal structure and permanent cultural elements; and, finally, the 'spirit,' that is, indigenous views, opinions and emotional reactions (Malinowski 1922: 18, 22). According to Malinowski, this combination would make it possible to obtain a complete and accurate picture of the indigenous culture, to grasp the 'native's point of view' and the 'native's attitude to life' and, in a way, to understand the indigenous view of the world.

Besides, *Argonauts* also contains still valid instructions on conducting intensive field research. The most important directives are very simple: live among the subjects of research long enough, learn their language and establish close relationships with them. Some other suggestions, dispersed in the book, are as follows: if the researcher lives among the natives and speaks their language, he (or she) should also try to share and understand their feelings; facts should be described, and speculative or hypothetical views should be avoided; the researcher should know in advance the basic rules of what he or she intends to observe; material culture is of interest to the researcher not for its own sake but because of its sociological aspect and the natives' emotional attitudes to it; the natives' statements should be tested against the researcher's own observations; and, the researcher should first analyse detailed data and then step away from particulars and take stock of the entire institution under study.

In *Argonauts*, the figure of the (capitalized) Ethnographer is evoked in such an emphatic way for the first time in the history of ethnographic writing. As a cultural concept, the Ethnographer is quite clearly defined: he is a representative of Science as a supranational entity, guided by its own principles. In *Argonauts*, the figure of the Ethnographer develops in a processual manner. In the first chapter, he is a beginner researcher who has trouble establishing contact with the natives but is also filled with deep interest and expectation when he enters the field. The 'Ethnographer's magic' is revealed when he is alone with the natives; he uses scientific methods of fieldwork, does not yield to popular opinions and makes an intellectual effort to fathom the motives behind the common views. The Ethnographer took part in the everyday life of the community he studied, but he looked at it as an outsider and insisted that only he, as the Ethnographer, could explain the entire system of connections between the various institutions of the Trobriand Islands. Direct participants could only see a fragment of that system.

The multiplicity of narrative methods employed in *Argonauts* is an interesting facet of the book that has considerably contributed to its ultimate success. At the core of the book is, of course, scientific ethnographic description, with its balanced and neutral style and a rather inconspicuous narrator. Intertwined with this matter-of-fact depiction, there is Malinowski's trademark narrative, which might be called a 'reportage' style. It is very characteristic and involves providing dates of the reported event, their places and portrayals of the individuals who took part in them and are identified by their names. Besides, landscapes are vividly pictured, including their colours, smells and even flavours, and vignettes of Trobriand art are drawn, which Andrzej Kisielewski interprets in this volume as exemplifications of ekphrasis. The figure of the narrator eloquently surfaces throughout *Argonauts* and often appeals to the readers' imagination. The combination of different types of narratives made Malinowski's writing unique and expressive (see Kubica 2024b). He was apparently aware of the significance of mixing styles of narration, noting that: 'The balance between dramatic presentation on the one hand, and scientific detachment, precision, and accuracy on the other, is a very fine one' (Malinowski 1932: XXVIII).

Malinowski's greatness in *Argonauts* is primarily based on his ethnographic craft. This was aptly assessed by Annette Weiner, an American anthropologist who, like Malinowski, carried out her fieldwork on the island of Kiriwina, half a century later, though. Writing about her famous predecessor, Weiner concluded:

> Yet, despite all the disclaimers, his Trobriand ethnography continues to enthrall each generation of anthropologists through its intensity, rich detail, and penetrating revelations. The distinctive quality and tone of Malinowski's ethnographic writing remain potent, emphatically and personally instructing

the reader how to enter into the lives of Trobrianders, cautioning them to beware of ethnocentric conclusions, and explaining how seemingly strange behaviors have pragmatic functions and must be understood on their own terms.

(1987: xiv–xv)

The success of *Argonauts* can also be measured by the number of its English editions, of which there have been more than a dozen. The book has been translated into many languages as well: German and French in 1963, Polish and Japanese in 1967, Portuguese in 1976, Italian in 1978, Croatian in 1979, Spanish in 1986, Russian in 2004 and Slovenian and Turkish in 2018 (some of these translations have had several editions; for example, the Polish one has had four). Seeing this, as the editors of this volume, we believe that the hundredth anniversary of the first publication of *Argonauts of the Western Pacific* marks an excellent occasion to reflect once again on Bronisław Malinowski's place in the contemporary social sciences and humanities.

Biographical Highlights

Bronisław Malinowski's life was multifarious, as befits an anthropologist. He was born on 7 April 1884 in Krakow, a former Polish capital, which was then part of Galicia, the Austro-Hungarian portion of partitioned Poland. His father, Lucjan Malinowski, who was a linguist, dialectologist and professor at the Jagiellonian University, the oldest university in this part of Europe, died when Bronisław was 14 years old. His mother, Józefa née Łącka, a cultivated woman of outstanding intelligence, played a great role in the education of her talented but very sickly son. Bronisław (called Bronio by his family and friends) studied at a classical gymnasium, a secondary school that offered general education, including Latin and Greek. His poor health often forced him to interrupt his studies, and he would take his exams as an external student. To improve his health, his mother arranged for them to spend long stints in southern Europe and North Africa (Kubica 2024a).

After graduating from his gymnasium, Malinowski began his studies at the Jagiellonian University. There were the Faculties of Law, Medicine, Theology and Philosophy at that time. The system of studies consisted in enrolling at a faculty and signing up for courses offered. Studying at the Faculty of Philosophy was to prepare future gymnasium teachers, and one could focus on mathematics, sciences, philosophy, history, languages, literature, etc. Malinowski enrolled at this faculty and chose courses in science (physics and chemistry), mathematics and philosophy. In 1906, he submitted his doctoral thesis *O zasadzie ekonomii myślenia* [On the Principle of the Economy of Thought], which is an analysis of the concepts of Ernst Mach and Richard Avenarius (Eng. transl. Malinowski 1993).[1] This work is discussed by Petr Skalník in this volume and referenced in the chapters by Adam Kuper, Krzysztof Łukasiewicz and Mateusz Stępień. Then, accompanied by his mother, Malinowski went to the Canary Islands for climatic treatment, where he began writing his diary, a practice he continued with some interruptions for the following ten years, until 1918 (Malinowski 2002). After his return to Krakow in 1908, he had a promotion *Sub auspiciis Imperatoris* [Under the auspices of the Emperor], which was a great distinction for the recipient (Kubica 1988).

Later, as customary at the time, he went abroad to hone his knowledge and skills at the University of Leipzig. He worked at laboratories and attended lectures given by outstanding local academics, like Wilhelm Wundt. In his contribution to this volume, Krzysztof Łukasiewicz discusses the importance of Malinowski's period at Leipzig for his future career. As a matter of fact, Malinowski's scientific interests underwent a fundamental change there. He abandoned science and went to the London School of Economics in 1910 to study ethnology under Charles Seligman, who would become his academic advisor, and sociology under Edward Westermarck.

Malinowski spent the year 1912 in Zakopane, a famous Polish health resort in the Tatra Mountains. He worked on his own and was in close touch with his youth friend Stanisław Ignacy Witkiewicz, a painter and writer. Natalija Jakubova explores the intellectual significance of this friendship and its effects in her chapter in this volume. At the time, Malinowski experienced his first encounter with psychoanalysis, which is discussed here in Lena Magnone's chapter. He also wrote an essay on Friedrich Nietzsche's *The Birth of Tragedy*, addressed in this volume in some detail by Andreas Lipowsky. Besides, Malinowski gave two talks at Krakow's Academy of Arts and Sciences and wrote *Wierzenia pierwotne i formy ustroju społecznego* [Primitive Beliefs and Forms of the Social System], a critical discussion of James George Frazer's *Totemism and Exogamy*. This study was to have been Malinowski's *habilitation* book.[2] Skalník analyses this work in this volume.

Having returned to London in 1913, Malinowski lectured at the LSE and worked on his following book, *The Family among the Australian Aborigines*. In 1914, he received a scholarship from industrialist Robert Mond to go and do research in the field. He was accompanied by Witkiewicz as a photographer and an illustrator of the expedition. When they were already in Australia, upon learning of the outbreak of World War I, Witkiewicz turned back to join the Russian Army, an episode discussed in Jakubova's chapter. Malinowski continued the journey alone. From September 1914 to March 1915, he conducted fieldwork on the island of Mailu, off the southern coast of New Guinea. Later, in Australia, he drew up the report, *The Natives of Mailu: Preliminary Results of the Robert Mond Research Work in British New Guinea* (1915). This work, together with *The Family among the Australian Aborigines*, earned him a D.Sc. degree in London (1916).

Malinowski undertook another field expedition in June 1915, heading to the Trobriand Islands, located north of the southern tip of New Guinea. He settled in the village of Omarakana, on Kiriwina Island, the largest island of the archipelago. He stayed there until May 1916. His second trip to the Trobriands spanned one year, from October 1917 to October 1918. Dariusz Brzeziński demonstrates in his chapter, Malinowski believed that the cultural reality he was researching would soon cease to exist as a result of dynamic civilizational changes. linus s. digim'Rina's chapter belies Malinowski's fears to a degree by analysing the continuity of the most important institutions he studied and their validity in the Trobriand Islands today. Importantly, between his expeditions and after their completion, Malinowski worked on his field materials while living in Melbourne.

In 1919, Malinowski married Elsie R. Masson, a writer and nurse, whose father was a professor of chemistry at the University of Melbourne. The Malinowskis had three daughters: Józefa, Wanda and Helena. Elsie was her husband's collaborator and the first critical reader, lector and editor of his texts. Their correspondence was published as *A Story of a Marriage* in 1995, a book edited by their youngest daughter, Helena Wayne. The memory of the Malinowskis among their daughters' children is examined in a chapter by Patrick Burke in this volume.

In 1920, Malinowski and his wife came back to Europe and settled in the Canary Islands, where he worked on his field materials and wrote his first monograph, *Argonauts of the Western Pacific*, which was published in 1922. At that time, Malinowski also returned to the London School of Economics. He applied for a position at the Jagiellonian University, but he ultimately did not accept the University's offer, which Grażyna Kubica discusses in her chapter. In 1924, Malinowski became a reader in anthropology, and in 1927, he was promoted to professorship and received the chair of social anthropology at the LSE. His subsequent books were based on the Trobriand field materials: *Crime and Custom in Savage Society* (1926), *Sex and Repression in Savage Society* (1927), *The Sexual Life of Savages in North-Western Melanesia* (1929) and finally the two-volume *Coral Gardens and their Magic* (1935).

Malinowski's famous seminar at the London School of Economics attracted large and diverse audiences (including numerous women and foreigners). Among his listeners were some later luminaries of anthropology (e.g. Raymond Firth, Audrey Richards and Edmund Leach) and politics (e.g. Jomo Kenyatta, a future leader and president of Kenya). A large group of Poles (including Józef Obrębski, Andrzej Waligórski, Feliks Gross and others) also attended the seminar, which is discussed in contributions by Grażyna Kubica and Anna Engelking.

In 1934, Malinowski spent several months in Central Africa, where he visited his students and himself carried out field research (Malinowski 1938, 1945). This research significantly influenced his functionalist approach and cultural theory. In both of these cases, he began to take into account the dynamics of cultural change to a much greater extent than before. Importantly, much of his findings at the time can be seen as a harbinger of later developments in anthropology, or in the social sciences and humanities more broadly. These issues are discussed in the chapters by Marta Songin-Mokrzan and Dariusz Brzeziński.

The following year, he became a widower after his wife Elsie succumbed to a long illness. In 1940, he married English painter Anna Valetta Hayman-Joyce, known as Valetta Swann.

In 1936, Malinowski was awarded an honorary doctorate by Harvard University. He spent in the United States the last years of his life, where the outbreak of World War II found him and where he decided to remain, taking up a visiting professor position at Yale University in New Haven. During the summer holidays of 1940 and 1941, he researched Zapotec peasant markets in Mexico (Malinowski and de la Fuente 1982).

In 1942, Malinowski was supposed to be tenured as full professor at Yale, a distinction which he did not live to see. He died on 16 May 1942, one day after the inauguration of the Polish Institute of Arts and Sciences in New York, of which he was President. This event is discussed in Kubica's chapter. Three of Malinowski's important anthropological books were published posthumously. *Freedom and Civilization* (1944a) and *A Scientific Theory of Culture and Other Essays* (1944b) were edited and prepared for publication by his wife. The third, *The Dynamics of Culture Change. An Inquiry into Race Relations in Africa* (Malinowski 1945), was edited by his student, Phyllis M. Kaberry. The widow's efforts also saw his diary notes written in New Guinea translated into English and published as *A Diary in the Strict Sense of the Term* in 1967.

Let us finish this part of our introduction by referring to Malinowski's mesmeric persona, that attracted the attention of those around him. This is well reflected in two passages in which the authors focused on Malinowski's corporeality and appearance. One comes from Witkiewicz's autobiographical novel *622 upadki Bunga* [622 Downfalls of Bungo], discussed by Jakubova in her chapter. Witkiewicz's description of the Duke of Nevermore, a character based on the young Malinowski, reads:

> His green, cold reptilian eyes, looking through the glasses of a seventeen-dioptre pince-nez, were a disturbing contrast to the childlike smile of his immense, red, beautifully formed lips… The Duke was sitting on a sofa, lolling about with an elusive nonchalance, which members of higher society tried to imitate in vain. Even in this posture, his appearance lost nothing of its self-assurance, and he gave the impression of a resting tiger.
> (Witkiewicz 1972: 64, 75; translated by GK)

The other description is by psychologist Józef Pieter, who participated in Malinowski's seminar in London in the 1930s and is mentioned by Kubica in her chapter. Pieter wrote on the Professor:

> He made an impression of Mephisto from *The Student of Prague*, starring Conrad Veidt as the "black archangel." A tall, slim man with brown hair, a greyish face and piercing eyes, wearing a black suit and a long black cape, he could at first arouse fear or at least intimidate. He spoke splendidly and wittily, his reflexes were brilliant, and it was a pleasure to listen to his voice, as 'human' as it could be.
> (Pieter 1986: 327; translated by GK)

Revisiting Malinowski's Life

Although the most important episodes of Malinowski's life are well known, new research on his biography – often underpinned by recently found sources – sheds new and very important light on him. This is amply shown by the contributions in the first part of this volume, titled **Bronisław Malinowski: Known and Unknown**.

Sociologist and anthropologist Grażyna Kubica emphasizes in the opening chapter of this section that although all anthropologists (and not only them) are well aware that Bronisław Malinowski was Polish, the nature of his Polishness is not known in any detail. Her chapter 'Bronisław Malinowski – the (Somewhat Anglicized and Cosmopolitan) Pole: The Biographical-Anthropological Reflections of His Polish Identity' analyses both what Malinowski himself said of his Polishness and what his contemporaries thought on the subject. Kubica considers other Poles' opinions to be the most authoritative source, as they were able to 'read' Malinowski's Polishness. However, as she stresses, the Polish reception of him was not uniform. On the one hand, Malinowski clearly irritated and provoked his nationalist compatriots, and on the other hand, he revealed his deep sentiment and nostalgia to those who were, like himself, cosmopolitan. Kubica also scrutinizes Malinowski's connections with the Polish Academia and its members as the most intense interactive dimension of his Polishness. She also argues (following Ernest Gellner) that Malinowski's own identity influenced his theoretical approach to the nation and nationalism. Moreover, she claims that Malinowski is a good example of Nigel Rapport's Anyone.

An important, though delicate, issue is addressed by political scientist Patrick Burke in his chapter 'Our Ancestors: Making Sense of Bronisław Malinowski and Elsie Masson.' As Malinowski's grandson, Burke reflects on how differently the process of 'making sense' works among the descendants of Bronisław and Elsie. Burke observes that while his American cousins (the children and grandchildren of Józefa) have a rather negative image of their grandfather, he and his sister (the children of Helena, who was the guardian of her parents' legacy and planned to write her father's biography) cherish a definitely more positive idea of him. His cousins express resentment and even talk of 'Malinowski's curse' in their texts and a documentary film about their famous grandfather, yet Burke himself does not share this view, despite being critical of Malinowski. He believes that the differences he analyses stem from the different attitudes of Malinowski's daughters. This idea can be taken further to suggest that it was Helena's exploratory approach to her parents' biographies and their legacy that triggered her empathy and understanding. Burke's article can also be regarded as an interesting resource for reflection on family memory and post-memory (Hirsch 2012).

The chapters in the next part of the book, entitled **Revisiting Malinowski's Intellectual Background**, mainly concern Malinowski's youth and early work. Social anthropologist Petr Skalník focuses in his chapter 'An Argonaut from Krakow: Pre-field Malinowski as a Theorist' on the theoretical significance of Malinowski's works preceding his field research and considers them decisive for his later accomplishments. Skalník starts his chapter on an autobiographical note, recalling that Soviet scholars' harsh critique of Malinowski made him, a young Czech student at the time, perversely interested in social anthropology and Malinowski. Skalník points out that Malinowski's doctoral dissertation speaks to his philosophical monism and attachment to the empiricist approach. Malinowski's subsequent anthropologically themed publications from that early period show that he had already rejected the popular idea of identifying the genesis of social institutions, and that his theory was thoroughly sociological.

The early stage of Malinowski's academic career is also covered in 'Bronisław Malinowski in the Laboratories of Leipzig,' a contribution by cultural studies scholar Krzysztof Łukasiewicz. The 15 months that Malinowski spent at Leipzig, still devoted to sciences but increasingly leaning toward other disciplines, marked a greatly important period in his life. The Leipzig School boasted a unique mode of investigating the development of nature, individuals, human collectives and history that was inductive and causally explanatory, while remaining historical and understanding. The principles the Leipzig School observed in defining human action were underlain by research rather than by speculation. Łukasiewicz considers the importance of this period to Malinowski in terms of the development and consolidation of epistemic virtues.

The next chapter, 'Malinowski: A Modernist in His Way,' written by eminent social anthropologist Adam Kuper, presents the broad historical and cultural context in which *Argonauts* was published. The year 1922 was momentous both for European culture in general (stamping the beginning of modernity) and for anthropology (seeing the publication of the main works of functional anthropology). According to Kuper, Malinowski's modernism partly lay in his involvement with the artistic bohemia of the time, alongside his friend Stanisław Ignacy Witkiewicz. However, Kuper also ponders what modernism means in ethnographic writing and argues that it primarily meant breaking with the model disseminated by *Notes & Queries on Anthropology*, a popular textbook for data collection in the field. The chapter also looks into Malinowski's own position as an Ethnographer who was a Polish emigrant in London and an outsider in Australia and New Guinea. In Kuper's view, modern ethnography is the 'product of a movement backwards and forwards between the field and various explicit and implicit sources of comparison' (102).

The third part of the volume is titled **Malinowski's Intellectual Relations: New Insights**. It contains chapters that rely on the latest research and records to explore Malinowski in his different roles – as a friend, a fellow intellectual and a teacher. In '"I Am Not Really a Real Character": Malinowski, Witkiewicz and the Pitfalls of Making Oneself a "Character,"' theatre scholar Natalija Jakubova investigates the complex, multidimensional relationship between Malinowski and Witkiewicz. Jakubova's explorations delve both into their mutual artistic and intellectual inspirations and into the moment when their paths diverged. Jakubova examines how Witkiewicz pictured Malinowski as a character in his works, particularly attending to Witkiewicz's novel *622 upadki Bunga* [622 Downfalls of Bungo]. She also reflects on the causes and consequences of the two intellectuals' key identity decisions. Central to Jakubova's chapter is her analysis of the last sentence of *A Diary in the Strict Sense of the Term* (which was wrongly translated into English) about Malinowski not being 'a character,' which she interprets with reference to Victorian literature.

The next chapter, authored by literary scholar Lena Magnone and titled 'Malinowski and the Disciples of Freud: Otto Rank, Ernest Jones and Wilhelm

Reich,' problematizes Malinowski's relationship with three prominent adherents of psychoanalysis. Magnone's contribution is based on Malinowski's papers and his correspondence. She screens these sources to provide some pioneering evidence for Malinowski's abiding interest in psychoanalysis and also of his growing opposition to Freudian orthodoxy. Her chapter thus offers an insight into the complicated relationship between functionalist anthropology and psychoanalytical thought. In this vein, Magnone's chapter highlights the connections between Malinowski's personal relationships and his work.

The last chapter in this part of the volume, titled 'Under the Wing of the Rockefeller Foundation: On the Cooperation of Bronisław Malinowski and His Polish Student Józef Obrębski,' portrays Malinowski in the role of a teacher. Its author, ethnologist and linguist Anna Engelking, discusses the long-standing acquaintance of Malinowski and Obrębski, who completed his doctoral studies at the London School of Economics under Malinowski's supervision. The chapter highlights the intellectual connections between the two intellectuals and captures the way in which their master-disciple relationship evolved. Engelking also analyses the dependence of knowledge production and acquisition in the social sciences on institutional conditions. Besides, Engelking's chapter is a fascinating testimony to how Malinowski's functional theory and the method of intensive field research were used by Józef Obrębski for the first time to study European peasants.

Revisiting Malinowski's Work

Eminent Austrian writer and playwright Thomas Bernhard repeatedly made creative practice and the legacy of artistic and intellectual creative work the subject of his writings. Their tone is often bitter and pessimistic. For example, the protagonist of a novel by Bernhard whose plot revolves around the virtuoso skills of pianist and composer Glen Gould states: 'Our great philosophers, our greatest poets, shrivel down to a single successful sentence (...), that's the truth, often we remember only a so-called philosophical cue' (Bernhard 2006 [1983]: 66). Further on, the protagonist mentions authors such as William Shakespeare, Arthur Schopenhauer, Friedrich Nietzsche, Heinrich von Kleist and Voltaire, who have been turned into 'classics' and 'locked up' in libraries, the extraordinary wealth of their work notwithstanding. Although this observation is patently hyperbolized, as is very often the case in Bernhard, it somehow captures the essence of selective and synthesizing individual and social memory. To some extent, this process is also discernible in the reception of Malinowski's work.

Although Malinowski authored a multitude of books and articles, comprising an extraordinary wealth of anthropological, sociological, cultural and philosophical analyses, only a small part of his oeuvre is the subject of intense scholarly debate today. Malinowski is mostly known as a one of the Founding Fathers of modern anthropology, the unsurpassed ethnographer and a prominent practitioner of functionalism, that is an already classic (and abandoned) approach in anthropology. Importantly, it is his synchronic – or ahistoric (Carrithers 1992) – vision of functionalism that is usually addressed, whereas, in the last decade of his life, he exerted himself to revise this approach with a view to problematizing the dynamics of cultural change (Malinowski 1938, 1945). On the one hand, Malinowski's synchronic functionalism must be foregrounded, as far as the exploration of much of his research is concerned. On the other hand, however, these 'canonical' interpretations end up with a reductive vision of his multidimensional, multithreaded and multivalent work. The analyses in the last two parts of this volume aim to contribute to redressing the imbalance.

The fourth part, titled **Reconsiderations of Interpretive Frameworks**, includes three chapters, each focused on a different aspect of Malinowski's work that is either overlooked or underappreciated. In the opening piece, 'Bronisław Malinowski: An Icon of a Body-centric Anthropology?' cultural scholar Andreas Lipowsky surveys Malinowski's work, from his very early papers to *Argonauts of the Western Pacific* and beyond, through the lens of the contemporary theories of embodiment. Lipowsky explores the sources and inspirations of Malinowski's thought on the body, notably in the context of the German *Lebensphilosophie* tradition. While illuminating the innovative nature of Malinowski's insights, Lipowsky points out that, surprisingly, they have failed to inspire or spark an intellectual debate among embodiment theorists although they mostly appreciate Malinowski's work. In trying to establish the reasons for this neglect, Lipowsky presents a novel interpretation of the theoretical and methodological aspects of Malinowski's work in the context of vitalist thought.

In the following chapter, titled '"The Gardens Are, in a Way, a Work of Art": Bronisław Malinowski's Social Anthropology as Anthropology of Art,' art historian Andrzej Kisielewski offers an innovative view of Malinowski's oeuvre from the perspective of art history and theory. Kisielewski reads Malinowski's Trobriand Islands studies – from *Argonauts of the Western Pacific* to *Coral Gardens and Their Magic* – for their descriptions of art. As already noted, he frames these passages as instances of ekphrasis. Kisielewski also explores Malinowski's sketch 'Art Notices and Suggestions,' which was found by Michael Young in the archives of the London School of Economics, and infers Malinowski's approach to art from it. In its concluding part, the chapter also refers to the Trobriand Islands' present-day realities as described by various researchers. It addresses the changes that have taken place in local art over the last century while also emphasizing the importance of the historical dimension of Malinowski's analyses.

Another interpretive framework for Malinowski's work reviewed in the fourth part of the book consists of his analyses devoted to law. In 'Exploring the Intersection of Law, Culture, and Biology: Tensions and Unfulfilled Potential in Malinowski's Legal Thought,' lawyer and sociologist Mateusz Stępień states that Malinowski's reflections on the role and significance of law are underestimated and often overlooked in legal science. Stępień provides a comprehensive and nuanced analysis of Malinowski's findings in this field, identified in his field monographs and in his theoretical works. He foregrounds both the analytical potential of Malinowski's legal reflection and the tensions and contradictions within it. Stępień also demonstrates the pioneering nature of Malinowski's references to the biology in the study of law and – more generally – social reality.

The fifth, and final, part of the book is titled **Malinowski and Anthropology Today**. The three chapters that it comprises study Malinowski's work from the perspective of recent empirical and theoretical developments in anthropology. The opening text, '*Gimwala* and *Kula*: Malinowski's Living Ethnography,' penned by anthropologist linus s. digim'Rina, brings into relief the continuing significance of reciprocal exchange in the Trobriands, the author's birthplace. The chapter begins by outlining the broad semantic fields of the terms 'Gimwala' and 'Kula' and highlighting the widespread and fundamental importance of the institutions these terms signify. The further analysis of these institutions is based on the present-day examples of the operations of Christian churches and the general election in the Trobriand Islands. linus s. digim'Rina's semi-autoethnographic chapter affords excellent insight into the Trobriand society of today and also demonstrates the salience of Malinowski's analyses.

While linus s. digim'Rina takes his readers to the Trobriand Islands, ethnologist Marta Songin-Mokrzan encourages hers to leave them. In her contribution 'What If We Had Followed Malinowski Instead of Staying on the Trobriand Islands? Notes on the Anthropological Multiverse,' Songin-Mokrzan focuses on Malinowski's research on African societies and his ideas of war, democracy, justice and freedom. She observes that these investigations are underrated or, rather, overshadowed by Malinowski's famous studies of Trobriand society. Songin-Mokrzan argues that these lesser-known works are highly valuable to contemporary anthropology, particularly to applied anthropology, and deliberates in more general terms on how knowledge is produced in anthropology. Her inspiring chapter is an excellent exemplification of the innovative concept of 'potential histories,' recently heralded by Ariella Azoulay (2019).

In the final chapter of this section, titled 'Bronisław Malinowski and the Anthropology of Nostalgia,' sociologist and cultural scholar Dariusz Brzeziński analyses Malinowski's work through the lens of the emerging perspective of the anthropology of nostalgia. Brzeziński first highlights the increasing importance of investigating the longing for the past in the contemporary humanities and social sciences, a development sometimes referred to as the 'nostalgic turn.' In discussing this trend in anthropology, he draws on David Berliner's recent typology of 'endonostalgia' and 'exonostalgia.' The former refers to an individual's longing for the past, while the latter addresses discourses about loss detached from any direct, personal experience. Brzeziński uses these concepts to examine Malinowski's books, diary and letters. As a result, he offers a new perspective on Malinowski's work, along with insights into the theory and methodology of nostalgia studies in anthropology and, more broadly, in the contemporary social sciences and humanities.

The authors of the texts in the fourth and fifth parts of this volume articulate observations similar to those of Bernhard's protagonist. For example, Lipowsky argues that 'canonization bears the unfortunate side-effect of promoting reductive readings of the authors whose statuses it elevates' (163). Songin-Mokrzan admits that Malinowski's readers' prevalent focus on his Trobriand studies 'may not offer a comprehensive or entirely accurate representation unless we complement it with

Malinowski's other works and accomplishments' (218). The editors of this volume share the contributors' belief that Malinowski's work must be reconsidered, reinterpreted and re-evaluated so that he can continue to be an inspiration for social scientists and humanities scholars today and in the future.

Conclusion

The field research depicted by Malinowski in *Argonauts of the Western Pacific* was conducted during World War I. The book was published four years after the end of the global conflict, when its consequences were still being felt and new social, cultural and political challenges were emerging. In this context, Malinowski notably argued in the last chapter of *Argonauts* that, besides portraying the life of Trobriand society and fostering readers' receptiveness to cultural diversity, his book also had another, more important purpose: 'yet our final goal is to enrich and deepen our own world's vision, to understand our own nature and to make it finer, intellectually and artistically' (Malinowski 1922: 517–518). The key role in the achievement of these goals was assigned to the improvement of individuals' understanding, tolerance and generosity.

Certainly, not only has this belief lost none of its relevance on the centenary of the publication of *Argonauts of the Western Pacific*, but, given the current civilization challenges, it has in fact gained in value. As the editors of this book, we hope that it will not only provide a novel insight into the life and work of one of the most important anthropologists ever or shed new light on the inspirations that his thought can offer to the contemporary social sciences and humanities, but also contribute to the dissemination of the values that he himself considered fundamental. We agree with Malinowski that 'the study of Ethnology (…) might become one of the most deeply philosophical, enlightening and elevating disciplines of scientific research' (Malinowski 1922: 518).

Notes

1 The length of the thesis (about 11,000 words) – quite typical at that time – was rather modest, and can be compared to a longer article.
2 *Habilitation* (*doctor habilitatus*) was a degree that gave its holder autonomy as an academic researcher (and is still valid in Central European countries). All in all, Malinowski was never habilitated because it was not necessary in British academia.

Bibliography

Azoulay, Ariella Aïsha. 2019. *Potential History: Unlearning Imperialism.* London: Verso.
Bartmański, Domnik. 2012. 'How to Become an Iconic Social Thinker: The Intellectual Pursuits of Malinowski and Foucault.' *European Journal of Social Theory* 15(4): 427–453. https://doi.org/10.1177/1368431011423577.
Bernhard, Thomas. 2006 [1983]. *The Loser: A Novel.* Translated by Jack Dawson. New York: Vintage Books.
Carrithers, Michael. 1992. *Why Humans Have Cultures: Explaining Anthropology and Social Diversity.* Oxford: Oxford University Press.

Clifford, James. 1988. *The Predicament of Culture: Twentieth Century Ethnography, Literature and Art*. Cambridge, MA: Harvard University Press.
Deliège, Robert. 2006. *Une histoire de l'anthropologie: écoles, auteurs, théories*. Paris: Seuil.
Ellen, Roy, Ernest Gellner, Grażyna Kubica, and Janusz Mucha, eds. 1988. *Malinowski between Two Worlds: The Polish Roots of an Anthropological Tradition*. Cambridge: Cambridge University Press.
Eriksen, Thomas Hyland, and Finn Sivert Nielsen. 2001. *A History of Anthropology*. London UK: Pluto Press.
Firth, Raymond, ed. 1957. *Man and Culture: An Evaluation of the Work of Bronislaw Malinowski*. London: Routledge & Kegan Paul.
Foks, Freddy. 2018. 'Bronislaw Malinowski, "Indirect Rule," and the Colonial Politics of Functional Anthropology, ca. 1925–1940.' *Comparative Studies in Society and History* 60(1): 35–57. https://doi.org/10.1017/S0010417517000408.
Geertz, Clifford. 1988. *Works and Lives: The Anthropologist as Author*. Stanford, CA: Stanford University Press.
Gellner, Ernest. 1998. *Language and Solitude: Wittgenstein, Malinowski and the Habsburg Dilemma*. Cambridge and New York: Cambridge University Press.
Hirsch, Marianne. 2012. *The Generation of Postmemory: Writing and Visual Culture after the Holocaust*. New York: Columbia University Press.
James, Wendy. 1973. 'The Anthropologist as Reluctant Imperialist.' In *Anthropology and the Colonial Encounter*, edited by Talal Asad, 41–69. London: Humanities Press.
Kubica, Grażyna. 1988. 'Malinowski's Years in Poland.' In *Malinowski between Two Worlds: The Polish Roots of an Anthropological Tradition*, edited by Roy Ellen, Ernest Gellner, Grażyna Kubica, and Janusz Mucha, 88–104. Cambridge: Cambridge University Press.
Kubica, Grażyna. 2024a. 'Cultural Capital and Economic Stringency: Reality and Myth of Bronisław Malinowski's Socio-economic Background.' In *One Hundred Years of Argonauts: Malinowski, Ethnography and Economic Anthropology*, edited by Deborah James and Chris Hann, 36–62. Oxford: Berghahn Books.
Kubica, Grażyna. 2024b. "A Notorious Diarist – Bronisław Malinowski, and His Sinful Publics. Polish Editor's Remarks." In: Aleksandar Bošković and David Shankland eds., *Argonauts of the Western Pacific and The Andaman Islanders: A Centenary Study in Social Anthropology*. Canon Pyon: Sean Kingston Publishing. [forthcoming]
Kuklick, Henrika. 1991. *The Savage Within: The Social History of British Anthropology, 1885–1945*. Cambridge: Cambridge University Press.
Kuklick, Henrika, ed. 2008. *A New History of Anthropology*. Malden, MA: Blackwell Publishing.
Kuper, Adam. 1973. *Anthropologists and Anthropology: The British School, 1922–1972*. New York: Pica.
Kuper, Adam. 2015. *Anthropology and Anthropologists: The British School in the Twentieth Century*. London: Routledge.
Malinowski, Bronisław. 1913. *The Family among the Australian Aborigines: A Sociological Study*. London: University of London Press.
Malinowski, Bronisław. 1915. 'The Natives of Mailu: Preliminary Results of the Robert Mond Research Work in British New Guinea.' *Transactions and Proceedings of the Royal Society of South Australia* 39: 494–706.
Malinowski, Bronisław. 1922. *Argonauts of the Western Pacific: An Account of Native Enterprise and Adventure in the Archipelagoes of Melanesian New Guinea*. London: Routledge & Kegan Paul Ltd.

Malinowski, Bronisław. 1926. *Crime and Custom in Savage Society*. London: Kegan Paul, Trench, Traubner, and Co.
Malinowski, Bronisław. 1927. *Sex and Repression in Savage Society*. London: Routledge and Kegan Paul.
Malinowski, Bronisław. 1929. *The Sexual Life of Savages in North-Western Melanesia: An Ethnographic Account of Courtship, Marriage, and Family Life among the Natives of the Trobriand Islands, British New Guinea*. London: George Routledge & Sons, Ltd.
Malinowski, Bronisław. 1932. 'Introduction.' In *The Sorcerers of Dobu*, by Reo F. Fortune, xv–xviii. London. George Routledge and Sons Ltd.
Malinowski, Bronisław. 1935. *Coral Gardens and Their Magic: A Study of the Methods of Tilling the Soil and of Agricultural Rites in the Trobriand Islands*, 2 volumes. London: George Allen & Unwin Ltd.
Malinowski, Bronisław. 1938. 'Introductory Essay on the Anthropology of Changing African Cultures.' In *Methods of Study of Culture Contact in Africa*, edited by Lucy Mair., vii–xxxviii. London: Oxford University Press.
Malinowski, Bronisław. 1944a. *Freedom and Civilization*. New York: Roy Publishers.
Malinowski, Bronisław. 1944b. *A Scientific Theory of Culture and Other Essays*. Chapel Hill: The University of North Carolina Press.
Malinowski, Bronisław. 1945. *The Dynamics of Culture Change: An Inquiry into Race Relations in Africa*, edited by Phyllis Kaberry. New Haven, CT: Yale University Press.
Malinowski, Bronisław. 1967. *A Diary in the Strict Sense of the Term*. Translated by Norbert Guterman. New York: Harcourt, Brace & World, Inc.
Malinowski, Bronisław. 1993. 'On the Principle of the Economy of Thought.' Translated by Ludwik Krzyżanowski. In *The Early Writings of Bronisław Malinowski*, edited by Robert J. Thornton and Peter Skalnik, 89–116. Cambridge: Cambridge University Press.
Malinowski, Bronisław. 2002. *Dziennik w ścisłym znaczeniu tego wyrazu*, annotated and prefaced by Grażyna Kubica. Kraków: Wydawnictwo Literackie.
Malinowski, Bronisław, and Julio de la Fuente. 1982. *Malinowski in Mexico: The Economics of a Mexican Market System*. London: Routledge & Kegan Paul.
Mills, David. 2008. *Difficult Folk? A Political History of Social Anthropology*. Oxford: Berghahn Books.
Mucha, Janusz. 1992. 'Problems of Freedom, Democracy and Peace in Bronisław Malinowski's Anthropology.' *The Polish Sociological Bulletin* 97: 69–82.
Pieter, József. 1986. *Czasy i ludzie*. Katowice: Śląski Instytut Naukowy.
Rapport, Nigel. 1990. 'Surely Everything Has Already Been Said about Malinowski's Diary.' *Anthropology Today* 6(1): 5–9.
Senft, Gunter. 2007. 'Bronislaw Malinowski and Linguistic Pragmatics.' *Lodz Papers in Pragmatics* 3(1): 79–96. https://doi.org/10.2478/v10016-007-0006-7.
Senis, Angela. 2023. 'Anthropology and Linguistics in Great Britain: Bronislaw Malinowski and John Rupert Firth.' *Histoire Épistémologie Langage* 44(2): 101–123. https://doi.org/10.4000/hel.3087.
Stocking, George W. Jr. 1992. *The Ethnographer's Magic and Other Essays in the History of Anthropology*. Madison: The University of Wisconsin Press.
Stocking, George W. Jr. 1995. *After Tylor: British Social Anthropology, 1888–1951*. Madison: The University of Wisconsin Press.
Sztompka, Piotr. 1988. 'From Malinowski to Merton: A Case-Study in the Transmission of Ideas.' In *Malinowski between Two Worlds: The Polish Roots of an Anthropological Tradition*, edited by Roy Ellen, Ernest Gellner, Grażyna Kubica, and Janusz Mucha, 52–64. Cambridge: Cambridge University Press.

Tauber, Elisabeth, and Dorothy L. Zinn, eds. 2023. *Malinowski and the Alps. Anthropological and Historical Perspectives*. Bolzano: Bozen-Bolzano University Press.

Wax, Murray L. 1972. 'Tenting with Malinowski.' *American Sociological Review* 27(1): 1–13. https://doi.org/10.2307/2093489.

Wayne, Helena, ed. 1995. *The Story of a Marriage: The Letters of Bronislaw Malinowski and Elsie Masson*, 2 volumes. London and New York: Routledge.

Weiner, Anette B. 1987. 'Introduction.' In *The Sexual Life of Savages in North-Western Melanesia*, by Bronisław Malinowski, xiii–xlix. Boston, MA: Beacon Press.

Weston, Gavin, and Natalie Djohari. 2020. *Anthropological Controversies: The 'Crimes' and Misdemeanours that Shaped a Discipline*. London and New York: Routledge.

Witkiewicz, Stanisław Ignacy. 1972. *622 upadki Bunga, czyli demoniczna kobieta*, edited by Anna Micińska. Warszawa: Państwowy Instytut Wydawniczy.

Young, Michael W. 2004. *Malinowski: Odyssey of an Anthropologist, 1884–1920*. New Haven, CT and London: Yale University Press.

Part I
Bronisław Malinowski
Known and Unknown

Illustration 2 Elsie and Bronisław Malinowski with their daughters: Józefa, Wanda and Helena in Oberbozen in 1926, photographed by Raymond Firth.

1 Bronisław Malinowski – The (Somewhat Anglicized and Cosmopolitan) Pole

Biographical-Anthropological Reflections on His Polish Identity

Grażyna Kubica

Introduction

It is a certain paradox that Bronisław Malinowski – a "notorious diarist" whose main preoccupation was striving for self-improvement and who quite early was interested in psychoanalysis[1] – as an anthropologist was not concerned with the problems of identity, just like other anthropologists of the time. According to his Polish disciple and colleague Feliks Gross,

> Malinowski did not consider self-identification, or what was called at that time 'national consciousness,' as relevant. As an anthropologist he saw the relevance of an objective, empirical approach to a cultural system and a cultural community, even if such communities did not share a broader national consciousness.
>
> (Gross 1978: xxv)

This can be explained by the functionalist paradigm, which assumed that identity resulted from social structure. Anthony Cohen pointed out that anthropologists were at most interested in how individuals interpret their belonging and how this influenced their actions (2014: 235). The identity of the social actor as an individual was not addressed as a research problem. Cohen believes that it was only under the influence of sociological theories of symbolic interactionism that Fredrik Barth and his colleagues showed that ethnic identity can be fluid and socially negotiated, and that it can be shaped by interaction rather than structure (Cohen 2014: 235).

However, Ralph Linton's and Abram Kardiner's reworking of the assumptions of the culture and personality school had already triggered a discourse on this topic in America. In Poland, it was Malinowski's student, Józef Obrębski, who in the 1930s put forward extremely innovative and important theoretical proposals that consisted in viewing ethnic groups in subjective categories and examining the processes of nationalization and the microstructural dimension of power. However, at that time, they were received ambivalently by the Polish scientific community (Lubaś 2019). Obrębski straightforwardly wrote: "the basic and essential fact that determines the existence of an ethnic group in general [is] the sense of separateness and awareness of existing differences in relation to the other groups of individuals of which this group consists"[2] (Obrębski 2005: 156–157). This can be seen as a significant departure by the student from the theoretical framework developed by the master.

Moreover, Malinowski himself in the 1930s wanted to consider the issue of "Culture as Personal Experience" in his research plans, i.e., he wanted to take into account this subjective aspect of cultural affiliation on the example of himself. That was in the outline of the never-written textbook *The ABC of Culture* (see Kubica 2023). There, he considered the impact on his identity as an anthropologist of the socio-cultural situation in which he grew up.

In this article, I have tried to collect statements by Malinowski himself regarding his identity, with particular emphasis on national identification, and – because the interactive dimension of national identity is important to me – statements on this subject by people who knew him. Here, I try to answer the question: What kind of Pole was Bronisław Malinowski? Another question that interests me here is what Malinowski's Polish academic contacts were like and how they can shed light on the issue of his identity. The analysis of this material will take into account the theoretical proposals of Malinowski himself, as well as more contemporary concepts. I have analyzed both published texts and previously unknown archival materials, mainly correspondence and memories from Polish, British and American resources.

What follows presents the discussion of the elements of Malinowski's national identity: his Polish-noble genealogy, his Austrian citizenship, his cosmopolitanism and his later plans to settle in the re-born Poland. Then, I will present other people's assessments of Malinowski's Polishness from the time of his British career, including his critical attitude towards Poles and Poland. The next part of the chapter discusses Malinowski's contacts with Polish academia as the most important interactional context of his Polishness. In the last part, I will refer to the present political situation in Poland as analogous to that of the 1930s, and also to Nigel Rapport's concept of Anyone as suitable to grasp Malinowski's "migratory identity."

Bronisław Malinowski's Genealogy and Its Relevance

In my assessment of Malinowski's own national identity, I would like to refer to an anthropologist who came from our region, namely Central Europe: Ladislav Holý (1933–1997), who studied the Berti people of Darfur in Sudan. Holý's theoretical contribution seems well suited to help in analyzing Malinowski's own identity. Holý concluded that two aspects of ethnic identity can be indicated. The first "includes specific cultural features, ways of behavior considered appropriate, as well as orientations to basic values and principles of assessing behavior as culturally appropriate" (Holý 1992: 109–110) – that is, what is transmitted in the process of upbringing and which may be (at least potentially) a matter of individual choice. The second aspect of ethnic identity concerns "properties and characteristic features that are perceived as given or unchangeable, the adoption or rejection of which is not a matter of individual choice" (Holý 1992: 110). For the Berti themselves, it was important to belong to one of the Berti lineages, i.e., to have the right genealogy. How can Malinowski himself be placed in this context?

He definitely had the "right genealogy": on both the sword and the distaff side, he was a descendant of old Polish-noble families that possessed old coats of arms. I have analyzed the issue of Malinowski's socio-economic background elsewhere (Kubica 2024a), and Michael Young also devoted a lot of space to it in his biography of this anthropologist (2004: 6–8). Here though, I want to focus on Malinowski's identity issues: his noble-Polish identification.

It should be added here that for centuries of Polish history, and especially during the First Polish Republic, which ended in the 1770s when the country was partitioned among neighboring empires, the idea prevailed that it was the nobility that created the "Polish nation." It was only from the second half of the 19th century that the peasants and burghers started to be "nationalized." The image of the history of Poland as the history of Polish nobility (and later also of intelligentsia) prevailed until quite recently, when the "peasant history of Poland" became popular with the reading public. Another new idea is seeing Polish expansion to the East as colonialism (Polish lords and local Ukrainian, Belarussian or Lithuanian peasants/serfs). This very issue had been raised by Józef Obrębski already in the 1930s, but his perspective has been appreciated only recently (Borkowska 2014).

Malinowski himself described the world in which he grew up in the above-mentioned outline of the textbook *The ABC of Culture* (in a somewhat sketchy way): I lived

> In a town and on estates owned by one or two of my Mother and Father's brothers and sisters (…). Shabby genteel withal a really cultured world not without dignity and heroism (J. Conrad's recollections[3]) (…) impoverished, dispossessed small Polish nobility shading into *inteligencja* [intelligentsia] professional world – after squeezed from land [and] political life. Lived in an old stone building, property of the University. (…) French language books, stories, *chansons*, *calambours*. Family traditions Warsaw Paris.[4]

Malinowski very accurately characterizes the social stratum of which his family was a part: the impoverished nobility who – using their education – had to take up professional work. He also emphasizes the important role of Frenchness as a cultural model. Malinowski refers here to the memories of Joseph Conrad (1857–1924), with whom he shared a common noble background and that was crucial here. However, Michael Young considers Malinowski's frequent references to Conrad as "a romantic avowal of his own Polish roots" (Young 2004: 4).[5]

He presented his Polish-noble identity to his Australian fiancée Elsie Masson, as she later reminded him in a letter: "It was there that you first disclosed that you were a Polish Noble and I really believe it is from that moment my regard for you must date" (a letter from 21 October 1917, Wayne 1995, vol. 1: 25). It wasn't that she fell in love with him because he was a nobleman but that he allowed her some intimacy by telling her about himself. He ended one letter to her ironically: "Your Bronisław Kasper z Kalnicy Pobóg-Malinowski, to show that I have blue blood also, though I'd have been blacklabelled even in Melbourne Club." "Pobóg" was his coat of arms, while "z Kalnicy" may be translated as "from Kalnica"[6] and can be seen as a 'clan' name.

Malinowski had to explain the nature of his identity to the Anglo-Saxons, but they later often claimed that he considered himself an aristocrat, which wasn't fair. He didn't have to explain anything to Poles because they usually had the same background or "understood" the position of the post-noble intelligentsia in the Polish social structure.

Ernest Gellner (1925–1995) described the issue of Malinowski's identity most briefly and at the same time very accurately, comparing him with another intellectual with a Habsburg background, Ludwig Wittgenstein. Gellner wrote that, unlike Wittgenstein: "Malinowski had no identity problem: he knew what he was, a member of the Polish gentry, and this was a prestigious thing to be" (Gellner 1998: 125). Gellner also aptly remarked that "Just because his personal identity was comfortable, he could allow himself doubts and indulge in rational thought about the political role of nation in general and his own nation in particular" (Gellner 1998: 126). Thus, in the case of Malinowski, the intersection of class and nationality was important. His noble origin gave him a sense of superiority and class-based distinctions of hierarchy.

Polish Nationality, Austrian Citizenship, Cosmopolitism & Anglomania

Bronisław Malinowski was born in 1884 in Kraków, when the Polish state had not existed for a century. His hometown, the former capital of the Polish–Lithuanian Commonwealth, was then experiencing a time of economic stagnation, but it culturally served as the capital due to the autonomy granted by the Habsburgs to the Austrian part of divided Poland, called Galicja. Malinowski himself, after many years, harked back to Kraków of his youth "which attracted everything that was best in Poland. Kraków radiated culture throughout the country, and not just any culture, but of the best sort, a great culture of unprecedented intensity" (Malinowski 1938: XIII). But it again has to be added here that the official capital of Galicja was Lemberg (Polish Lwów, now Ukrainian Lviv), and the autonomy was only for Poles, not for non-Poles (like Ukrainians in East Galicja).

When the Great War found him in Australia, his Austrian citizenship made him an enemy-alien and caused a number of problems, including restrictions on movement (Young 2004: 365). However, Malinowski did not intend to change his citizenship. In a letter to his London mentor Charles Seligman (1873–1940), he tried to explain the situation: "We [Poles] had the best treatment in Austria and as a confederation of fairly autonomous peoples. A[ustria] was one of the most possible states" (a letter of 3 November 1914).[7]

This Polish–Austrian identity was difficult for the English to grasp, even for his own daughter, Helena Wayne (1925–2018), who observed that in his letters he wrote "in quick succession, 'I am a Polish national' and 'I am an Austrian national'" (xiii). In fact, Malinowski's real letter read something else: he listed possible reasons for Elsie's parents not to agree to their daughter's marriage, which – as he wrote – they could have done in two ways: "kindly (health, lack of money, no prospects of career, nationality (Polish)), or unkindly ((...), nationality (Austrian))" (Wayne 1995, vol. 1: 113). Malinowski used one English word here, which, however, can mean two different identifications: national and state. For Poles, this distinction is quite obvious.

According to Gellner, Malinowski felt "undisguised admiration and affection" towards the Habsburg Empire (Gellner 1987: 558). Some confirmation of that can be found in his letter to Wilhelm Koppers (1886–1961), thanking him for the honor of electing him corresponding member of the Anthropological Society in Vienna:

> It is a very great honor for me as a late Austrian and a D.Ph. sub auspiciis Imperatoris[8]. I frankly do not like republican institutions and my heart is still in the old Austrian monarchy, but we have to be satisfied with what we can get nowadays.
> (a letter of 24 May 1932)[9]

Gellner claimed that Malinowski considered the political arrangement under which Polish cultural autonomy and military security were guaranteed by Austria-Hungary to be an optimal situation (resembling indirect rule) and referred to the anthropologist's posthumously published book *Freedom and Civilization* (Malinowski 1944). However, a careful reading of this work does not allow us to draw such a conclusion. Nowhere does Malinowski explicitly write about Austria-Hungary as an ideal superstate, nor does he give such an example.[10] Gellner must have obtained such information from personal communication with some of Malinowski's students. There is no doubt, however, that Malinowski considered nationalism to be the greatest threat to peace, and he postulated the separation of the nation from the state.

The *fin de siècle* in Austria-Hungary also had another interesting feature. The historian Marci Shore analyzed Mitteleuropa's cosmopolitanism. She claims that although nationalisms became fashionable at that time, some of the intelligentsia still shared the traditional aristocratic idea that the world, or at least Europe, belonged to them (Shore 2010). Shore cited Stefan Zweig, who remembered his youth in Vienna: "It was sweet to live here, in this atmosphere of spiritual conciliation, and subconsciously every citizen became supernational, cosmopolitan, a citizen of the world" (Zweig 1943: 21–22). These words could have been Malinowski's – talking about the Kraków of his youth. Later, he wrote to his Australian fiancée in a more sad mood about being a Citizen of the World, about his "tragedy of cosmopolitanism," and about his own homelessness and detachment (a letter of 19 May 1918, Wayne 1995, vol. 1: 150). In a letter to his future father-in-law, he explained: "as a Pole brought up with a cosmopolitan point of view I may plead an almost entire absence of any narrow national prejudices & conventionalities & a great capacity for adaptation."[11]

He would later consider cosmopolitanism an important dimension of his discipline. In his essay about war, published in "The Atlantic," he wrote: "Now to be an anthropologist really means to be a citizen of the world, past and present"

(Malinowski 1936: 659). This attitude can be seen already in *Argonauts of the Western Pacific*, where his "Ethnographer" is deprived of any nationality and mentions his background only once: "perhaps the Slavonic nature is more plastic and more naturally savage" (Malinowski 1922: 21). He refers here to his "racial," not cultural, outfit, and it is rather ironic.

In 1910, Malinowski went to England, because, as he later put it, while traveling in Europe and North Africa, he got "highly developed Anglomania, some almost mystical cult for British culture and its representatives," he wrote in 1913 to a Polish friend. He admitted that after moving to London he adopted English culture as "second spiritual homeland" and he got already "Anglicized to some extent." He observed with self-irony that he was in a "contemptible and comical" category of the "masquerade of foreigners," who live in England and are superficially Anglicized. "It's easy to recognize them at first glance!" (Malinowski 2002: 128–129, 135).[12]

Polish Plans for the Career

After the end of the Great War, the independent Polish state was established on 11 November 1918. When it later appointed consular representatives in Australia, Malinowski applied for Polish citizenship. Nothing happened and only Seligman sent him a Polish passport from London (Young 2004: 602). Elsie Masson, who in the meantime had become his wife, also took Polish citizenship because at that time, according to the law, a wife had to accept her husband's citizenship.

Even earlier, when they were planning their life together, they considered settling in the future independent Poland. Elsie wrote in December 1917: "I am all ready to love Poland, but not uncritically" (Wayne 1995: 86) and she started learning Polish. And Bronio, as he was called by his friends, made plans: "I should be able to find an academic position in Poland as soon as the war is over, which would be very poorly endowed (...) but we both do not mind poverty, do we?" (a letter of 14 May 1918, Wayne 1995, vol. 1: 147–148).

In his diary, which is itself a performative act of Polishness because it is written from beginning to end in Polish,[13] he makes comments about his plans to return to the country:

> pleasantly ambitious thought: I'll surely be 'an eminent Polish scholar'. This will be my last ethnological escapade. After that, I'll devote myself to constructive sociology: methodology, political economy, etc., and in Poland I can realize my ambitions better than anywhere else.
> (entry of 21 December 1917, Malinowski 1967: 160)

And finally:

> Thought about Poland, about 'Polish woman'; for the first time, deep regret that E.R.M. is not Polish. But I rejected the idea that perhaps our engagement is not definitive. I shall go back to Poland and my children will be Poles.
> (entry of 15 April 1918, Malinowski 1967: 253)

This last phrase, however, sounds like a magic spell or wishful thinking, rather than a binding resolution.

The young couple certainly considered living in Poland, but their plans were more about moral obligation towards the country that had just regained its sovereignty than about specific plans (although there were some, as I will explain in the next part of this chapter). After the death of his mother, Józefa Malinowska, in 1918, Bronisław felt that his connection with the country had weakened. He wrote about it to his fiancée:

> lately I've felt more and more that I should like to return with you to Poland and that our duty and our happiness also lay that way. Now it almost frightens me to think of my return to my country. It will never be the same.
> (a letter of 11 June 1918, Wayne 1995, vol. 1: 155)

After choosing a British academic career and buying a family house in South Tyrol (then awarded to Italy), where Elsie lived with their children due to the good climate, and to where Bronisław commuted for holidays,[14] his ties with Poland as a country weakened even more, but personal contacts were still important: family and friends, as well as academic relationships.

Malinowski's Kraków sentiments and nostalgia for home[15] are revealed in a letter to Maria Laskowska, a Polish student of Vassar College he met in America. The letter begins in English and ends in Polish:

> Meeting you was a very attractive experience, and also a little melancholy; it made me think of many things long past slept behind: spring in Krakow – spring in the planty, chestnuts still green in buds and then in dense leaves and flowers. Błonia and these villages (what are they called?) under Mount St. Bronisława on the way to Skały Panieńskie. That's how it passed a long time ago (for me?), that's all that I've lost...
> (letter of 30 April 1935, cited in: Pudłocki 2015: 215)

Malinowski mentions a park built on the site of the city walls (the Planty), a large meadow (Błonia), which was then located on the outskirts of the city, and villages near Kraków on the way to the picturesque limestone hills (Panieńskie Skały).[16] During World War II, when he was living in America, he met his childhood friend, Zofia Smoluchowska, who had taken refuge overseas. Later, he received from her a map of Kraków, hand-drawn by her son, "which has been filed in my personal and sentimental archives. It allows me to remember many things which I had forgotten," as he wrote to her in gratitude a few weeks before his death.[17]

Malinowski's Polishness in the Eyes of Others

How did others perceive his Polish identity? This issue arose only when Malinowski had been living in London for a while after 1910. The later-great novelist Maria Dąbrowska (1889–1965) wrote to her husband: "When I remember all the

Czaplickas[18] and Malinowskis from their emigration career, it seems so faded, withered, just squeezed out of the soul" (letter of 22 April 1914, Głębicka 2005: 362). Dąbrowska's point may have been that Czaplicka and Malinowski were preoccupied with academic matters that took them mentally away from Poland.

Malinowski's closest friend, Stanisław Ignacy Witkiewicz, an avant-garde painter and writer, who was to accompany him on his "expedition to the tropics" but, upon learning of the outbreak of war, returned to Europe and enlisted in the Russian army, wrote in a similar tone: "It's just that Malinowski doesn't exist for me anymore. I'm writing to Bronio about Malinowski" (letter of mid-October 1914, Witkiewicz 2000: 276). That is, he did not accept the changes he had observed in his friend, Bronio, when he became the London scholar Malinowski. And years later, he wrote about him in one of his literary works: "Malinowski, that cursed, Anglicised, untamed dreamer" (Witkiewicz 1972: 552).[19]

In her *Foreword* to the volume *Malinowski between Two Worlds. The Polish Roots of an Anthropological Tradition*, Helena Wayne wondered: "why was there so little Polishness in the household in which my sister and I grew up?" (Wayne 1988: xi). And she mentioned only the figure of her remarkable Polish grandmother and "a mystical place called Zakopane in some magic mountains" from her father's Polish youth that he told her about. She also remembered the Szymberskis,[20] her father's friends whom they visited often in Paris. But one may ask: what else did she expect the Polishness in their family to be like? The language is an obvious thing. None of the Malinowski's daughters could speak Polish.[21] But Helena did not mention that, in fact, the Malinowskis had a plan to send each daughter to Poland (and Australia) for a year to learn about their motherland and fatherland (Wayne 1995, vol. 2: 210–212), but this plan was never realized, mostly due to Elsie's illness and her early death in 1936.[22] I heard this from Helena in personal communication sometime in the 1990s. Helena also did not mention that all three daughters had Polish (or Polish spelled) names: Józefa (after Bronisław's beloved mother), Wanda and Helena. Thus, they carried Polishness in their very personal "labels." Moreover, Malinowski always addressed his wife by her Polonized name in the vocative case: Elsusiu, and she addressed him with Polish diminutive name: Bronio.

In her *Foreword*, Helena wrote about the Polishness of her father, mostly based on what she had learned from her parents' correspondence and other peoples' recollections, like in this piece:

> In England, when it suited him, Malinowski used his Polishness, his continental past, instrumentally and in the spirit of self-mockery. So he did his Britishness, and sometimes in tandem. There is a little story that illustrates this from the summer of 1931, when he was granted British nationality. His graduate students and listeners-in were waiting for him in the seminar room at the London School of Economics, a room crowded and very stuffy because no one had dared to open the windows: Malinowski's dislike of unnecessary fresh air indoors was well known, a dislike in those days that was an instant divider between the Anglo-Saxon 'fresh air fiend' and the continental

foreigner. Malinowski strode into the room, demanding as he arrived: 'Open the windows! Wider!! Wider!! Wider!! [gesture of open arms]. Today, you see, I have become a British gentleman.'

(Wayne 1988: xiii)

I still vividly remember Helena telling me that story and her gestures showing opening windows. She apparently liked the anecdote, perhaps because it was very British with its strong self-ironic flavor. Other hints of his Polishness might have escaped her.

Malinowski's eminent student and successor at LSE, Raymond Firth (1901– 2002), pointed out the fact that: "While he always retained a sentimental affection for Poland and a benevolent interest in Polish doings, Malinowski did not seem to be particularly conscious of himself as a Pole in any politically nationalist sense" (Firth 1959: 14). Firth is certainly right: Malinowski was not a nationalistic Pole, but it must have been difficult for a New-Zealander to grasp the shade of his master's identity. He simply could not "read" his Polishness.

The best person to elaborate on that would be Feliks Gross (1906–2006), Malinowski's compatriot and later collaborator. This is not only because of their mutual Cracovian background (though Gross came from a Jewish intelligentsia family) but also because he had researched the problems of ethnic identity. Gross referred to his master's case in the introduction to his book *Ethnics in a Borderland*:

> He was born, raised, and educated in Poland; wrote a book and his doctoral dissertation in Polish; became an English anthropologist, if nationality matters at all in this case; and had admiration for English and American institutions. In his last days he told me once, 'I feel now that I am a citizen of the world.' And still he was British and Polish, and in his sympathies, he was Italian. (…) he had more than one identity and felt comfortable – so it seems to me – and knew how to reconcile them in an honest, ethical way. His early Polish bond was local in its nature, tied to his friends and landscape, to the memory of those who were kind and understood his work from the beginning.
>
> (Gross 1977: xxv)

In an interview carried out by Petr Skalník in 1979, Gross added:

> He was very much attached to Poland, as you are attached to the place you were born, you know, your friends, this type of patriotism that is very local, very regional. (…) he was very Polish in the sense of the generation. He was always very touched when I brought him greetings from Żuławski, from his friends. (…) In the objective sense, he was very much a part of the European culture of his time. He had a very strong trace of the generation, especially of Krakow's intellectual generation of his time. (…) He always spoke Polish [with me]. (…) I felt with him like a colleague, you could joke. I still have

a letter in which he wrote: 'your uncle Bronio'. He was very pleasant and very witty.[23]

In another interview carried out in Polish Gross characterized Malinowski as follows: "he was a real Krakauer, no professorial moods, but Cracovian sentiments, a sense of humor; he was sometimes nasty in an intelligent way" (Bator, Łukasiewicz 2000: 18).

In his Polish paper, Gross also wrote:

Conversations in London began with matters concerning the country and friends, so he asked about Stanisław Estreicher, about Zygmunt Żuławski (...) – and here he began to reminisce, alternately, once about his time in Krakow, about Zakopane, memories of past times, discussions and people.

(Gross 1961: 79)

And significantly, as Gross recalled: "In his house in London at 6 Oppidans Road, there was only one picture that decorated the walls: Stryjeńska's Taniec Zbójnicki [Robber Dance]" (Gross 1961: 79). The painter Zofia Stryjeńska (1891–1976) is famous for her very decorative works that depict folk motifs in the art deco style. She painted a series of images presenting Polish folk dances in 1927. It is not known whether Malinowski bought one of them during his stay in the country, or maybe he got it from someone. But it is significant that it was the only painting in his house, or at least that is how Gross remembered it. The painting combined modernity of form with folkloric content, which must have appealed to Malinowski, who spent a large part of his childhood and youth in the mountains, and what is more, he was interested in contemporary art inspired by primitive art.[24]

Another Polish student in London, future eminent psychologist Józef Pieter (1904–1989), remembered:

Thanks to Waligórski's protection, I actually got into Malinowski's seminar and met him personally. He made an impression of Mephisto from the movie 'The Student of Prague', with Conrad Veidt as the 'black archangel'. A tall, slim man with brown hair, a grayish face, piercing eyes, a black suit and a long black cape could at first arouse fear or at least intimidation. He spoke splendidly and wittily, his reflexes were brilliant, it was a pleasure to listen to his voice, as 'human' as it could be. (...) Malinowski treated me kindly, with a clear note of sentiment for his home country, especially Kraków. He once invited me for a snack at an underground railway kiosk. At the same time, he asked me in detail about my affairs and informed me about his scientific views and undertakings. Of course, in Polish.

(Pieter 1986: 327–333)[25]

Pieter was my Silesian-Cieszyn compatriot, and like all Slavonic autochthons he was of peasant background. Malinowski might have made him feel intimidated, but this dissipated due to the professor's accepting attitude when he got to know him better.

Malinowski's Critical Attitude towards Poles and Polishness

Gross mentioned in his interview (but not in his published texts) that Malinowski "was very critical of Polish people as such, like Joseph Conrad [was] (…) He said to me that the only good thing we have produced is music." Gross tried to convince Malinowski to appreciate Polish workers, suggesting that they were a "very attractive element." Gross was involved in the socialist movement, which was quite strong after the 1905 revolution, but he failed to convince Malinowski.[26]

One example of this attitude was provided by his youth colleague, English literature scholar, supporter of National Democracy, Władysław Tarnawski (1885–1951), who described their meeting in 1925 in London:

> having once met Mr. Malinowski in the street, I entered into a conversation with him about politics. I developed the thesis that England, by supporting Germany, was accelerating its own decline. He took the opposite position, citing English exports to Germany, which amounted to 25% of its total exports before the war. Finally, I lost patience and reminded him of his nationality. (…) a few days later, me and Prof. Dybowski received an invitation from him to lunch in the refectory of the School of Economics. (…) This time the conversation was more polite because we were host and guests. We talked about the Polish political system, and when I presented England as a relative ideal, Malinowski said that Poland follows the German model (hierarchy and obedience) rather than the English one (civil liberties).
>
> (Tarnawski 1997: 17–18)

As can be seen from this story, Malinowski analyzed problems impartially, taking into account the facts, without a "Polish bias." His interlocutor could not accept that. What's more, Tarnawski believed that as a Pole he should have this distortion – it would even prove his Polishness. Malinowski's desire to provoke nationalist Poles is also visible here. This critical attitude of Malinowski towards Poles and Poland can be traced in various sources.

Another example of his critical attitude may be found in his letter to Elsie in which he described a ceremonial dinner at the Polish Embassy in honor of an Austro-Hungarian diplomat, Count Adam Tarnowski (1866–1946), "a really charming Pole, not very young any more (67) but intelligent, well-mannered and reminding me of old Polish things at their best" (letter of 24 October 1933, Wayne, vol. 2: 185). However, Tarnowski's lecture the next day was "touching but not convincing. Still patriotism – and nothing more" (ibid: 185). Talking solely about patriotism had no value for Malinowski.

Another thing that Malinowski distanced himself from was the anti-Semitism that was rising in Poland (and not only there, of course). Andrzej Waligórski

(1908–1974), his Polish student, reported his master's mocking of another Polish participant of the seminar, a linguist called Jerzy Kuryłowicz (1895–1978): "We live together in great harmony, only we disagree a little politically. Prof. Malinowski constantly addresses [Kuryłowicz's] spontaneous anti-Semitism, claiming that Bronisław Malinowski is only an embellishment, because he really is Berek Malinower."[27] Malinowski impersonating a Jew must have irritated Kuryłowicz because it ridiculed his beliefs.

Of a similar nature is Malinowski's earlier letter to Jan Michał Rozwadowski (1867–1935), a Kraków linguist, in which he writes about his stay in the former capital: "Vienna is now completely Jewished, but now I can stand only the Jews and I have best friends among them." He also asks the addressee to help a certain Denis Cohen, who was coming to Poland to investigate Zionist emigration to Palestine: "It would be good for him to meet decent and not very National Democratic Poles" (letter of 12 December 1923).[28] Malinowski uses the anti-Semitic term here, "zżydziały," meaning "Jewished," but he does so in a subversive way.

Gross also addressed this issue in the context of Malinowski's accusations of racism after the publication of the English translation of his diary:

as I knew him in the late 1930s and during the war years, he was a courageous opponent of fascism, racism, and any form of totalitarianism. He helped and assisted victims of antisemitism; his convictions were not reduced to words only.

(Gross 1986: 563)

The author of these words experienced this help himself. When he could not obtain a habilitation[29] at any Polish university due to being a Jew, and the Rockefeller Foundation refused to grant him a scholarship (probably due to his socialist activism), Malinowski suggested he should conduct fieldwork under his supervision in the Jewish district of Kraków and give lectures at the LSE; later – in America – he tried to help in his academic career.[30]

The account of the linguist Antonina Obrębska-Jabłońska (1902–1994) (Malinowski's student, Józef Obrębski's sister), who, together with her sinologist husband Witold Jabłoński, visited Malinowski in London, is very interesting. She reported to Kazimierz Nitsch (1974–1958), a linguist from Jagiellonian University, a friend of Malinowski's from his Kraków days:

And then at 11 p.m. he started showing us London: the entire Soho district, divided into ethnic districts, favorite wineries, more interesting tenement houses, until we reached the place where he lived in London for the first time 27 years ago, before setting out to conquer English science. It was extremely pleasant. He asked a lot about you, Professor, and Polish matters. He is not informed in detail, but he listens willingly and a lot. Once he and Witold had a prank fight. Malinowski said that he didn't feel very Polish, that he couldn't stand many Polish things, various national advantages and disadvantages, and that he got great satisfaction in irritating and shocking Polish opinion, etc. Witold replied: 'Then you are a real Pole'. Therefore, Malinowski's Polishness has been conclusively proven, to the great satisfaction of both parties and the rest of the gathered public.

(letter of 2 February 1937)[31]

Similar in tone is the account of Theodore Abel (1896–1988), a Pole from Łódź of German origin who was a professor of sociology at Columbia University and lived in New York, where he met his fellow countryman, who had come for a lecture tour in America. In his diary on 21 April 1933, Abel wrote:

> Malinowski greeted me in Polish – he speaks the language perfectly. I was pleasantly surprised for I was told that he makes it a point to show that he is an Englishman now by avoiding Polish contacts and culture, and expressing a cynical attitude towards Poland. I found him delightful, full of wit and good humor, a lover of life, Rabelaisian to a considerable extent, fond of women. (…) [I] Took Malinowski to my house for the night. I felt he was delighted to be able to speak Polish and to find Polish hospitality. He after all is quite sentimental about his origins in spite of his cynicism.[32]

But there were also times when contact with Poles was not satisfactory, as Malinowski wrote to his wife:

> For supper I had invited *pan* Borowy, a lecturer of Polish literature at the School of Slavonic Studies, his wife and a Polish woman, Maria Słomczanka, who is a freelance journalist (…) I find, however, speaking Polish a little straining, and I was glad when after 2 ½ hours they went.
> (letter of 3 February 1935, Wayne 1995, vol. 2: 214)

Słomczanka was a translator. They all belonged to the Anglo-Polish Circle in London.[33]

These accounts show that Malinowski apparently took a provocative attitude towards some Poles (as towards the National Democrat Tarnawski), and contact with some Poles rather tormented him (like Borowy and Słomczanka), but with others (like Gross, Pieter, Abel, the Jabłońskis and also Waligórski and Obrębski) he happily gave in to his Polish sentiments. The latter group were the "non-National Democratic" Poles, not only members of post-noble intelligentsia but also intelligentsia of Jewish, German and peasant origin.

As can be seen from these accounts, Malinowski's contacts were mainly with representatives of Polish academia.

Malinowski and Kraków Academia before 1914

Bronisław Malinowski was the son of a Jagiellonian University professor, Lucjan Malinowski (1839–1898), a distinguished linguist and dialectologist. The bond of friendship connected them with other professorial families. Moreover, the

Malinowski family and their son lived in the Bursa Akademicka [Academic Dormitory], of which Lucjan was a senior. Though the father orphaned his son early (he was 14 years old), Bronio and his mother were still part of the "professional clan" (Kubica 1988).

The academic career path was obvious for young Bronisław. He was prepared for it by his education at a classical gymnasium (with Latin and Greek) and his studies at Jagiellonian University, which then consisted of four faculties: Law, Medicine, Theology and Philosophy. The latter faculty covered a very wide spectrum of disciplines: from mathematics and science to humanities and philosophy. Back then, one didn't study specific disciplines: one studied at the Faculty of Philosophy and could choose any courses. Young Malinowski matriculated at the Faculty of Philosophy and chose courses in science and philosophy. His doctoral dissertation "On the Principle of the Economy of Thought" (in Polish) was a critical discussion of the concepts of Ernst Mach and Richard Avenarius (Malinowski 1993 [1906]).

And it was there that the concept of function, so important for his later theoretical concepts, appeared. My colleagues proved that the "roots of Malinowski's anthropology" lay in his "Polish background" and the education he received in Kraków during Austrian times (Paluch 1981; Flis 1988), and they showed Malinowski's connections with the artistic movement of Young Poland (Jerschina 1988). The role and importance of Malinowski's early work for the development of anthropology was also demonstrated by Robert Thornton and Peter Skalník (1993), who published English translations of these early works.[34] Ernest Gellner developed these themes in his brilliant book *Language and Solitude. Wittgenstein, Malinowski and the Habsburg Dilemma* (which I have already quoted here), where Gellner shows the originality of Malinowski's work, that derives from his early years. Michael Young elaborates on this issue in his biography of Malinowski (Young 2004).

Particularly important for the young scholar were his speeches before the Academy of Arts and Sciences in Kraków, later published in its proceedings. They were "a gateway to a scientific career," as Feliks Gross put it. Malinowski presented the results of his scientific work undertaken at the London School of Economics. The paper on "Tribal male associations" can be considered the first study on gender issues in Polish (Kubica 2019).

Later, the Academy undertook to publish his book *Wierzenia pierwotne i formy ustroju społecznego* [Primitive Beliefs and Forms of Social Organization], which was to be his habilitation book. The book was published in 1915, when the author had already been to the other side of the world. The editorial work was undertaken by Stanisław Estreicher (1869–1939).[35] It should also be noted that Malinowski received a scholarship from the Academy of Arts and Sciences "for research in the field of sociology."[36]

And after His Return to Europe

After returning to Europe from his fieldwork in New Guinea and a stay in Australia, Malinowski applied for a chair at Jagiellonian University. Based on archival materials, I managed to determine how this process took place.[37] The initiator was Malinowski, who in the fall of 1921 wrote to Rozwadowski, former dean of the Faculty of Philosophy, presenting his readiness to undertake academic work at this university. The university authorities began the procedure of establishing the chair: a special commission was appointed, experts' opinions were collected, and an application was sent to the ministry to appoint Malinowski as an associate professor of ethnology and ethnography. However, in the end, Malinowski did not accept this offer because – as he wrote to the dean of the Faculty of Philosophy – although it was an honor for him,

> I cannot accept any new teaching duties at the moment because I have a very large stock of ethnographic materials that I must immediately elaborate. (…) my refusal is not caused by the unwillingness to return from the country with a pound and a penny flowing into the country of already diluted material conditions.
> (letter of 12 September 1922)[38]

He also wrote that he accepted a teaching sinecure at LSE, which took up little of his time, but the income allowed him to live modestly abroad.

According to Helena Wayne, this decision was influenced by the young Dr. and Mrs. Malinowski's visit to Poland in the summer of 1922 with their second daughter Wanda. The difficult economic situation of the newly established country and the fear of harsh winters made the young family decide "not to take up a life there, despite Bronio's feelings of loyalty towards his country and his old university in Kraków" (Wayne 1995, vol. 2: 27). Nevertheless, Malinowski maintained correspondence with Kraków academics all the time. These were not only the professors already mentioned – Estreicher, Rozwadowski, Nitsch – but also Franciszek Bujak, Kazimierz Moszyński, Stanisław Kutrzeba, Kazimierz Stołyhwo, and Jerzy Smoleński.

In 1926, Malinowski was elected a member of the Ethnographic Commission of the Polish Academy of Arts and Sciences; in 1929, elected a corresponding member of the Polish Academy; and in 1938, elected an active member of the Polish Academy, as was officially approved, and the decree was sent to the Polish embassy in London. He also served as a representative of the Polish Academy several times at various events, for example at the centenary of the University of London, about which he reported to the President of the Polish Academy, ending with: "Since I was the only Polish representative, I felt that it was quite useful to have our country somewhere on the map on such an occasion."[39]

Malinowski worked for the Polish Academy but also expected help from them. At the end of the 1930s, he turned to his colleague from Kraków, the physical anthropologist Kazimierz Stołyhwo, with an unusual case, albeit characteristic for that time. Sometime earlier, an article by Professor Luiggi Cipriani had been published in the Italian magazine "Corriere della Sera" with the information that only Jews deal with the study of sexual problems: Freud, Adler and Malinowski. The latter asked the editorial office for a correction, but to no avail, so he then asked his Kraków colleagues that the Polish Academy would intervene with the Italian Academy in this matter. He ended his letter to Stołyhwo as follows:

> The difficulty, as you can gather, consists in the fact that I would not like to associate myself with any anti-semitic manifestation, in other words I would like simply to lay stress on the factual error and not to imply that being called a Jew is an insult.[40]

The president of the Polish Academy, Stanisław Kutrzeba, sent a letter to the Italian Academy stating that Malinowski "is not a Jew at all" and comes from "a noble family of purely Polish origin" [emphasis in the original] and asked to influence the editors of "Corriere della Sera" to include a correction. It turned out that only the intervention of the Italian Ministry of Culture achieved this aim. When I asked Helena Wayne why Malinowski took such trouble to correct this information in the Italian magazine, she replied that being accused of being a Jew at that time in Italy could have resulted in the family being persecuted and having their home in South Tyrol confiscated.

Contacts with Poznań University

His contacts with Kraków professors did not exhaust Malinowski's contacts with Polish academia. He met an outstanding Polish sociologist who would later become the known American sociologist, Florian Znaniecki (1882–1958), in the 1920s. These two scholars met in Berlin in the fall of 1926 during the First International Congress for Sex Research (Wayne 1995, vol. 2: 82). They must have quickly found a common language, not only because it was Polish, but also because they had a similar way of sociological thinking. Znaniecki's "humanistic coefficient"[41] can be seen as an equivalent of Malinowski's principle of research from the "native's point of view." Znaniecki wrote to Malinowski in January 1930, thanking him for an article for the first issue of "Przegląd Socjologiczny" [Sociological Review] he edited:

> For the sake of the readers, we have not indicated that it is a translation from English; I hope you will not be offended by this because it only proves how highly everyone here values you – that they cannot regret that Polish science has lost you. To tell the truth, I am not surprised at you at all; in Poland, you would never have such opportunities for research and such broad horizons as in England.[42]

However, the following anecdote seems to indicate something completely different. Znaniecki's student Zygmunt Dulczewski (1916–2004) revealed the existence of an interesting plan in a book about his mentor:

> When in 1929,[43] the Universal Country Exhibition in Poznań was organized and the famous Polish scholar Bronisław Malinowski came from London to visit it, Znaniecki persuaded him of the need for him to return to Poland to organize in Poznań – in cooperation with Znaniecki – a great world center of

social studies. Malinowski agreed and waited for an official invitation from the Chancellor of Poznań University. Unfortunately, Znaniecki's departure for two years to the USA, the threat of war by Hitler's Germany, and, to a certain degree, some opposition from the circle of conservative professors, caused a delay in the decision, and in the meantime World War II broke out.

(Dulczewski 1992: 143)

In the earlier Polish version of this book, the author illuminated the reasons for this opposition: "opinions of clerical-conservative circles not to 'enlarge the circle of the Poznań professorship by another Freemason'," because Znaniecki was also considered to be such (Dulczewski 1984: 218). The rumor about Malinowski's freemasonry must have been popular in National Democratic circles, because a few years later, he was labeled as such by the magazine "Prosto z Mostu" [Straight Forward].[44] The project of bringing Malinowski to Poznań apparently did not go beyond informal conversations between Poznań scholars, because there is no mention of it in the minutes of the Senate meetings (Domanalus et al. 2020). If at all, it was just an urban legend of the Poznań sociological community.

Malinowski and Znaniecki remained in close relations; the former wrote about the latter: "I reckon him a friend of mine,"[45] which does not mean, however, that he studied the other's works diligently. Gross recalled "When I asked whether he had read any of his works, he said No, but he added: 'Tomorrow we shall go for a walk, you will tell me whatever you know about Znaniecki's work'" (Gross 1986: 566).

Theodor Abel gives a very interesting picture of the relationship between the two scholars in his diary. In the years 1931–1933, Florian Znaniecki lectured at Columbia, and Malinowski, in turn, was invited to a series of lectures by Cornell University. They met in New York. In the already quoted entry from 21 April 1933, Abel wrote also:

> Party at Znanieckis in honor of Malinowski. [Robert] MacIver, [William] Casey, [Edmund] Brunner, [George] Counts and [Edward] Korwin Lewiński were there. (...) The gathering, at which some excellent wines were served, engaged mainly in telling of snappy stories. There was a prolong dispute over characteristics and meritts of various nations, which amused me highly, for here was one of the greatest living anthropologists and several of the best minds in sociology, engaging in sweeping generalizations about nations, such as that the French are contemptible, cruel, etc. (Malinowski), disregarding the elementary principle of caution in generalizing from individual experience. MacIver and Znaniecki were just as bad as Malinowski expressing definite judgments.

The next day, Abel wrote:

> [I] Took an early morning train with Malinowski to Philadelphia. [I] Discussed with him for two hours general problems of sociology. He approved of my definitions of culture in functional terms. [We] Attended a seminar on current theories in sociology conducted by Howard Becker.

A few days later, Abel wrote that he drank Bruderschaft with Malinowski.[46]

In Poznań, Malinowski had another colleague, Czesław Znamierowski (1888–1967), a philosopher and lawyer. They knew each other from the time they both studied in Leipzig (1908–1910), when Malinowski was still interested in sciences.[47] In the 1920s, Znamierowski wrote to him that he was following his works, which were sent to him by a bookseller from Cambridge, and referred to the old times: "Your works are confirmation for me (...) that one also needs to have mathematical and philosophical culture to be able to write sociological things of such high value." He added:

> Reading on page 105 of Sex and Repression the extensive collection of lewd locutions, I encountered, not without a certain historical sentimentality, a sonorous yet inappropriate 'me cago dios', which reminded me of your inexhaustible, multilingual resource of anecdotes and locutions. Only now I see that these were the beginnings of your ethnographic interests.[48]

In later years, Znamierowski would play the role of a popularizer of Malinowski's work in Poland: in February 1937, he would talk about Malinowski on national radio in the program "What Poland has contributed to culture,"[49] and he would publish an article about him in the literary magazine "Marchołt" (Znamierowski 1937), where Malinowski's essay *The Deadly Issue* (translated by Józef Obrębski) would be published. Znamierowski would also write a foreword to the Polish edition of *Crime and Custom*. In 1937, a translation of Malinowski's article "Culture as a determinant of behavior" was published in the Poznań scientific journal "Ruch Prawniczy, Ekonomiczny i Socjologiczny" [Legal, Economic and Sociological Movement].

Offer of the Chair at the University of Warsaw

As I have only recently discovered, a plan to offer Malinowski a chair also arose at the University of Warsaw, and it was even implemented, as his cousin reported to him in a letter of 27 December 1933:

> The news spread like wildfire throughout the scientific world – and with joy and pride in the collective heart of the family – about the appointment of Professor Bronisław Malinowski to the chair of ethnology at the University of Warsaw! I wonder if this will be possible and how: perhaps at least in the form of coming for a few weeks to give lectures?.[50]

Indirect confirmation of this information can be found in a letter from the Dean of the Faculty of Humanities at the University of Warsaw, Marceli Handelsman, dated 18 April 1934: "Some time ago you reported that you could not accept our choice, which filled us with sadness; you wrote that you intended to come to Warsaw in May" and he asked if Malinowski would give one or more lectures while in Warsaw.[51] Malinowski replied that he was going to Central Africa for fieldwork, but he would come to Warsaw next year, and he added: "I am afraid, however, it will be very difficult for me to lecture in Polish now, as all the technical language of sociology and ethnography is familiar to me mostly in English."[52]

Thus, it seems that the Faculty of Humanities of the University of Warsaw decided to establish a chair of ethnology and general ethnography in the fall of 1933 and appoint Bronisław Malinowski to it. It is unknown whether he was consulted beforehand. In any case, he refused. Only then was Stanisław Poniatowski (1884–1945), a researcher of Siberia and a diffusionist, appointed, and at the same time the chair of Polish ethnography was established and the first woman, Cezaria Baudouin de Courtenay Ehrenkreutz Jędrzejewiczowa (1885–1967), was appointed. The "prehistory" of institutional ethnology related to Malinowski is not known at all to my Warsaw colleagues (see Engelking 2006).

Polish Students in London

In the 1930s, Polish students began to arrive in London, sent there by the Polish National Cultural Fund and later also financed by the Rockefeller Foundation. They came under Malinowski's wing. This was the case of Józef Obrębski (1905–1967) (Anna Engelking writes about it in this volume) and Andrzej Waligórski, and later also of Feliks Gross (although he was not financed by these institutions).

Malinowski's seminar also attracted other participants: the already mentioned psychologist Józef Pieter and the linguist Jerzy Kuryłowicz; Kraków sociologist and ethnologist Kazimierz Dobrowolski (1894–1987); Maria Ossowska (1896–1974) and Stanisław Ossowski (1897–1963), later outstanding Warsaw sociologists. As their student Stefan Nowakowski (1912–1989) recalled:

> Ossowski became more familiar with Malinowski's research and methodological approach in London during his studies there in 1933–1935. At Malinowski's seminars, he learned his functional method, although he did not participate in any of Malinowski's scientific expeditions. During his classes in the post-war period, as well as in private conversations, he often referred to many matters related to Malinowski's research workshop and recalled various details from meetings and contacts with the participants of this seminar, including the famous independence politician and ethnologist Kenyatta.
> (Nowakowski 1992: 187)

In the late 1930s, Malinowski's Polish students, Józef Obrębski and Andrzej Waligórski, after returning to the country, worked at the Polish Institute of Rural Culture in Warsaw, headed by Józef Chałasiński (1904–1979), Znaniecki's student. They edited the magazine "Przegląd Socjologiczny," founded in Poznań by Znaniecki, and encouraged Malinowski to cooperate.[53] An article translated by Obrębski was published there, as well as reviews of Malinowski's books written by young sociologists. Waligórski, Obrębski and Chałasiński also translated his books. In 1938, *The Sexual Life of the Savages* was published by Przeworski, a popular publishing house, in a wonderful translation by Waligórski with the help of Chałasiński. This publication was accompanied by a real promotional campaign, which contributed to Bronisław Malinowski's name becoming widely known by the Polish reading public.

They managed to launch the "Biblioteka Socjologiczna" [Sociological Library] publishing series at the Institute of Sociology in Poznań and intended to publish several of Malinowski's works there. This was achieved in the case of *Crime and Custom*, which was published in Obrębski's translation in 1939. Further plans were prevented by the outbreak of World War II. It should be emphasized here that the social anthropology practiced by Malinowski found resonance in Poland mainly among sociologists, but not that much among ethnologists.

Malinowski also promised cooperation to the (still-existing) magazine "Organon,"[54] which served to promote Polish science abroad (the Ossowskis, Znaniecki and many other outstanding scholars published there). Before World War II, two volumes of this magazine were published, but the third one, of 1939, which most likely contained Malinowski's article,[55] was destroyed during the Warsaw Uprising.[56]

A good summary of this part of the article is a fragment of Malinowski's introduction to the Polish edition of *The Sexual Life of the Savages*, where he wrote with rare pathos: "I have always served Polish academia, no less than others, only in a different way. And it required such services abroad. But I have never ceased to feel Polish and, if necessary, I was able to emphasize it" (Malinowski 1984 [1937]: 109).

The Polish Institute of Arts and Sciences in New York – The Last Chord

World War II annihilated Polish academia: the German occupying authorities closed all universities and the Polish Academy. In the *Sonderaktion Krakau*, the professors of Jagiellonian University and other Kraków universities were arrested and deported to concentration camps (Stanisław Estreicher, mentioned here, died on 28 December 1939 in Sachsenhausen, followed shortly by Jerzy Smoleński). It was similar at other academic centers. Jewish scholars suffered great losses. The remnants of the Polish scientific community reached the United States. Malinowski had landed there earlier because from the fall of 1938, he was there on sabbatical leave with his second wife, the painter Valetta Swan, and became associated with Yale University.

The last important event for Malinowski, a scholar and a Pole, was his election as the President of the Polish Institute of Arts and Sciences in New York. Gross described the context: "To be honest, he was quite hesitant about accepting the presidency." There were other candidates.

> However, leading persons in London [the Polish emigree government] thought that Malinowski would be far better suited to chair the continuation of the Polish Academy of Sciences if people cared to elect him. I conveyed this information to him and tried to convince him. (…) Valetta said to me

later that deciding this matter was psychologically stressful for him. It was, however, a moral imperative to which he was sensitive.

(Gross 1986: 567)

Theodore Abel described in his diary the opening ceremony that took place on 15 May 1942 in New York:

> Yesterday I attended the first board meeting of the Polish Institute of AS, at which Bronek was elected chairman. He then presided brilliantly at the opening ceremony in the Morgan Library. An impressive gathering that made me feel really proud of Poland. For in spite of the greatest adversity, the Polish government has provided funds to carry on the work of the Polish Academy – the best possible propaganda and a symptom of great vitality. After the ceremony I asked Bronek to come for a drink. He said that he felt bad and wanted to lie down, but he came to the dinner at the Biltmore and talked animatedly throughout the evening.[57]

The draft of the inaugural Presidential address survived. Malinowski started it as follows:

> This is an impressive and historic moment: the founding of a New Polish Centre. [I am] deeply moved – our country has no universities, no libraries, no centers of learning. Think of those of our colleagues who died in concentration camps under persecution, on the field of battle, or simply starved to death or fell fatally ill.[58]

Malinowski died of a heart attack the day after returning home to New Haven. (The same age and the same cause as his father.) The Institute received dozens of letters and telegrams of condolence from all over the world, from both academic and diplomatic institutions.[59] Valetta Malinowska took care of her husband's legacy and prepared subsequent volumes for publication. But it is not widely known that she was financially supported by funds obtained from the Polish government in exile.[60] The first volume to be published was *Freedom and Civilization* by the Polish publishing house Roy, whose owner Roman Kister was in exile in New York.

Conclusions and Reflections on the Present

When tracing Bronisław Malinowski's Polish contacts, it becomes obvious that his most intense relationships were with representatives of the Polish academia, a circle of close friends from his youth, and a wide extended family circle. What is significant in this context is the lack of any connections between Malinowski and the then-Polish state authorities.[61] Only his occasional visits to the Polish embassy in London on the occasion of visits of personalities from the country, or his equally occasional participation in the Anglo Polish Society[62] can be considered participation in relations with the Polish state. The chairmanship of the Polish Institute of Arts and Sciences had a different character because it took place in wartime.

The current political situation in Poland may make it easier to understand Bronisław Malinowski's identity and its interactive dimension. The situation is similar to the one in the 1930s: at that time, Poland was ruled by the Sanacja, an autocratic political formation that took power in 1926 as a result of a coup d'état. Although it came from the socialist movement, it became more and more nationalistic. In recent years, contemporary Poland has also seen the rule of the populist-nationalist right, and national megalomania and xenophobia have been treated by those in power as a measure of patriotism. Malinowski then, like many scholars today, distanced themselves from this attitude of closed nationalism and did not agree to the abridgements of democracy. I think that many of us contemporary scholars in Poland perfectly understand and sympathize with Malinowski in his aversion to the xenophobic form of Polishness. Unlike Poland in the 1930s, which ended with World War II, in our contemporary case, the matter is less dramatic: the democratic opposition won the democratic elections in autumn 2023 (but there is still a war behind the Polish border: in Ukraine).

Malinowski must have been irritated by the political situation in Poland after regaining independence, and certainly after the coup d'état in 1926, as well as by those of his compatriots who participated in the nationalist discourse of that time, which pervaded public space and even the academy. As Gellner wrote:

> Malinowski's attitude was really quite unusual amongst, so to speak, his own people. His reaction to the Polish question, and in general to ethnic issues, *is* untypical: it is to be found in his remarkable freedom from *political* nationalism, combined with an acute sense of and love of *culture*.
> (Gellner 1998: 139)

Malinowski was not "very untypical" in this respect. When he met Poles who, like him, were not political nationalists, their interaction gave birth to Victor Turner's *communitas*, i.e., an alternative institution of community that is spontaneous, direct and concrete. *Communitas* is a shared experience. It must have been felt by the young Jabłońskis, whom Malinowski took around London at night, discussing his Polishness, as well as by other Poles like them who appreciated his sympathy and help. As Turner wrote, one aspect of *communitas* – the existential one – is being on the border of some community, a social or cultural border, on the border of different nations, for example (Turner 1969). In this context, it is worth recalling that Turner was inspired by Znaniecki's theory, especially his understanding of community, i.e., the humanistic reality that also includes phenomena such as the development of new ideals in culture (Znaniecki 1934).

Such an ideal could be Malinowski's Polishness, devoid not only of political nationalism, as Gellner wanted, but also of xenophobia, and merging with Catholicism, but Polishness that is open, pluralistic, progressive and European (the embodiment of Malinowski's idea of a superstate is the European Union). This is the Polishness that the majority of Poles voted for in the 2023 elections with the highest turnout in the history of Polish democracy, 74%, sometimes queuing for several hours and feeling not only a sense of democratic responsibility but also some joyful *communitas* (as was also experienced at huge demonstrations organized by the opposition before the election). This can be seen as the first aspect of ethnic identity in Ladislav Holý's concept, i.e. "cultural features considered appropriate" and "orientations on basic values."

Thus, there are two kinds of Polishness, as each new generation of Poles becomes aware. In 1938, the Polish-Jewish poet Antoni Słonimski wrote a poem "Two homelands" (for which he was slapped in public by a right-wing journalist). It is comforting that Bronisław Malinowski, despite his "noble craze," located himself in the homeland of Słonimski, Znaniecki, the Ossowskis, Gross, Obrębski and others. Malinowski's posthumously published book *Freedom and Civilization* is the best proof of that.

Although I have been trying to present the Polishness of Malinowski, I would now like to bracket it by referring to Nigel Rapport's concept of Anyone. The principle of immersion that Malinowski postulated in his *Argonauts* and employed even earlier in his life while traveling extensively, and later when entering the world of British Academia, is very important here. Rapport writes about "passing" as individuals purposely and strategically traversing social identifications and adopting other identities. "Passing occurs *by virtue* of individual capacities and the will to dissemble and ironize identities" (Rapport 2014: 162). Malinowski was a master of "passing," which was even easier for him because he spoke Polish, English and probably several other languages without an accent. He was an incarnation of Rapport's Anyone, or a "migrant of identity" who had the power of free passage. Malinowski was being a Pole, but he treated this identity with irony and could leave it to be British, or Anyone.

Acknowledgments

This chapter derives from a project sponsored by Poland's National Science Center (2019/33 / B / HS3 / 00272). I would like to thank Janusz Mucha for his comments and discussion, and Michael Timberlake for improving my English.

Notes

1 Lena Magnone investigates this issue in her chapter in the present volume.
2 Unless otherwise stated, all translations from Polish are of my authorship.
3 Malinowski referred to Joseph Conrad's *A Personal Record* as a work available in English on the peculiarities of the Polish nobility.
4 Bronisław Malinowski Papers, Culture 1/139, British Library of Political and Economic Science, London School of Economics (later MP LSE). Malinowski in this text points to the fact that he had been exposed to two entirely different cultural worlds: city intelligentsia and highlanders (see Kubica 2023).
5 Malinowski knew Conrad personally. The young anthropologist was taken to the writer at the beginning of 1914 by Otolia Retingerowa (the former's lover at that time and the latter's friend, Kubica 2006). Interestingly, Zdzisław Najder (1930–2021), the writer's Polish biographer, told me that he had found at an auction of books from Conrad's home library a copy of *The Family among Australian Aborigines* by Bronisław Malinowski, with a Polish dedication from the author. He must have brought it to Conrad then. Comparisons of Malinowski to Conrad are a common topic among researchers; see

especially Clifford (1988), Thompson (1995). Kuper also refers to Conrad in his paper in the present volume.
6 Kalnica is a village in Podlasie, north-eastern Poland.
7 A letter from Malinowski to Seligman of 3 November 1914; Malinowski/27/2, MP LSE; also cited in Firth 1957: 13.
8 The promotion *Sub auspiciis Imperatoris*, i.e., under the auspices of the emperor, was a great distinction. Austrian universities could present only one candidate to the emperor per year (and only the University of Vienna – three candidates); the emperor himself approved this candidacy, signed a decree, and presented the recipient with a gold signet ring with diamonds.
9 Letter from Malinowski to W. Koppers in English, 24 May 1932, Malinowski Papers, Yale University Library (later MP YUL).
10 Janusz Mucha did not find any such case in his insightful study of Malinowski's understanding of freedom, democracy and peace (Mucha 1992).
11 A letter from Malinowski to Professor Masson, undated, sent probably on 17 October 1918; MP LSE.
12 A letter-essay written by Malinowski for Aniela Zagórska of 25 February 1913 in Polish. It was probably never sent, published in Polish edition of the diary (Malinowski 2002: 128–141) and cited by Young (2004).
13 Malinowski's diary was written between 1908 and 1918 and was published in the original language, i.e., Polish, under my editorship in 2002 (Malinowski 2002). Only the last two parts, written in New Guinea, were published in English translation (Malinowski 1967), see Kubica 2024b.
14 See Wayne 1995, vol. 2: 28; and Kubica 2024a.
15 Malinowski's nostalgia is analyzed by Dariusz Brzeziński in this volume.
16 Malinowski was very sensitive to the landscape, as is especially visible in his diary (Kubica 2023).
17 Letter from Malinowski to Zofia Smoluchowska of 27 April 1942, MP LSE. Michael Young saw this map in Helena Wayne's papers, later donated to the LSE Archives, but I have not yet been able to find it there.
18 This is about Maria Czaplicka (1884–1921), a Warsaw friend of Malinowski who studied at LSE and Oxford, led the Yenisei Expedition, and after her return she was a lecturer at the Oxford School of Anthropology and the University of Bristol (Kubica 2020).
19 Natalija Jakubova analyzes Malinowski as a character in Witkiewicz's literature in her article in this volume.
20 Tadeusz Szymberski was an underrated poet, and his wife Zofia was an amateur painter. The Yale archives contain extensive correspondence between the Szymberskis and Malinowski (MP YUL).
21 The case of the Malinowski family is quite typical of mixed marriages. Research undertaken by migration studies shows that the most common model is acculturation and integration of a mixed family in the country of settlement (see Brzozowska 2017).
22 Only Józefa went to Australia in 1936.
23 An interview between Petr Skalník and Feliks Gross in English, 1979. A cassette in Feliks Gross's Papers, Archive of the Polish Institute of Arts and Sciences in America, New York (later GP PIASA).
24 Kisielewski in this volume writes about art in Malinowski's works.
25 There is a letter from Pieter to Malinowski of 15 November 1931 in Polish, MP YUL. Pieter's project was psychological and sociological; it concerned the study of young people and the impact of social and biological conditions on intelligence.
26 An interview between Petr Skalník and Feliks Gross in English, 1979. GP PIASA.
27 Letter from Waligórski to Stanisław Kot in Polish of 3 December 1935; sygn. przyb. 170/83 t. 29, Dział Rękopisów, Jagiellonian Library, Kraków.
28 Letter from Malinowski to Rozwadowski of 12 December 1923 in Polish, sygn. 2571, vol. 1, Library of Polish Academy of Arts and Sciences, Kraków.

29 Habilitation is an academic degree that entitles one to lecture at universities in Central European academic systems.
30 I wrote more about it in the paper *"The study of the ghetto" in the time of antisemitism* (Kubica 2014).
31 Letter from Obrębska-Jabłońska to Nitsch in Polish of 2 February 1937; in: Skarżyński, Smułkowa 2018: 316–317.
32 Theodor Abel, Journal of Thoughts and Events, Theodore Fred Abel Papers, Columbia University Archives (later AP CUA).
33 In Malinowski Papers is a letter of Hilda Buckmaster confirming his subscription from December 1931 to December 1932. MP YUL. The association changed its name later to: Anglo Polish Society.
34 Skalník analyzes them in his chapter in this volume.
35 Letter from Estreicher to Malinowski of 10 June 1914 in Polish, MP YUL.
36 Decision of 12 January 1914, sygn. tymcz. PAU I – 81, nr 738/1913, Polish Academy of Sciences Archives, Kraków.
37 Some authors writing on this subject suggest that the initiative was on the side of Jagiellonian University, and Malinowski did not accept it.
38 All documents in: teczka WF II-96, Jagiellonian University Archives, Kraków.
39 Letter from Malinowski to Stanisław Kutrzeba in English of 9 July 1936, sygn.tymcz. PAU 1–157, Polish Academy of Sciences Archives. Writing to Polish recipients in English Malinowski always added a hand written postscript justifying himself that he could not type himself and had no Polish typist.
40 Copy of a letter from Malinowski to Stołyhwo in English of 11 September 1938, MP YUL. Malinowski also wrote about the problem to Richard Turnwald, MP YUL.
41 The concept of the humanistic coefficient, i.e., a methodological perspective defining the research attitude towards the subject of research, was developed by Znaniecki in his *Introduction to Sociology* in the early 1920s.
42 Letter from Znaniecki to Malinowski of 30 January 1930 in Polish, Malinowski/29/21, MP LSE. It was a paper on kinship which was published in the first issue of "Przegląd Socjologiczny".
43 Malinowski visited Poznan in July 1930 (Wayne 1995, vol. 2: 155); he also visited Warsaw, Kraków and Zakopane then.
44 Press clipping at MP YUL.
45 He used this phrase in a letter to Gross in English, dated 4 October 1938, MP YUL.
46 Theodore Abel, Journal of Thoughts and Events, AP CUA.
47 Krzysztof Łukasiewicz writes more about this in his chapter in the present volume.
48 Letter from Znamierowski to Malinowski in Polish of 4 October 1928, MP YUL.
49 The information was sent to Malinowski by a "nephew" in a letter of 14 February 1937 in Polish, MP YUL.
50 Letter from Stanisław Brzeziński to Malinowski, in Polish, of 27 December 1933, MP YUL.
51 Letter from Handelsman to Malinowski in Polish, of 18 April 1934, MP YUL.
52 Copy of a letter from Malinowski to Handelsman, in English, MP YUL. Not much earlier than this correspondence, in March 1934, Dean Handelsman was attacked with brass knuckles in the university courtyard by the National Radical Camp's militia. He was also attacked by the National Democratic press.
53 Correspondence at MP YUL.
54 Letter of Stanisław Michalski, chief editor of "Organon," in Polish of 20 December 1934, MP YUL.
55 This is evidenced by Michalski's letter to Malinowski of 30 March 1938, thanking him for agreeing to write his autobiography, MP YUL.
56 See https://www.ejournals.eu/Organon/ [accessed 25 October 2023].
57 Theodore Abel's diary, AP CUA.
58 Hand written "Opening Remarks Polish Institute", Malinowski40/7, MP LSE. There is a whole folder of correspondence concerning the Institute, and also earlier Kościuszko

Association-Committee of Polish Scholars in America, of which Malinowski was a vice-president.
59 The Archive of the Polish Institute of Arts and Sciences in America, New York.
60 The Archive of the Józef Piłsudski Institute, New York.
61 That is why the appearance of Malinowski in the book by Krakow historian Tomasz Pudłocki about the contribution of intellectuals to promoting a positive image of Poland in Great Britain in 1918–1939 (Pudłocki 2015) is quite surprising. Presenting Malinowski as a promoter of the "positive image of Poland" is quite some abuse.
62 There is a photograph taken at the Anglo Polish Society Dinner at Hyde Park Hotel, 8 March 1938. Malinowski, who chaired the event, sat next to the Duke of Kent and Lady Granville, MP LSE.

Bibliography

Bator, Joanna, Sławomir Łukasiewicz. 2000. "Najgorsze jest okrucieństwo," an interview with Feliks Gross *Gazeta Wyborcza*. 2–3 (X): 18.

Borkowska, Grażyna. 2014. "A Post-Colonial Perspective on Polish Soil: Some Questions of a Sceptic," *Teksty Drugie*, 1 (special issue): 41–54.

Brzozowska, Anita. 2017. "Mixed Marriages in a Super-Diverse Society. The Case of Polish–British Couples in the Cities of the West Midlands." *Studia Migracyjne – Przegląd Polonijny*, 166 (4): 13–35.

Clifford, James. 1988. "On Ethnographic Self-Fashioning: Conrad and Malinowski." In: James Clifford., *The Predicament of Culture. Twentieth Century Ethnography, Literature and Art*. Cambridge, MA: Harvard University Press: 92–114.

Cohen, Anthony P. 2014. "A Personal History of the Anthropology of Identity." In: Michał Buchowski and Arkadiusz Bentkowski eds., *Colloquia Anthropologica. Issues in Contemporary Social Anthropology*. Poznań: Wydawnictwo Nauka i Innowacje: 233–252.

Domanalus, Anna, Irena Mamczak-Gadkowska, Monika Sak, Aleksandra Wysokińska eds. 2020. *Protokoły posiedzeń Senatu Uniwersytetu Poznańskiego 1919–1939*. Poznań: Wydawnictwo Naukowe UAM.

Dulczewski, Zygmunt. 1984. *Florian Znaniecki: życie i dzieło*. Poznań: Wydawnictwo Poznańskie.

Dulczewski, Zygmunt. 1992. *Florian Znaniecki. Live and Work*. Poznań: Wydawnictwo Nakom.

Engelking, Anna. 2006. "Józef Obrębski – etnolog i socjolog warszawski." *Sprawy Narodowościowe*, 29: 91–106.

Firth, Raymond. 1959. "Introduction: Malinowski as Scientist and as Man." In: Raymond Firth ed., *Man and Culture. An Evaluation of the Work of Bronisław Malinowski*. London: Routledge & Kegan Paul: 1–14.

Flis, Andrzej. 1988. "Cracow Philosophy of the Beginning of the Twentieth Century and the Rise of Malinowski's Scientific Ideas." In: Roy Ellen, Ernest Gellner, Grażyna Kubica, Janusz Mucha eds., *Malinowski between Two Worlds: The Polish Roots of an Anthropological Tradition*. Cambridge: Cambridge University Press: 105–127.

Gellner, Ernest. 1987. "The Political Thought of Bronisław Malinowski." *Current Anthropology*, 28 (4): 557–559.

Gellner, Ernest. 1998. *Language and Solitude: Wittgenstein, Malinowski and the Habsburg Dilemma*. Cambridge, New York: Cambridge University Press.

Głębicka, Ewa, ed. 2005. *Ich noce i dnie. Korespondencja Marii i Mariana Dąbrowskich 1909–1925*. Warszawa: Wydawnictwo Iskry.

Gross, Feliks. 1961. "Bronisław Malinowski." In: Feliks Gross, *O wartościach społecznych. Studia i szkice*. New York: Polski Instytut Naukowy: 73–80.
Gross, Feliks. 1978. *Ethnics in a Borderline. An Inquiry into the Nature of Ethnicity and Reduction of Ethnic Tensions in a One-Time Genocide Area*. Westport, CT, London: Greenwood Press.
Gross, Feliks. 1986. "Young Malinowski and His Later Years." *American Ethnologist*, 13 (3): 556–570.
Holy, Ladislav. 1992. "Kulturowe tworzenie tożsamości etnicznej: Berti z Darfur." In: Zdzisław Mach, Andrzej K. Paluch eds., *Sytuacja mniejszościowa i tożsamość*. Kraków: Zeszyty Naukowe UJ: 105–122.
Jerschina, Jan. 1988. "Polish Culture of Modernism and Malinowski's Personality." In: Roy Ellen, Ernest Gellner, Grażyna Kubica, Janusz Mucha eds., *Malinowski between Two Worlds: The Polish Roots of an Anthropological Tradition*. Cambridge: Cambridge University Press: 149–163.
Kubica, Grażyna. 1988. "Malinowski's Years in Poland." In: Roy Ellen, Ernest Gellner, Grażyna Kubica, Janusz Mucha eds., *Malinowski between Two Worlds: The Polish Roots of an Anthropological Tradition*. Cambridge: Cambridge University Press: 88–104.
Kubica, Grażyna. 2006. *Siostry Malinowskiego, czyli kobiety nowoczesne na początku XX wieku*. Kraków: Wydawnictwo Literackie.
Kubica, Grażyna. 2014. "The Survey of the Ghetto in the Time of Anti-Semitism: Feliks Gross and His Unfinished Fieldwork on the Jewish Quarters of Krakow and Vilna, 1938–1940." *East European Politics and Societies*, 28 (2): 318–340. https://doi.org/10.1177/0888325413511662
Kubica, Grażyna. 2019. "Sex, Gender and Polish Socio-Cultural Anthropology – A Historical and Reflexive Account." In: Michał Buchowski ed., *Twilight Zone Anthropology. Voices from Poland*, The RAI Country Series. Herefordshire: Sean Kingston Publishing: 74–104.
Kubica, Grażyna. 2020. *Maria Czaplicka. Gender, Shamanism, Race. An Anthropological Biography*. Translated by Ben Koschalka. Lincoln: The University of Nebraska Press.
Kubica, Grażyna. 2023. "The Two Worlds of Bronisław Malinowski's Polish Youth in His Own Writings: The Anthropologist's Historical Autoethnography." Unpublished Manuscript.
Kubica, Grażyna. 2024a. "Cultural Capital and Economic Stringency: Reality and Myth of Bronisław Malinowski's Socio-Economic Background." In: Deborah James, Chris Hann eds., *One Hundred Years of Argonauts: Malinowski, Ethnography and Economic Anthropology*. Oxford: Berghahn Books: 36–62.
Kubica, Grażyna. 2024b. "A Notorious Diarist – Bronisław Malinowski, and His Sinful Publics. Polish Editor's Remarks." In: Aleksandar Bošković and David Shankland eds., *Argonauts of the Western Pacific and The Andaman Islanders: A Centenary Study in Social Anthropology*. Canon Pyon: Sean Kingston Publishing. [forthcoming]
Lubaś, Marcin. 2019. "Dokument myśli otwartej. Studia poleskie Józefa Obrębskiego a rozważania o grupach etnicznych i stosunkach narodowościowych w polskiej etnologii i socjologii." *Sprawy Narodowościowe*, 51: 1–20.
Malinowski, Bronisław. 1922. *Argonauts of the Western Pacific: An Account of Native Enterprise and Adventure in the Archipelagoes of Melanesian New Guinea*. London: Routledge & Kegan Paul Ltd.
Malinowski, Bronislaw. 1936. "The Deadly Issue." *The Atlantic*, 158 (December issue): 659–669.

Malinowski, Bronisław. 1938. "Przedmowa do wydania polskiego." In: Bronisław Malinowski, *Życie seksualne dzikich w północno-zachodniej Melanezji*. Warszawa: Wydawnictwo Przeworskiego: XIII–XIV.
Malinowski, Bronislaw. 1944. *Freedom and Civilization*. New York: Roy Publishers.
Malinowski, Bronislaw. 1967. *A Diary in the Strict Sense of the Term*. Translated by Norbert Guterman. New York: Harcourt, Brace & World, Inc.
Malinowski, Bronisław. 2002. *Dziennik w ścisłym znaczeniu tego wyrazu*, annotations and introduction by Grażyna Kubica. Kraków: Wydawnictwo Literackie.
Mucha, Janusz. 1992. "Problems of Freedom, Democracy and Peace in Bronisław Malinowski's Anthropology." *The Polish Sociological Bulletin*, 97: 69–82.
Nowakowski, Stefan. 1992. *Sylwetki polskich socjologów*. Warszawa: Instytut Filozofii i Socjologii PAN.
Obrębski, Józef. 2005 (1936). "Problem grup i zróżnicowań etnicznych w etnologii i jego socjologiczne ujęcie." In: Anna Engelking ed., *Dzisiejsi ludzie Polesia i inne eseje*. Warszawa: Wydawnictwo IFiS PAN: 153–172.
Paluch, Andrzej. 1981. "The Polish Background to Malinowski's Work." *Man. The Journal of the Royal Anthropological Institute*, 16 (2): 276–285.
Pieter, Józef. 1986. *Czasy i ludzie*. Katowice: Śląski Instytut Naukowy.
Pudłocki, Tomasz. 2015. *Ambasadorzy idei. Wkład intelektualistów w promowanie pozytywnego wizerunku Polski w Wielkiej Brytanii w latach 1918–1939*. Kraków: Towarzystwo Wydawnicze "Historia Iagellonica."
Rapport, Nigel. 2014. "Apprehending Anyone: The Non-indexical, Post-cultural and Cosmopolitan Human Actor." In: Michał Buchowski, Arkadiusz Bentkowski eds., *Colloquia Anthropologica. Issues in Contemporary Social Anthropology*. Poznań: Wydawnictwo Nauka i Innowacje: 153–178.
Shore, Marci. 2010. "On Cosmopolitanism and the Avant-Garde, and a Lost Innocence of Mitteleuropa." In: Michael Gordin, Helen Tilley, Gyan Prakash eds., *Utopia/Dystopia. Conditions of Historical Possibility*. Princeton, NJ: Princeton University Press: 176–202.
Skarżyński, Mirosław, Elżbieta Smułkowa eds., 2018. *Korespondencja Kazimierza Nitscha i Antoniny Obrębskiej-Jabłońskiej 1925–1958*. Kraków: Księgarnia Akademicka.
Tarnawski, Władysław. 1997. "Brytyjczycy o Polsce i Polakach." *Rocznik Przemyski*, 33 (1): 7–22.
Thompson, Christina. 1995. "Anthropology's Conrad: Malinowski in the Tropics and What He Read." *The Journal of Pacific History*, 30 (1): 53–75.
Thornton, Robert and Peter Skalník eds. 1993. *The Early Writings of Bronisław Malinowski*. Cambridge: Cambridge University Press
Turner, Victor. 1969. *The Ritual Process. Structure and Anti-structure*. Abingdon, New York: Routledge.
Witkiewicz, Stanisław Ignacy. 1972. "Metafizyka dwugłowego cielęcia." In: Stanisław Ignacy Witkiewicz, *Dramaty* vol.1. Warszawa: Państwowy Instytut Wydawniczy.
Witkiewicz, Stanisław Ignacy. 2000. „Letters to Bronisław Malinowski." Translated by Michał Kłobukowski and Daniel Gerould. *Konteksty*, 248–251 (1–4): 240–290.
Wayne, Helena. 1988. "Foreword." In: Roy Ellen, Ernest Gellner, Grażyna Kubica, Janusz Mucha eds., *Malinowski between Two Worlds: The Polish Roots of an Anthropological Tradition*. Cambridge: Cambridge University Press: xi–xviii.
Wayne, Helena ed. 1995. *The Story of a Marriage: The Letters of Bronisław Malinowski and Elsie Masson*. London, New York: Routledge.
Young, Michael W. 2004. *Malinowski. Odyssey of an Anthropologist, 1884–1920*. New Haven, CT, London: Yale University Press.
Znamierowski Czesław. 1937. "Etnograf i socjolog." *Marchołt* 3 (4): 539–543.
Znaniecki, Florian. 1934. *The Method of Sociology*. New York: Rinehart & Company.
Zweig, Stefan. 1943. *The World of Yesterday*. London: Viking Press.

2 Our Ancestors

Making Sense of Bronisław Malinowski and Elsie Masson

Patrick Burke

It can be hard to write about how one's extended family has tried to make sense of its ancestors. Some family members, now dead, cannot tell us their views, and they may not have written down their thoughts; children's accounts of a parent's views of their ancestors are tied up in the children's relationships with the parent; family members may recall, or interpret, the same events and relationships differently. On top of all that, the descendant who is collating the available evidence – as I am here – cannot be detached; his views are both part of, and shape his understanding of, the story he is trying to tell. He is also trying to make sense of Bronisław Malinowski and his first wife, Elsie Malinowska (née Masson).

Malinowski and Elsie had three daughters: Jozefa, Wanda and Helena (my mother). Neither Jozefa nor Wanda, to my knowledge, committed to paper, nor are there any recorded interviews with them about, their views about their parents. We rely, therefore, on second-hand accounts. In Jozefa's case, we have above all the memories of three of her children, David, Sebastian, and Rebecca Stuart. These memories – along with the children's own claims and opinions about their maternal grandparents – are recorded in *Savage Memory: how do we remember our dead?* (2012), the documentary about Malinowski's legacy by Zachary Stuart (a great-grandson – one of David Stuart's children) and Kelly Thomson. Zachary and his brother Dan also contribute their views to the documentary; as does Zachary to a later discussion about the making of *Savage Memory* (Astacio 2013). Memories and views are also to be found in Sebastian Stuart's memoir, *What Wasn't I Thinking? A memoir of rebellion, madness, and my mother* (2021), and in Lucy Ulrich and Rebecca Stuart's 'Prologue' in *Gender and Genre in Ethnographic Writing* (2021). They have also been passed on in private conversations.

We know much less about what Wanda and her children thought about Malinowski and Elsie: there are a few comments in Sebastian's book; and, again, there are family conversations. For Helena's views, I can draw on interviews with my mother in *Savage Memory*; on my memories, and those of my sister, Lucy Ulrich, of what our mother told us, and how she felt about, Malinowski and Elsie (some of these recounted by Lucy in 'Prologue' (2021)); and on three publications: an article my mother wrote about women in Malinowski's life (Wayne 1984), her foreword to a book on Malinowski's Polish roots (in which she wrote about the lack of 'Polishness' in the household in which she and her sisters had grown up) (Wayne 1988), and – to a lesser extent – on the editorial matter in *The Story of a Marriage* (Wayne 1995), the correspondence between Malinowski and Elsie.

The 'making sense' has, for most descendants, been of Malinowski and Elsie as our forebears: their character traits; their marriage; their relationships with their daughters; their influence on the following generations. Malinowski-the-anthropologist's work and status has largely been taken as given. (Though an exception is Dan Stuart, whose work in the field of religious studies has been influenced 'in a variety of ways' by Malinowski's work and its reception (conversation with the author, 17 September 2023).) Malinowski's fieldwork diary – because of what it seems to reveal about his character – has also featured in descendants' accounts of the man.

Malinowski's Curse

In a discussion of what the Malinowskis' descendants think of their forebears, the obvious place to start is *Savage Memory*. The documentary, drawing heavily on the views of contemporary Trobrianders, anthropologists, and Malinowski family members, investigates Malinowski's legacy for the Trobriand Islands, for anthropology, and for his family. The co-director and narrator Zachary Stuart's own questions about Malinowski are a central element in the film. The directors bind together the three strands, and frame the documentary, with the idea that our forebears, though dead, are present in our lives. Malinowski's words – from his essay 'Magic, science and religion', published in 1926 – open the documentary: 'Now the soul obviously continues to lead an existence after death, for it appears in dreams, haunts the survivors in memories and in visions, and apparently influences human destinies' (Stuart & Thomson 2012, 0:0:10).

Savage Memory was not the first time the descendants had expressed publicly their views about Malinowski and Elsie. Helena published her pieces in the 1980s; *The Story of a Marriage* appeared in the 1995. But it was the first occasion on which so many descendants had done so; and the first time explicitly negative assessments – of Malinowski's relationships with Elsie and the daughters, and of the harm Malinowski's behaviour has allegedly passed down the generations – had been aired publicly.

Malinowski the anthropologist emerges for the most part well from *Savage Memory*. Less so Malinowski the husband, father, grand-, and great-grandfather. In the legacy-for-the-family strand the documentary explores the claim that Malinowski behaved with – in some versions, extreme – selfishness towards his wife and daughters: that he neglected, even abandoned, them; and that this damaged the girls, and through them their children, perhaps even their grandchildren. Malinowski was 'definitely ... a kind of negative force in the family', says Rebecca (Stuart & Thomson 2012, 0:5:30). In only partly ironic hyperbole, Sebastian casts Malinowski as a 'huge ... psychological nightmare cloud from Hell hanging over the whole family' (0:46:40). Zachary Stuart summarizes these views thus: 'There are those in my family who think that my great-grandfather's legacy has crippled all of the following generations' (0:6:00).

Malinowski's self-centredness kept him apart from his family. He was a 'powerful figure who was in ... [but not] engaged in' his daughters' lives, David states (Stuart & Thomson 2012, 0:55:35). He was, for all three daughters, 'a very distant figure because he wasn't there [in Oberbozen]', says Rebecca. 'They never actually had this man as a father, just as this father *figure*', she continues (0:22:40). Sebastian puts it baldly: 'There were three daughters, their mother got sick with multiple sclerosis, and Malinowski bought a house in Northern Italy and put the three daughters there with their dying mother and went off to pursue his career' (0:23:05). (In fact, Malinowski and Elsie bought the house together in 1923 – before the first symptoms of Elsie's multiple sclerosis appeared (in 1924), and before the birth of the youngest daughter, Helena, in 1925; nor is it clear that Malinowski imposed on Elsie and the girls, rather than deciding with her, the arrangement in which he spent the teaching terms in London and returned to the South Tyrol in the holidays. But the core meaning of Sebastian's statement remains: that Malinowski put career before family and his wife's health.)

Malinowski's distance from his wife and daughters left the girls 'feeling undervalued, unappreciated', says David (Stuart & Thomson 2012, 0:55:40), who presents this behaviour also as an expression of Malinowski's attitude to women as whole: 'He treated women badly .... He didn't value women for their intellectual capacity' (0:58:40). (A claim Sebastian echoes in his memoir: 'Bronio was condescending, especially to women' (Stuart 2021: 260).) (These last two comments illustrate how family members' accounts of a forebear may contradict each other: my mother – see below – offers a more positive assessment of Malinowski's attitude to women.)

After Malinowski's sudden death in 1942, and his second wife, Valetta Swann's, departure for Mexico City, the daughters – who, says David, in England had been 'acknowledged as part of [an] elite group' (0:56:35) – were now, at the ages of just 21, 20, and 17, respectively, in the United States, and penniless. ('The story is', says Rebecca, that Valetta 'literally ... stole the family silver' (0:57:30). Valetta, Rebecca writes elsewhere, was 'known universally in the family as "the wicked stepmother", as in a fairy tale' (Ulrich & Stuart 2021: 5).) The abandonment, one might say, was complete. The way they dealt with this, David suggests, was to 'assert' the 'only thing' they had: their 'intellects and their status' as the children of a 'great man' (0:56:50). Only in this way, David implies, could the three daughters, now orphaned (Elsie having died in 1935), create a sense of security and belonging for themselves.

In a sometimes caustic memoir that traces his fraught relationship with Jozefa, Sebastian states that being Malinowski's daughter was not just a key component of his mother's identity: it gave her a sense of superiority. She would, he writes, describe Malinowski as an '"arrogant shit" who could be "cold and cutting as ice" and "had little time for his daughters"' (because he '"desperately wanted a son"'). (Rebecca Stuart comments that Jozefa 'in many ways resented' Malinowski – 'feeling that he was not present enough after [Elsie] started to become ill, and then for virtually abandoning her to take care of her two younger sisters after their mother died' (Ulrich & Stuart 2021: 2).) But, Sebastian writes, she also 'wrapped herself in his reflected glory …'. Malinowski 'gave her … cachet, entrée, an aura of intellectual superiority' (Stuart 2021: 20). (In a somewhat kinder tone, Sebastian writes that his aunt, Helena, was '"terribly bright" in that Malinowski way that let you know she knew it' (280).) In Sebastian's childhood, Jozefa, who 'talked about "Daddy" *all the time*', recounted 'stories and gossip' about Malinowski to 'eager' dinner-party guests, and 'exalted and revered' Malinowski in the family (20). On holiday in the house in the South Tyrol that the Malinowskis had bought in 1923 (the 'Villa Malinowski'), 'Malinowski's spirit was ever-present and "Daddy-this, Daddy-that" was a continual chorus' (31). (This is another example of how family members may have different memories of the same people: Sebastian's sister, Rebecca, recalls that her mother *never* talked about Malinowski (conversation with author, September 2022).)

This trait – a sense of superiority derived from being a daughter of Malinowski – is the essence of the burden Malinowski has placed on his descendants. It is, the Stuart grandchildren tell us in the documentary, the 'Malinowski Curse': in Sebastian's words, 'a lot of intelligence and no common sense', allied with an 'unearned, condescending grandiosity overlayered over a crippling insecurity' (Stuart & Thomson 2012, 0:45:15). Or, more succinctly, as Rebecca and David put it, being a 'know-it-all' (0:45:40).

'Family dynamics … reproduce generation after generation', says David (Stuart & Thomson 2012, 0:58:25). (Sebastian in his memoir: 'Mom had a *compulsion* to feel superior to other people and … she … passed it down to me' (Stuart 2021: 260).) And so this 'curse' has been passed on, by the daughters, to the next generation: 'I've been a know-it-all all my life', says David (0:45:50). Rebecca: 'I think David has the worst of the Malinowski Curse and I'm second. He's a bigger know-it-all than I am' (0:45:45). Sebastian: 'I think I certainly got a little of it … I've worked very hard [to] do voodoo and undo the curse, but it's a long process' (0:45:15). Even a great-grandchild, Dan Stuart, Zachary's twin, 'know[s]' that he is a know-it-all, 'but I'm a know-it-all with a grain of salt' (0:46.00). (Though, unlike other family members interviewed, Dan is sceptical of, even dismisses, the claim that there is a 'Malinowski Curse': 'It's just a great myth you've all created [in order] to blame your problems on someone' (0:59:05).)

At the same time, there was – in David's recollection – no encouragement at home to read Malinowski's work: 'We weren't really introduced to Malinowski … nobody said … your grandfather was a great man, here are his works, you should know them and understand them' (Stuart & Thomson 2012, 0:4:20). (It was later, as a university undergraduate, that David read Malinowski; and, in the 1970s, was influenced in his work as a disarmament campaigner by *Freedom and Civilization* (1947) (conversation with the author, 18 June 2023).) 'I knew of [Malinowski] much more', says Sebastian, 'as this huge, looming presence in the family, than from any familiarity with his work' (0:4:40). Zachary Stuart comments more than once on what he sees as his family's unfamiliarity with Malinowski's work: 'I began reading Malinowski's books well aware that I was one of the few descendants who's taken an interest in his work' (0:11:20). This ignorance of Malinowski's work seems to be for him symbolic of his family's difficult relationship with their forebear – the relationship which the documentary is trying to explain.

Malinowski's Diary

Zachary talks with admiration of Malinowski's work: 'I'm amazed by the topics he takes on: mythology, sex, and magic rituals, spirits of the dead, flying witches and sorcery, to name a few' (0:11:30). But one element of Malinowski's writings discomforts – even angers – him (Stuart & Thomson 2012, 0:39:45): what he calls the 'racial aspects' of Malinowski's fieldwork diary, *A Diary in the Strict Sense of the Term* (Astacio 2013).[1] The directors quote from the diary: 'On the whole my feelings towards the natives are decidedly tending towards "Exterminate the brutes"' (Stuart & Thomson 2012, 0:39:30); 'I see the life of the natives as utterly devoid of interest or importance, something as remote from me as the life of a dog' (0:38:30). This Malinowski, the 'racist tyrant' as he calls him, leaves Zachary 'shocked and disgusted'; even more so, it seems, because Malinowski is a relative: this is '*my ancestor* revealing his most savage side' (0:39:40). The documentary includes explanations, or defences, of the diaries: 'what an honest document it is', says Malinowski's biographer, Michael Young, 'he keeps on trying to ransack the bottom of his soul, as he says – something like that – to "look into the farthest corners of my mind"' (0:41:05). Zachary finds it 'hard to include' statements such as these, 'because I feel like that lets him off the hook' (0:41:05). Yet include them he does; and he ends a later interview about the making of *Savage Memory* thus

> Racism is a plague on the psyche of all mankind ... Becoming less racist is a process that can only come through understanding history, exploring other cultures ... Malinowski understood this more than many of the scholars of his time. He was a humanist and what he chose to write and publish years after writing the damning diary was a body of work that looked at our common humanity ... that is what I personally see as Malinowski's intended legacy.
>
> (Astacio 2013)

Elsie's Curse

For one descendant, Sebastian Stuart, there is also another family 'curse'. It overlaps with the first, but has a different origin and a distinct character. In his memoir, Sebastian tells us that, after reading the correspondence in *The Story of a Marriage*, he came to see that it was 'Elsie, not the exalted Bronio, who was the linchpin in our family story (Stuart 2021: 248)'. It was Elsie's 'gruesome death [from multiple sclerosis] for eleven long years' (55),[2] and its effect on the daughters as they watched her decline – coupled (the overlap) with Malinowski's being 'gone for long stretches', and, 'when he was around', having 'little time for his daughters' (260) – that did damage, first to the daughters, and then to their children.

The pain of watching Elsie die a '"slow and agonizing death"' was compounded by the fact that, after her death, the daughters (or at least Jozefa and Wanda; Helena is not mentioned by name in these passages) never talked about this 'trauma': '"they just stuffed it all down ... [and] they're *still* stuffing it down"' (Stuart 2021: 83).[3] Jozefa said nothing about Elsie, Sebastian writes: 'Mom never mentioned her Australian mother, Elsie Masson Malinowski' (31). On holiday in Oberbozen, sitting on the veranda of the Villa Malinowski, Jozefa 'must have felt close to [Elsie] .... But Mom never said a word to us. There were no photographs of Elsie in the house'. Sebastian, his father Walker told him, was not to '"bring Elsie up to your mother"' (32) Elsie's slow wasting-away and death from multiple sclerosis was such a painful memory, Walker seems to be implying, that Jozefa could not bear to discuss her mother.

Sebastian suggests that Elsie's decline was worst for Jozefa, because she loved her mother even more than the others did (he quotes Elsie: 'I feel that Jozefa loves me really, deep down, more than anyone') but Elsie could not return her love: fighting her disease, 'her marriage growing tenuous, wanting to shield her daughters from witnessing her painful decline ... Elsie simply couldn't return Mom's love in kind' (254).[4]

The destructive effects on the next generation of *this* curse have been much worse than the mere 'know-it-all'-ness of the other version. The 'three girls watching their mother slowly degenerate with multiple sclerosis' (Stuart & Thomson 2012: 0:23:10), and their repression of what this meant for them, has had a profoundly damaging effect on the grandchildren's mental health: it played a role in Sebastian's own 'self-destructive behaviour and roiling insecurity'; and in the schizophrenia, drug abuse, 'disturbing fits' and 'zero impulse control' of other members of the extended family (Stuart 2021: 83). Elsie's illness 'generated monster waves that swamped, to one extent or another, her children and grandchildren' (84).

Helena's Stories

Savage Memory and *What Wasn't I Thinking?*, as well as Rebecca Stuart's comments in 'Prologue', tell us something about what Jozefa's children think about Malinowski and Elsie; and provide second-hand accounts of what Jozefa felt about her parents. We have no comparable record of Wanda's feelings and thoughts, or of those of her children. Wanda's youngest son, David Allan, has said that his mother never talked about Elsie; and rarely about Malinowski. David himself has expressed scepticism about the 'Malinowski Curse' (conversation with the author, 22 August 2022). Sebastian recalls discussions that he and Tina, Wanda's third child, had about the impact of Elsie's death (Stuart 2021: 82–84); but these are snippets only, and remembered over a distance of almost 60 years. In short, there is little material with which to build up a picture of how Wanda and her children have 'made sense' of Malinowski and Elsie.

It is easier to form a picture of Helena's thoughts and feelings about her parents: from her publications; from interviews; and from what she told her children – my sister Lucy and me – about Malinowski and Elsie.

My mother's writings about her father and Elsie have their origins – as far as I know – in the research she conducted for a biography of Malinowski. I am not sure when this work began. My sister and I became aware she was conducting biographical research at around the time of her first visit to Poland in 1970. Did she want to write about her father much earlier, but only started when she and her family were – from December 1965, after some nine years of travelling – finally settled in one country, England? Was the publication of Malinowski's fieldwork diary in 1967, with the unflattering picture it presented of the man, a catalyst? In the end, my mother did not write the biography. That task fell, of course, to Michael Young, whose magnificent *Malinowski: Odyssey of an Anthropologist 1884–1920* appeared in 2004. But the work my mother began in the late 1960s, and which carried on until she was incapacitated by illness in the mid-2000s, bore fruit in various publications.

In both the article about the influence of women on Malinowski and the foreword about Polishness in the Malinowski household (Wayne 1984, 1988), my mother paints vivid portraits of different aspects of Malinowski's life, illuminated by memories of her childhood, of her sisters and mother, family friends, and of Malinowski himself. In these writings, she casts Malinowski – for the most part – in a positive light. In places the light shines very brightly: for example, my mother emphasizes that Malinowski 'expected women to be intellectually equal to men' (Wayne 1984: 193). Citing his student Audrey Richards, she writes that, in the England of the 1920s, 'there was a horror of the clever woman, but Bronio didn't have it at all'; his women students 'blossomed in this atmosphere of being taken completely seriously' (199). This attitude extended to his daughters, to whom he gave the 'gift of never feeling that women are inferior to men. This was by no means a common gift in my youth' (193).

My mother's positive account of Malinowski includes happy memories of her father at home when she was a child. In *Savage Memory*, prompted by the place where she is being interviewed – the verandah of the Villa Malinowski in Oberbozen – my mother describes watching Elsie (whose multiple sclerosis would have been advanced) lying on 'her chaise longue' on the verandah; and 'Daddy' coming up the steps from the garden, sitting down at the end of the chaise longue, and saying, 'in the most wonderful tone of voice, "how are you, darling? How are you, Elsiusu?"'[5] This filled me with a great feeling of joy, somehow, it was so lovely to hear him talking like that to her' (Stuart & Thomson 2012, 0:19:35).

In places, though, I am struck by how my mother treats what some might regard as character flaws rather tolerantly. In the article, she describes my grandfather leaving the care of his three daughters after Elsie's death to Rosa Decall, Elsie's carer and companion, and a 'safety net of women relatives and friends who met us at trains, took us shopping, fed and entertained us'; and then explains that this was 'probably the only way for a very busy man, so often away, to cope with motherless girls'. The role of the father may have changed in the last century; but this seems to me altogether too tolerant, too understanding of my grandfather's behaviour. (It is not made less so by my mother writing that Malinowski was 'not a neglectful father' in the years after Elsie's death: that 'he kept up a steady correspondence' with his daughters when they were 'separated from him' (Wayne 1984: 199).)

Some of my mother's stories about Malinowski *are* obviously less flattering: for example, that Malinowski did not invite his three daughters to the civil ceremony at which he married Valetta Swan in 1940 (201); or that 'neither Valetta nor, more curiously, my father considered making a home for his daughters [in New Haven]: we lived with, and I'm glad to say were befriended by others, mostly in New York' (202). But even here it seems to me that my mother is pulling her punches. The tone of the second passage, for example, contrasts with how sad, even upset, she seemed when, later, she told *me* that same story: how, aged 14, she arrived in America, where she knew no-one apart from her father and sisters; how – living in a boarding house in New York – she asked her father if she couldn't come to live with him in New Haven; and how, in reply, he said 'no' – he was too busy, or words to that effect. That refusal seems, to this descendant, to be simply heartless.

I think that, in private conversation with her grown-up children my mother felt able to be frank in her views about her father. This might also have been true of her discussions with Michael Young. He writes, in *Odyssey of an Anthropologist*, that in their conversations, 'at times Helena took a more uncompromising view of [Malinowski's] shortcomings than I was inclined to do ... I found myself in the curious position of defending him against her critical judgement' (Young 2004: xiii).

But not in public: my mother would, I think, have regarded public discussion of the intimate aspects of family affairs as unseemly. I would not have been surprised that, if she had seen *Savage Memory*, or read *What Wasn't I Thinking?*, or read *this* chapter, she would have disapproved of her nephews, niece, great-nephew and son washing the family's dirty linen in public. That my mother did express critical views about Malinowski in *Savage Memory* need not undermine this point: it is possible that she regarded her comments as a contribution to a conversation with a family member.

Another point must be made here. As my mother found out more about her father – above all as she read her parents' letters – she does seem to have changed her views, to some extent, about her father's character. In *Savage Memory*, she tells Zachary that

> I don't remember actually ever blaming Daddy for how he was with my mother – until I read his letters. That was when I did begin to see that he didn't give her enough time and attention ... and that his letters became thinner in content. He tried hard. But he was moving away from her [as he pursued his career and she became increasingly ill], and she knew it. And that was what was so wrong. But that came later to me.
>
> (1:04:25)

Elsewhere in the documentary, her unhappiness at Malinowski leaving her in New York as a 14-year-old is much more evident than in her earlier, published, account

> It was very strange ... plonked into a new society – never been to America, hardly knew anything about it – and then we [were] parcelled out with

strangers, strangers, strangers ... I still think that was wrong of Daddy: he should have worked out something better than that.

(0:57:05)

My mother certainly presented our grandparents to me and my sister in a positive light when we were children. Lucy and I were brought up with stories about our maternal grandparents. Though we learnt about Elsie's death from multiple sclerosis – and that our mother was only ten when this happened – the stories painted a picture of a happy childhood. I remember anecdotes about Malinowski (some of which have appeared in print): Malinowski placing buckets of water around the Christmas tree in case one of the candles on the tree set fire to the branches (Wayne 1995: 153); his quipping to a Finnish friend, as they were heading out to a party , 'I'll provide the polish and you provide the finish' (Young 2004: 176)[6]; and – for its pointless pedantry, still my favourite – Malinowski asking, when he wanted to hear what was in a newspaper or on the wireless, not 'What's the news?' but 'What are the news?' We grew up, as I remember – one's memory of childhood can be as much a general feeling as a recollection of distinct anecdotes and tales – with the idea that our grandparents had been, well, just parents, much like our own.

Perhaps my mother was making a conscious effort to paint a positive portrait of her parents and her childhood. My sister has suggested that our mother 'sanctified her parents in her own memory'. If this is so, it makes sense that she would have passed on this sanctified view to her children. My sister again: 'Having lost her parents young and not having known her own grandparents, Mummy wanted to create [for her children] a little bit of a perfect world with grandparents in it' (conversation with the author, 20 August 2022).

There is another reason, I think, why our grandparents seemed 'normal' to me and my sister – and part of our lives. As children, Lucy and I, with one or both of our parents, stayed frequently (most years once, sometimes twice a year) in the Villa Malinowski in Oberbozen. It was our family home for 12 months, in 1964–1965, when Lucy and I also attended the village school. The house then was almost unchanged since our grandparents and their daughters had lived there: we sat on the furniture, ate off the plates, slept in the beds (and, by the feel of them, on the mattresses) with which Malinowski and Elsie had furnished the house some 40 years before.

I broadly share my Stuart cousins' critical view of Malinowski as husband and father. The correspondence gathered in *The Story of a Marriage* has shaped that view; as it has made me feel deep admiration of and affection for Elsie, my grandmother. But I do not feel burdened by having had Malinowski as a grandfather; nor do I feel scarred by Elsie's early death. (Some might say this still leaves me as a know-it-all. They would, of course, be wrong. I know that I am not a know-it-all.)

Concluding Remarks

A self-centred, ambitious grandfather who loved his wife but increasingly neglected her as her health worsened, and who did not give his daughters the attention they needed; and a loving and attentive grandmother whose early death was a profound rupture in her daughters' lives. One set of grandchildren who feel these relationships and events have been a source of disruption, even trauma, in their own lives; and another grandchild – though broadly agreeing with his cousins' assessment of the grandparents' characters – who does not feel 'cursed' by what his ancestors did or by how they suffered. The explanation for this difference lies, I think, in how the respective daughters, as mothers, transmitted to their children – how they interpreted for their children – the difficult, sometimes damaging, events of their childhood.

I have wished, writing this chapter, that I had talked to my mother more about her parents; and tried to understand better her relationship with – and her memory of – them. *The Story of a Marriage*, for example, reveals so much about Malinowski and Elsie: I wish – after I'd read it – that I had sat my mother down, with the tape recorder on, and pressed her to tell me more, not just about what she remembered, but about what she thought and felt, as a child, and as a grown-up, about Malinowski and Elsie.

Acknowledgements

The author is grateful to Lucy Ulrich, David Allan, David Stuart, Rebecca Stuart, Sebastian Stuart, Dan Stuart, Zachary Stuart, and Mark Thompson for their comments. None of them is responsible for what I have written.

Notes

1 Much has been written, of course, about the diary and the controversies to which it gave rise. See, for example, Clifford Geertz, 'Under the mosquito net', *New York Review of Books*, Vol. 9, No. 4, 14 September 1967, 12–13; Nigel Rapport, 'Surely everything has already been said about Malinowski's diary!', *Anthropology Today*, Vol. 6, No. 1, 1990, 5–9; Grażyna Kubica, 'A notorious diarist: Bronisław Malinowski and his sinful publics. A Polish editor's remarks.' Unpublished paper.
2 The first symptoms of Elsie's multiple sclerosis appeared in 1924; she died in September 1935.
3 The words in double quotation marks Sebastian attributes to our cousin, Tina Montemora, Wanda's third child.
4 David Stuart comments that Jozefa was also the oldest of the three daughters and thus most aware of what was happening to Elsie. Conversation with the author, 18 June 2023.
5 Malinowski used this, the vocative case in Polish, to address Elsie. I am grateful to Grażyna Kubica for pointing this out.
6 I discovered from the biography that this was Tancred Borenius.

References

Astacio, Patricia Alvarez. 2013. *Screening room: Savage memory* (10 July 2013). Accessed 1 June 2023.
Stuart, Sebastian. 2021. *What wasn't I thinking? A memoir of rebellion, madness, and my mother*. New York: Querelle Press.
Stuart, Zachary and Kelly Thomson, directors, 2012. *Savage memory: How do we remember our dead?* DVD. Boston, MA: Sly Productions.

Ulrich, Lucy and Rebecca M. Stuart. 2021. 'Prologue.' In *Gender and genre in ethnographic writing*, edited by Elisabeth Tauber and Dorothy L. Zinn, 1–6. Cham: Palgrave Macmillan.

Wayne, Helena. 1984. 'Bronislaw Malinowski: The influence of various women on his life and works.' *Journal of the Anthropological Society of Oxford* XV (3), 189–203.

Wayne, Helena. 1988. 'Foreword.' In *Malinowski between two worlds: The Polish roots of an anthropological tradition*, edited by Roy Ellen, Ernest Gellner, Grażyna Kubica and Janusz Mucha, xi–xviii. Cambridge: Cambridge University Press.

Wayne, Helena, ed. 1995. *The story of a marriage: The letters of Bronislaw Malinowski and Elsie Masson.* 2 volumes. London and New York: Routledge.

Young, Michael W. 2004. *Odyssey of an anthropologist, 1884–1920*. New Haven, CT and London: Yale University Press.

Part II
Revisiting Malinowski's Intellectual Background

Illustration 3 Bronisław Malinowski photographed after his doctoral promotion at the Jagiellonian University in Kraków in 1908.

3 An Argonaut from Kraków

Pre-field Malinowski as a Theorist

Petr Skalník

Dedicated to the memory of Leif Korsbaek (1941–2023)

Prologue

I grew up in communist ruled Czechoslovakia which was a satellite country of the Soviet Union. Information about the West and social anthropology was quite distorted and mostly negative. Thus I became aware of Malinowski via a 1951 article by Soviet Russian authors Dmitri Olderogge and Ivan Potekhin entitled "Functional school in ethnography in the service of British imperialism". There the two eminent Soviet Africanists wrote

> functional school as to theory is revulsive synthesis of everything backward, reactionary and antiscientific from all preceding ethnography as well as sociology. It rejects from the heritage everything that was positive in it, progressive and maintains all reactionary: biologisation of social life in the spirit of Spencer and Bastian, racism in its refined and therefore above all dangerous Anglo-Saxon forms, utmost antihistorism, etc. Functional school represents a complete break with science, it is antiscientific reactionary school.
>
> (Olderogge, Potekhin 1953: 73).

The authors continue by presenting functionalism as a product of the crisis of capitalist colonial system. They refer at length to the 'field marshall' Smuts whose philosophical work *Holism and Evolution* (Smuts 1926) they consider racist. After several pages of exposition and criticism of holism as a philosophy hanging above matter and spirit, the authors conclude that "[I]n substance can Smuts' holism hardly be called philosophy. It is an attempt to support philosophically his reactionary political views" (op. cit., p. 81). Functional school is an attempt to put into reality Smuts's ideas. The exposé about Malinowski in the article is very detailed and well-informed. His latest posthumously published works such as *Scientific Theory of Culture* (Malinowski 1944a) and *Dynamics of Culture Change* (Malinowski 1945) are branded as "biological-racist" (op. cit., p. 94). Main tenet of functionalism was according to the two authors to save imperialism and "the need to keep

DOI: 10.4324/9781003449768-6

in colonial subjugation many millions of masses" (op. cit., p. 95). Malinowski, according to the chapter, had no clear theoretical position. The result was "hopeless compilation of behaviouralism, holism, psychoracism and other kinds of contemporary American sociology...functionalism embraced all most reactionary teachings of the epoch of imperialism" (ibid.).

The vitriolic tone of the article had something substantial in itself because it predicted by more than 20 years the self-criticism of colonial social anthropology (Asad 1973). Needless to say the utterly negative assessment of Malinowski caused suspicion in me and I began to be interested in the substance: social anthropology and Malinowski as one of its founders. While I was a refugee in the Netherlands (1976–1982), Adam Kuper invited me to contribute with an article on Malinowski to a series of articles on the vocation of anthropology. In it, I dubbed Malinowski an "argonaut from Cracow" and stressed his humanism, love of freedom, his innovative fieldwork method, his teaching, activism but also his contribution to the theory of anthropology (Skalník 1982).

Introduction

Bronisław Malinowski was a child of his epoch and at the same time one of those spirits who surpassed it with his legacy in several fields. He was an unusual blend of several quests. On the one hand, the status of science and scientific civilisation was very high on his agenda. Science was the moving force of modernity and has enjoyed highest status among all educated people of his time. On the other hand, art and especially avant-garde around the turn of the 19th into the 20th century appealed to him. As I have tried to argue in one of my earlier texts (Skalník 1995), he was marginally involved in the Young Poland artistic movement which put art at the pinnacle of human creativity. For reasons of 'economy of thought', i.e. least effort, Malinowski decided to channel his career towards science. He revolutionised ethnology and made it de facto obsolete by postulating social anthropology. By his dogged strivings to establish a scientific theory of culture, he influenced the course of cultural anthropology in the USA.

I should not forget acknowledgment of the importance of writings on Malinowski by Grażyna Kubica (1988), Raymond Firth (1981, 1988), Ernest Gellner (1988), Adam Kuper (1973 and subsequent revised editions), Andrzej Paluch (1981), Janusz Mucha (1988) and Michael Young (2004). During the decades since Kuper's *Anthropologists and Anthropology* (Kuper 1973), Malinowski's work has been slowly but surely re-discovered in its many aspects. In this modest chapter, I would like to show that the formation of Malinowski during his first 30 years has determined in a decisive way what Malinowski turned into – a path-breaking social anthropologist. His youth prepared him for scientific thinking. Especially his university studies were mostly a combination of philosophy with mathematics, chemistry and physics. With his mother, he undertook a host of travels to southern European, north African and Middle East countries. He learned not only European languages such as French, Italian and Spanish but also English and Russian besides the then ubiquitous German. He was a cosmopolitan already at the early age. His

Ph.D. thesis dealt with the economy of thought and that was the first step towards his economic anthropology. Malinowski was however surrounded by art, literature and music. His close friend was Stanislaw Ignacy Witkiewicz alias Witkacy, a talent of all arts whose example was not to be matched. Malinowski was a very ambitious young man who realised pretty soon that he is not an artistic genius. Instead he chose social sciences, namely ethnology, as a subject in which he would excel and made himself famous by transcending it through his fieldwork in Melanesia. That decision however alienated him from his native country, from his friends and ultimately from his beloved mother.

Cosmopolitanism means citizen of the world and Malinowski felt himself at home in at least most of Europe, eventually Australia, Africa and North America. Malinowski was also *homo politicus* because he clearly distinguished between the democratic values and totalitarianism. The decision not to fight for the Emperor Franz Joseph was very political and patriotic as well. He was clearly aware of his Polishness which he proved during the war when he was considered an enemy subject. The very fact that he managed to carry out his fieldwork plans practically without delay and at the cost of a break with Witkacy (who as Russian subject decided to travel from Australia to Russia in order to fight Germans and Austrians) is a proof that he managed to persuade the Australian colonial officials, especially A. Atlee Hunt, that he was a *bona fide* person. Was Mailu field experience a test of his loyalty? I think that it was an elegant test if such at all (see Young 1988).

His lukewarm or even agnostic relation to religion did not prevent him to be interested in the theory of religion. Before he left for Australia and the Papua fieldwork, he established himself as a theorist by publishing the book *The Family among the Australian Aborigines. A Sociological Study* (1913). This was a major result of his study at the London School of Economics and served as a partial requirement for a D.Sc. thesis. Still achieved in April 1914, just before the departure for Australia, was his large manuscript in Polish. Entitled *Wierzenia pierwotne i formy ustroju spolecznego* (*Primitive Beliefs and Forms of Social Order*) with a subtitle "A view on the genesis of religion with special emphasis on totemism", it was to be submitted as a habilitation thesis to his alma mater, Jagiellonian University of Kraków. The Academy of Arts in Kraków published it in the book form in 1915 when Malinowski was already in the southern hemisphere. This major work has 356 pages and references are made not only to 88 works in German, French and English, mainly dealing with religion and magic but also to general works such as Wundt's *Völkerpsychologie* (1912). Unfortunately, it was never translated into English.

These major pre-fieldwork works prove that Malinowski was exceptionally well prepared theoretically. Malinowski went to the field with the idea to find enough data to fit into his pre-field theoretical framework (Malinowski 1967: 158). In Kiriwina he found such data. They concern economy, magic, agriculture, psychology and politics. His books are a clear proof of success. The success of his first field monograph, *Argonauts of the Western Pacific* (1922), can be seen already in the main title. Argonauts were subject of an ancient Greek myth and they went across the Black Sea in order to find a golden fleece. What a romantic parallel!

Malinowski's prose is an attempt at a literary piece of art on a scientific note. He wrote it, with the substantial help of his young wife, herself a literary talent, in another romantic place, Canary Islands. Once it was clear that his book will be published in London by Routledge, a reputable Publisher, he was free to make the most important decision: to cut the umbilical cord with Poland. In the same year as the publication, he took his wife to Poland. The trip helped him to decide not to take an offer of a teaching position in his alma mater. Malinowski did not buy a summer house in Zakopane but acquired a spacious villa in Oberbozen/Soprabolzano located on the southern slopes of the Alps in South Tyrol (Tauber and Zinn 2023). That country, similarly to Galicia, Malinowski's homeland, belonged to Austria as its portion of partitioned Poland until 1918. Italy as a victorious power in the Great War received it through the peace process of Versailles. It should be stressed that Mussolini marched on Rome also in 1922 and that ominous event must have prepared Malinowski for his politics perhaps more than the Great War. His opposition to Fascism, National Socialism and Communism climaxed by his last book *Freedom and Civilization* written 20 years later (Malinowski 1944c). I shall now continue with four parts of the chapter.

Malinowski 1884–1914

The first 30 years of his life, Bronisław Malinowski spent in Europe with short recreational trips to North Africa and the Near East. The fieldwork followed by his teaching and writing career was shorter, only 28 years. His pre-fieldwork writings are essential for his anthropological career (Malinowski 1993g). Malinowski's young years can be divided into three stages (Korsbaek 2016). The first period was his studies at the Jagiellonian University of Kraków when he studied subjects such as philosophy, mathematics, physics. The second stage was his study sojourn in Leipzig that brought him in touch with Wundtian psychology and Bücher's economy. Finally, between 1910 and 1914, he studied sociology and ethnology at the London School of Economics (though two years out of four he spent in his native country).

The question of a fieldwork in non-European areas emerged within first two years in London. The fieldwork examples of his teachers Westermarck and Seligman influenced his planning. Especially Seligman inspired him to go to the areas of his expertise. First the northeastern Sudan was suggested by him as Malinowski's fieldwork site. Malinowski was to learn Arabic and should have worked among the coastal peoples such as Bisharin. But that intention was thwarted by the rejection of funding (Young 2004: 192–194). Though Seligman did not give up searching for funds and eventually he suggested that Malinowski goes to "Melanesia", concretely Papua, southern part of the Australian administered New Guinea. Considerable financial means were found and Malinowski was to become the key figure in the expedition named after Robert Mond, a philanthropist without whose endowment Malinowski's research would never materialise (Young 2004: 245–246). Once the prospect of the field research in the fifth continent was settled, Malinowski concentrated on theoretical works with special emphasis on Australian data. But before embarking on his European studies, he finished two important theoretical works, namely his Ph.D. Thesis "On the principle of the economy of thought" and a long essay "Observation on Friedrich Nietzsche's *The Birth of Tragedy.*"

The Kraków thesis (see Flis 1988) is an apology of science against metaphysical speculations (Nietzsche's nihilism). It is a critical analysis of the views of physicists such as Ernst Mach (1898) and philosophers such as Richard Avenarius (1888, 1890), influential in the epoch, i.e. up to the beginning of the 20th century. Malinowski dissects a concept of the least effort in economy and other human activities. This concept is a human ability and here he differs from Darwinian conceptualisation. But Malinowski is a philosophical monist with emphasis on empiricist approach. Whereas Mach is interested in physical phenomena, Avenarius analyses mind whose task is apperception. Malinowski defines the least effort as derived from the concept of mathematical minimum. In practice, it means good management and economy specifically means thrift. "At any rate, both the concept of least effort and that of economy may be reduced to the concept of a minimum" (Malinowski 1993a: 91). Mach understands the essence of philosophy as the economy of thinking. Avenarius's psychological argumentation concerns the question of "solving tasks by means of the least effort" the latter being "the expenditure of physiological strength accompanying the psychological process" (Malinowski 1993a: 98). But Avenarius cannot avoid reification and metaphysics of his psychological theory. In his thesis, Malinowski introduces the concept of a function in the sense that "any consideration of maximum-minimum becomes fruitful only when it is applied to functions" (op. cit., p. 92). He gives an example of an economic enterprise with an annual budget. The expenditures, a maximum-minimum, have no meaning unless we know the purposes, i.e. "functional connection between the expenditures and the items purchased." Then, a scientific examination of the enterprise is possible. The principle of univocal determinism, writes Malinowski, means that there is no spontaneity in nature, "all factors of every process are exactly and unequivocally determined" and laws of nature can be sought, formulated and applied (op. cit., p. 93). Here, I can discern Malinowski's potential application of the concept of function in the social sciences.

Malinowski is strongly convinced about the power of scientific laws. These laws are objective and do not require approval or plebiscite of mankind. He writes:

> Even if only one normal man remained on the earth, and all other had lost the ability to make judgments…that one man would not need to doubt the value of the material and scientific conquests of mankind. …The tremendous practical importance of the former and the latter instruments would enable him to completely annihilate his adversaries. The attitude of the white man to his less civilized, coloured fellow men illustrates this point sadly and significantly.
>
> (op. cit., p. 112)

Though Malinowski refers to 'less civilized, coloured fellow men,' he is not propagating racist views but stresses the power of science as an instrument of conquest of the non-European world that was not equipped with the scientific knowledge and therefore could not prevent its subjugation. The attitude of Europeans to their 'less civilized, coloured fellow men' he views as sad but also significant. Significant means that being armed with science enables colonisation.

Malinowski was originally attracted to ethnology and anthropology by listening to his mother's reading (because of his bad eyesight) to him of Frazer's *The Golden Bough* during his university studies (1902–1906). First, it was reading as entertainment, later he proceeded with the critical survey of Frazer's theories of magic and religion. Malinowski believed that less civilised fellow men are equipped with magic which is "completely different from science." Magic "does not perceive in the world of objective things but relates emotionally, subjectively" (Malinowski 1993b: 117). He noted that "magic, as a form of human activity based on experience, is an equivalent of science." However, "[S]cience is something more than belief; it is a principle in which we believe, and moreover which we understand." Whereas religion "is a system of tradition explaining and justifying the world" as well as a system of norms regulating human conduct, "[D]ogmatics and ethics are the two components of religion" (op. cit., p. 118).

Critique of Frazer

Malinowski's review article of four volumes of Frazer's *Totemism and Exogamy* was undertaken because he considered it "undoubtedly the most important publication in the social sciences which appeared in English in recent years" (op. cit., p. 123). The review was written in Polish in London and it is certain that its contents were never revealed to Frazer. The importance of totemism consists in its quality as a religious conception as well as social institution. Malinowski appreciates Frazer's "unusual erudition, his great ability to illuminate facts and to demonstrate essential connections between them." He elegantly praises Frazer's 'invaluable treasury' and 'mine of facts' but at the same time suggests that other scholars would be able "to formulate more precise and more scientific theories than the original author." Himself, Malinowski states bluntly that "the theories set forth by Professor Frazer in the present work cannot stand up to serious criticism" as "they possess all the advantages and defects of the English anthropological school" (op. cit., p. 125). As if to milden this devastating judgment, Malinowski reproduces Frazer's definition of totemism and adds "[W]e are here dealing with a brilliant empirical treatment of the subject, which constitutes such an outstanding virtue of the English anthropological school" (ibid.). There are different types of totems but "only clan totems have an almost exclusively sociological significance" (ibid.). Malinowski went to London to study explicitly sociology. Nevertheless, he refers to his studies as ethnographical, ethnological and anthropological as if in dependence to what audience he speaks. I will give examples of it later. The exposé of totemism is very rich and Frazer introduces data from the whole world and "his work may be read with interest as a colourful anthropo-geography. However, in the systematic listing of facts, we are struck by the lack of a clearly formulated, purposeful method, the lack of posing a problem and tracing the course of research" (op. cit., p. 126). Malinowski laments that lack of method in 'comparative ethnology' and criticises evolutionist assumptions of the author. "The fewer hypothetical assumptions and postulates to be found in a given description of facts, the greater the value of description...every description and classification must thus be based of necessity on theoretical formulation" and "it is necessary to formulate precisely a method for comparing ethnographic phenomena" (op. cit., p. 127). Malinowski's principal and fundamental reproach against Frazer's method is that

> he does not give us a clear and objective picture of the state of things, independently of any hypotheses or theories. On the contrary, when describing facts Frazer constantly employs concepts drawn from purely hypothetical and, as it were, personal assumptions and dogmas. He makes no clear line of demarcation between facts and inferences from facts.
> (op. cit., p. 135)

Frazer follows the general tone of Australian ethnography of the period where "ethnological methods are based on evolutionism" and argues for example for 'primitiveness' of the Arunta tribe (op. cit., p. 136). As a result "neither Frazer's general reasoning nor the facts mentioned by him stand up to criticism. His general reasoning is always arbitrary with references to social organization and culture..." (op. cit., p. 137). Malinowski admits that Australian material which Frazer introduces is rich but at the same time is not dependable scientifically because he elevates legends and guesses to historical truths. Malinowski remarks that

> the aims of exact science do not consist in constructing theories and hypotheses concerning areas beyond the limits of experience, but rather in an exact and accurate description of facts. The interest of an exact scientist should focus on understanding and penetrating the mechanism and essence of social phenomena as they exist at present and are accessible to observation, and not in order that these phenomena should serve as a key to solving the riddle of a prehistoric past about which we cannot know anything empirically.
> (op. cit., p. 140)

I am convinced that here, during his pre-field period, Malinowski postulated his methodological presentism and positivism that in combination with functionalism completed his theoretical equipment.

> The ultimate goals of any scientific investigation are to discover the facts, to acquire a knowledge of their connections and interdependence, and consequently to gain the ability to deal with them comprehensively. All of this would be a banal truth for a natural scientist, but in the sociological sciences the interesting but inexact chats about the origins of various social institutions and beliefs should be replaced at last by less attractive but more exact investigations of sociological laws.
> (op. cit., pp. 140–141)

Part I of Malinowski's review closes with the assertion that "beyond the naively presented problem of evolution there are a number of sociological problems which possess more certain foundations and whose theoretical significance is not less" (op. cit., p. 144).

Part II of the review first concerns totemism among the Torres Straits islanders and then the 'ethnology' of the New Guinea island where totemism 'unquestionably' exists but "we do not have a clear and accurate picture of the totemism of even one tribe" (op. cit., p. 149). Malinowski proceeds further into Melanesia and Oceania where Frazer does not always find totemism. Samoan totemism, for example, is not really a totemism because Samoans worship gods. Religion is defined unsatisfactorily by Frazer because he stresses the psychic criteria as decisive (ibid., pp. 160–161). Frazer, according to Malinowski, mentions sociological facts as differentiating between religion and magic. But he

> does not take sociological criteria into account at all, and this is a fundamental error. Religion is just as much a form of social organization as it is a collection of beliefs, and the latter is conditioned in each man by his living together with other members of a society.
>
> (op. cit., p. 163)

"Psychological concepts cannot serve to define religion and relationship to magic"..."Religion, as a social term for all of man's transactions with the supernatural world, also permeates every section of social life" (op. cit., pp. 164–165). Eventually, Malinowski comes with his own definition of religion as "any collection of beliefs and practices referring to supernatural powers and bound into an organic system, which are expressed in social life by a series of acts of a cult which is systematic, public, obligatory and based on tradition" (op. cit., p. 166). If applied to the facts, Australian totemism is a form of religion, "for it possesses a system of organically connected traditions permeating the whole social organization" (op. cit., p. 167). Malinowski goes through several areas of Frazer's research such as Africa and in particular the kingdom of Buganda where totemism is highly developed as a social phenomenon than religious. He also points out the developed totemism among particular peoples of North America such as the Omaha who have eleven animal totems, one plant and four inanimate objects. Especially, bison and its bodily parts were taboo for a number of Omaha clans whose ancestors were believed to be bisons. As to the Iroquois, whom Frazer studied from Morgan, "the famous American ethnologist", but "because of the one-sided interest of this researcher in the social organization exclusively, we know nothing about the religious aspect of the totemism of the Iroquois" (op. cit., p. 178). Malinowski continues to comment on Frazer's characterisations of totemism among the Prairie and Pueblo Indians.

Part III of this extended review article surveys totemic phenomena. Malinowski characterised the whole work as a compilation, based on 'great erudition'

> but not digested and not grasped within a theoretical framework...The author, in fact, has done nothing to facilitate our orientation with a clear and concise

look at the facts. If we view the task of science to be close and succinct description and comprehension of the facts, achieved through the precise classification of those facts, the creation of generalizations, and the inclusion of the specific facts under the general concepts created, in this case Frazer's work, which does none of this, is not, in the proper sense of the word, a scientific work.

(op. cit., p. 184)

This devastating criticism opens for Malinowski the section of the compendium that deals with the origins of exogamy. Here, Frazer criticises and rejects the theories of McLennan, Westermarck and Durkheim on the origins of exogamy while he accepts 'more or less' Morgan's views. His own theory includes the prevention of incest as the motivation for overcoming of 'promiscuity'. 'Disgust over' incest was caused by a belief in its harmful influences on the fertility of both people and animals. But Malinowski finds that Frazer's idea that all this "was the result of a conscious reform, is entirely contrary to the scientific principles..." (op. cit., p. 186). Malinowski criticises Frazer for dismissing the varieties of totemism and therefore underestimating comparative research. To search for the 'most primitive' form and then to think that the definition of totemism is best to be found in it, is considered by Malinowski as 'naïve'. Frazer's theorising on totemism as a 'logical deduction from a given belief' ignores that totemism is an extremely fundamental and complicated form of social organisation, and 'does not merit discussion' (op. cit., p. 193). Malinowski rejects one Frazer's theory of totemism after another. "Frazer's fundamental error...is that he considers totemism to be an integral whole, a cultural unity, as if it came from a single casting" (op. cit., p. 197). Finally, Malinowski arrives at "a rejection of Frazer's conception of totemism as well as his manner of explanation" (op. cit., p. 199).

The exhaustive review of Frazer's *Totemism and Exogamy* is to my mind the first and essential evidence for what Ernest Gellner characterised as "the replacement of Sir James Frazer by Bronisław Malinowski as *the* paradigmatic anthropologist" (Gellner 1998: 113) even before social anthropology replaced ethnology. "The move from Frazer to Malinowski constitutes a complete break, a *coupure*" (op. cit., p. 114). Gellner brilliantly shows pros and cons of Frazer and concludes uncompromisingly

[T]he succession of the kingship or priesthood of the Sacred Grove of Anthropology passed from Frazer to Malinowski precisely in the manner in which things had once been acted out in Nemi. Intellectually speaking, Malinowski slew Frazer and thereby succeeded him.

Frazer, who had no idea about the devastating contents of Malinowski's review of his four volumes opus on totemism and exogamy,[1] unwittingly confirmed his own defeat if not execution in 1922 by writing the laudatory preface to *Argonauts of Western Pacific*. There, he not only calls Malinowski his "esteemed friend" but approves of his research methods, "Both by theoretical training and by practical experience he was well equipped for the task which he undertook." Frazer approves of Malinowski's 'theoretical training' as it was exemplified by his book on the family among the aborigines of Australia (see below] and of his 'practical experience' shown by his first fieldwork among the Mailu of New Guinea (Frazer 1922: vii).

Australian Studies

That Malinowski was 'esteemed' long before going to do his New Guinea fieldwork is evidenced by fact that his first monograph published in London in 1913, though based 'only' on library research, was included as volume 2 of the University of London series Monographs on Sociology edited by none other than professors L.T. Hobhouse and E. R. Westermarck. To the Festschrift for his London teacher Westermarck (see Shankland 2022), Malinowski contributed a chapter based on Australian material (Malinowski 1993c: 209–227). By 1912, Malinowski was pretty sure that his forthcoming fieldwork will be situated in Oceania. Therefore, from now onwards, he spent time and energy on studying various aspects of social order and religion in Australia. The above-mentioned contribution to the Westermarck Festschrift was one of them. Another was a paper "Tribal male associations in Australia", read by Malinowski before the Kraków Academy which develops his thoughts on kinship organisation that, according to him, has two aspects: the family and individual kinship. Malinowski stresses that "the old men wield the real power, but to understand the basis of this power, an investigation into the organization of the tribal society of males is necessary" (Malinowski 1993d: 201). The paper describes the initiation ceremonies as the main aspect of the secret male associations. But that description serves Malinowski as a basis for theoretical and critical remarks. He criticises evolutionist approaches. "An institution is considered as explained when its 'origins' are found and its evolution is traced" (op. cit., p. 204). "We often find that these very answers to the question of 'origins' are not really evolutional" but sociological, biological and even metaphysical.

"The sociological reason, the function or task that a given institution performs in society, is often confused with its aim as subjectively conceived by society" (op. cit., p. 205). Therefore, the task of the researcher is "to show what the chief social functions of these male societies are, what part they play in the integration of the various other institutions and wherein lies their general importance for the whole social structure" (ibid.). Malinowski concludes that the male associations

> are the basis of sexual separation…males only can be initiated…highly developed magico-religious cult (some of which possess a distinct economic aspect) …are the duty of the initiated exclusively. The whole public and political life of the tribe rests upon this organization; by its means women are consequently secluded from public life.
>
> (ibid.)

Here we can see that Malinowski operates with the functionalist or even structural-functionalist mode of thinking. In London, he acquired the sociological toolkit that he is going to employ in the major study of the Australian aboriginal family.

Malinowski's first monograph *The Family among the Australian Aborigines* was written during his early time in London. Eventually, it was published in 1913. In 1916, together with his *The Natives of Mailu* (Malinowski 1915b), this book earned him a D.Sc. from the London School of Economics (University of London) (Firth 1957: 3). Its subtitle is "A Sociological Study" which symbolises the conversion of the writer to the primacy of the study of social problems. (Eventually, he arrived at "social anthropology" as an independent discipline whose link to sociology is evident.) The Family book of more than 300 pages is divided into nine chapters preceded by author's foreword. In the latter, he argues for a detailed study of Australian family because of the importance of Australian kinship. But at the same time, Malinowski stresses 'sufficiently wide theoretical scope' and the need "to demonstrate some general principle upon the particular example treated" and also points out "plenty of subjects of great theoretical importance, some of which, as yet not fully considered by Sociologists." While he avoids the reconstruction of origin and evolution of the family institution, he also points out the importance of the study of hitherto neglected social phenomena such as "facts of daily life, the emotional side of family relations, the magico-religious ideas of the aborigines about kinship and sexual relations, customary as well as legal norms" must be also included (Malinowski 1913: v). Malinowski's research credo was that, in one sentence, "each social institution must be studied in all its complex social functions as well as in its reflexion in the collective psychology" (op. cit., p. vi). The whole book follows it literally. His foreword refers to his predecessors such as Bachofen, Morgan, McLennan and Cunow. While he praises these classics, he considers their work as lacking of the pure sociological approach. For example, when reading Cunow, "one has the impression that the Australian tribes were a museum of sociological fossils from various ancient epochs of which the petrified form has been rigidly preserved, but into whose inner nature it is quite hopeless to inquire" (op. cit., p. vii). But Tylor and Westermarck surpassed the speculations of the preceding researchers. Especially, Westermarck in his *The History of Human Marriage* resolved "the problem of marriage into that of family" (op. cit., p. viii). Therefore, I presume Malinowski wrote his book on the family while meaning also kinship and marriage. He actually characterises his task as follows

> I shall avoid making any hypothetical assumptions, or discussing general problems which refer to the origin or evolution of the family. I wish only to describe in correct terms and as thoroughly as possible all that refers to actual family life in Australia. In other words I intend to give in outline the social morphology of the Australian family.
>
> (op. cit., p. 1)

While going through various authors before him, Malinowski approves with a statement of Ernst Grosse: "chief sources of error in sociology is speculating on the origins and prehistory of an institution before this institution is thoroughly known in the present state" (op. cit., p. 4). And he further stresses: "we have to look for the connection between the facts of family life and the general structure of society and forms of native life" (op. cit., p. 8). This he does throughout the whole of his book. He also dwells on the right of the reader to "fully to judge and exercise his criticism" (op. cit., p. 33). All facts mentioned in the book are supported by references to all serious ethnographies existing to the moment of Malinowski's writing. There is no place for conjecture and speculation in this library monograph. All the statements had to be critically evaluated. "In general the chief methodic rule in utilizing the evidence was to arrange the whole argument and inferences in the clearest possible manner" (op. cit., p. 294). Malinowski is well aware of the fact that 'the Australian Aborigines' are not an ethnic unit. But "many general, fundamental features of family life" are common for all Australian tribes (ibid.). As to marriage, Malinowski found that "institution of marriage is the object of definite collective ideas, consequently is firmly established in the social organization" (op. cit., p. 296). The individual family was described in great detail while kinship organisation would need further elaboration. Such comprehensive analysis had to wait until Malinowski's special monograph from the Trobriands, namely *The Sexual Life of Savages.*

Primitive Beliefs and Social Organisation

As his fieldwork was approaching, Malinowski concentrated ever more on the social organisation in relation to the belief system, especially totemism. In October 1913, he presented his thoughts concerning this relationship in a Kraków Academy of Arts lecture session. I can consider this lecture an appetizer for his large monograph which Malinowski (1915a) presented to the academy in the Spring of 1914, just before his departure for Australia (cf. Young 2004: 240, 243–244). Malinowski attempts to establish the theory of totemism through both the definition of the essence of totemism and the genesis of totemism. The essence of totemism has a religious aspect and the social aspect. By comparing 62 totemic tribes, he arrives at the preponderance of animal totems. Most totems, whether animals or plants, are edible. And indeed, the totems are eaten at special ceremonies which express "the assimilation of man with his totem" (Malinowski 1993e: 233). His approach is again "in favor of scientific undertakings" by "achieving maximum results with a minimum of effort and risk" and where "speculation must reckon more and more with the toilsome collecting and comparing of facts" (op. cit., p. 242). In the foreword to his 1915 monograph, dated in London in April 1914, Malinowski stresses again that "with emphasis to note that theories here postulated are not a priori speculations, but they are result of detailed researches on concrete problem" (Malinowski 1915a: vi). The author used 88 references to both theoretical and descriptive works on totemism. When summarising his findings contained in five long parts of the book, Malinowski stresses that his analysis of the "genesis" of totemism does not construct "beginnings" of totemism as an institution as it is usually presented. He instead analysed the relationship of beliefs to social elements and psychological needs. "I wish to emphasize that my limitation to such modest and partial translation is conscious and intentional and that from principle and conviction I waived the pretense of deciphering of all possible riddles, connected with totemism" (op. cit., p. 325). He adds that scientific work does not produce the 'philosophical stone'. It does not allow to find a key, which would open the locks of all secrets of the world, especially when it concerns primitive humankind.

> The construction of 'beginnings' as concrete history of prehistorical institutions, beliefs and customs, is always something very risky. Ethnological data in the projection on the schemas of historical evolution of humankind is leading only to very unfirm solutions of only most general problems.
>
> (ibid.)

That is why many problems were left without solution. Malinowski is strongly positivist here, because he is well aware of lack of data that would allow conclusions about origins. Especially he is an opponent of those 'theories' that totemism emerged in a particular place and then spread around the world. This thought, expressed namely by Fritz Gräbner, is according to him 'unscientific in the highest degree'. Also, the lack of data does not allow to answer the question how clan emerged and what is the genetic relation between the clan and totemic beliefs. Even if not unscientific, there is lack of data that would help answer such questions. Malinowski sees that lack of data does not allow to resolve concrete historical problems and leads to 'absolute bankruptcy of attempts in that direction.' All those theories that should answer such problems can be characterised by the Latin proverb 'quot capita tot sensus' meaning as many heads, so many opinions (op. cit., p. 327).

Clan system is genetically independent of totemism. To postulate whatever hypothesis how lineage, family or local group turned into clan is only a toy of imagination. But only clan is found in relation with exogamy and totemism. Exogamy was explained by Westermarck as a biological phenomenon, but Malinowski is not interested in its genesis but in its social function, The link between clan and exogamy is an expression of its social basis. Malinowski is opposed to exact answer to the question of how different clans acquired particular religions connected with particular totems. It is impossible to describe concrete factors leading to it. 'Ethnological material and general speculations' cannot give answer to such question (op. cit., p. 344). "Religion in general, especially the primitive one, is principally a social matter and an individual cult would be in primitive conditions a complete impossibility" (op. cit., p. 346).

Malinowski also prepared a short paper read at the meeting of the British Association for the Advancement of Science, held in 1914. That was his last written piece before his fieldwork-based writings (Malinowski 1993f: 243). Malinowski considers this question 'of utmost importance for the general theory of religion'. He rejects Durkheimian dichotomy of sacred and profane (Durkheim [1912] 1976) which he considers 'dogmatic' and also Crawley's viewpoint that 'for savage everything has got a religious dimension' (Crawley 1902). Spencer and Gillen (1904), who at the time of Malinowski's writing were the best ethnographers of religion in central Australia, found that that there was sharp division of everyday life from magico-religious activities. On the other hand, he refers to the writings of the Seligmans (Seligman and Seligman 1911) and Thurnwald (1913) who through their fieldwork experience among the Veddas and the people of the Bismarck Archipelago and Solomon Islands respectively found that there was no radical opposition between religious and profane. Thus, Malinowski concludes that

> religious life can be different amongst various peoples, depending as it does upon various social conditions...the division into *religious* and *profane* is not an essential and fundamental feature of religion...it is an accidental feature, dependent chiefly upon the social part played by religion. (Malinowski 1993f: 244–245)

Conclusion

The purpose of the present chapter was to document the thesis that Malinowski's intellectual preparation during the first half of his life that preceded his famous field researches in Melanesia was decisive for the success of the second half of his life. Malinowski's intellectual formation was not primarily anthropological. He studied various fields including mathematics and philosophy. Then, he proceeded with the study of psychology and economy. And finally, during the last four years before his fieldwork, he embarked on the study of sociology and ethnology. That brought him to the vast literature on Australian Aborigines and the problem of totemism.

I have tried first to characterise Malinowski's philosophy. He is convinced about the decisive power of scientific method. This power consists in maximum achievement through minimum effort. Social facts are best understood by way of their function. Malinowski's functionalism that dominated social sciences and other human undertakings such as architecture throughout several decades around the middle of the 20th century was first discovered during the first 15 years of that century when he studied in Kraków, Leipzig and later in London. Malinowski relied on his meticulous study of the most recent works. Therefore, he could not avoid major works by Frazer and Durkheim. His analysis of Frazer's four volumes on totemism and exogamy showed clearly that the conclusions Frazer arrived at were not really scientific because they were not based on facts but speculations.

Altogether is the whole pre-field period in Malinowski's scholarly development marked by the rejection of the search for origins of social institutions for which there is no proof. The Soviet criticism of Malinowski's approach missed the point. Malinowski is a positivist who searches for scientific laws based on the knowledge of facts. Because he is not satisfied with the theories of his older contemporaries, he eagerly prepares for his own fieldwork among the 'savages' that would provide his own data. The quality of the data would then prove his theories. His two pre-fieldwork books are brilliant examples of detailed but critical treatment of published material on mostly Australian Aborigines. Malinowski eventually arrives at the sociological functions of primitive religion. His theoretical anthropology is sociological, leading logically towards social anthropology and away from ethnological reconstructivism.

Note

1 When Frazer died in 1941, Malinowski wrote a long essay, 'a biographical appreciation', where he highly praises him as 'great humanist', but also noted that "Frazer never read adverse criticisms or reviews of his books" (Malinowski 1944b: 183).

References

Asad, Talal, ed. 1973. *Anthropology and the colonial encounter*. London: Ithaca Press.
Avenarius, Richard. 1888, 1890. *Kritik der reinen Erfahrung*. 2 vols. Leipzig: Reisland.
Crawley, Alfred Ernest. 1902. *The mystic rose: A study of primitive marriage and of primitive thought in its bearing on marriage*. London: Methuen.
Durkheim, Emile. 1912. *Les formes élementaires de la vie religieuse, le système totémique en Australie*. Paris: F. Alcan.
Firth, Raymond. 1957. "Introduction: Malinowski as scientist and as man". In *Man and culture. An evaluation of the work of Bronislaw Malinowski*, edited by Raymond Firth. London: Routledge and Kegan Paul, 1–14.
Firth, Raymond. 1981. "Bronislaw Malinowski". In *Totems and teachers. Perspectives on the history of anthropology*, edited by Sydel Silverman. New York: Columbia University Press, 101–140.
Firth, Raymond. 1988. "Malinowski in the history of social anthropology". In *Malinowski between two worlds. The Polish roots of an anthropological tradition*, edited by Roy Ellen, Ernest Gellner, Grażyna Kubica, and Janusz Mucha. Cambridge: Cambridge University Press, 12–42.
Flis, Andrzej. 1988. "Bronislaw Malinowski's Cracow doctorate". In *Malinowski between two worlds. The Polish roots of an anthropological tradition*, edited by Roy Ellen, Ernest Gellner, Grażyna Kubica, and Janusz Mucha. Cambridge: Cambridge University Press, 195–200.
Frazer, James. 1922. "Preface". In *Argonauts of the Western Pacific. An account of the native enterprise and adventure in the archipelagoes of Melanesian New Guinea*, by Bronisław Malinowski. London: Routledge, vii–xiv.
Gellner, Ernest. 1988. *Language and solitude: Wittgenstein, Malinowski and the Habsburg dilemma*. Cambridge: Cambridge University Press.
Korsbaek, Leif. 2016. *El joven Malinowski*. México: Escuela Nacional de Antropología e Historia.
Kubica, Grażyna. 1988. "Malinowski's years in Poland". In *Malinowski between two worlds. The Polish roots of an anthropological tradition*, edited by Roy Ellen, Ernest Gellner, Grażyna Kubica, and Janusz Mucha. Cambridge: Cambridge University Press, 89–104.
Kuper, Adam. 1973. *Anthropologists and anthropology. The British school 1922–1972*. New York: Pica Press. Revised editions published as *Anthropology and anthropologists*.
Mach, Ernst. 1898. *Popular scientific lectures*. Trans. Thomas J. McCormack. Chicago, IL: Open Court Publ. Co.
Malinowski, Bronislaw. 1913. *The family among the Australian Aborigines. A sociological study*. London: University of London Press.
Malinowski, Bronisław. 1915a. *Wierzenia pierwotne i formy ustroju społecznego. Pogląd na geneze religii ze szczególnem uwzględnieniem totemizmu* (Primitive beliefs and forms of social order. A view on the genesis of religion with special emphasis on totemism). Kraków: Akademia umiejętności.

Malinowski, Bronisław. 1915b. "The natives of Mailu: Preliminary results of the Robert Mond research work in British New Guinea". *Transactions and Proceedings of the Royal Society of South Australia*, vol. 10, pp. 494–706. Issued in 1988 in a separate book form edited with an introduction by Michael Young as *Malinowski among the Magi. 'The Natives of Mailu'*. London: Routledge.

Malinowski, Bronisław. 1922. *Argonauts of the Western Pacific. An account of the native enterprise and adventure in the archipelagoes of Melanesian New Guinea*. London: Routledge.

Malinowski, Bronisław. 1944a. *A scientific theory of culture and other essays*. With a preface by Huntington Cairns. Chapel Hill: The University of North Carolina Press.

Malinowski, Bronisław. 1944b. "Sir James George Frazer: A biographical appreciation". In *A scientific theory of culture and other essays*, by Bronisław Malinowski. Chapel Hill: The University of North Carolina Press, 179–221.

Malinowski, Bronisław. 1944c. *Freedom and civilization*. New York: Roy Publishers.

Malinowski, Bronisław. 1945. *The dynamics of culture change. An inquiry unto race relations in Africa*, edited by Phyllis Kaberry. New Haven, CT: Yale University Press.

Malinowski, Bronisław. 1967. *A diary in the strict sense of the term*. London: Routledge and Kegan Paul.

Malinowski, Bronisław. 1993a. "On the principle of the economy of thought (1906)". In *The early writings of Bronisław Malinowski*, edited by Robert J. Thornton and Peter Skalník. Cambridge: Cambridge University Press, 89–115.

Malinowski, Bronisław. 1993b. "Review of Frazer, J.G. 1910. *Totemism and exogamy*", 4 vols. London. In *The early writings of Bronisław Malinowski*, edited by Robert J. Thornton and Peter Skalník. Cambridge: Cambridge University Press, 123–199.

Malinowski, Bronisław. 1993c. "The economic aspects of the *intichiuma* ceremonies". In *The early writings of Bronisław Malinowski*, edited by Robert J. Thornton and Peter Skalník. Cambridge: Cambridge University Press, 209–227.

Malinowski, Bronisław. 1993d. "Tribal male associations in Australia". In *The early writings of Bronisław Malinowski*, edited by Robert J. Thornton and Peter Skalník. Cambridge: Cambridge University Press, 201–208.

Malinowski, Bronisław. 1993e. "Relationship of primitive beliefs to social organization". In *The early writings of Bronisław Malinowski*, edited by Robert J. Thornton and Peter Skalník. Cambridge: Cambridge University Press, 229–242.

Malinowski, Bronisław. 1993f. "A fundamental problem of religious sociology". In *The early writings of Bronisław Malinowski*, edited by Robert J. Thornton and Peter Skalník. Cambridge: Cambridge University Press, 243–245.

Malinowski, Bronisław. 1993g. *The early writings of Bronisław Malinowski*, edited by Robert J. Thornton and Peter Skalník. Cambridge: Cambridge University Press.

Mucha, Janusz. 1988. "Malinowski and the problems of contemporary civilization". In *Malinowski between two worlds. The Polish roots of an anthropological tradition*, edited by Roy Ellen, Ernest Gellner, Grażyna Kubica, and Janusz Mucha. Cambridge: Cambridge University Press, 149–163.

Olderogge, Dmitri A. and Ivan I. Potekhin. [Russian original 1951] 1953. Funkcionální škola v ethnografii ve službách imperialismu [Functional school in ethnography in the service of imperialism]. In *Anglo-americká ethnografie ve službách imperialismu*, edited by Ivan I. Potekhin. Praha: Nakladatelství Československo-sovětského institutu, 73–112.

Paluch, Adam K. 1981. The Polish background to Malinowski's work. *Man* 16, 276–285.

Seligman, Charles Gabriel and Brenda Zara Seligman. 1911. *The Veddas*. Cambridge: The University Press.

Shankland, David. 2022. "Edward Westermarck, a Master Ethnographer, and His Monograph *Ritual and belief in Morocco* (1926)". In *Ethnographers before Malinowski. Pioneers of anthropological fieldwork, 1870–1922*, edited by Frederico Delgado Rosa and Han Vermeulen. New York-Oxford: Berghahn Books, 117–149.

Skalník, Peter. 1982. "Bronislaw Malinowski (1884–1942)". In *Beroep: Anthropoloog. Vreemde volken, visies en vooroordelen*, edited by G. Banck and B. Van Heijningen. Amsterdam-Brussel: Uitgeverij Intermediair, 29–41.

Skalník, Peter. 1995. "Bronislaw Kasper Malinowski and Stanislaw Ignacy Witkiewicz: science versus art in the conceptualization of culture". In *Fieldwork and footnotes. Studies in the history of European anthropology*, edited by Han F. Vermeulen and Arturo Alvarez Roldán. London and New York: Routledge, 129–142.

Smuts, Jan Christiaan. 1926. *Holism and evolution*. London: Macmillan.

Spencer, W. Baldwin and Francis James Gillen. 1904. *The northern tribes of Central Australia*. London: Macmillan.

Tauber, Elisabeth and Dorothy Zinn (eds). 2023. *Malinowski and the Alps – anthropological and historical perspectives*. Bozen-Bolzano: BB University Press.

Thurnwald, Richard. 1913. Ethno-psychologische Studien an Südseevölkern auf dem Bismarck-Archipel und den Solomon-Inseln. *Zeitschrift für angewandte Psychologie und psychologische Sammelforschung*. Beiheft 6. Leipzig: Barth.

Wundt, Wilhelm. 1912. *Elemente der Völkerpsychologie*. Leipzig: Kessinger.

Young, Michael. 1988. "Malinowski among the Magi. Editor's Introduction". In *Malinowski among the Magi. 'The Natives of Mailu'*, edited by Michael Young. London: Routledge, 1–76.

Young, Michael. 2004. *Malinowski: Odyssey of an anthropologist, 1884–1920*. New Haven, CT and London: Yale University Press.

4 Bronisław Malinowski in the Laboratories of Leipzig

Krzysztof Łukasiewicz

Introduction

Why Leipzig? Why did the young Jagiellonian University doctor, Bronisław Malinowski, decide in 1908 to continue his studies at Leipzig University instead of some other university in Germany or elsewhere? He already held a degree and was quite familiar with the allures of Europe on account of his earlier travels. Studying at a foreign university, sort of an academic *Wanderjahre,* was de rigueur in academia at the turn of the 20th century. It was devised as a test of, and supplement to, the knowledge already acquired, and its strictly educational purposes were coupled with formative aspects. Although rapid changes were observed in the early 20th century, there were still few universities, professors and students at that time. Even leaving aside financial considerations, the choice of a university or professor was only made after much thought on the part of a student (Molik 1989). The rapid advances in philosophical and scientific thought, and the emergence of new directions in the former and new disciplines in the latter, should also be taken into account. For Malinowski, the son of a university professor, surrounded by a caring mother and attentive academic teachers, a young man whose diary evidences a great deal of self-reflection and intentional work on himself, the decision on the next stop on his life's path could not have been made lightly.

He decided to choose Leipzig not only for family reasons but on account of his education to date, and his hopes and plans for the future (Young 2004: 128). His father, Lucjan Malinowski, was awarded a doctoral degree by the local university in 1872 and his dissertation *Beiträge zur slavischen Dialectologie. Über die oppelnsche Mundart in Oberschlesien* [Contributions to Slavic dialectology. About the Opole dialect in Upper Silesia] was published by the Leipzig publishing house Bär & Hermann a year later (Bubak 2000). Two other reasons are related to what the Saxon university was primarily famous for, and what turned out to be the less obvious but more long-lasting and far-reaching consequences of having studied there. Based on the biographical notes of Polish thinkers who studied in Leipzig at the turn of the 20th century, let me first focus on the distinctive features of the local university, where the "Leipzig School" was active. Then, following those who emphasized the importance of the three semesters Malinowski spent there, in a third step, I will argue that what proved to be more important than the ideas to

DOI: 10.4324/9781003449768-7

which he was exposed and which he partly adopted were the epistemic virtues he acquired in its chemical and physical laboratories and which he respected in his further research work.

Leipzig in the Intellectual Biographies of the Polish Intellectuals

One of the leading Polish positivists, philosopher, social activist and writer, Aleksander Świętochowski (1849–1938), who prepared his doctoral dissertation *Ein Versuch die Entstehung der Moralgesetze zu erklären. Eine ethische Analyse* [An attempt to explain the origins of moral laws. An ethical analysis] (Świętochowski 1876) under the guidance of the famous Leipzig psychologist and philosopher Wilhelm Wundt in 1876, praised German scientific life as the model to follow in his journalistic texts, which were published in the highly influential Polish *Przegląd Tygodniowy* [Weekly Review]. Years later, he summarized his stay in Leipzig:

> From listening to the lectures of Wundt, Heinze, Windelband, Peschl, Leuckert (who lectured on Darwin's theory) and, in general, the year and a half of study at Leipzig University, I reaped enormous intellectual benefits that continued to have an impact throughout all my later life, and my doctoral degree was of least importance among them.
> (Świętochowski 1966: 45)

Among similar autobiographical testimonies, we find that of Julian Ochorowicz (1850–1917), a precursor of Polish psychology and a friend of Świętochowski, who studied under Wundt, worked in his famous laboratory and under his guidance, wrote his own doctoral dissertation *Bedingungen des Bewusstwerdens, eine physiologisch-psychologische* [Conditions of becoming conscious, a physiological-psychological one], which was published by the Leipzig publishing house Heinrich Matthias in 1874. He wrote of Leipzig that it was "[A] city of merchants, learned booksellers and students" (Ochorowicz 1876: 152). He estimated that there were 3,000 students and was struck by the scant interest of German students in their education and the ease of obtaining a diploma. This was unacceptable for someone who had come there lured by the fame of the university with an aim to ensure that his research was grounded in science and reason. In keeping with the spirit of the times, Ochorowicz was convinced that it was psychology, having achieved the status of a science, that would form the basis for solving philosophical problems (Gęsikowska 2022; Hatfield 2010). Like Świętochowski, Ochorowicz wrote a series of five "letters from Leipzig" (Ochorowicz 1874), although for another important journal, viz. *Niwa* [Field], in which he diagnosed the state of German philosophy at that time.

Ochorowicz denied, albeit quite unconvincingly, that Leipzig University was an obvious choice for further education. Nonetheless, there were many Polish students there due to a confluence of external circumstances. This was the case with Bogdan Nawroczyński (1882–1974), later an eminent Polish educator and philosopher of culture. Nawroczyński went to Saxon Leipzig in 1906 as a result of a ministerial ban on Russian citizens studying in Prussia. He had moved from Berlin, where he had attended lectures by Georg Simmel, Alois Riehl, Max Dessoir, Alexander Brückner, as well as classes at Carl Stumpf's Institute of Psychology and training courses in nervous system anatomy.

> The city, shrouded in thick fog, did not make a favorable impression on us. Somehow it was quiet and provincial here. However, I realized pretty soon that this was to be cherished. Berlin was so crowded that students, especially foreign ones, did not have ready access to professors. It was much easier in Leipzig.
>
> (Nawroczyński 2020: 307)

Nawroczyński was most interested in working under Wundt, but the latter was only giving lectures at that time, and delegated laboratory classes to his students. Nawroczyński enrolled in these, along with exercises in experimental physics, the methodology of history and philosophy.

A number of later well-known early 20th-century Polish thinkers and scholars, including Jan W. Dawid, Edwin W. Katzen-Ellenbogen, Stanisław Kobyłecki, Adam Mahrburg, Bolesław Mańkowski, Marian Massonius, Witold Rubczyński, Stefan Rudniański and Kazimierz Twardowski, studied and trained under Wundt for shorter or longer periods. Wundt had 32 Polish doctoral students from Poland. It should be mentioned that some Polish students returned from Leipzig discontented. One such was Władysław Witwicki (1878–1948), who was keen to improve his psychological skills. He was allowed to work in Wundt's laboratories, although in a letter he wrote to Twardowski on 9 May 1902, the founding father of the famous Lvov-Warsaw School of philosophy, he stated that while it was good to get to know Wundt, "[…] it is unkind that they treat me here like missionaries treat a savage. Indeed, there is something religious in the strength of their conviction, or rather the sanctity of these convictions" (Rzepa 1991: 86; Witwicki 1902). The metaphorical nature of this statement primarily reflects on the rigorous and doctrinaire nature of Wundt's school and, at the same time, a lingering sense of disrespectful treatment of outsiders. Wundt's condescending tone continued to rankle Ludwik Hieronim Morstin (1886–1966), a poet, playwright and literary critic, years after their initial conversation. Morstin had wanted to explore aesthetic issues under Wundt's guidance. It can be assumed that despite his academic standing and international exposure, Malinowski also encountered such situations in Leipzig. Nawroczyński, years after studying in Germany, emphasized the enormous energy it required. This was not balanced by intensive social contacts with compatriots studying in Leipzig, concerts at the Thomaskirche and Gewandhaus, or performances of Richard Wagner's operas. It should be added that Poles studying natural history outnumbered those studying the humanities. The scientific achievements of the Nobel laureate in chemistry, Leipzig University professor Wilhelm Ostwald, along with his thriving laboratories, and the philosophical concepts and activities of the *Deutscher Monistenbund* [German Monist Union], were reported by his Polish students in all the specialist and popularizing natural history journals.

As he was primarily interested in literature and art, Morstin ultimately did not become a student of Wundt, while Stefan Kołaczkowski (1887–1940), later a well-known literary historian, studied under him, but gained very little from this experience. His subsequent academic path took him to Munich and Paris. He attended lectures by e.g., Hans Cornelius, Heinrich Wölffin, Henri Bergson and Pierre Janet. However, it was not until he studied under Brückner in Berlin that he abandoned his conviction that he had a flair for philosophy and focused on literary studies. Czesław Znamierowski (1888–1967), later an eminent philosopher of law, with whom Malinowski was in close contact in Leipzig, knew Kołaczkowski from high school, but only established a deep and durable bond with him there in 1907. In his memoirs about his friend, describing his human and intellectual life, he explained:

> At the time, Leipzig did not offer an environment for acquiring philosophical culture. In particular, no philosopher there could act as a guide to someone who explored philosophy solely with a view to find food for thought for his future work on literature.
> (Znamierowski 1962: 1109)

After two years, Kołaczkowski left the city and the university while Znamierowski returned there to continue his studies, including in psychological laboratories. Before focusing on the philosophy of law, his early work was on social psychology, and he continued to take a keen interest in sociology between the wars, as evidenced by his reviewing activity.

Between Leipzig and Reborn Poland: Malinowski's Intellectual Affinities

The acquaintanceship of Znamierowski and Malinowski, formed in Leipzig, paid off for a long time. For many years, Znamierowski, as a professor at the University of Poznań, established after Poland had regained its independence in 1918, edited the sociological section of the quarterly *Ruch Prawniczy, Ekonomiczny i Socjologiczny* [Legal, Economic and Sociological Movement] together with ethnographer and sociologist Jan Stanisław Bystroń. In 1927, he published a review of two books of Bronisław Malinowski: *Myth in Primitive Psychology* and *Crime and Custom in Savage Society*, in which he wrote that it was very "symptomatic" that their author was only known in his homeland because of the publicity he had received abroad:

> He [Malinowski] points out, on the one hand, that there is no qualitative difference between the Polish and Western European minds. The Pole has a bright mind and his vivid and unique intellect often, if not usually, surpasses that of a Western European intellectual. On the other hand, academia is not as organized in Poland as it is in the West. Just look through the prefaces to English works: authors usually give credits to a whole host of people who

assisted with advice, criticism or joint discussions. Almost every book is a collective effort. Great scientific talents thrive in such an environment.

(Znamierowski 1927: 445)

To a large extent, this resonates with the views expressed by the eminent physical anthropologist and ethnographer Jan Czekanowski (1882–1965) nearly a decade earlier, which will be discussed below, and proves that Malinowski's research talents required appropriate conditions. Znamierowski greatly appreciated his fellow Leipzig scholar's works:

[…] [they] provide extremely valuable material for the sociologist, although by no means per se. Dr. Malinowski is too much of a philosopher to limit himself to merely reporting facts. The author always seeks, with true philosophical caution and restraint, a sociological construct that will link and explain the facts.

(Znamierowski 1927: 456)

In this statement, the emphasis on sociology refers to the reviewer's own interests and how ethnography and ethnology, which were treated as descriptive sciences, were understood in Poland at that time. In another review, penned a year later, similarly evaluating two works by Malinowski, Znamierowski acknowledged that they used the material that was collected for *Argonauts of the Western Pacific* (Znamierowski 1928). When a decade later *Ruch Prawniczy, Ekonomiczny i Socjologiczny* published, definitely as a result of his efforts, a translation of the speech Malinowski delivered on the occasion of being awarded the honorary doctorate, the editors felt obliged to include an introductory explanation (in a footnote) that, whenever anthropology is mentioned, it means ethnology as understood in Poland. The editorial endnote added: "The entire reasoning is a consistent demonstration of functionalism, i.e., that position in ethnology, whose spiritual leader is Prof. Malinowski himself" (Malinowski 1937a: 127).

The work was translated by Jerzy Piotrowski and proofread by Znamierowski and Tadeusz Szczurkiewicz, who became a co-editor of the sociological section in 1931. In general, he was associated with Znaniecki's school, with which Znamierowski vigorously polemicized. Szczurkiewicz was also the editor of *Przegląd Socjologiczny* [Sociological Review], the second, after *Ruch Prawniczy, Ekonomiczny i Socjologiczny*, most serious Polish sociological journal of the time. The periodical was founded by Florian Znaniecki (1886–1958). He also served as head of the publishing department of the Polish Sociological Institute. Translations and reviews of Malinowski's works were published by *Przegląd Socjologiczny* (Malinowski 1938a, 1938b) and volume four of the Institute's *Sociological Library* series was Malinowski's work *Crime and Custom in Savage Society* (1939), for which Znamierowski was asked to provide a foreword. The authors or co-authors of the Polish translations were Znaniecki's students. This is quite remarkable, as many of their master's English works were still awaiting translation. Znaniecki's magnanimity seems to be of less importance here than the need to debate. Polemics on the understanding and research of culture between Polish sociologists and exponents of philosophy and pedagogy in the interwar period favoured the ideas of the author of *A Scientific Theory* of *Culture* over that of the author of *Cultural Sciences* (Znaniecki). Moreover, as the status of sociology became entrenched, Malinowski was increasingly recognized as its representative.

Kołaczkowski should also have been mentioned above because he was made editor-in-chief of the quarterly *Marchołt* in 1934. This was a very important journal for the humanities, as it was willing to publish translations of significant works of the time and present the latest methodological approaches. Presumably again on Znamierowski's initiative, Malinowski's lecture *The Deadly Issue,* translated by Józef Obrębski, was published in the fourth issue of 1937 (Malinowski 1937b). It was accompanied by an article by Znamierowski in which he recalled the biography of the author of *The Sexual Life of Savages in North-Western Melanesia* and briefly described his ideas. He considered it important to emphasize that Malinowski had studied "mathematical sciences" at the Jagiellonian University and to recognize that "[t]he second stage of his studies was Leipzig, where, in contact with Felix Krüger, he was preoccupied with psychology without neglecting the sciences" (Znamierowski 1937: 539). Although a misprint caused *Argonauts of the Eastern Pacific* to appear in the article, Znamierowski, referring mainly to that book, reliably presented the methodology of its author, whose most memorable achievement was to ensure that field studies were conducted scientifically. There were three primary factors behind this:

> First, his mathematical and philosophical background has given him a subtle precision of thinking and a clear awareness of methodological intentions. [...]
> Second, an important regulator of Malinowski's reflections is his common sense [...]. Science, according to his explicit statement, is a manifestation of common sense, refined and brought to the fullest conceptual clarity possible.
> Third, the cult of common sense demonstrated by Malinowski is related to, or perhaps even stems from, his artistic attitude towards the reality under his review.
> It is great praise for a scientist if it can be said of him that he sees reality not through theoretical constructions but in its vivid picture examined by an artist.
> (Znamierowski 1937: 541)

To a large extent, this is a development of Znamierowski's opinions expressed in the reviews cited above from the late 1920s that Malinowski owed his clarity of mind and critical thinking abilities to his natural history studies, his acute powers of observation to his psychological studies, and that his "high mental culture" translated into an impeccable aesthetic writing style. The same applies to the presentation of ethnography versus sociology because Znamierowski believed that for the author of *Argonauts of Western Pacific* ethnographic descriptions became:

> [...] the starting point for broad generalizations about social structure, in which he is a sociologist. It is not surprising: he never ceases to be a prudent philosopher who seeks general laws (Znamierowski 1937: 543).

The wide array of possible directions for the research passions of the young Malinowski that dominates the literature is further complicated once sociology and its growing social recognition and struggle for academic standing is added to the picture. In 1903, Feliks Młynarski (1884–1972), one of its Polish precursors, commenced his studies at the Jagiellonian University, and in 1908, received his doctoral degree for a dissertation titled *Socyologia wobec teorii poznania* [Sociology towards the theory of knowledge]. Młynarski later focused on economics, but at the beginning of his academic career, he showed great persistence and determination to pursue sociology. As this was not possible at Austrian universities, Młynarski took classes in history, natural history and law. As did Malinowski and Znaniecki, he had to obtain his diploma from the philosophers Maurycy Straszewski and Stefan Pawlicki.

> The first one gave me a rather unkind and grouchy welcome. He accused me of not applying to his seminar and not agreeing on the topic of the thesis. I explained to him that I was a sociologist, and self-taught due to there being no such faculty. The other, however, received me kindly and politely. He was clearly interested in my self-education.
> (Młynarski 1971: 29)

It seems that there was more to this than his admiration for the student's independence, commitment and diligence. The rapid transformation of social life at the time fostered an interest in sociology and an appreciation of its achievements and potential. This was the case with Pawlicki, Malinowski's doctoral thesis supervisor, who quite successfully tried his hand at it (Mylik 1991). However, this did not lend itself to Malinowski; sociology had a much lower status as an academic discipline than anthropology in the early 20th century. Malinowski was not involved in social issues and it was this kind of commitment, often politically motivated, that steered scholars toward sociology at the turn of the 20th century.

Despite the various ups and downs documented in his diaries, Malinowski was clearly driven by the need to run his own life. In this respect, he was the antithesis of the great historian of philosophy, and friend from his youth, Władysław Tatarkiewicz (1886–1980), who retrospectively admitted: "In any case – my life was not a life planned at all" (Tatarkiewicz 1979: 126). Before he ended up in Marburg, after the closure of the University of Warsaw following the failure of the 1905 revolution, he studied in Zürich and then in Berlin, where he was fascinated by the lectures of Simmel (whose works Malinowski admittedly found very difficult to read).

> And at the same time, I attended lectures on political history, classical archaeology, art history, sociology, experimental psychology, diligently completed the course in chemistry, even attended lectures at the medical faculty: anatomy and psychiatry.
> (Tatarkiewicz 1979: 123)

Tatarkiewicz did not have a good opinion of himself as a student at that time; the variety of classes was enormous. The large number of natural history courses among them, however, is not surprising, because they promised stability in life, as the parents of the future author of *History of Aesthetics* tried to convince him.

Some light is shed on the situation in which Malinowski contemplated and made important life decisions a dozen or so years later, when Czekanowski dispassionately diagnosed the status and prospects of Polish anthropology at the beginning of the 20th century. Czekanowski subscribed to a historical trend, in contradistinction to Malinowski's ideas, and he already enjoyed international recognition. In the inaugural issue of *Nauka Polska* [Polish Science], a magazine launched at the time of the rebirth of Poland in order to breathe new life into its academia, Czekanowski drew attention to the negative selection among Polish researchers resulting from Poland's disrupted statehood.

> They are more or less inferior addition to foreign science, primarily German and Russian, and our country remains, scientifically no less than politically, *a dependent province*. Our society does not quite grasp how humiliating this is. The public should not be indifferent to the fact that, for the majority of outstanding scholars who return to their homeland out of a sense of civic duty, this step means, under current conditions, a resignation from their academic career in Europe. The creation of elementary conditions that foster independent science must remain a matter of constant concern of the citizenry, if only for political reasons.
> (Czekanowski 1918: 202–203)

Certainly, having studied in Leipzig as well as in London, and later – after years of field research, Malinowski was aware of this and factored it into his professional plans.

Referring to the distinction accepted in the philosophy of science, it can be said that the "context of discovery" of Malinowski's idea of going to Leipzig has been discussed above and that it is now necessary to consider its "context of justification". For this reason, his diagnosis of the intellectual atmosphere of the time, as presented in his doctoral dissertation, deserves to be emphasized: "A stubborn war on metaphysics has been declared on all sides, beginning with Nietzsche [...] and ending in the laboratories of chemistry and physics" (Malinowski 1993: 89). The combination of the concepts of the author of *Unzeitgemässe Betrachtungen* [Untimely meditations] and the achievements of physical chemistry, *Lebensphilosophie* and natural history in one sentence is strikingly modernistic (Lipowsky 2020). Ostwald distinguished *Lebenswissenschaften* in his "pyramid of sciences", which included physiology, psychology and sociology/culturology (*Kulturologie, Kulturwissenschaft*). For Malinowski, natural history had a role to play by virtue of having a methodological basis rooted in the assumptions of empiriocriticism. Such a prevailing conviction among Kraków scholars and philosophers shaped the young Malinowski's epistemology and influenced its further development, which in his case did not result from declarations or even from purely theoretical considerations, but was tested in laboratory research. According to Andrzej Waligórski, Malinowski's doctoral student, his mentor was supposed to attend lectures by Ernst Mach in Vienna in the end of 1909

(Waligórski 1973: 282). This has not been confirmed by later researchers of the life and works of the author of *Argonauts of Western Pacific*. Moreover, Mach ceased giving classes in 1898 and resigned his professorship at the University of Vienna in 1901. What is more important here is that Waligórski considered it obvious in view of the theoretical bases of epistemology and the development of Malinowski's ideas, despite the lack of confirmation from any source. Malinowski chose Leipzig instead of Vienna for his further education. Given the interests in methodology and the search for an adequate epistemology, this was quite plausible. The widely known laboratories of physical chemistry and psychology at the Leipzig university blazed a trail for new methods of doing science and Ostwald, who increasingly audaciously delved into the theory of cognition, agreed on many issues with Mach, with whom he maintained a lively correspondence (Blackmore 1972). Students from all over the world headed to the laboratories of the Leipzig-based chemist and promoter of energeticism. As a side note, it is worth mentioning that empiriocriticism also influenced American anthropology (Lowie 1916), and Ostwald's work *Energetische Grundlagen der Kulturwissenschaft* [Energetic foundations of culturology] (1909) was directly referenced by Leslie A. White in his book *The Science of Culture* (1949). Malinowski, however, proved resistant to the evolutionist thinking espoused by many Leipzig scholars.

Malinowski and the Leipzig School

Compared to other German universities, Leipzig University was distinguished by its positivist orientation, the strong position accorded to natural history, its organizational and institutional innovation, pro-modernity and characteristic cosmopolitanism. The recognition, fame and intellectual nature of the university should be attributed primarily to Wundt and Ostwald, as mentioned above, but also to Karl Bücher, Karl Lamprecht and Friedrich Ratzl, who formed the Leipzig School with them. This does not meet all the prerequisites that the restrictive definition of a scientific school implies, although it well deserves its name (Smith 1991; Chickering 1995, 1997; Űner 1998; Espagne 2009). Doctrinal unity was missing but its distinctive discourse community was well formed and the advocacy of methodological unification led to various forms of interdisciplinary cooperation, agreement on research purposes, methods of achieving them, communication and presentation to the public. Scientific work, forms of studies and didactic methods were supported financially. With all the internal differences within the circle of the above-mentioned scholars, the idea was to research the development of nature, individuals, human communities and the past in such a way that, while remaining historical and understanding, would provide both inductive and causal-explanatory reasoning. These attempts to combine culture, history and psychology were clearly recognized and even commented on in the press (Hewitson 2018: 138). The nomothetic approach of each member of the Leipzig School had different tones and shades, but what they had in common was the search for the principles that define human action. Synthesis was treated as the final outcome of a painstaking research process rather than the product of speculative thinking. Dissimilarities in the objects of interest and approaches of chemists, psychologists, geographers, economists or historiographers deserved to be respected while the principles applicable to all of them were observed. This brought quite experienced scholars from Europe and America to Leipzig for research visits, including Emil Durkheim (academic year 1885–1886) and William James (de Wolf 1987; Dias Durate 2004; Wolfradt 2010; Feuerhahn 2014). This can be described as a "laboratory effect", i.e., an effect that was a result, a means and a method. Its essence was the acquisition and consolidation of epistemic virtues (Pels 2014).

The term "Leipzig School" was not used in the early 20th century, but the set of assumptions, beliefs and actions that came to be known by this name over time was identified in philosophical and scientific circles quite well. This concerned not only what was associated with the high level of Leipzig's natural history and psychology, of which Malinowski's Kraków professors were aware, but also the spread of the worldviews that accompanied it. The outcomes of Ostwald's energeticism (Rabinbach 2018) or, more broadly, monism, were commented on in the pages of the influential Kraków-based journal *Krytyka* [Criticism], and Pawlicki, Malinowski's mentor, even dedicated a separate paper to that issue (Pawlicki 1912). However, the future author of *Argonauts of Western Pacific* was not all that interested in these contexts and activities of the representatives of the Leipzig School. He focused on his laboratory work on the principles of thermodynamics and may have visited psychological laboratories. His Leipzig diary does not mention Ostwald, who had already retired, although Malinowski worked under his student Herbert Freudenlich. Ratzel is also omitted, although the anthropogeography that he developed included critical notes on ethnological evolutionism. There is a minor remark about the founder of the Insitut für Kultur- und Universalgeschichte [Institute for Cultural and Universal History], Lamprecht, author of the monumental 12-volume *Deutsche Geschichte* [German History] (1891–1909), whose *kulturhistorische Methode* [cultural-historical method], based on a supraindividual viewpoint and seeking to establish regularities, stirred up fierce controversy among historians (Chickering 1993). In April 1909, after visiting an exhibition of paintings by Arnold Böcklin, Malinowski noted:

> Lamprecht's method of searching for guidelines. The right historical thread gives us a very serious starting point, nevertheless, these are purely superficial connections, not running parallel to an important developmental moment.
> (Malinowski 2002: 87)

This can hardly be considered as an opinion on the *Methodenstreit* [Method dispute] introduced by the historian although its subject was familiar to Malinowski. When he compiled the entry on Anthropology for the *Encyclopaedia Britannica* in 1926, he included Lamprecht among those representatives of "modern empirical philosophy" who were greatly influenced by anthropology (Malinowski 1926: 138). However, such verbal and mental shortcuts, partly forced by the form of an encyclopaedic entry, do not warrant attention. More important than the standard emphasis on anthropology's links with other sciences, including history represented by Lamprecht, was Malinowski's great scepticism about the certainty of the latter's research results. In *A Scientific Theory of Culture*, a 1944 work published posthumously, he concluded that it had not yet reached the status of science, so only "intelligent and illuminating partial reconstructions" were possible (Malinowski 1960 [1944]: 20), as formulated by Lamprecht along with Hyppolite Taine and Max Weber.

Among all Leipzig positivists, Bücher and Wundt had the most intensive and long-lasting influence on Malinowski's concept of man and culture, the latter in particular as the father of the collective psychology concept. The former was credited with Malinowski's better understanding of the role of economic factors and, above all, their multiple and complex relationships with other human activities (Spittler 2013), nevertheless, he refused to factor economic development in. For the future author of *Coral Gardens and Their Magic*, who chose to take musicology classes in Leipzig as well, Bücher's old and popular book *Arbeit und Rhythmus* [Work and rhythm] (1892) was very informative. In Poland, the views of this scholar were known thanks to the translation of his selected works published in 1906 (Bücher 1906). As a renowned scholar, however, the author of *Argonauts of Western Pacific* most often cited Wundt, whose introspective and volitional psychology or inductive metaphysics he never accepted while he appreciated his approach to language and myth. Despite his many reservations, he recommended that students read Wundt's multi-volume *Völkerpsychologie*, which significantly influenced the development of anthropology (Klautke 2013, 2020; Hahn 2022).

Conclusion

Due to a high degree of independent thinking and a desire to develop a comprehensive concept, Malinowski did not embark on any in-depth analysis of the views he rejected. Therefore, in his works, there were only rare and perfunctory references to the representatives of the Leipzig School. Nowhere did he summarize his study at the Leipzig university either. Michael W. Young is right, that for Malinowski "Leipzig represented the best of German science, but in the very guises that he was about the relinquish" (Young 2004: 130). However, his diary entries from those years (Malinowski 2002: 75–118) prove that his focus on laboratory work was deliberate and whether it was research into thermodynamics or mental processes, the most important thing for him was to form a proper research approach and truly scientific conduct. In light of the foregoing, the dilemma of choosing between natural history and anthropology fades and the long-standing preoccupation with the former is no longer a remnant of a bygone era but rather seems to be in harmony with the plan to modernize positivism in order to achieve plausible research results. Therefore, it is not surprising that the German propaedeutics to ethnology portray Malinowski as a "trained natural historian" (*ausgebildeter Naturwissenschaftler*) who became one of the initiators of the "empirical turn" (*empirische Wende*) in anthropology (Kaschuba 2012: 66). In this sense, the promises he made to himself to focus on work in the laboratory and the admonitions to persevere in this, which keep recurring in his Leipzig notes, were a subjective expression of the desire to achieve an objective research attitude and a kind of declaration in favour of a certain concept of science. Malinowski treated his studies in Leipzig rather instrumentally (Young 2004: 130), he was more concerned with perfecting the appropriate forms of work, achieving certain research qualities and traits rather than acquiring any new piece of erudition. In his introduction to *Argonauts of Western Pacific*, Malinowski made readers aware that to obtain satisfactory research results it is necessary first – to set real scientific goals, second – to provide adequate working conditions and third – to implement strict data collection methods. His laboratory work experience proved that all these matters were valid and indicated how they should be resolved. It was not just about proficiency in applying certain techniques, inventing new research tools or conducting clever experiments, or more precisely, not primarily about that. The laboratory turned out to be a place for achieving epistemic virtues that were instrumental in all research progress. It can therefore be argued that without his studies at Leipzig University, Malinowski's anthropology would not have been what it eventually became.

Translated by Magdalena Szyc

Bibliography

Blackmore, John T. 1972. *Ernst Mach. His Work, Life, and Influence*. Berkeley: University of California Press.

Bubak, Józef. 2000. "Lucjan Malinowski (1839–1898)." In *Złota księga Wydziału Filologicznego*, edited by Jan Michalik and Wacław Walecki, 77–83. Kraków: Księgarnia Akademicka.

Bücher, Karl. 1906. *Szkice ekonomiczne*. Translated by Maria Gomólińska. Warszawa: Księgarnia Naukowa.

Chickering, Roger. 1993. *Karl Lamprecht. A German Academic Life (1856–1915)*. Atlantic Highlands, NJ: Humanities Press.

———. 1995. "Der "Leipziger Positivismus"", *Comparativ* 5 (3): 20–31.

———. 1997. "Das Leipziger "Positivistenkränzchen" um Jahrhundertwende." In *Kultur und Kulturwissenschaften um 1900. Band II. Idealismus und Positivismus*, edited by Gangolf Hübinger, Rüdiger vom Bruch, and Friedrich W. Graf, 227–245. Stuttgart: Franz Steiner Verlag.

Czekanowski, Jan. 1918. "W sprawie potrzeb nauk antropologicznych w Polsce." *Nauka Polska* 1: 201–223.

Dias Durate, Luiz Fernando. 2004. "The romantic drive and human sciences in western culture." Translated by Plinio Dentzien, *Revista Brasileira de Ciências Sociais* 19 (55): 5–18.

Espagne, Michel. 2009. "Le cercle positiviste de Leipzig: une anthropologie en germe?" *Revue Germanique Internationale* 10: 81–95.

Feuerhahn, Wolf. 2014. "Zwischen Individulismus und Sozialismus: Durkheims Soziologie und ihr deutschen Pantheon." In *Europäische Wissenschaftskulturen und politische Ordnungen in der Moderne (1890–1970)*, edited by Gangolf Hübinger, 79–98. München: De Gruyter Oldenbourg.

Gęsikowska, Kamila. 2022. "Man and his History in the Evolutionary Approach: The Theory and Sources of the Rudimentary Symptoms of Julian Ochorowicz." *Lietuvos Etnologija. Lithuanian Ethnology* 22: 13–31.

Hahn, Hans-Peter. 2022. "Wilhelm Wundt et la phase de formation de l'ethnologie de langue allemande. Une critique de la «psychologie des peuples»" *Revue Germanique Internationale* 35: 171–184.

Hatfield, Gary. 2010. "Psychology and Philosophy." In *The Routledge Companion to Nineteenth Philosophy*, edited by Dean Moyar, 522–553. London, New York: Routledge.

Hewitson, Mark. 2018. *Germany and the Modern World 1880–1914*. Cambridge: Cambridge University Press.

Kaschuba, Wolfgang. 2012. *Einführung in die Europäische Ethnologie*. München: Verlag C. H. Beck.

Klautke, Egbert. 2013. *The Mind of the Nation*. Völkerpsychologie *in Germany 1851–1955*. New York: Berghahn Books.

———. 2020. "*Völkerpsychologie: Völkerpsychologie* in 19th-Century Germany: Lazarus, Steinthal, Wundt". In *Doing Humanities in Nineteenth-Century Germany*, edited by Efraim Podoksik, 243–263. Leiden, Boston, MA: Brill.

Lipowsky, Andreas. 2020. "*Lebensphilosophy* and the revolution in anthropology. Uncovering the original «turn to life»". *HAU: Journal of Ethnographic Theory* 10 (3): 800–812.

Lowie, Robert H. 1916. "Ernst Mach: the messiah of scientific thought." *The New Republic* 6: 335–337.

Malinowski, Bronisław. 1926. "Anthropology". In *Encyclopaedia Britanica*, edited by J.L. Garvin, Supplementary Volume 1, edition XIII, 131–140. London: The Encyclopaedia Britannica, Inc.

———. 1937a. "Kultura jako wyznacznik zachowania się". Translated by Jerzy Piotrowski. *Ruch Prawniczy, Ekonomiczny i Socjologiczny* 17 (1): 101–127.

———. 1937b. "*Śmiertelny problemat*". Translated by Józef Obrębski. *Marchołt* 3 (4): 429–451.

———. 1938a. "Prawo i zwyczaj". Translated by Józef Obrębski. *Przegląd Socjologiczny* 6 (1–2): 1–50.

———. 1938b. "Zwyczaj i zbrodnia w społeczności dzikich". Translated by Józef Obrębski. *Przegląd Socjologiczny* 6 (3–4): 307–380.

———. 1939. *Prawo, zwyczaj, zbrodnia w społeczności dzikich*. Translated by Józef Obrębski and prefaced by Czesław Znamierowski. Poznań: Polski Instytut Socjologiczny.

———. 1960 [1944]. *A Scientific Theory of Culture*. New York: Oxford University Press.

———. 1993 [1906]. "On the Principle of the Economy of Thought". In *The Early Writings of Bronislaw Malinowski*, edited by Robert Thornton and Peter Skalnik, 89–116. Cambridge: Cambridge University Press.

———. 2002. *Dziennik w ścisłym znaczeniu tego słowa*. Annotated and prefaced by Grażyna Kubica. Kraków: Wydawnictwo Literackie.

Młynarski, Feliks. 1971. *Wspomnienia*. Warszawa: Wydawnictwo Naukowe PWN.

Molik, Witold. 1989. *Polskie peregrynacje uniwersyteckie do Niemiec 1871–1914*. Poznań: Wydawnictwo UAM.

Mylik, Mirosław. 1991. "Stefan Pawlicki – jeden z prekursorów socjologii w Polsce." *Studia Socjologiczne* 120–121: 7–13.

Nawroczyński, Bogdan. 2020. *Oddech myśli. Archiwalia główne*. Kraków: Oficyna Wydawnicza "Impuls".

Ochorowicz, Julian. 1874. "Listy z Lipska o współczesnej filozofii niemieckiej." *Niwa* 3 (5): 30–34, 78–81, 125–128, 149–152, 269–274.

———. 1876. *Z dziennika psychologa: wrażenia, uwagi i spostrzeżenia w ciągu dziesięciu lat spisane*. Warszawa: Nakładem i drukiem Władysława Dębskiego.

Ostwald, Wilhelm. 1909. *Energetische Grundlagen der Kulturwissenschaft.* Leipzig: Verlag Dr Werner Klinkhardt.
Pawlicki, Stefan. 1912. *Spinoza i dzisiejszym monizm.* Kraków: Nakładem Towarzystwa Filozoficznego.
Pels, Peter. 2014. "After objectivity an historical approach to the intersubjective in ethnography." *Hau: Journal of Ethnographic Theory* 4 (1): 211–223.
Rabinbach, Anson. 2018. *The Eclipse of the Utopias of Labor.* New York: Fordham University Press.
Rzepa, Teresa. 1991. *Psychologia Władysława Witwickiego.* Poznań: Wydawnictwo UAM.
Smith, Woodruff D. 1991. *Politics and the Sciences of Culture in Germany 1840–1920.* Oxford: Oxford University Press.
Spittler, Gerd. 2013. "Beginnings of the Anthropology of Work: Nineteenth-Century Social Scientists and Their Influence on Ethnography." In *Work in a Modern Society: The German Historical Experience in Comparative Perspective*, edited by Jürgen Kocka, 37–53. New York: Berghahn Books.
Świętochowski, Aleksander. 1876. *Ein Versuch die Entstehung der Moralgesetze zu erklären. Eine ethische Analyse*, Kraków: A. Dygasiński's Verlagsbuchhandlung.
———. 1966. *Wspomnienia.* Wrocław: Zakład Narodowy im. Ossolińskich.
Tatarkiewiczowie, Teresa i Władysław. 1979. *Wspomnienia.* Warszawa: PIW.
Thornton, Robert J. 1985. "«Imagine yourself set down… ». Mach, Frazer, Conrad, Malinowski and the role of imagination in ethnography." *Anthropology Today. Journal of the Royal Anthropological Institute* 1 (5): s. 7–14.
Üner, Elfriede. 1998. "Kulturtheorie an der Schwelle der Zeiten. Exemplarische Entwicklungslinien der Leipziger Schule der Sozial- und Geschichtswissenschaften." *Archiv für Kulturgeschichte* 80 (2): 375–416.
Waligórski, Andrzej. 1973. *Antropologiczna koncepcja człowieka.* Warszawa: Wydawnictwo Naukowe PWN.
Witwicki, Władysław. 1902. "Rzut oka na kierunek W. Wundta w dziejach filozofii." *Tygodnik Słowa Polskiego* 9: 5–8; 10: 7–8.
Wolf de, Jan J. 1987. "Wundt and Durkheim. A reconsideration of a relationship." *Anthropos* 82 (1/3): 1–23.
Wolfradt, Uwe. 2010. *Ethnologie und Psychologie. Die Leipziger Schule der Völkerpsychologie.* Berlin: Reimer Dietrich Verlag.
Young, Micheal W. 2004. *Malinowski. Odyssey of on Anthropologist 1884–1920.* New Haven, CT and London: Yale University Press.
Znamierowski, Czesław. 1927. [rec.:] "R. Malinowski, «Myth in primitive psychology; Crime and Custom in Savage Society". *Ruch Prawniczy, Ekonomiczny i Socjologiczny* 7 (3): 445–461.
———. 1928. [rec.:] "B. Malinowski, «The father in primitive psychology; Sex and Repression in savage society". *Ruch Prawniczy, Ekonomiczny i Socjologiczny* 8 (1): 125–132.
———. 1937. "Etnograf i socjolog." *Marchołt* 3 (4): 539–543.
———. 1962. "Stefan Kołaczkowski. Wspomnienie." *Znak* 14 (97–98): 1108–1128.

5 Malinowski
A Modernist in His Way

Adam Kuper

1922

Ezra Pound proclaimed 1922 Year One of Post-Christian Modernism. His touchstone was literature, in fact Anglophone authors: his magical year began with the publication of James Joyce's *Ulysses* and ended with T. S. Eliot's *The Waste Land.*

1922 was also a landmark year for anthropologists. The publication of Malinowski's *Argonauts* and Radcliffe-Brown's *Andaman Islanders* heralded a new ethnographic research programme. Ironically, the abridged one-volume edition of the Victorian bestseller, the *Golden Bough* by James George Frazer, was also published in 1922. Malinowski invited Frazer to write a preface for *Argonauts*, but he and Radcliffe-Brown were breaking with the evolutionists and diffusionists. Radcliffe-Brown wrote:

> I believe that at this time the really important conflict in anthropological studies is not between the "evolutionists" and the "diffusionists", nor between the various schools of the diffusionists, but between conjectural history on the one side and the functional study of society on the other.
> (Radcliffe-Brown 1929: 53)

And in the closing pages of *Argonauts*, Malinowski contrasted the various historical schools with what he called 'a new type of theory' that would address 'the influence on one another of the various aspects of an institution, the study of the social and psychological mechanism on which the institution is based' (Malinowski 1922: 515–516).

Functionalism

There was a very general shift from historical to 'functional' studies across the social sciences in the aftermath of World War One, as social scientists were drawn into policy studies. Dorothy Ross, points to 'the growing power of professional specialisation, and the sharpening conception of scientific method,' which together produced a 'slow paradigm shift in the social sciences ... away from historico-evolutionary models ... to specialised sciences focused on short-term processes' (Ross 2003: 388).

Functionalism was a legacy of the organic analogy in social theory: the idea that a society was like natural organism, each part making a particular, crucial contribution to the greater good. Functionalism, however, came in different forms. Malinowski's version was influenced by his teacher in Leipzig, the pioneering social psychologist Wilhelm Wundt, whose *Elemente der Völkerpsychologie*, published in 1912, drew from ethnographic sources and expounded on *Kultur*: 'those mental products which are created by a community of human life and are, therefore, inexplicable in terms merely of individual consciousness, since they the presuppose the reciprocal action of many'. The

> various mental expressions, particularly in their early stages, are so intertwined that they are scarcely separable from one another. Language is influenced by myth, art is a factor in myth development, and customs and usages are everywhere sustained by mythological conceptions.

At each evolutionary stage 'there are certain ideas, emotions, and springs of action about which the various phenomena group themselves' (Wundt [1904] 1923: 5).

The aim of functionalism was to discover laws, on the model of laws of nature. In Kiriwina in the Trobriands, on 22 December 1917, waking after a disturbed night, Malinowski wrote in his diary:

> ... I thought about the relation between the historical *point of view* (... causality as in respect of *extraordinary,* singular things) and the sociological point of view (in respect of normal course of things, the sociological *law* in the sense of laws of physics and chemistry). "Historicists" a la Rivers = investigate geology and geological "history," ignoring the laws of physics and chemistry. The physics and chemistry of history and ethnology = social psychology. Sociological mechanics and chemistry = the individual soul in relation to collective creations.

The themes begin to emerge: there are regularities in nature – laws, even – that endure without change. There are laws too of human psychology.

Malinowski then mused about the individual (the hero of Modernism), who must be understood in the context of collective rituals, beliefs, and language. The passage continues:

> thought about language as a product of collective psychology. As a '*system of social ideas.*' Language is an objective creation, and as such it corresponds to the institution in the equation: social imagination = institution + individual ideas. On the other hand, language is an instrument, a vehicle for individual ideas, and as such it must be considered first when I study the other component of the equation.
>
> (Malinowski 1967: 161)

Functionalists not only turned their back on 'speculative history'. They were also impatient with any kind of history and uninterested in social change. While Malinowski promised an account of the realities of Kiriwinian life, it was a highly selective account. The Government Officer, the Missionary and the Trader appear as shadowy stereotypes in his academic texts. His diaries 'permit a better view of the colonial context of his fieldwork than do any of his monographs', Malinowski's biographer, Michael Young, remarks (2004: 316).

This reluctance to consider the real political situation was perhaps politically convenient. British colonial policy in Africa and Oceania addressed the inexorable social, economic, ideological and political changes by trying to turn the clock back. 1922 was also the year in which the colonial grandee, Lord Lugard, set out the policy of 'Indirect Rule' in *The Dual Mandate in British Tropical Africa*. This advised that 'tribes' should be governed through their 'chiefs'. Malinowski scribbled a triumphant note to himself, "[Lord Lugard's] Indirect Rule is Complete Surrender to the Functional Point of View" (Cell 1989: 483). And indeed the Trobriand monographs were written as though the society was closed off from outside influences, its institutions set in aspic.

In a confessional appendix to his final Trobriand monograph, *Coral Gardens and Their Magic*, published in 1935, Malinowski wrote: 'The empirical facts which the ethnographer has before him in the Trobriands nowadays are not natives unaffected by European influences but natives to a considerable extent transformed by these influences'. His neglect of the colonial reality was, he admitted, 'perhaps the most serious shortcoming of my whole anthropological research in Melanesia'. At the LSE in the 1930s, he promoted a new brand of anthropology, which he called 'the anthropology of the changing native' (Malinowski 1935: 479–481).

W. H. R. Rivers, whose diffusionist study of Melanesia was scorned by Malinowski, was much more ready to discuss radical, perhaps catastrophic, social changes in the islands of the South Pacific. In 1922, that magic year once more, T. S. Eliot, no less, noted:

> In a most interesting essay in the recent volume of *Essays on the Depopulation of Melanesia* the great psychologist W. H. R. Rivers adduces evidence which has led him to believe that the natives of that unfortunate archipelago are dying out principally for the reason that the 'Civilization' forced upon them has deprived them of all interest in life. They are dying from pure boredom.
>
> (Eliot 1922: 662–663)

In all its varieties, functionalism fell out of favour in the social sciences in the 1950s. When Malinowski's loyal disciple, Raymond Firth, orchestrated a volume of reflections on Malinowski's contribution to anthropology, *Man and Culture*, published in 1957, his distinguished former students could find little of value in Malinowski's theoretical legacy. But they had no doubt that Malinowski created a new and enduring paradigm for ethnographic field work. *Argonauts* and *Coral Gardens* provided a model for the ethnographic monographs of the future.

Malinowski and Modernism

Is there any connection between Malinowski's new ethnographic paradigm and 'modernism' in philosophy and the arts and sciences?

What was modernism about? What was its programme? Pound himself offered the motto – *Make it New*. Ironically, perhaps, he drew this slogan from the French translation of a Confucian anecdote about the first king of the Shang Dynasty in the 18th century BC, who had a washbasin inscribed with the maxim (North 2013). Quite what form the *new* might take was, naturally, disputed. In any case, it is not easy to find common tendencies across the graphic arts, music, literature and theatre, psychoanalysis, ethnology, physics, and radical political programmes. Easier, perhaps, to say what modernism was against: Christianity, traditional authority, prudery and sexual repression, and classical models in the arts. At a minimum, modernists were against everything that the English call Victorian values.

'Modernist' movements appeared in Europe at the turn of the 19th century (notably in Austro-Hungarian philosophy, German physics, British natural history, and French art and literature). Before World War One, the young men and women in Malinowski's bohemian milieu were passionately involved in modernist movements in the arts. Bronio's closest friend, Stanislaw Ignacy Witkiewicz (Staś, Witkacy), was an artist, poet, novelist, and playwright. As students, the two young men lived together in an apartment of Bronio's mother. Bronio was dabbling in poetry. His essay on Nietzche's *Birth of Tragedy* explored the forms taken by mythical narratives. Meanwhile, Staś became a fan of Frazer. He drew on *The Golden Bough* in several plays and even developed an idiosyncratic theory of totemism (Young 2004: 242–243). And he accompanied Bronio to the fateful scientific meeting in Australia in the summer of 1914, the two young men travelling via Ceylon.

Between 1910 and 1911, Staś wrote an absurdist, proto-surrealist novel, *The 622 Downfalls of Bungo*. Malinowski featured as Edgar, Duke of Nevermore. After a series of improbable adventures and hair-raising liaisons:

> The Duke was deported to New Guinea for certain unheard-of crimes he committed in the byways of Whitechapel with a pair of lords and while he was there wrote such a brilliant work about the perversions of those supposedly savage peoples contemptuously called Papuans [*The Golden Bough of Pleasure*, Cambridge University Press] that he returned to England as a Member of the British Association of the Advancement of Science and a Fellow of the Royal Society. The rest of his life was nothing but a series of wild and improbable triumphs.
>
> (cited in: Young 2004: 106)

In the 1920s, the fraught decade between the senseless slaughter in the trenches of World War One and the Great Depression, a new version of modernism appeared, first in the arts. Dubbed *primitivisme* by modern historians of art, it abandoned the European cult of civilisation and made a cult of the arts of Africa and Oceania (Dagen 2019, 2021).

Leading anthropologists in the 1920s were very much aware of new directions in intellectual life. Radcliffe-Brown moved in advanced artistic circles in Sydney. His mentor, Rivers, was a pioneering, if critical, Freudian. He founded a club, the Socratics, which included Sassoon and the novelists H. G. Wells and Arnold Bennett. Robert Graves, one of the leading poets of his generation, wrote a critical study, *On English Poetry*, which also appeared in 1922. It was dedicated 'To T. E. Lawrence of Arabia and All Souls College, Oxford, and to W. H. R. Rivers of the Solomon Islands and St John's College, Cambridge, my gratitude for valuable critical help'.

In Paris Surrealism and Ethnology emerged in tandem (Mauss 2011). The Surrealist Manifesto was published in 1924. André Breton and Georges Bataille were fascinated by primitive art and by what they called fetishes. In 1925, Marcel Mauss set up the *Institut d'Ethnologie* and relaunched the *Année Sociologique*. The first volume carried his *Essay on the Gift*, which reworked Boas on the Potlatch and Malinowski on the Kula. One of Mauss's first students, Michel Leiris, a poet, was drawn to ethnology by his ties with the Surrealist movement, 'which represented for me the rebellion against the so-called rationalism of Western society and therefore an intellectual curiosity about peoples who represented more or less what Lévy-Bruhl called at the time the *mentalité primitive*. It's quite simple'. (in: Price, Jamin 1988: 158). A short-lived, breakaway Surrealist magazine, *Documents*, was edited by Georges Bataille, assisted by the deputy director of the Trocadéro Museum of Ethnography, Georges Rivière. *Documents* had a remarkably eclectic remit. According to the journal's strapline, it covered 'Doctrines, archaeology, fine arts, ethnography'. 'In its illustrations', Rivière recalled, 'could be seen side by side a Zapotec urn and a scene from the Folies Bergères' (Riviere 1968: 18).

The Conrad of Anthropology

How helpful is it to read *Argonauts* as a modernist literary production? After all, Malinowski himself said that he would be the Conrad of anthropology while Rivers would be the Rider Haggard.

Malinowski's field diaries and letters reveal a fascination with the 'realist' novels of Joseph Conrad and Émile Zola. In a letter to Malinowski, in August 1917, his fiancée Elsie wrote that she had begun to read Zola's *La Terre* (1887), which immediately

> interested me a hundred times more than the Balzac ... I see already what you mean about the Zola resembling your work. It has a tremendous central idea, and everything expresses this idea, and has a bearing on it ... nothing

seems trivial ... everything is explanatory of the main theme. The reader is not just presented with a jumble of fact but a philosophy is constantly placed before him. It *is* just the same in your work ...

(in: Wayne 1995: 20)

That is the best capsule account I have come across on Malinowski's expository style.

Christina Thomson (1995) reviews Malinowski's bouts of novel reading in the field, for which he regularly castigated himself, but argues that it is the *Diaries* rather than *Argonauts* that echoes Conrad's narrative style. One entry quotes the words of a raging Kurtz in *The Heart of Darkness*: 'At moments I was furious at them, particularly because after I gave them their portions of tobacco they all went away. On the whole my feelings toward the natives are decidedly tending to "*Exterminate the brutes*"' (Malinowski 1967: 69).

Frazer titled his *Golden Bough* after a myth in the Aeneid. Malinowski took his title *Argonauts* from Homer. Marc Manganaro points out that (ironically perhaps) it was also Frazer's example that inspired Malinowski to introduce pace and drama into the *Argonauts*. 'Much of the power of the book', he writes, 'has to do with how the momentum of anthropological knowledge gathering on the one hand and of narrativized voyaging (both of the native and of the anthropologist) on the other so fittingly and complexly combine' (Manganaro 2002: 78). And indeed, *Argonauts* is structured as a leisurely account of a typical Kula expedition, beginning in the Trobriands and moving out across the ring of Kula islands. Every stopping place is vividly evoked, and Malinowski explains its place in mythology, the local specialties, the sexual preferences of the women, the character of their men as Kula partners and as traders. Digressions explore the meaning of gifts, the techniques of boat building and sailing, the practice of magic. Gradually the complex panorama unfolds, the extraordinary system of ceremonial exchange begins to make sense. With Malinowski as guide, one has the sense of seeing the Kula as the Trobriander experiences it.

A Modernist Ethnography

In what ways did *Argonauts* make ethnography new? The answer surely lies in part in the ethnographic method, participant observation as it came to be called, that Malinowski laid out so brilliantly in the opening chapter, 'Subject, Method and Scope'.

Malinowski's experiment with new methods was partly born out of the accident of his forced sojourn in the antipodes, which led him to undertake an exceptionally long stint in the field. It also followed a failed experience of fieldwork, in Mailu, on mainland New Guinea, which made him disillusioned with the *Notes and Query* method of fieldwork that was current at the time.

Published by the Royal Anthropological Institute, *Notes and Queries on Anthropology*, went through four editions between 1870 and 1920. In effect an extended questionnaire, it was addressed to 'men in the field': colonial administrators, missionaries and scientific travellers. They were expected to summon native experts to their verandahs and take them through the check-list of queries about food taboos, totems, ghosts and witches, funeral customs, or ideas about conception, as required. Professionally trained ethnographers went into the field in the first decades of the 20th century, but they seldom spent more than a few weeks in any one field site, and they still relied on native experts, whom they questioned with the help of translators.

Before going to the Trobriand Islands, Malinowski undertook an apprentice field study on mainland New Guinea. Writing it up, he organised his material to fit the standard format of *Notes and Queries*. However, as a student of Wundt, Malinowski was not comfortable with the treatment of institutions as independent silos. The mechanical listing of customs and beliefs may have facilitated cross-cultural comparisons, but it obscured the connections between different activities and institutions. In a small-scale society without a developed division of labour, it was necessary to tease out the various strands – magic, economics, kinship, politics – that were woven together in even the most ordinary activities, such as house building, sailing or gardening.

Notes and Queries was designed to elicit rules of conduct. Malinowski instructed his students to pay special attention to the ways in which people bent or broke the rules and manipulated customs, myths and rituals to their own advantage. Getting the rules from some expert did not tell you how the game was played. Witch doctors disagreed among themselves, like medical doctors. And people tend to say one thing but do another: 'Whenever the native can evade his obligations without the loss of prestige, or without the prospective loss of gain, he does so, exactly as a civilised businessman would do', Malinowski wrote (1926: 30). To understand what was really going on, the ethnographer 'must relinquish his comfortable position on the verandah', pitch a tent in the village, cultivate a garden, exchange gifts, listen in to conversations, flirt, argue, and generally hang about. Intimate personal histories, neighbourhood feuds, the tug of a man's emotional loyalties against his legal obligations, all this was accessible only to an observer who was immersed in the everyday life of the village (Malinowski 1922: 6–7).

In a letter to his fiancée, Elsie Masson, Malinowski described his delight at going fishing with 'real *Naturmenschen*' and remarked:

> It was another cardinal error in my previous work that I talked too much in proportion to what I saw. This one expedition ... has given me a better idea of Kiriwinian fishing than all the talk I heard about it before. It was also a more fascinating though not necessarily an easier method of working. But, it is *the* method.
>
> (in: Wayne 1995: 84–85)

In the opening pages of *Argonauts*, Malinowski made a claim for 'the ethnographer's magic, by which he is able to evoke the real spirit of the natives, the true picture of tribal life'. Malinowski 1922: 5). Yet, fieldwork was not simply a matter of immersion or participation. In the introductory chapter of *Argonauts*, Malinowski distinguished three distinct classes of ethnographic documentation. '*The organisation of the tribe, and the anatomy of its culture* must be recorded in firm, clear outline'. Then, since people say one thing and do another, 'the *imponderabilia of actual life*, and the *type of behavior* have to be filled in. They have to be collected through minute, detailed observations, in the form of some sort of ethnographic diary, made possible by close contact with native life'. Third, 'a collection of ethnographic statements, characteristic narratives, typical utterances, items of folklore and magical formulae has to be given as ... documents of native mentality'. All this was in the service of 'the final goal, of which an Ethnographer should never lose sight. This goal is, briefly, to grasp the native's point of view, his relation to life, to realise *his* vision of *his* world' (Malinowski 1922: 23–24).

But Malinowski was not a vulgar fact grubber. Working in the Trobriands, he sometimes felt himself 'almost swamped by detail' (Young 2004: 558). Experience had to be shaped; theory must come before description.

As a student in Kraków, studying physics and chemistry, Malinowski specialised in the philosophy of science. He wrote a thesis on the ideas of Ernst Mach, an Austrian physicist and philosopher. Mach influenced Einstein. He became a central figure in the Vienna Circle of neo-positivists. His reflections on individual perception made him a father figure to Gestalt theorists in psychology. Boas, who also studied physics, drew on Mach for his doctoral thesis on the perceptions of individual experimenters in the physics of water.[1]

From Mach, Malinowski took a crucial lesson. Facts are constructs. Reviewing Frazer's *Totem and Taboo* in a Polish publication, he wrote:

> The fewer hypothetical assumptions and postulates to be found in a given description of facts, the greater the value of this description, but because every precise description of facts requires precise concepts, and these can be provided only by theory, every description and classification must thus be based of necessity on a theoretical formulation.
> (in: Thornton, Skalnik 1993: 127)

How innovative was this kind of ethnographic research? Frederico Delgado Rosa and Han F. Vermeulen (2022) together with authors of the volume edited by them document several hundred ethnographic studies carried out by individual fieldworkers in the half century before 1922. In the early 20th century, attempts were made to break with the *Notes and Queries* style of research, typically carried out on short expeditions, often by teams. Shortly before Malinowski went to the Pacific, proposals to reform field methods were published by two of the leaders of anthropology in Britain: by R. R. Marett in 1912, and W. H. Rivers in 1913.

Instead of survey studies, Rivers advocated 'intensive work'.

> A typical piece of intensive work is one in which the worker lives for a year or more among a community of perhaps four or five hundred people and studies every detail of their life and culture; in which he comes to know every member of the community personally; in which he is not content with

generalized information, but studies every feature of live and custom in concrete details and by means of the vernacular language ... It is only by such work that it is possible to discover the incomplete and even misleading character of much of the vast mass survey work which forms the existing material of anthropology.

(Rivers 1913: 7)

Rivers and Marett agreed that this type of research would recast the way in which social life was understood. Rivers suggested that the ethnographer who undertook 'intensive work' would soon come to recognise that 'among peoples of rude culture, a useful art is at the same time a series of religious rites, an aesthetic occupation, and an important element in the social organisation' (Rivers 1913:11). Marett was even more specific. He argued that intensive immersion in the life of a community would make the ethnographer conscious of individual variation and changing mores: 'even where the regime of custom is most absolute, the individual constantly adapts himself to its injunctions, or rather adapts these to his own purposes, with more or less conscious and intelligent discrimination. The immobility of custom, I believe, is largely the effect of distance. Look more closely and you will see perpetual modification in process ... manifesting itself through individuals as they partly compete and partly cooperate one with the other' (quoted by Wallis 1957: 790).

This reads almost as if it were a vision of a book review of *Argonauts*, which was published ten years later. Indeed, Malinowski rephrased Marett's argument in the introduction to *Argonauts*. In 'survey work', he remarked:

we are given an excellent skeleton, so to speak, of the tribal constitution, but it lacks flash and blood. We learn much about the framework of their society, but within it, we cannot perceive or imagine the realities of human life ... In working out the rules and regularities of native custom ... from the collection of data and native statements, we found that this very precision is foreign to real life, which never adheres rigidly to any rules. It must be supplemented by the observation of the manner in which a given custom is carried out, of the behaviour of the natives in obeying the rules so exactly formulated by the ethnographer, of the very exceptions which in sociological phenomena almost always occur.

(Malinowski 1922: 17)

The Ethnographer as Emigré

If the post-modernist critique taught us anything about ethnographic studies, it is that the ethnographer's situation and personal background require interrogation. Lévi-Strauss described this immersion in the field as a technique for deracination. The ethnographer, anywhere, is very like any immigrant – a young Polish intellectual, for example, making his way in London. In a letter to Frazer, written from the Trobriand islands in 1917, Malinowski remarked that a foreigner coming to

England would need to understand the language, become familiar with current ideas, tastes and fads, learn to enjoy native sports and amusements: in short, he had to make himself at home if he was 'to penetrate into the depths of the British mentality. The same refers, *mutatis mutandis*, to native society, as far as I can see' (Young 2004: 475).

The ethnographer is a displaced person, a professional émigré – a role to which Malinowski was born. He once wrote that his family belonged 'to the dispossessed, impoverished small Polish nobility, shading into the *inteligencja*' (in: Young 2004: 15–16). He grew up in Kraków, in the province of the Austro-Hungarian Empire. Graduating from the Jagiellonian University, Malinowski was awarded the Imperial Prize for his doctoral thesis, and like his father went on to the University of Leipzig. But educated Poles were at best ambivalent in their attitudes to Vienna and to German culture. Their allegiance was to a vanishing Poland, and they imagined that its authentic spirit might still be captured in isolated villages. The intellectuals of Kraków spent long summer holidays in the mountain resort of Zakopane, where they admired and imitated local crafts; Malinowski's father collected folk-tales in Silesia; some artists and writers married peasant women. As a sickly child, Malinowski was packed off to live with peasants in a reputedly healthy but remote Carpathian village.

> By the time I was eight I had lived in two fully distinct cultural worlds, speaking two languages, eating two different kinds of food, using two sets of table manners, observing two sets of reticencies and delicacies, enjoying two sets of amusements. I also learned two sets of religious views, beliefs and practices, and was exposed to two sets of morality and sexual mores.
> (in: Young 2004: 16)

In his student days in Kraków, Malinowski mixed in Young Poland circles, but he did not become a Polish nationalist. In 1923, he turned down a chair at the Jagiellonian University in order to take up a permanent position at the LSE, and in a letter to his future wife, he confessed that he had a 'highly developed Anglomania, an almost mystic cult of British culture and its exponents' (in: Wayne 1985: 532).

Malinowski was an outsider many times over in Australia and New Guinea. He went to Australia in 1914 to attend a grand imperial meeting of the British Association for the Advancement of Science. Trapped by the outbreak of war, he found himself an enemy alien. The Australian authorities allowed him to carry out his research as planned in their colonial territory of Papua, and even helped to finance his work, but although he talked of his 'voluntary captivity' he was under continual surveillance. The colonial boss of Papua remarked that there was 'something wrong about him'. Local gossip reported that he was a spy, a seducer and a pederast. His future father-in-law, a distinguished Australian professor, was set against what he called 'mixed marriages' (see: Young 2004: 289–328).

Malinowski never tried to go native. In London, he liked to play the part of the Central European intellectual. In Melbourne, his closest friends were fellow exiles. In the Trobriand Islands, he spent more time with white traders than he later admitted. He lodged for weeks at a time in the rowdy compound of the pearl trader Billy Hancock. Hancock's wife was the daughter of another trader, Mick George, and his Trobriand wife. Malinowski's closest friends were Raphael Brudo and his wife: French-speaking Levantine Jews, in whose house he would eat French food, listen to readings from Racine, Hugo and Chateaubriand, and daydream over back numbers of *La Vie parisienne*. Even when he found himself at last in the middle of a *kula* trading expedition, he broke off to spend an afternoon with a Finnish trader, who played Viennese waltzes on a portable gramophone.

A good case can be made that an ethnographer should maintain something of an outsider's point of view. Modern ethnography is the product of a movement backwards and forwards between the field and various explicit and implicit sources of comparison. Malinowski kept a diary intermittently for years, since reading Frederic Amiel as a teenager (see: Kubica 2024). Now it became an instrument of research, as he monitored his physical and spiritual condition and urged himself to work harder. 'Main thing to do', one note reads, 'is to reflect on the two branches: my ethnological work and my diary. They are well-nigh as complementary as complementary can be' (in: Young 2004: 484).

Detachment could shade into revulsion. Malinowski's diary and his letters to Elsie were punctuated with outbursts of irritation, even rage, against the Trobrianders:

> I had a row with some of the niggs – they crowd round the tent: to ask them to get away is of no avail, to swear at them in fury or to hit them is dangerous, because they'll swear back or even hit back & as you have more to lose by loss of prestige than they have, you are the weaker in the contest. No, Elsie, I see no way out of this problem – it is either slavery for them or for us & out of the two, I prefer slavery for them.
>
> (in: Wayne 1995: 161)

Malinowski could be equally scathing about colonial officials, missionaries, colonists, and Australian professors. Nor did he spare himself. 'I know my character is not very deep', he wrote to Elsie. 'Small ambitions & vanities & a sense for intrigue & spite are more rampant there than the real, true feelings' (in: Wayne 1995: 161). Witkiewicz accused him of cynicism – 'a total lack of faith in any noble impulses whatsoever ... and the conviction that at bottom human motives are always petty and mean' (in: Young 2004: 305–306). Malinowski did not dissent. Nor did he doubt that the Trobrianders were much like everyone else. Self-reflection and observation fed off each other, yielding not only aversion and self-disgust but also new insights.

> What is the deepest essence of my investigations? To discover what are [the native's] main passions, the motives of his conduct, his aims? ... His essential, deepest way of thinking. At this point we are confronted with our own problems: What is essential in ourselves?
>
> (Malinowski 1967: 119)

Despite his refusal to address contemporary reality in the Trobriand Islands, the cosmopolitan Malinowski regarded the Trobriander as being essentially rather like himself. The ethnographer in Papua and the immigrant in London are similarly situated. Above all, he insisted that all societies have a great deal in common. When he started as an anthropologist, Malinowski once remarked, the emphasis had been on the differences between peoples. 'I recognised their study as important, but underlying sameness I thought of greater importance & rather neglected. I still believe that the fundamental is more important than the freakish' (Malinowski 1967: 119).

Note

1 For a fascinating account of what Boas and Malinowski took from their studies of physics, see Simon Schaffer, *From Physics to Anthropology and Back again*, Prickly Pear Pamphlet No. 3, 1994.

References

Cell, John W., 1989, 'Lord Hailey and the making of the African survey', *African Affairs*, 88, 481–505.
Dagen, Philippe, 2019, *Primitivismes: Une invention modern*, Paris : Gallimard.
Dagen, Philippe, 2021, *Primitivismes 2: Une Guerre Moderne*, Paris : Gallimard.
Eliot, Thomas S., 1922, 'London letter', *The Dial*, LXXIII (6), 659–663.
Kubica, Grażyna. 2024. "A Notorious Diarist – Bronisław Malinowski, and His Sinful Publics. Polish Editor's Remarks." In: Aleksandar Bošković and David Shankland eds., *Argonauts of the Western Pacific and The Andaman Islanders: A Centenary Study in Social Anthropology*. Canon Pyon: Sean Kingston Publishing. [forthcoming]
Malinowski, Bronislaw, 1922, *Argonauts of the Western Pacific: An account of native enterprise and adventure in the archipelagoes of Melanesian New Guinea*, London: Routledge & Kegan Paul Ltd.
Malinowski, Bronislaw, 1926, *Crime and custom in savage society*, London: Kegan Paul, Trench, Traubner, and Co.
Malinowski, Bronislaw, 1935, *Coral gardens and their magic: A study of the methods of tilling the soil and of agricultural rites in the Trobriand Islands*, 2 volumes, London: George Allen & Unwin Ltd.
Malinowski, Bronislaw, 1967, *A diary in the strict sense of the term*, Translated by Norbert Guterman, New York: Harcourt, Brace & World, Inc.
Manganaro, Mark, 2002, *Culture, 1922, the emergence of a concept*, Princeton: Princeton University Press.
Mauss, Marcel, 2011, 'L'ethnographie en France', *European Journal of Social Sciences*, 49 (1), 209–234.
North, Michael, 2013, *Novelty: A history of the new*, Chicago: University of Chicago Press.
Price, Sally and Jean Jamin, 1988, 'A conversation with Michel Leiris', *Current Anthropology*, 29 (1), 157–174.
Radcliffe-Brown, A. R., 1929, 'A further note on Ambryn', *Man*, 29, 50–53.
Rivers, W. H. R., 1913, 'Report on anthropological research outside America', In: *The present condition and future needs of the science of anthropology*, Washington, DC: Carnegie Institution, 5–28.

Riviere, G. H., 1968, 'My experience at the Musée d'ethnographie', *Proceedings of the Royal Anthropological Institute*, 17–21. https://www.jstor.org/stable/i352011

Rosa, F. D. and Han Vermeulen, 2022, *Ethnographers before Malinowski*, New York: Berghahn Books.

Ross, Dorothy, 2003, 'Changing contours of the social science disciplines', In: *The modern social sciences*, vol. 7 of *The Cambridge History of Science*, edited by Theodore Parker and Dorothy Ross, Cambridge: Cambridge University Press, 205–237.

Schaffer, Simon, 1994, *From physics to anthropology and back again*, Cambridge: Prickly Pear Press.

Thomson, Christina A., 1995, 'Anthropology's Conrad: Malinowski in the tropics and what he read', *The Journal of Pacific History*, 30 (1), 53–75.

Thornton, Robert and Peter Skalník, 1993, *The early writings of Bronislaw Malinowski*, Cambridge: Cambridge University Press.

Wallis, Wilson D., 1957, 'Anthropology in England early in the present century', *American Anthropologist*, 59 (5), 781–790.

Wayne, Helena, 1985, 'Bronislaw Malinowski: The influence of various women on his life and works', *American Ethnologist*, 12 (3), 529–540.

Wayne, Helena, 1995, *The story of a marriage: The letters of Bronislaw Malinowski and Elsie Masson*, volume 1, London and New York: Routledge.

Wundt, Wilhelm, (1904) 1923, *Elements of Folk Psychology: Outlines of a Psychological History of the Development of Mankind*, London: Allen & Unwin.

Young, Michael, 2004, *Malinowski: Odyssey of an anthropologist, 1884–1920*, New Haven, CT: Yale University Press.

Part III
Malinowski's Intellectual Relations
New Insights

Illustration 4 Portrait of Bronisław Malinowski photographed by Stanisław Ignacy Witkiewicz in Zakopane in 1912.

6 'I Am Not Really a Real Character'
Malinowski, Witkiewicz and the Pitfalls of Making Oneself a 'Character'

Natalija Jakubova

Stanislaw Ignacy Witkiewicz, alias Witkacy (1885–1939), was arguably the most important friend of Bronisław Malinowski's youth. It was he who connected the young anthropologist with the field of literature and art. Many documents show that they elaborated a common language to evaluate the works of art and even the events of life from the aesthetic point of view, with the accent to the criteria relevant for the newest trends in the modernist art (see Jakubowa 2002). It is mostly because of this friendship that Malinowski expressed doubts if he should become a scientist and not an artist instead. Indeed, his diary shows that in their youth they lived in a sort of artistic competition with each other: Malinowski even tried to follow his friend's receipt for attaining a better quality of his nightdreams (11 August 1912, Malinowski 2002: 160). The most telling probably is this diary entry: "Does Staś see me from within? This is what concerns me. At the moment it is *Existenzfrage* for me – for, I do not see myself from within!" (11 August 1912, Malinowski 2002: 159–160).

Witkiewicz often mentioned Malinowski in his work, so, in fact, it is mostly in *his* work that Malinowski appears as a "character" and even as an "iconic figure". This paper starts with the analysis of Malinowski's early diaries that give insight into the world of a young man who stood very close to the character of Witkiewicz's novel *662 upadki Bunga* [622 Downfalls of Bungo] (1910–1911) the Duke of Nevermore. Further on, however, the article proceeds with questioning Witkiewicz's strategies of making Malinowski-based characters epitomic representations of "objective"/"pragmatic" scientist.

The Artificial World of *622 Downfalls of Bungo* – with Malinowski as Both Its Character and One of Its Authors

For me, as a theatre scholar and a "witkacologist", the Polish edition of Malinowski's diaries (Malinowski 2002) meant revelation. I realized that the artificial world depicted in Witkiewicz's early novel *622 Downfalls of Bungo* (1910–1911), had existed in reality.[1] Although the prototypes of the heroes had been identified by the researchers, I used to think about the inhabitants of this world as "characters in search of an author". In other words, I did not doubt that the prototypes had existed, but I did doubt that they could have used the same language and thought in the

DOI: 10.4324/9781003449768-10

same concepts as the characters in the novel, because this language and these concepts seemed to be too artificial. The main concern of the characters was a kind of experimental play with their own personalities and with the personalities of other people. Reality did not exist for them or counted very little.

Although one could assume that this kind of representation of the real persons did reflect the exaggerated aestheticization of life in the circle of the friends of the author, but the same it was clear, that this representation itself was an exaggeration, too. One was tempted to perceive the characters of the novel as epitomes of certain life-styles (if not like caricatures) that are unlikely to exist beyond the boundaries of this text.

In the early diaries of Malinowski, however, we actually met another author of the novel's world and could read about the way he articulated his ambitions, intentions but also his failures and his so called "downfalls". To be one's own author is a kind of obsession of Malinowski, the diarist. His early diaries are full of evidence that he was thinking in terms of "life's forms", "pacts with oneself", "life dogmas", "inner campaigns", "downfalls", "justifications", "overcoming" and the need of "vita nuova" (see Jakubowa 2002: 158). All aspects of life, including science or love are understood as material to be used in the unique masterpiece. Its essence is articulated in one of the entries (21 May 1908) as follows: "Does not the change of oneself, an inner metamorphosis constitute the essence of my creativity?" (Malinowski 2002: 66).[2]

The diary provides insight into the exercises Malinowski assigned himself in order to achieve his goals, as for example the following ones: "mastering associations, mastering impressions" (9 January 1908, Malinowski 2002: 41), confrontation with the unpleasant impressions (13 February 1908, Malinowski 2002: 45), "to ignore completely the change of place and the milieu" (29 March 1909, Malinowski 2002: 86), "to mingle into the crowd, inner concentration: to remain always oneself. To use it exclusively as trials" (25 February 1908, Malinowski 2002: 51).

In this way, Malinowski articulates his discipline of "remaining oneself" in any circumstances. Obviously, it cannot be enough. Malinowski seems to understand any interpersonal relations as a constant battle for one's own personality so his decisions concern not only "defense" of oneself but also "attacks" against other people: "A wish to destruct with the thought. To act in an evil manner" (13 February 1908, Malinowski 2002: 44), "To raise skepticism" (14 November 1908, Malinowski 2002: 45), "I am born to go against the current" (14 April 1909, Malinowski 2002: 91).

Malinowski as a "Real Zakopanian"

Once, in a gesture of closing a certain period of his life, Witkiewicz wrote a text that problematized the Zakopanian milieu to which Malinowski also used to belong and which had formed both of them so much. It is *Demonizm Zakopanego* [Demonism of Zakopane], a sarcastic article written in 1919 about the place in Tatra mountains where both spent much of their youth (Witkiewicz 1976: 494–501). The famous resort attracted representatives of the intellectual and artistic elite of all generations, but Witkiewicz's text seems to concentrate on the younger ones – no doubt, on his own friends.

The type of personality analysed in this text resembles the hero of Malinowski's diary in quite an astonishing way. "Real Zakopanians", as Witkiewicz states in this article, turn life into art: they "combine the events into a complex that have a character of abstract beauty". They think in such terms as:

> general composition of life, experience of this evening, suspension of direct impressions, artistic justification of one's downfalls, the term of downfall itself (with the specifically highlighted clarification that it concerns ‚an inner downfall'), metaphysics of billiards or chess, contradictions between the simplest sensations, for example experiencing hunger when at the same time having appetite, both physical and spiritual one.
> (Witkiewicz 1976: 499–500)

By that time when these statements are written, Witkiewicz himself claims to have made his own choice for "art" against "life-as-art". According to him, the Zakopanian style of life reduces human existence to the attempts "during the conversation with one's double, with one's friend or with Her (with the capital letter H) to transform reality in such a way that it would become worth to be part of the great Zakopanian symphony of life". These words are written by a man who has become an artist and wants to detach himself from the people who make "art" out of the life accidents.

But it is long before writing this essay that Witkiewicz, in *622 Downfalls of Bungo*, had already constructed the Malinowski-based character called the Duke of Nevermore as an epitomic example of the spirit of Zakopane. The artistic attitude to life is common to *all* friends of the autobiographical hero Bungo (who is alter ego of the author), but it is the Duke of Nevermore who is claimed to be "a wonderful mechanism to work out the life strength" (Witkiewicz 1996: 26) and it is he who predicates to Bungo in the following manner:

> Life is either a masterpiece or a farce, which we create out of the raw material of our ego, starting, broadly speaking, with the subtlety of our conscience and ending with the elasticity of our ankles. [...] But, my dear boy, we must have the raw material, a kind of wild strength. Beyond that, it is necessary to understand what life amounts to. In this respect you must consider art the chief means. Art will give you the possibility of obtaining certain material needed for acquiring strength. Understand that life per se – to rot, screw, conquer, struggle, work, break and be broken – is both the goal and the means.
> (Witkiewicz 1992: 55–57, translated by Daniel Gerould)

Bungo's reaction follows:

> Bungo looked at him with true artistic delight. His own personal experiences struck him as something vastly insignificant measured against the immensity of the tasks the Duke imposed on him. Although the concept of art as a means of acquiring strength in life was almost repulsive to him, he felt that the

Duke's words had awakened his consciousness of the metaphysical strangeness of life – a feeling he so often lost in the chaos of events.
(Witkiewicz 1992: 57, translated by Daniel Gerould)

Some pages later the Duke of Nevermore says the words that surely the author of the *Diary in the Strict Sense of the Term* wanted to say about himself: "I can say of each moment of my life that I have created it myself. From the most to the least important things" (Witkiewicz 1992: 62, translated by Daniel Gerould).

The Duke of Nevermore as Bungo's Double Responsible for His "Downfalls"

At the same time, the Duke of Nevermore is depicted with a great deal of irony. For example, after his predication, he is said to walk

crushing invisible obstacles between his jaws. Time after time his mouth assumed the shape of a frightful sucker and his whole being resembled a huge tapeworm attached to the stomach of the universe.
(Witkiewicz 1992: 57, translated by Daniel Gerould)

The Duke of Nevermore is also depicted as a person who tends to dedicate himself to the fanatical work (in chemistry, mechanics and mathematics) of which he finally gets bored and then needs treatment for his nerves.

But Witkiewicz also uses other means to make readers question the life strategies of the Duke of Nevermore. Part I of the novel is dedicated to so-called "essential conversations" with Bungo's male friends, and the Duke of Nevermore is one of the most important of them. "Essential conversations" are opposed to the adventures with women (which are only talked about but not contribute to the plot in part I of the text, i.e. the women who are mentioned participates neither in the action nor in the conversations, see Kubica 2006: 157).[3] With these adventures, however, some "downfalls" mentioned in the title of the novel are brought into connection, for this sphere of life is presented as dangerous for the development of the spiritual life of all participants of the "essential conversations". However, it is precisely the Duke of Nevermore who betrays this order by seducing Bungo into a homosexual adventure, which is also classified by Witkiewicz as Bungo's downfall. In a way, the narrator presents the Duke of Nevermore as a person who can be claimed responsible for Bungo's spiritual development and even guilty for anything that deviates him from this path. Sexuality, generally, is presented as such a deviating factor (the parts II and III of the novel are dedicated almost exclusively to this topic).

Bungo's disappointment with the Duke of Nevermore is summarized in the following words:

From afar he [Bungo] perceived the abyss into which he could have fallen had he gone on living from day to day in his former style and permitted

himself everything for the sake of purely artistic experiences. Once and for all the artistic justification of one's transgressions had to be crossed off the list of real-life theories. Bungo had come to understand the impossibility of exploiting every situation, even the most demonic, for the goals of art.
(Witkiewicz 1992: 68, translated by Daniel Gerould)

The narrator says that Bungo finally felt "hatred for the Duke and his system of conquering life" (Witkiewicz 1992: 68, translated by Daniel Gerould).

The Doubles of the Main Heroes of Witkiewicz's Mature Work – Malinowski's Shadow?

In Witkiewicz's later works, it is not rare that a friend of the main hero claims himself more advanced in attaining the mastering of life (and turning it into the work of art) and promises to initiate him into the most mysterious secrets of being. But when it comes to this initiation, he betrays quite mundane sexual instincts. In this respect, the closest to *622 Downfalls of Bungo* is the play titled *Nadobnisie i koczkodany, czyli Zielona pigulka* [Lovelies and Dowdies, or the Green Pill], 1922, Witkiewicz 1998: 465–512).

Edgar Nevermore is also mentioned by name in the "spheric tragedy" *Kurka wodna* [The Water Hen], 1923, where his widow, Duchess Alice of Nevermore plays quite an important role in the plot. Her late husband was the friend of the main hero whose name is also Edgar. In this way, the Duke of Nevermore is perceived as his double (he later marries Alice). The Duke, however, is already dead when the action of the play begins and the spectator is to gain knowledge on him only from the conversations of other characters. According to his widow, the Duke had been eaten by the tiger in the jungle. The reason was that he

> constantly had been putting his courage on trial, until the dam of patience of the Highest Being was finally broken. He was dead within two days after the accident and […] he died in a beautiful way. He […] suffered immensely. But till the last moment he read the work by Russel and Whithead: *Principia Mathematica*.
> (Witkiewicz 1998: 302)

This absent Duke of Nevermore might be a joke (after all, he is not essential for the action of the play; the raison d'etre of this character is rather to give a hint at Malinowski). To my opinion, however, other plays written by Witkiewicz contain a group of characters based on the same construction as the Duke of Nevermore in *622 Downfalls of Bungo* and in this way connected to Malinowski. They have different names and may even lack a touch of the exotic. Yet, I would speak of "Malinowski's shadow" present in the characters of this group who are a kind of doubles of the main hero: namely, his friends who are claimed to achieve the perfection in turning life into the work of art. Witkiewicz, however, needs these doubles mainly to demonstrate that this claimed perfection is but an illusion. His main interest is not a "perfect hero" but a hero who displays doubts and goes through crises. These doubts and "downfalls" are the reasons why this central hero is criticized by a Malinowski-like character. To greater or lesser degree "Malinowski's shadow" is present in characters such as, for example, Franz von Telek from *Pragmatyści* [The Pragmatists], 1919, Witkiewicz 1996: 177–207; Hyrkan in *Mątwa, czyli Hyrkaniczny światopogląd* [The Cuttlefish or the Hyrkanic Worldview], 1922, Witkiewicz 1998: 421–463; or Pandeusz in *Nadobnisie i koczkodany, czyli Zielona pigułka* [Dainty Shapes and Hair Apes or the Green Pill], 1922, Witkiewicz 1996: 465–512.

It is worth to ask how much these characters (or, rather, constellations of characters) can add to our knowledge on Bronisław Malinowski, the person, since they seem to be rather intentional constructions which the scheme of Witkiewicz's work simply implies. One may assume that through this constellation of the heroes, Witkiewicz elaborates a trauma of not-becoming-such-an-artist-of-life like that one epitomized by Malinowski over and over again. Witkiewicz makes his central hero to confront a seduction of a "perfect artist of life" and then through his disenchantment celebrates his choice of being a desperate outcast, one of the last creatures on this planet who would have chance to access a metaphysical secret of being. In the plots of Witkiewicz's work, this kind of hero finally does access this metaphysical secret in a sort of momentary revelation, but then understands that these moments cannot last.

"I am not really a real character" (1918)

Witkiewicz wrote almost all his dramas within a short period right after the year 1918 (only one play – *Szewcy* [The Shoemakers] – was finished later, in 1934). So, one could say, in this respect, that Malinowski becomes an iconic figure of the cultural texts and a character in Witkiewicz's dramas right after he has written down in his diary on the 18th July of 1918: "I am not really a real character" (Malinowski 2002: 657).[4] Characteristically, these are the very last words of his diaristic endeavour (1908–1918).

What is interesting, in this last sentence of the Polish original diary Malinowski either makes a grammatical mistake or uses an anglicized word "character" for speaking of himself as about a character in a work of literature or art.[5] Malinowski began to write this very diary in October 1917, and, in fact, only this notebook was titled *Dziennik w ścisłym znaczeniu tego wyrazu* [A Diary in the Strict Sense of the Term]. It is clear from the beginning of this text that its author meant to return to the self-discipline elaborated in his earlier notebooks (the first one we know was written on Canary Islands in 1908, the rest – before 1914 – in various locations in Europe).[6] At the same time, this last diary already lacked extreme formulations as for the experiments with one's own self. Its aim was much more modest than in the diaries written in 1908 in Breña Baja, in 1909 in Leipzig or in 1912 in Zakopane. Now it was articulated, for example, in this way: "I must collect myself, go back to writing the diary, I must deepen myself. My health is good. Time to collect my strength and be myself. Overcome insignificant failures and petty material losses, etc., and *be* yourself!" (Malinowski [1967] 1989: 120, translated by Norbert Guterman, underlined in the original).

Anyway, to "be oneself" *is* the aim of writing the diary, and it would be logical to assume that if Malinowski sums up these attempts on the very last page of it with the statement that, after all, he is not "really a real character", these words refer to the failure to achieve his goal. Particularly, before putting down these final words, Malinowski makes a series of sorrowful confessions that also sound like summing up at least a major time period if not the whole life. In short, he writes that too much of what used to belong to his personality somehow has vanished from the horizon of his existence. This feeling is connected with the loss of his mother, of whose death in Europe, due to the war, he got to know only after six months after it had happened. The reminiscences of the past associated with the mother also reminds him of his youth, his friend Witkiewicz and his former fiancée (Nina Stirling), whom he feels he betrayed. It is in this context that Malinowski could have accused himself of lacking character: instead of "remaining oneself" he simply eliminated the people and events that did not fit into his current life.

Yet, in the original text, Malinowski does not write of "*lacking* character", but instead of it he writes of "not *being* really a real character". For understanding the reason, why it is so, I think that the aforementioned terms of the Zakopanian "symphony of life" can be of little use, because at this stage, Malinowski feels already quite distanced from that world that turned life into a work of art. Is it not possible, that for him, who, besides the ethnographic studies, continuously read the works by Charlotte Bronte, Joseph Conrad or Rudyard Kipling, the terms elaborated by the Victorian culture would be equally relevant?

Nina Auerbach, a prominent researcher of the Victorian culture, calls attention to the specific status of "character" in this age. Particularly, she writes of "transcendent attributes" of character and that the criticism of the epoch "imagines character as art's sole link with eternity". As her examples show, a literary character can be understood "as a multidimensional figure with a range of choices and identities beyond" her or his role in the particular work of literature (Auerbach 1982: 191). In other words, what is written in the book is never enough for the reading audience; in its imagination, this character receives new lives, new pasts and new futures. Moreover, to do this additional work of imagination becomes almost compulsory for the Victorian reading audience. "This intense concentration on a figure who was never quite alive has come to seem naïve or eccentric, but these acts of aesthetic idolatry produced intense and diverse varieties of worship", writes Auerbach (Auerbach 1982: 190–191). But her analysis goes beyond the cases of such an idolatry. She also connects it to the "nonliterary sense" of the word "character". She observes that the Victorian authors who write about character beyond literature, in fact, develop a similar concept:

> that character, like fiction, is created, formulated, constructed. A person of character is not endowed by birth or circumstances; he is an artist over his own

human nature. Once character erects itself, its possessor is transfigured [...]
into an empowered and transcendent being.

(Auerbach 1982: 193)

Finally, Auerbach concludes: "In life as well as literature character is transfiguration, the transcendence of temporal conditions" (Auerbach 1982: 193). Thus, in the Victorian understanding of the term, *character* does not mean a limitation or a set of peculiarities that make person strikingly recognizable but rather refers to a vast field of potentiality.

One may say that it is the loss of something from this field that Malinowski perceives as a loss or deficiency of "character" he writes about in the last sentence of his diary. These torments accompanied him through the whole diaristic endeavour. He could state that he was "born to be an artist" (21 December 1912, Malinowski 2002: 274), and he often articulated that the academic activities he was involved in seemed uncreative to him. He also could name "scientific work the least appropriate way to wear not one's own costume at the life masquerade" (22 August 1912, Malinowski 2002: 180).

In 1912, Malinowski was preparing two essays: one on the novel by Wacław Berent *Ozimina* [Winter Crop][7] and another on Nietzsche's *The Birth of Tragedy*.[8] Most probably he considered them an intellectual experiment beyond the frames of his core academic interests. In his lifetime they remained unpublished (and the first one also unfinished). Available now in the Polish edition of Malinowski's diaries, these two texts give an insight into some solutions he was thinking about: how would it be possible to defy the limitations of being a scientist and, by this, to retain one's artistic potential? In these essays, while writing about his subjects, Malinowski also reflects on the way a piece of academic writing – be it a review of a novel or a philological work on the origin of theatre – can transcend the norms prescribed for a scientific work and come closer to art. Referring to Nietzsche he defines this kind of creativity as myth-making (Malinowski 2002: 676–677). In the text on *Ozimina* he coins the term "subtle dilettantism" (Malinowski 2002: 701). The hero of this essay is already not the author of the novel, but the author of the essay on the novel: a scientist who writes about a piece of art in such a way that himself becomes an artist.

It is easy to suggest, that he could have felt that, unlike the purely scientific activities, these routes of myth-making or of subtle dilettantism could enable him to preserve the potentiality needed for "character" in Victorian understanding. By July 1918, however, Malinowski probably had no illusion that he could escape making his choice "at the life masquerade", and this choice would be for the academic career.

Of course, it might be an exaggeration, that, when reading the published diaries, we perceive them as a unity. And of course, it just can be a coincidence that after having stated that he was not "a character", Malinowski stopped to write his diary at all. Is it only me, a reader, who ascribes the special meaning to this coincidence? Probably. Yet, I cannot but be astonished that he ended his diary with these very words. In what sense are they true and in what sense are they not?

Malinowski – Witkiewicz: A Virtual Competition for Remaining Versatile?

From the perspective of individual development, it is Malinowski who suffers a failure, because he realizes just one of the life possibilities: makes his choice for becoming a scientist. It is Witkiewicz who remains a versatile individual: he paints and becomes a playwright; later on, after declaring the death of the art of the Pure Form, he writes novels (which, according to his theory, belong to the genre that escapes the rigors of the Pure Form). In 1925 he also founds so called *Portrait Firm S. I. Witkiewicz* as a complex artistic enterprise that produces works of art in different styles but more importantly problematizes the functioning of art in the 20th century. At the same time, he publishes original sociological essays (*Narkotyki* [Narcotics], 1932, *Niemyte dusze* [Unwashed Souls], 1936) and a major philosophical treatise *Pojęcia i twierdzenia implikowane przez pojęcie istnienia* [The Concepts and Principles Implied by the Concept of Existence], 1935) but does not submit to the rigors of academic writing retaining his unique artistic style also in these texts.

In his dramas, Witkiewicz depicts the failures of the type of people to whom he belongs himself. According to his vision of the future, there is no place left for them in the unified and mechanized society that is about to come. At the same time, as a genius outcast, he seems to celebrate the victory over the stand he ascribes to Malinowski: the characters that remind us of the latter are constantly accused of having utilized their creative potentials in a too pragmatic way. This construction of the fictional heroes may probably reflect Witkiewicz's opinion that Malinowski belongs to the persons who claim to be infinitely versatile, but in fact only cultivate an image of such a versatility. Unlike the multi-faceted outcast like Witkiewicz himself, these people fit perfectly into the society that expects something quite different from a human being: namely, to play a limited, specific role in the whole societal mechanism. In a way, in Witkiewicz's art "Malinowski" is able to become a character precisely because his features can become *iconic*. If in 1908 Malinowski identified the essence of his creativity as "the change of oneself, an inner metamorphosis", Witkiewicz, by the constructions of Malinowski's doubles in his texts, somehow declares that this change and this metamorphosis had already ended for good.

Probably Witkiewicz felt that in this virtual competition for "remaining versatile", the victory was his. Was it however a fair victory? What did Witkiewicz get to know – essentially – about his friend after they parted in 1914? He read some of his books, but the way he referred to them in his works betrayed that he either used some stories about "savages" for his own ends (in his plays) or used the example of Malinowski as epitomic figure of "scientist" (he rather used the label of "pseudo-scientist") who denied metaphysics and reduced human experience to such objective states as hunger, sexual desire, fear, etc. (see Baker 1973). Even if one can accept some of this criticism (see Baker 1973: 82), such reductive reading of Malinowski's work means that it did not interest Witkiewicz too much and that the core ideas of Malinowski, the anthropologist, did escape him.

There remains, however, Malinowski, the person. In the 1920–1930s, from time to time, two old friends resumed attempts to communicate in letters (see Witkiewicz 2000). Above it, sometimes Witkiewicz wrote about Malinowski in his correspondence to other persons (first of all to his wife, see Witkiewicz 2005, 2010, 2015, 2016). The way Witkiewicz wrote to his old friend or referred to him in the correspondence with other people showed that in spite of the fact that he tended to present his friend's career as exoticized and thus distanced himself from Malinowski, "the professor", he was also able to reanimate the tone of "essential conversations", the joy of role-playing and linguistic games that used to be so specific for the Zakopanean milieu of the early 20th century. Moreover, Witkiewicz's letters betrayed the feeling of genuine compassion to Malinowski regarding his illness or the death of his first wife. Thus, one might say that Witkiewicz's attitude to Malinowski constantly went through phases of objectifying him into a "character" (i.e. a "character" that has its function in the artificial world of a play or any other piece of creative writing but not necessarily has much in common with the reality of the person to whom it refers) – and through a more direct attitude. Comparing, however, "a vision of Malinowski created by Witkiewicz" with the works and life documents of real Malinowski, one gets the impression that the above mentioned vision was too dear to his creator to let the knowledge of the real person interfere with it too much. In other words, even if Witkiewicz could have felt sympathy for Malinowski, the person, "Malinowski as an iconic figure" was much more important for him in the field of ideology construction (that I believe, he realized through his fiction, drama and quasi-academic works).

Returning to the Year 1914

To my mind, however, the most decisive act of objectification of Malinowski in Witkiewicz's writings took place not even in *622 Downfalls of Bungo* or in his plays, but in his letters written in 1914 when he left his friend in the tropics and decided to go back to Europe and take part in the Great War. For me, it is also the moment when Witkiewicz becomes a "character" himself (in a sense that puts limits to the infinite potentiality and defines a person as a distinct actor in a social drama). This construction necessitated the construction of "an objectified Malinowski" to be opposed to.

What kind of "character", however, did Witkiewicz envision for himself in 1914? This is a complicated story with specific Polish overtones. Both Witkiewicz and Malinowski seem to inherit the torments of Polish modernists of the turn-of-the-century over the problems whether to remain on the territory of the pure potentiality or to take action that would somehow define the self, and by this, limit it. This antinomy was passionately discussed by the main representatives of the movement of "Young Poland" and its critics. Still a teenager, Witkiewicz dedicated his first philosophical manuscript titled *Marzenia improduktywa* [*Dreams of an Non-productive Person*] (1902–1904) to this issue. Later on, it is with this antinomy that Witkiewicz tends to explain his own quite long period of coming of age as an artist.

In Poland, divided between three foreign empires, however, the choice for "the pure potentiality" would also have meant a betrayal of the tradition of the national romanticism, according to which art ideally was to transform into the art of life, although not in that dandy version as practiced by the Zakopanians of the early 20th century. Instead, art was expected, ideally, to shape the life of large human collectives for which this kind of artist was to become a spiritual leader. This stand was retaken by some of the representatives of the "Young Poland" movement, who, despite all the pessimism of the late 19th and early 20th century, came to the conclusion, that even if the modern artists could hardly expected to become prophets, the artistic attitude to life should lead to the action in the real world with the potential to have a significant impact on the life of the nation.

I would like to suggest, that in his letter to Malinowski written in October of 1914 from the then Russian capital, Witkiewicz adopts a "character" that refers precisely to this tradition of the Polish romanticism. For, it is from the position of an artist who finally can fulfil himself in the modus prescribed by the Polish romantics that Witkiewicz writes to Malinowski from Petrograd: about "the spirit of the nation", "the hope of fighting" and most notably about converting his thought into action (Witkiewicz 2000: 274–276). In the same letter, he writes about the attempts to enrol into the Russian army that he would succeed to do somewhat later that year. He says good-bye to his past: "good old days when the dialectics of emptiness and the spewing of significant lies used to cover up the mediocrity of what we did" (Witkiewicz 2000: 274). Even the fact of the suicide of his beloved fits now in the pattern of the romantic hero's fate: in Polish romanticism, it is common that only the deeds for the sake of the nation make the hero forget the torments of the unhappy love. I would argue that it is the way Witkiewicz juxtaposes his new decision of becoming a man who immediately confirms his thoughts with action to his previous life with its concentration on words, thoughts and personal feelings makes the author of the letter written from Petrograd a heir to Polish romantics.

In his new state of thought, Witkiewicz criticizes everybody who is unable to think and act at the same sublime level. First of all, of course, he criticizes his addressee

> Your claim that I have taught you how to be cynical is a terrible lie: it was from you that I have learnt to view the whole world and myself with cynicism. [...] That comfortable attitude of yours, no faith at all in any noble impulse, your cold little smile and the conviction that there is always meanness at the bottom of things. It is very easy to view life in this way if one chooses to. Flowers grow in mud. One can look at them without sticking one's nose in the mire. I was alone and suffered terribly. Now I see that everybody is like this.[9]

Without any obvious connection, Witkiewicz, however, proceeds to the confession that now he believes that Russia is the best friend of the Poles, so, in fact what he labels as "cynicism" of other people (including the addressee) is their disbelief in the Russian solidarity with the Polish national interests in this war. Witkiewicz is at pains to assure Malinowski that he came to these conclusions entirely independently, although he mentions several times Russian newspapers as something that impressed him. (An excellent example of the way the war-time propaganda works.)

All this is quite peculiar, because Witkiewicz had previously distinctly distanced himself both from the politics and from the questions of the Polish fight for independence, although his father had been making persistent attempts to engage him with these issues. Moreover, Witkiewicz Senior surely had expected his son to share his anti-tsarist attitude.

The Russian episode of Witkiewicz's biography (that finally lasted until 1918) fascinated his fans and researchers. Thanks to his decision to leave Malinowski in the tropics and go precisely to Russia, Witkiewicz finally went through the crucial experience of his life – that of two Russian revolutions (February 1917 and October 1917). It helped him to formulate his pessimistic vision of the development of mankind and the role of art in this catastrophic process. This sociocultural vision became the foundation for his own art. There is also a kind of mystery around the experience he went through in these years. The stories that from time to time he had told his friends but never had written down were later retold by these people with otherwise identifiable mistakes and distortions. As a result, they are hardly reliable.[10] A letter to Malinowski written on the 17th of October 1914 remains an outstanding document of this period. I may probably exaggerate the importance of this letter, but the conclusions I draw from it are also supported with some other indirect evidence.

For example, most probably it is after receiving this very letter (on 29 October 1914), Malinowski wrote down in his diary about his friend:

> I see almost no possibility of reconciliation. I also know that however many faults I have committed, he acted very ruthlessly toward me; all the time having gestures and airs of persecuted greatness and moralizing in accents of deep, mature, objective wisdom.
> (Malinowski [1967] 1989: 29, translated by Norbert Guterman)

Yet, it is a sort of "deep, mature and objective wisdom" that admirers of Witkiewicz want to find in "the Russian episode" of his biography, in a quite illogical way. In other words, although Witkiewicz has become famous as a "tragic clown" of the Polish culture of the 20th century, for many "the Russian episode" provides a reason to represent him as "(simply) tragic" in a sublime way, at least during this short stage of his life. Should, however, this stand taken in Petrograd be celebrated (despite the fact that "iconic Witkacy" of the 1920s and 1930s would distance himself from any "mature wisdom")? Should not the irritation that Malinowski felt because of this tragic pose of his friend alarm the student of Polish culture of the time?

Malinowski invited Witkiewicz to join his ethnological expedition because the latter had found himself in a state of severe depression after the suicide of his fiancée in February of 1914 and had been thinking about suicide himself. Responding to the suggestion of Witkiewicz's mother, Malinowski surely counted that the change of milieu could save his friend, and his desperate friend should have had the same hope, despite the constant laments about himself as a lost man. Already at this stage, during the preparations for the expedition, Witkiewicz begins to write – and most probably also to speak – with a great pathos unknown to him previously. These moments of pathos, however, remain intermingled with the actor-like cynicism, as one can judge on the base of Witkiewicz's correspondence and the events of Witkacy's life that are depicted there.

This is important to understand the change of Wikiewicz's behaviour that takes place in Russia. In his letters to Malinowski, Witkiewicz constantly registers that despite the tragic state of affairs, he would fall in an actor-like behaviour and blames himself for this habit ("I've spent my life squandering my energies on trifles […]", March 1914, Witkiewicz 2000: 244, translated by Michał Kłobukowski). In turn, the depiction of him written by his paternal aunt Aniela Jałowiecka who resided in the Russian capital, seems to confirm, that the sublime projection of the "man of action" that the October letter to Malinowski contained, was becoming a reality. Particularly, on 13 February 1915, she wrote to Witkiewicz's mother:

> Before he never was the way he is now. Calm, almost joyful, he holds himself straight with his head raised high – he has completely shaken off the despairing state of apathy in which we first saw him when he arrived. He's preparing for his theoretical exams remarkably well, and he's holding up under the rigors of army life splendidly. His health is excellent. He looks very well in his uniform, neither the heavy boots, not the thick coat, not the saber bother him at the least.
> (Witkiewicz 1992: 105, translated by Daniel Gerould)

The photography of him in a Russian uniform known as *Multiple Self-Portrait in Mirrors* (1915–1917) that illustrates most of the publications on Witkiewicz of this period confirms this description perfectly.

From "Man of Action" to the Spectator in a Theatre Box

What is so appealing in this story to those who so willingly (and mostly uncritically) cite Witkiewicz's aunt or choose precisely the "cool" officer of the tsarist army as the best illustration of this period? Probably, it is the fact that in these representations Witkiewicz has a distinct role and becomes a character in a great historical drama.

Until today, however, it is the only period in Witkiewicz's life in which he, as a character, seems to merge into the background, to melt into the mass of other people. For many decades, everything that had been happening during these four years with Witkiewicz in Russia was the object of reconstruction by his biographers and other authors who wrote about him on the basis of unreliable legends and misty speculations. In his profound work *Wojna Witkacego* [Witkacy's War] (Dubiński 2015), Krzysztof Dubiński plausibly demonstrated that virtually all attempts that had been made by the "witkacologists" to imagine how the war and the revolutions could have looked like for their hero, had contradicted the concrete reality of the historical facts. Dubiński's own hypothesis of "how it could have looked like" is much more advanced, of course, and creates a factual ground for further investigations. Yet, the overall result remains the same: even such a detailed reconstruction of the relevant events as that of Dubiński cannot help but be based on the facts about what *others* did at the same time and at the same place. In other words, even after this profound historical research we still do not know what *Witkiewicz* did in that historically important time and in those historically important locations.

It seems that, paradoxically, after proclaiming himself "a man of action", Witkiewicz stops to leave individual traces. Is he still a character, or just a figurant? This question should be put, despite all the signs of his active participation in the battle at the river Stokhod (July 1916) and even in some events of the February revolution that are now reconstructed by Dubiński in all detail.

Years later, Witkiewicz himself articulated his position as something completely different than that of a "character" or a "figurant". In 1936, he wrote in the essay *Niemyte dusze* [Unwashed Souls]:

> More recently I have had much food for thought in the spectacle of the Russian Revolution from February 1917 to June 1918. I cannot call it anything but a spectacle since unfortunately, I watched it as though from a box at the theatre, not being able to take an active part owing to my schizoid inhibitions.
> (Witkiewicz 1992: 320, translated by Daniel Gerould)

So, not a "character", not a "figurant", but a "spectator"?

Witkiewicz's Letters to Malinowski as a "Downfall" and Its Consequences

When some 25 years ago I worked on my dissertation on Witkacy's connections with the legacy of "Young Poland" movement and had to make an overview of the biography of my hero, I wrote that the pathetic letters to Malinowski marked a much more profound downfall than all other downfalls that Witkiewicz himself was eager to identify. When he wrote about the errors of those who perceived Germans or Austrians as reliable allies in the fight for the Polish independence that they turn their merits "into crimes against the spirit of the nation" (Witkiewicz 2000: 274), he might have been right but was not he himself up a blind alley thinking that he *had* found the way to express "the spirit of the nation"? Was not it the deepest downfall to see oneself as an accomplished character that had "no contradictions [...] within [his] consciousness", as he wrote in the same letter (Witkiewicz 2000: 276)? Luckily, he failed to become "a man of action", he returned from Russia to Poland not in this quality but as an artist. This was a downfall, but it would have been even deeper if Witkiewicz had succeeded in pursuing the character of "man of action".

This was a conclusion I came to in my dissertation on Witkiewicz and "Young Poland". But now, in connection with Malinowski's diaries, I see the problem a little bit differently. For, I think that just like Witkiewicz by the end of the Great War, Malinowski failed to become what he hoped to (and what he called "a real character"). He did become a "character" in Witkiewicz's writings, and it is a bitter irony, that in these writings, Malinowski's role as "a character" is completely foreign to that sense that he himself most probably ascribed to this word. To analyse in what way "the fictional Malinowski" contradicts "the real one", however, is not a very interesting task, because Witkiewicz rather uses his "Malinowski(s)" (both in letters and in fiction) to create doubles that help to define his own position and/or the position of his fictional *alter ego*.

Much more interesting is to look at both "failures" that occur by the year 1918. Witkiewicz fails to become "a man of action" but becomes a versatile artist. After having observed the drama of the revolution as from a theatre box, he proclaims a true artist to be per definition alienated from other people who – by the virtue of not-being-artists – are less resistant to the ongoing processes of mechanization and unification of individual human beings within the contemporary society. Ultimately, this "true artist" is to confront "a grey mass", for all "not-artists" are bound sooner or later to join it.

At the same historical moment, Malinowski states his failure of becoming a "character", that most probably means inability to become "an empowered and transcendent being", as Nina Auerbach defined the essence of the Victorian understanding of this term. He has no ambition to form reality around him; he comes to the conclusion that he can hardly manage his own inner reality. Instead of trying to become a "transcendent being" he chooses a limited role of a researcher (in Witkiewicz's vocabulary: "a scientist"). What is his role in the society, then? I think, that once again, Witkiewicz and Malinowski found themselves in a dispute. One can hardly find any traces of this dispute in Witkiewicz's work, even if from time to time, he referred to Malinowski's research (doing it in his usual tone of exoticization, exaggeration and parody, see Baker 1973). Yet, are these two visions – one about the role of the artist in the society, another one about that of the anthropologist – not comparable?

As a researcher, Malinowski distinctly situates himself vis-à-vis a human *collective*, but this is not a *mass* anymore, but a cultural *organism*. He is an observer, but a participant observer. By this, he, in some sort, invents quite an interesting type of "character" in the social drama of the 20th century. And, hopefully, gives an effective answer to Witkacian "theatre box" and "grey mass".

This is about the difference between these two visions. From the historical perspective, however, one can also catch some important affinities.

"Nietzsche breaking with Wagner", – wrote down Malinowski in his diary after the rupture with Witkiewicz (Malinowski [1967] 1989: 34). By this, he referred to one of the epitomic failures of the union between "thought" and "art". But, as we, from our perspective, also know, he also named two iconic figures that would be utilized by the totalitarian system that was about to come. Both "a spectator from a theatre box" and "a participant observer" proved to be immune to this fate.

Using the terminology Malinowski elaborated in his essays of 1912, one may say that Witkiewicz choose the route of "the subtle dilettantism", that is, of course, something just opposite to "becoming a Wagner". In turn, Malinowski restrained himself from becoming a "myth-maker". This "Nietzsche" broke with this "Wagner" just in time. Somehow each of them also understood the dangers of becoming "a Nietzsche" or "a Wagner".

Notes

1. By the end of the 1960s, the novel *622 Downfalls of Bungo*, still unpublished but available in manuscript preserved in the Ossolineum Library, Wrocław, raised attention of the researchers (Micińska 1967; Wojnowska 1970). In Anna Micińska's article, the prototypes of the most of the characters were identified. The novel was published with her preface in 1972. In spite of this fact, however, for a longer time, it was assumed that the peculiar language the characters spoke with each other and the system of values they elaborated was rather the result of the imagination of the novel's author, as there were hardly known any autobiographical texts derived from the persons identified as the characters prototypes (as for Malinowski's diaries, only the diaries from 1914 to 1918 were published in English translation). However, after the publication of Malinowski's diaries in the original language (initiated by Grażyna Kubica as early as in 1997–1999 in the journal "Konteksty", and then published in the book form in 2002 (Malinowski 2002)), some other relevant texts by the authors who are considered to be the prototypes of the characters of *622 Downfalls of Bungo* (Helena Czerwijowska, Zofia Dembowska, Tadeusz Szymberski) were also published. The diaries of Leon Chwistek are currently expecting their publication.
2. If not mentioned otherwise, the translations are my own.
3. Kubica writes: "Witkacy's woman, to use a chemical comparison, does not appear as an element, but only as part of a compound that she creates together with a man".
4. This phrase is translated differently in the published English translation of the diary: "Truly I lack real character" (Malinowski [1967] 1989: 298, translated by Norbert Guterman).
5. In Polish, one cannot "be" a character (for this word does not refer to a character in a work of literature or art) but can only "have" a character.
6. In her preface for the Polish edition of the diaries, Grażyna Kubica names it "the diarist's slavery" and gives examples how Malinowski himself understood what she calls "this vivisection, sometimes very detailed and brutal" (see Kubica 2002: 19–21).
7. [Uwagi o *Oziminie* Wacława Berenta], published in: Malinowski 2002: 695–701. The essay concerned the book that had been just published: Berent, Wacław. Ozimina. Warszawa – Lwów, J. Mortkowicz, 1911.
8. *Uwagi o Geburt d[er] Tragedie Fr. Nietzshego*, published in: Malinowski 2002: 675–694. English translation: Thornton and Skalnik 1993: 67–88. This essay concerned the dissertation of Friedrich Nietzshe first published as a book in 1872. Malinowski probably used this edition: Friedrich Nietzsche: *Die Geburt der Tragödie*. Rauman Verlag, Leipzig 1906. By that time, however, the Polish translation (by Leopold Staff) was also available: Nietzsche Fryderyk, *Dzieła*, t. IX, *Narodziny tragedii, czyli hellenizm i pesymizm*, przeł. Leopold Staff, Warsaw: J. Mortkowicz 1907.
9. This letter was written in Petrograd (as St. Petersburg was renamed with the beginning of the Great War) allegedly on 17 October 1914 (see: Witkiewicz 2013: 391). Translated by Michał Kłobukowski in: Witkiewicz 2000: 276.
10. For the detailed criticism of these mistakes and distortions, please consult Dubiński 2015.

References

Auerbach, Nina. 1982. *Woman and the Demon. The Life of a Victorian Myth.* Cambridge, MA, and London: Harvard University Press.

Baker, Stuart. 1973. "Witkiewicz and Malinowski, The Pure Form of Magic, Science and Religion." *The Polish Review* 18 (1–2): 77–111.

Dubiński, Krzysztof. 2015. *Wojna Witkacego, czyli Kumboł w galifetach.* Warszawa: Wydawnictwo Iskry.

Jakubowa, Natalia. 2002. "Język 'Prawdziwych Zakopiańczyków' w 'Dzienniku' Bronisława Malinowskiego." *Pamiętnik Literacki* 93 (4): 155–172.

Kubica, Grażyna. 2002. "Wstęp." In: Malinowski, Bronisław, *Dziennik w ścisłym znaczeniu tego wyrazu*, edited by Grażyna Kubica. Kraków: Wydawnictwo Literackie, 5–39.

———. 2006. *Siostry Malinowskiego, czyli kobiety nowoczesne na początku XX wieku.* Kraków: Wydawnictwo Literackie.

Malinowski, Bronislaw. [1967] 1989. *A Diary in the Strict Sense of the Term.* Stanford, CA: Stanford University Press.

———. 2002. *Dziennik w ścisłym znaczeniu tego wyrazu* . Kraków: Wydawnictwo Literackie.

Micińska, Anna. 1967. "622 upadki Bunga, czyli Demoniczna kobieta." *Miesięcznik Literacki* 12 (8): 34–44.

Thornton, Robert J., and Peter Skalnik, eds. 1993. *The Early Writings of Bronislaw Malinowski.* Translated by Ludwik Krzyzanowski. Cambridge: Cambridge University Press.

Witkiewicz, Stanisław Ignacy. 1976. *Bez kompromisu.* Warszawa: Państwowy Instytut Wydawniczy.

———. 1992. *The Witkiewicz Reader.* Evanston, IL: Northwestern University Press.

———. 1996a. *Dramaty.* Tom I. Warszawa: Państwowy Instytut Wydawniczy.

———. 1996b. *622 upadki Bunga, czyli Demoniczna kobieta.* Warszawa: Państwowy Instytut Wydawniczy.

———. 1998. *Dramaty.* Tom II. Warszawa: Państwowy Instytut Wydawniczy.

———. 2000. "Letters to Bronisław Malinowski". Translated by Michał Kłobukowski and Daniel Gerould. *Konteksty* 248–251 (1–4): 240–290.

———. 2005. *Listy do żony. (1923–1927).* Warszawa: Państwowy Instytut Wydawniczy.

———. 2010. *Listy do żony. (1928–1931).* Warszawa: Państwowy Instytut Wydawniczy.

———. 2013. *Listy.* Tom I. Warszawa: Państwowy Instytut Wydawniczy.

———. 2015. *Listy do żony. (1932–1935).* Warszawa: Państwowy Instytut Wydawniczy.

———. 2016. *Listy do żony. (1936–1939).* Warszawa: Państwowy Instytut Wydawniczy.

Wojnowska, Bożena. 1970. "Problem artysty w powieści Stanisława Ignacego Witkiewicza 622 upadki Bunga." *Pamiętnik Literacki* 61 (3): 39–76.

7 Malinowski and the Disciples of Freud
Otto Rank, Ernest Jones and Wilhelm Reich

Lena Magnone

Introduction

This chapter originates from my research on the cultural transfer of psychoanalysis to the Polish intelligentsia before the Second World War (Magnone 2016, 2023) and is informed by the methods developed by Michel Espagne and Michael Werner to study historical conditions of the transmission and circulation of ideas (Espagne 1999). Instead of elaborating on the influence of psychoanalysis on Malinowski's thought or the theoretical essence of his discussions with Freudians, I will focus on his personal and intellectual relationships with a few representatives of the psychoanalytical movement. The widespread tendency to treat psychoanalysis as a philosophical monolith disregards the fact that the beginning of the 20th century was a period of passionate theoretical discussions during which what became classical Freudian thought crystallized. My interest is in the actors of these conflicts, as their turbulent personal paths and rejected theoretical propositions inform about the directions not taken by the psychoanalytical movement. I believe the encounter between Malinowski and psychoanalysis is just one of those missed opportunities.

However, first of all, I need to stress Malinowski's exceptionally early interest in psychoanalysis. In contrast to William Rivers and Charles Seligman, who were both trained as medical doctors and entered into contact with psychoanalysis in the context of war neuroses treatment (Pulman 1986, 1989), Malinowski's was more of personal interest. It can be dated back to 1912, the year Malinowski spent in Zakopane in the company of his closest friend, Stanisław Ignacy Witkiewicz. Witkiewicz was undergoing analysis with a local physician and family friend, Karol de Beaurain, and he discussed the details with Malinowski. He also diagnosed him with "*Mutterkompleks*" and urged him to record his dreams (Malinowski 2002: 232).[1] Early parts of Malinowski's diary – which unfortunately are missing from the English-language edition – contain several descriptions of dreams and attempts at interpreting them, as well as a reference to a Polish disciple of Carl Gustav Jung, a psychiatrist Stefan Borowiecki (Łuniewski 1933; Herczyńska 2004), whom he may have consulted in this period (Malinowski 2002: 342).

This is all the more impressive because, before the First World War, the reception of psychoanalysis was still generally limited to medical circles. The situation was not different in the Polish lands that were, until 1918, partitioned between the neighboring powers of Prussia, Russia, and Austria-Hungary. It was only the Second Congress of Polish Psychiatrists, Psychologists, and Neurologists in Kraków in December 1912, during which a whole section was devoted to psychoanalysis – with, among others, Karol de Beaurain and Stefan Borowiecki as participants – that gained a little curiosity for Freudian ideas among broader circles of the intelligentsia (Magnone 2023: 194–207).

Nevertheless, Malinowski's public involvement with psychoanalysis begins much later and can appear very short-lived.[2] While *Argonauts of the Western Pacific* (1922) still lacks any mention of psychoanalysis, the author's preface to *Sex and Repression* indicates that by 1927 Malinowski had already overcome his dalliance with Freudian ideas.[3] During these five years, he published three articles titled "Psychoanalysis and Anthropology." One should not get confused by their identical titles, for each documents a different phase of his involvement with the Freudian movement, from a prospect of exciting mutual inspiration to the rejection and open hostility.

Psychoanalysis and Anthropology: Malinowski between Rank and Jones

The first one is an open letter to the editors of *Nature*, which appeared in early November 1923.[4] Here Malinowski distances himself from Freud's followers, whose "missionary zeal" is marked by "dogmatism and aggressiveness," as well as from critics who "go as far as to dismiss all anthropological contributions of Freud and his school as 'utterly preposterous' and 'obviously futile'" (Malinowski 1923: 650). His stated goal is "to consider impartially, without enthusiasm or prejudice, the scope, importance, and value of Freud's contribution to anthropology" (Malinowski 1923: 650).

He goes on to explain that he had a unique opportunity to test the applicability of the psychoanalytic theory to the "savage" psychology and customs during his fieldwork in Eastern New Guinea. What the anthropologist saw as Freud's unquestionable achievement was that he "has given us the first concrete theory about the relation between instinctive life and social institution" (Malinowski 1923: 650). Although Malinowski's fieldwork led him to refute the universality of the Oedipus complex, which turned out to be linked exclusively with one concrete form of the patriarchal family, with a stern father and a mother embodying love and kindness, the gathered ethnographic evidence, at the same time, remarkably confirmed the Freudian theory. Even if the exact constellation described by Freud was nowhere to be found on the antipodes – continues Malinowski – the structure of the family on the Trobriand Islands, so entirely different from the European family model, also had its own unique complex. Repressive authority and sexual taboo are differently distributed (the person with the greatest power over a young boy is the maternal uncle, and the incest taboo concerns mainly his sister), but they are still present, and they structure both individual psychology and the collective imagination. Malinowski announces his hope to demonstrate the fruitfulness of Freud's theory for anthropology in his upcoming book on the sexual life and family organization of the native groups he studied.

This article opened the possibility of a collaboration between psychoanalysts and anthropologists. Royal Anthropological Institute was intrigued enough to invite a representative of the Freudian movement for one of its scientific meetings. Thus, on February 19, 1924, Ernest Jones, the President of the International Psychoanalytic Association, delivered a paper titled *Psychoanalysis and Anthropology*. He presented concisely the major elements of psychoanalytical thinking and pointed to their convergence with the most recent anthropological field discoveries, referring, among others, to Malinowski. In his view, the nature of what psychoanalysts have found is that it can "only be true of mankind in general or else not true at all" (Jones 1924: 51).

His text appeared soon after in *The Journal of the Royal Anthropological Institute*, next to the presidential address on the points of contact between anthropology and psychology by Charles G. Seligman, read before the Institute the previous month (Seligman 1924). It also opened the ethnological issue of *Imago*, a journal dedicated to the psychoanalysis of culture, founded by Freud in Vienna in 1912.

The same issue of *Imago* contained a piece by Malinowski (1924b). "Mutterrechtliche Familie und Ödipus-Komplex: Eine psychoanalytische Studie" is a German translation of the second article that Malinowski published under the title "Psycho-Analysis and Anthropology," which appeared in April 1924 in Charles K. Ogden's journal *Psyche* (Malinowski 1924a). Under the title "The Formation of a Complex," it will form the first part of *Sex and Repression in Savage Society*. The same year, the International Psychoanalytic Press also published this German version in book form (Malinowski 1924c).

Here, Malinowski goes even further in arguing against the universality of the Oedipus complex, which does not result from biological determinism but has a social underpinning. It "corresponds essentially to our patrilineal Aryan family with the developed *patria potestas*, buttressed by Roman law and Christian morals, and accentuated by the modern economic conditions of the well-to-do bourgeoisie" (Malinowski 1924c: 5). He repeats his conviction that psychoanalysis ought to study "every type of civilization, to establish the special complex which pertains to it" (Malinowski 1924c: 82). This time he also touches on the issue of sexual repression, which is central to psychoanalysis but which he was unable to identify in the Trobriands. He highlights the need also to polemicize with the claims of psychoanalysts pertaining to myths, religions, and cultures. He will take on this task in his next article in *Psyche*, titled "Complex and Myth in Mother-Right," (Malinowski 1925) and reprinted later as the second part ("The Mirror of Tradition") of *Sex and Repression* (Malinowski 1927: 83–135). Based on rich material, the article is an attempt to prove that Melanesian folklore reflects the matrilineal complex; "it is just the difference in the actors, in the cast of the play, which distinguishes the matriarchal from the patriarchal myth," Malinowski argues. "The foundations of the psycho-analytic explanations of myth we have in no way shaken. We have merely corrected the sociology of this interpretation" (Malinowski 1927: 117).

The fact that the psychoanalytic press published so far-reaching a criticism of the very foundations of the Freudian theory comes as a surprise. After the First World War, Freud's disciples had already formed a highly institutionalized international movement that stood guard over the theoretical orthodoxy. As early as 1920, Freud wrote that recognizing the Oedipus complex "has become the shibboleth that distinguishes the adherents of psycho-analysis from its opponents" (Freud 1953: 226). To reject this central concept simply meant ex-communication – not so long before, Alfred Adler was forced to stop calling himself a psychoanalyst for this reason (Stepansky 1983: 112–149).

So how did it come about that as revisionary an article as Malinowski's appeared in the official outlets of the psychoanalytical movement?

It happened on the initiative of Otto Rank, the editor of *Imago* and the director of the International Psychoanalytic Press. In doing so, Rank followed his own agenda. Once the most beloved student of Freud, he fell out of favor after publishing, in December 1923, a work Freud saw as an unacceptable departure from his theoretical positions. Indeed, in *Das Trauma der Geburt* (*The Trauma of Birth*), Rank questions the importance of the Oedipus complex, shifting the original trauma from the discovery of sexual difference to the very moment of birth, thus undermining Freud's fundamental discovery. He goes even further when he argues that the pre-Oedipal phase is most important to a child's development and privileges the role of the mother over the father, who until then had appeared as the crucial figure (Rank 1924).

Malinowski's challenging of the universality of the Oedipus complex supported Rank's theory, just as Rank's Polish wife Beata's article, titled "Zur Rolle der Frau in der Entwicklung der menschlichen Gesellschaft" [On the Role of Women in the Development of Human Society], published in the same issue of *Imago* (Rank 1924). Beata Rank, born in 1896 in Nowy Sącz as Betty Münzer, is worth recalling on account of her initiatives regarding the transfer of psychoanalysis to Poland. In the International Psychoanalytic Press, she launched a series, "Polish Psychoanalytic Library." The first volume was her translation of Freud's book *Über den Traum* (*On Dreams*), which appeared in 1923 under the title *O marzeniu sennem*. Her idea was also to include a section devoted to Poland in the *Internationale Zeitschrift für Psychoanalyse*. She used the column to regularly inform the Freudians about the development of psychoanalysis in Poland. The anthropological article she published in *Imago* was presented there as an introduction to her future research. The first part of the study was to focus on women in mythical tradition, the second – on women in prehistoric societies, and the third – on the role of women in history. Unfortunately, the planned study was never published in full. In the part that appeared next to Malinowski's article in 1924, Beata Rank boldly modifies Freud's myth of the genesis of culture, as presented in his *Totem and Taboo* from 1913. Drawing on the theory of the matriarchy proposed by Johann Jakob Bachofen, as well as Jules Michelet's *The Women of the French Revolution* and many works by her husband, she offered two hypotheses: first, that matricide preceded patricide described by Freud, and second, that after the death of the primal father, women tried to regain power and were eventually defeated by a clan of brothers. As a result, there were not two but four stages in the development of human society: the primal rule of the mother, the law of the father, a period marked by the rule of "masculine daughters," and finally, the seizure of power by the sons.

In his discussion with Freud, Otto Rank certainly needed allies, which explains why he promoted Malinowski's work. At the same time, Malinowski could have been influenced by Rank. Indeed, they met in Vienna in 1923. Rank offered Malinowski a copy of *The Trauma of Birth*, which the anthropologist not only cited at length in his works but also referred to in his private communications (Wayne 1995: 38). Their correspondence also proves that he consulted the first few chapters of his book on sex and repression with both Ranks (Rank 1934).

Malinowski's association with Rank gravely affected his dealings with the psychoanalytic movement. Following his heresy, Rank had to separate from Freud. He left the Vienna Psychoanalytic Society and was divested of his functions at the psychoanalytical publishing house. After getting rid of Rank, the psychoanalytic movement also needed to distance itself from Malinowski.

The person who defended Freudian orthodoxy against the anthropologist was Ernest Jones. At a meeting of the British Psychoanalytical Society on November 19, 1924, he gave a paper titled "Mother-Right and the Sexual Ignorance of Savages," which he had previously consulted with Freud.[5] Standing up for Freud's theory of the Oedipus complex as a universal and timeless phenomenon, he declared that Malinowski was naive to take locals' narratives at face value. Jones believed they were aware of the physiological mechanisms of procreation: the fact that they had pushed it into their unconscious only shows how much the father was hated in the societies under investigation. Their hatred of the father was so strong that it not only led to the negation of his role but to dividing the paternal figure into the good, sensitive father (the mother's husband) and the strict one who monopolized wealth (the uncle). The whole matrilineal system, Jones argued, was a defense mechanism against primordial Oedipal tendencies, and Malinowski, rather than having revised Freud's theory, had once again confirmed it (Jones 1925, 109–130).[6] According to the report published in the *Internationale Zeitschrift für Psychoanalyse*, rendered most probably by Jones himself, the anthropologist, who was present at the meeting along with Seligman, was forced to acknowledge that Jones was correct in that the ignorance of physiological paternity he had observed was rooted in neurotic repression (Bryan 1925: 133).

Malinowski responded to Jones's criticism in 1927 in his third and last text titled "Psychoanalysis and Anthropology," which constitutes the third part of *Sex and Repression*.

He presents Jones's argument as a typical example of the psychoanalysts' relationship to the problems of primitive societies. He outlines what he sees as the most important methodological difference, clearly outlining his point of view:

[T]o Dr. Jones and other psycho-analysts the Oedipus complex is something absolute, the primordial source, […] *fons et origo* of everything. To me on the other hand the nuclear family complex is a functional formation dependent upon the structure and upon the culture of a society. It is necessarily

determined by the manner in which sexual restrictions are molded in a community and by the manner in which authority is apportioned. I cannot conceive of the complex as the first cause of everything, as the unique source of culture, of organization and belief; as the metaphysical entity, creative, but not created, prior to all things and not caused by anything else.
(Malinowski 1927: 142–143)

This time Malinowski also presents a sharp critique of *Totem and Taboo*. The very hypothesis of a collective unconscious, he argues, is a "metaphysical fallacy" (Malinowski 1927: 157) that scientific anthropology cannot admit; his most important attack, however, concerns the fact that Freud, trying to reconstruct the birth of human culture, explained its origin "by a process which implies the previous existence of culture and hence involves a circular argument" (Malinowski 1927: 153). The totemic crime could not have happened in the state of nature. In Freud's account, he goes on, "the primeval horde has been equipped with all the bias, maladjustments and ill tempers of a middle-class European family, and then let loose in a prehistoric jungle to run riot in a most attractive but fantastic hypothesis" (Malinowski 1927: 165). The patricidal sons could not have had the conscience that made them perform the cannibalistic feast and then implement the sexual taboo, for conscience is "a most unnatural mental trait imposed upon man by culture" (Malinowski 1927: 165). Nor could a single act have allowed them to establish laws, moral values, religious ceremonies, and social ties. The transition from the state of nature to culture was not a sudden change, a forceful jump, but "a very laborious and very slow process achieved in a cumulative manner by infinitely many, infinitely small steps integrated over enormous stretches of time" (Malinowski 1927: 166).

In the introduction and throughout the book, Malinowski forsakes his former attraction to psychoanalysis.[7] He even rejects *The Trauma of Birth*, which he had once commended, in one of the footnotes he added to the extract previously published in *Imago*: "Needless to say, the conclusions of Dr. Rank's book are entirely unacceptable to the present writer, who is not able to adopt any of the recent developments of psychoanalysis nor even to understand their meaning" (Malinowski 1927: 22).

However, when Otto Rank contacted the anthropologist at the beginning of 1934 to pay his respects and recruit him for the Summer Institute in the Psychological Center, an organization he founded the previous year in Paris, Malinowski responded very favorably. He kindly wrote that he remembered their meeting in Vienna very well and followed Rank's work closely, "noting with regret that the orthodox Freudians did not have enough plasticity of mind and width of outlook to remain in touch" with him (Malinowski 1934b). He also assured Rank of his interest in participating in the activities of the Psychological Center.

Unfortunately, the Center did not survive Rank's emigration to the US later that year. Still, Malinowski was in other ways in contact with the French psychoanalytic milieu. During a visit to the South of France in 1932, he met the French analysts René Laforgue and Marie Bonaparte. He became close friends with the latter, and they exchanged letters for several years.[8] It was probably she who invited him to attend a meeting of the Société Psychanalytique de Paris on October 14, 1934, as he was returning from a research trip to southern and eastern Africa (a vote was held during this meeting to decide if Jacques Lacan should join the society (Leuba 1935: 159). The following year Bonaparte's son, Pierre de Grèce, a member of the SPP himself, went to study with Malinowski at the London School of Economics (Roudinesco 1994: 355).

At this time, it must have been clear to Malinowski that the psychoanalytical movement went far away from its initial revolutionary zeal, becoming a rigid institution on the way to professionalization within the medical field. Nevertheless, he kept the highest esteem for Freud as a thinker. In 1938, Malinowski was among the first British intellectuals to welcome the father of psychoanalysis, who, with the help of Marie Bonaparte, had arrived in London after leaving Nazi-occupied Austria. In a short letter addressed to his daughter Anna, Malinowski presented himself – to the astonishment of Freud, who had thought of the anthropologist as a fierce opponent (Freud 1938) – as his "devoted admirer" (Malinowski 1938). Malinowski also tended to sympathize with the movement's dissidents, sensing that it is in their work that any advance in psychoanalysis in its relations with other social sciences was still possible. After his brief relationship with Rank, his decade-long friendship with Wilhelm Reich merits closer presentation.

"My dear Willy": Malinowski's Correspondence with Reich

This Marxist psychoanalyst, *enfant terrible* of both the psychoanalytic and communist movements, is perhaps best known for his 1933 book *Massenpsychologie des Faschismus* (*The Mass Psychology of Fascism*), where he portrays the working class's participation in fascism as a consequence of the authoritarian character structure, shaped through sexual inhibition in patriarchal conditions (Reich 2020). Because of political radicalism and his moving away from Freudian orthodoxy, a year after the publication, he was debarred from the official structures of the international psychoanalytical movement by its president Ernest Jones, who rejected the political dimension of Freudian thought and discouraged analysts from any direct political involvement. Soon after, Reich was also discarded from the Communist Party. Following Hitler's rise in power, he went into exile, finding temporary refuge in Norway before emigrating to the United States. In Reich, Malinowski's theories found the most unusual supporter and propagator.

Reich agreed with Malinowski that the Oedipus complex is not a biological fact but an expression of specific social conditions. For him, sexual inhibitions that result in mental illness are related to the organization of patriarchal bourgeois society and the capitalist system, and neuroses can only be eliminated through a complete reorganization of family life (Robinson 1969: 9–75).

In Malinowski's work, he found evidence that contrary to Freud's belief, humanity is not condemned to sexual repression to prevent a relapse into the state of nature. For Freud, the pain related to repression is the price that humankind must pay for civilization's progress; through sublimation, sexual energy is harnessed into cultural activities. For Reich, on the Trobriands example, Malinowski demonstrated that it is possible to have an organized society capable of cultural activity despite a relationship with eroticism much freer than in Western Europe (Reich 1971: 38–69). Culture does not necessarily feed off suppressed urges. It can develop even when people are able to fulfill their needs without any guilt and if they never experience sexual frustration. Reich referred to the concept of archaic matriarchy as proposed by Engels in his theory of primitive communism. He argued that by introducing the institution of marriage, patriarchy restricted the sexual freedom that had prevailed until then and paved the way for class society. Reich suggested that the root of social inequality lies in the authoritarian patriarchal system, which is why no real change in the relations of production can be achieved without a sexual revolution. Ultimately, unrestricted sexual gratification should be accessible to all age groups, as in Trobriand society.

As early as 1931, Reich wrote an enthusiastic review of the German translation of Malinowski's *The Sexual Life of Savages* for *Internationale Zeitschrift für Psychoanalyse* (Reich 1931a). Shortly afterward, he sent him the manuscript of his book, *Der Einbruch der Sexualmoral: Zur Geschichte der Sexuellen Ökonomie* (The Invasion of Compulsory Sex Morality, 1932), based mainly on the anthropologist's findings. In the accompanying letter, he shared his problems with its publication (the book was refused by the publishing houses and eventually printed at his own expense in his newly founded Verlag für Sexualpolitik) (Reich 1931b). Malinowski suggested translating the book into English and promised to ensure a review appeared in England (Malinowski 1932). In a letter to Elsa Lindenberg, his partner at the time, Reich slightly exaggerates the anthropologist's reaction, reporting that Malinowski expressed his great excitement about the book, used it in his lectures, and praised it wherever he went (Reich 1994: 33).

This was the beginning of a friendship that lasted for a decade. From 1932 until Malinowski's death in 1942, Malinowski and Reich regularly exchanged long letters written alternately in English and German.[9]

For Reich, these were very tumultuous years. After Hitler's rise in power, he left Germany for Denmark, from where he was expelled after a few months. He found temporary refuge in Sweden, but here, too, his visa was soon revoked. Finally, after a detour via Denmark, in October 1934, he settled in Norway, where he stayed until August 1939.

During this time, he regularly confided to Malinowski, whom, not without reason, he saw as his ally against the psychoanalytic establishment. The anthropologist continually reassured him: "As you can well imagine, your book and your point of view are extremely congenial to me, and that in spite of the fact I do not agree with all your conclusions" (Malinowski 1933). Complaining about the lack of support from the movement, Reich solicited Malinowski's help in finding a position in London (this plan did not come to fruition, not least because of the opposition from Ernest Jones) (Reich 1933). Reich also turned to Malinowski in his polemic with Géza Róheim, a Hungarian psychoanalyst and anthropologist whom the Freudians sent on a research trip to Normanby Island in 1928 so that he might find evidence against Malinowski's concepts. His supposed confirmation of the existence of the Oedipus complex in matrilineal societies was published in 1932 in another ethnological issue of *Imago* under the title *Die Psychoanalyse primitiver Kulturen* (Róheim 1932). When, in 1933, Róheim wrote for *Imago* a critical review of Reich's book (Róheim 1933), Reich consulted Malinowski to help him evaluate the validity of Róheim's ethnological arguments (Reich 1934a). The anthropologist did not keep his promise to look at the review and give Reich his opinion. He only wrote evasively that Róheim's mode of expression appeared to him at times so technical as to become almost obscure. "Not knowing always what he wants to say, it is not always easy for me to criticize him fairly" (Malinowski 1934a). He never responded to Róheim's criticism of his own work either. As for Reich, having not heard from Malinowski, he decided to publish a sharp critique of Róheim's book in his *Zeitschrift für politische Psychologie und Sexualökonomie*, later reprinted in the second edition of *Der Einbruch der Sexualmoral* (Reich 1971: 171–210). Here, not only did he defend Malinowski against Róheim, but he also took the Hungarian's results as a broadening of the empirical basis for his theses.

On October 10, 1934, Reich was proud to announce to Malinowski that he made his ten-year-old daughter read the German translation of *The Sexual Life of Savages in North-Western Melanesia*, which she allegedly found very much to her tastes and wanted to write about for a journal Reich started in exile, *Zeitschrift für Politische Psychologie und Sexualökonomie*. He asked the author to send the girl a dedicated copy (Reich 1934b). In exchange for this service, Malinowski requested Reich's recent book, *Der sexuelle Kampf der Jugend* [The Sexual Struggle of Youth] (Malinowski 1934c).

Their relationship became much warmer after Malinowski's five-month stay in Oslo, where he lectured at the Institute for Cultural Research and spent much time with the Reichs. Henceforth, the two gentlemen were on first-name terms. Reich addressed Malinowski as "Dear Bronislaw," adding: "We think of you often and fondly. Please write as often as you can" (Reich 1994: 220). Malinowski, meanwhile, addressed his friend as "My dear Willy" (Malinowski 1936).

Malinowski put much effort into tutoring Reich in his dealings with scientific institutions. In 1936, he contacted the Rockefeller Foundation on his behalf, and in 1937, the World League for Sex Reform. His help could have been crucial in prolonging Reich's residency permit in Norway. In March 1938, when the psychoanalyst was being threatened with expulsion after a vehement discussion in the Danish press about his more and more dubious research methods, Malinowski wrote a sort of recommendation letter for him, which was published in *Dagbladet*:

> I have known Dr. Wilhelm Reich for five years, during which period I have read his works and also, on many occasions, had the opportunity of conversation and discussion with him in London and Oslo. Both through his published work and in the personal contacts, he has impressed me as an original and sound thinker, a genuine personality, and a man of open character and courageous views. I regard his sociological work as a distinct and valuable contribution to Science. It would, in my opinion, be the greatest loss if Dr. Reich were in any way prevented from enjoying the fullest facilities

for the working out of his ideas and scientific discoveries. I should like to add that my testimonial may have some additional strength, coming as it does from one who does not share Dr. Reich's advanced views nor yet his sympathies with Marxian philosophy – I like to describe myself as an old-fashioned, almost conservative liberal.

(cited in: Higgings and Raphael 1972: 219)

After the Anschluss, the situation in Austria, the need to facilitate Freud's emigration, and the impact of the political crisis on the world of sciences are recurrent topics of the correspondence. While Malinowski went for a cure to the United States, where he would eventually settle, Reich also decided to leave Europe. In a letter from November 17, 1938, Reich, sensing that Norwegian authorities were about to end his stay there and determined to find a safe haven for continuing his research, devoted a whole letter to describing his work in detail (Reich 1938a). Perhaps only then could Malinowski realize the absurdity of his friend's pursuit. Reich was illegally keeping in his basement hundreds of mice on which he performed experiments, hoping to drive forward the search for a cure against cancer. Crucial was his discovery of "bions" – supposedly the most primitive, nebulous forms of life, clusters of the vital energy he later named "orgone."

Reich explains his hope to establish himself in the United States and continue his experimental work, which would require transferring his lab to a university or hospital. In the following letter, he sends samples of mice tissues to Malinowski, asking him to get them examined by a specialist in the US (Reich 1938b). Malinowski was more than skeptical. Still, he remained loyal to his friend, giving him the benefit of the doubt. Sending the samples to a colleague at Johns Hopkins Hospital, he comments:

If my friend from Norway is suffering under a delusion, you will be carrying out a useful psychopathological act. If he has made an important discovery, you will be helping the advancement of medical knowledge. In either case, you will earn my gratitude.

(Malinowski 1939)

Completely baffled, the pathologist excluded the existence of any "Bion-Cell-Cultures" in the presented specimens (Leighton 1939).

Malinowski's help was also valuable in Reich's emigration. As Reich wished to arrive outside the established quota (i.e., not as an ordinary emigrant, but on the invitation of a scientific institution), Malinowski promised to do what he could to find an academic position for him in the United States – a task made more difficult by the fact that the psychoanalytical milieu in the US was dominated by émigrés from Vienna and Berlin whose opinion of Reich tended to be less than favorable. In 1939, Reich could finally join the New School of Social Research, where he would stay till 1941. Besides teaching, he was busy developing his orgone theory, conducting experiments at his home in Queens, and building orgone accumulators – modified Faraday cages that he claimed were beneficial for cancer patients.

Surprisingly, once both men settled in the United States, they had a hard time scheduling a meeting. Each of them seemed to blame the other for their estrangement. In October 1941, Malinowski wrote to Reich: "Dear Willy, it is ages since we have met. Do you still like, appreciate, and estimate me? Are you at least prepared to tolerate me? If so, let me know and we shall try to arrange a meeting" (Malinowski 1941a). Reich responded, returning the argument: "Did you have some reason to keep away for such a long time? I, of course, did not change" (Reich 1941). Malinowski quickly reassured his friend:

> No, I have no reason whatsoever to avoid your presence, company, and exchange of ideas. We always had one or two fundamental differences of opinion, which did not bother me, nor did they seem to bother you. I like people whose company is amusing to me and stimulating, and that is certainly the case in our relations.
>
> (Malinowski 1941b)

He also invited Reich to visit him in New Haven.

Before they could meet, on December 12, 1941, Reich was taken to Ellis Island by the FBI, who arrested him for alleged pro-Nazi tendencies (Wayne 1995: 251). Contacted by Reich's second wife, Ilse Ollendorff, Malinowski produced an affidavit testifying his friend's anti-Fascist views (Malinowski 1942). It helped to liberate Reich after almost a month of the arrest.

In the last exchange, Reich announces the publication of his book, *The Discovery of the Orgone* (Reich [1942]). Malinowski would not have a chance to become aquatinted with this new wing of Reich's activities, nor with his settling a research center, Orgonon in Rangeley, Maine (now hosting Wilhelm Reich Museum). After Malinowski died in May 1942, Reich wrote a lengthy obituary in his newly founded *International Journal of Sex Economy and Orgone Research* (Reich 1942a). Reich died 15 years later while serving a two-year term following an investigation by the US Food and Drug Administration regarding his claims about the health benefits of orgone.

Conclusion

The life trajectory of Wilhelm Reich illustrates in a very tangible way the two dimensions of psychoanalysis. His ideas, fringe as they were, had roots in the original, emancipatory aspect of Freudian thought that, at the beginning of the 20th century, attracted many theoretical nonconformists who critically assessed the state of society and wanted to bring about a radical change. His destiny, however, manifests the psychoanalysis' increasing need for social recognition, which eventually resulted in successfully repressing those unruly impulses by the movement's leaders. After the Second World War, the professionalization of psychoanalysis and its theoretical stiffening were completed. In the United States, psychoanalysis has ultimately lost its dimension of radical social thought and established itself as a form of therapy in service of reactionary public policy (Jacoby 1983; Adorno 1986; Parin 1990; Hale 1995; Bergman 2000).

I would argue that Malinowski – like Otto Rank, Wilhelm Reich, or any other "political Freudian" (Jacoby 1983) – was indeed a victim of this process. His involvement with psychoanalysis and willingness to explore its utility for anthropology ending abruptly in 1927 was not related to his loss of interest in Freudian hypotheses. It was rather due to the rigidity of the psychoanalytic movement, over which Freud had little personal control at the time.

Reviewing Malinowski's *Sex and Repression in Savage Society* for the *International Journal of Psychoanalysis*, Ernest Jones expressed his regret over the fact that this "man of unquestioned eminence in anthropology," who "has shown himself to be a shrewd observer in sociology and a keen natural psychologist," nevertheless "denies altogether or reduces to the most shadowy proportions the [...] most fundamental tenets of psycho-analysis" (Jones 1928: 373). "If only he had some personal acquaintance with the unconscious" – continues Jones – "some knowledge of psycho-analytic practice as well as psycho-analytic theory, he would have unrivaled opportunities opened up to him" (Jones 1928: 373). I am tempted to join Jones in his resentment but with a slightly different argument. Indeed, what could have happened if the psychoanalytic establishment had been less interested in protecting its status and opened itself to Malinowski's suggestions? What could the history of psychoanalysis and anthropology in the 20th century have looked like had the two disciplines developed in closer collaboration?

Notes

1. I refer to the Polish original diaries as, contrary to the English-language edition, which only begins in 1914, it includes passages dated 1908–1914. After 1914, there is only one mention of Freud in the diary: in April 1918, Malinowski compares his affection for his fiancée to a child's affection for the mother, adding in parentheses "vide Freud's theory" (Malinowski 1967: 245).
2. George W. Stocking suggested there might have been a pragmatic dimension to Malinowski's decision to join the debate on psychoanalysis and anthropology in the early 1920s. After the sudden death of William Rivers, a dominant figure of British anthropology who, in his last years, became highly interested in psychoanalysis and produced a series of publications on Freudian topics, "the intellectual leadership of the discipline was there for the capturing – more easily, perhaps, by picking up one of the central strands of Rivers' own anthropological interests" (Stocking 1986: 33). Considering Malinowski's previous deep interest in psychoanalysis, I do not share this opinion.
3. Malinowski distances himself from his former attraction to psychoanalysis in the very first paragraph: "The present writer [...] was for a time unduly influenced by the theories of Freud and Rivers, Jung, and Jones. [...] subsequent reflection soon chilled the initial enthusiasms. [...] I have never been in any sense a follower of psycho-analytic practice, or an adherent of psycho-analytic theory; and now, while impatient of the exorbitant claims of psycho-analysis, of its chaotic arguments and tangled terminology, I must yet acknowledge a deep sense of indebtedness to it for stimulation as well as for valuable instruction in some aspects of human psychology" (Malinowski 1927: vii).
4. It was republished in the collection of Malinowski's contributions *Sex, Culture and Myth*, New York: Harcourt, Brace & World 1962.
5. Cf. Jones' letter to Freud dated May 30, 1924: "I presume that Malinowski sent you a copy of his recent anthropological paper in *Psyche*. It interested me greatly and helped to embolden me to formulate a theory to which at the moment I'm inclined to attach

some importance. It is to the effect that the whole system of matriarchy was devised as one means of meeting the difficult Oedipus situation by decomposing the *Urvater* into a kind paternal nurse and a stern maternal uncle. The same explanation would also account for the supposed ignorance of paternity to which Malinowski like most anthropologists subscribes. As soon as I have any time, I shall attempt to work this out and see if it accords with the facts before publishing it" (Paskauskas 1993: 545).
6 In more recent years, such a polemic was presented by M.E. Spiro in *Oedipus in the Trobriands* (Chicago: University of Chicago Press, 1982). Using data provided by Malinowski himself, Spiro demonstrates that the Oedipus complex does exist in Trobriand society. The same approach is found in B. Pulman, *Anthropologie et Psychanalyse. Malinowski contre Freud*, Paris: PUF, 2002. Pulman writes that it is not a question of an absence of knowledge but of a socially instituted defensive formation (*"formation défensive socialement instituée"*). Both researchers thus continue Jones's line of argument.
7 Interestingly, at the time of the book's publication, in May 1927, he followed Lady Frazer's recommendation and consulted an unnamed psychotherapist or psychiatrist in London (Wayne 1995: 90). Malinowski socialized with the Bloomsbury Group, so the person in question may have been Freud's translator, James Strachey, or Virginia Woolf's brother, Adrian Stephen.
8 A bulk of letters from Malinowski to Princess Marie Bonaparte from the period 1932–1940 is stored in the archives of the London School of Economics and Political Science (MALINOWSKI/31/1). Bonaparte's letters to Malinowski are located at Yale University Library (Manuscripts and Archives, MS19, Series I, Box 1, Folder 62–63). Malinowski's daughter Helena Wayne recalls having attended "elegant dinners at the mansion of Princess Marie Bonaparte" during their visits in Paris (Wayne 1988: xviii).
9 Only a few of those letters have been published (Reich 1994: 219–226). I consulted the original typescripts kept at the London School of Economics and Political Science archive under the reference numbers: MALINOWSKI/29/15, MALINOWSKI/13/14, MALINOWSKI/36/32, MALINOWSKI/40/19.

References

Adorno, Theodor. 1986. "Die revidierte Psychoanalyse." In *Gesammelte Schriften*, edited by R. Tiedermann, 20–41. Frankfurt am Main: Suhrkamp, t. 8.
Bergman, Martin S., ed. 2000. *The Hartmann Era*. New York: Other Press.
Bryan, Douglas. 1925. "British Psycho-analytical Society. IV Quartal 1924." *Internationale Zeitschrift für Psychoanalyse* 1: 132–134.
Espagne, Michel. 1999. *Les transferts culturels franco-allemands*. Paris: PUF.
Freud, Sigmund. 1953. "Three Essays on the Theory of Sexuality." In *Standard Edition*. Translated and edited by James Strachey. Vol. VII, 125–244. London: The Hogarth Press and the Institute of Psychoanalysis.
Hale, Nathan G. 1995. *The Rise and Crisis of Psychoanalysis in the United States. Freud and the Americans, 1917–1985*. New York: Oxford University Press.
Herczyńska, Grażyna. 2004. "Stefan Borowiecki (1881–1937)." *Postępy Psychiatrii i Neurologii* 1: 1–8.
Higgings, Mary and Chester M. Raphael, eds. 1972. *Reich Speaks of Freud: Wilhelm Reich Discusses His Work and His Relationship with Sigmund Freud*. New York: Farrar, Straus & Giroux.
Jacoby, Russell. 1983. *The Repression of Psychoanalysis. Otto Fenichel and the Political Freudians*. New York: Basic Books.

Jones, Ernest. 1924. "Psychoanalysis and Anthropology." *The Journal of the Royal Anthropological Institute of Great Britain and Ireland* 54: 47–66.
———. 1925. "Mother-Right and the Sexual Ignorance of Savages." *International Journal of Psychoanalysis* 6: 109–130.
———. 1928. "*Sex and Repression in Savage Society* by Bronislaw Malinowski." *International Journal of Psychoanalysis* 9: 364–374.
Leuba, John. 1935. "Société Psychanalytique de Paris. IV Quartal 1934." *Internationale Zeitschrift für Psychoanalyse* 1: 159.
Łuniewski, Witold. 1933. "Prof. Stefan Borowiecki. Życie i człowiek." *Rocznik Psychiatryczny* 32: 1–7.
Magnone, Lena. 2016. *Emisariusze Freuda. Transfer kulturowy psychoanalizy do polskich sfer inteligenckich przed drugą wojną światową*. Kraków: Universitas.
———. 2023. *Freud's Emissaries. The Transfer of Psychoanalysis through the Polish Intelligentsia to Europe 1900–1939*. Genève-Lausanne: Sdvig press.
Malinowski, Bronisław. 1923. "Psychoanalysis and Anthropology." *Nature* 2818: 650–651.
———. 1924a. "Psycho-Analysis and Anthropology." *Psyche* 4: 293–332.
———. 1924b. "Mutterrechtliche Familie und Ödipus-Komplex: Eine psychoanalytische Studie." *Imago* 2/3: 228–276.
———. 1924c. *Mutterrechtliche Familie und Ödipus-Komplex: Eine psychoanalytische Studie*. Leipzig, Vienna, Zurich: Internationaler Psychoanalytischer Verlag.
———. 1925. "Complex and Myth in Mother-Right." *Psyche* 5: 194–216.
———. 1927. *Sex and Repression in Savage Society*. London: Kegan Paul.
———. 1962. *Sex, Culture, and Myth*. New York: Harcourt, Brace & World.
———. 1967. *A Diary in the Strict Sense of the Term*. London: Routledge & Kegan Paul.
———. 2002. *Dziennik w ścisłym znaczeniu tego wyrazu*, edited by Grażyna Kubica. Kraków: Wydawnictwo Literackie.
Parin, Paul. 1990. "Die Beschädigung der Psychoanalyse in der angelsächsischen Emigration und ihre Rückkehr nach Europa." *Psyche* 3: 191–201.
Paskauskas, Andrews R., ed. 1993. *The Complete Correspondence of Sigmund Freud and Ernest Jones 1908–1939*. Cambridge, MA, London: Harvard University Press.
Pulman, Bertrand. 1986. "Aux origines du débat anthropologie/psychanalyse: W. H. R. Rivers (1864–1922)." *L'Homme* 100: 119–142.
———. 1989. "Aux origines du débat anthropologie et psychanalyse: Seligman (1873–1940)." *Gradhiva. Revue d'histoire et d'archives de l'anthropologie* 6: 35–49.
———. 2002. *Anthropologie et psychanalyse. Malinowski contre Freud*. Paris: PUF.
Rank, Beata. 1924. "Zur Rolle der Frau in der Entwicklung der menschlichen Gesellschaft." *Imago* 2/3: 278–295.
Rank, Otto. 1924. *Das Trauma der Geburt*. Leipzig, Vienna, Zurich: Internationaler Psychoanalytischer Verlag.
Reich, Wilhelm. 1931a. "Malinowski, Bronislav: Das Geschlechtsleben der Wilden in Nordwestmalanesien (Grethlein & Co, Leipzig)." *Internationale Zeitschrift für Psychoanalyse* 3: 403–404.
———. 1932. *Der Einbruch der Sexualmoral: Zur Geschichte der Sexuellen Ökonomie*. Berlin, Leipzig, Wien: Verlag für Sexualpolitik.
———. 1934. "Roheims Psychoanalyse primitiver Kulturen." *Zeitschrift für politische Psychologie und Sexualökonomie* 3/4: 169–195.
———. 1942a. "In Memoriam: Bronislaw Malinowski 1884–1942." *International Journal of Sex Economy and Orgone Research* 2: 173.
———. 1942b. *The Discovery of the Orgone*. New York: Orgone Institute Press.

———. 1971. *The Invasion of Compulsory Sex-Morality*. New York: Farrar, Straus and Giroux.

———. 1994. *Beyond Psychology: Letters and Journals 1934–1939*, edited by Mary B. Higgins. New York: Farrar, Straus, and Giroux.

———. 2020. *Massenpsychologie des Faschismus. Der Originaltext von 1933*, edited by Andreas Peglau. Giessen: Psychosozial Verlag.

Robinson, Paul A. 1969. *The Freudian Left: Wilhem Reich, Géza Róheim, Herbert Marcuse*. New York: Harper & Row.

Róheim, Géza. 1932. "Die Psychoanalyse primitiver Kulturen". *Imago* 3/4: 297–563.

———. 1933. "Reich, Wilhelm: Der Einbruch der Sexualmoral. Berlin, Verlag für Sexualpolitik, 1932." *Imago* 4: 552–561.

Roudinesco, Élisabeth. 1994. *La bataille de cent ans. Histoire de la psychanalyse en France*, vol. 1. Paris: Fayard.

Seligman, Charles G. 1924. "Presidential Address. Anthropology and Psychology: A Study of Some Points of Contact." *The Journal of the Royal Anthropological Institute of Great Britain and Ireland* 54: 13–46.

Spiro, Melford E. 1982. *Oedipus in the Trobriands*. Chicago: University of Chicago Press.

Stepansky, Paul E. 1983. *In Freud's Shadow. Adler in Context*. Mahwah, NJ: Lawrence Erlbaum.

Stocking, George W. 1986. "Anthropology and the Science of the Irrational. Malinowski's Encounter with Freudian Psychoanalysis." In *Malinowski, Rivers, Benedict, and Others. Essays on Culture and Personality*, edited by George W. Stocking, 13–49. Madison: The University of Wisconsin Press.

Wayne, Helena. 1988. "Foreword." In *Malinowski between Two Worlds: The Polish Roots of an Anthropological Tradition*, edited by Roy F. Ellen, Ernest Gellner, Grażyna Kubica, and Janusz Mucha, XIX–XXIV. Cambridge: Cambridge University Press.

———. ed. 1995. *The Story of a Marriage: The Letters of Bronislaw Malinowski and Elsie Masson. Vol. 2: 1920–1935*. London, New York: Routledge.

Unpublished Archival Sources

Freud, Sigmund. 1938. *Letter to Bronisław Malinowski, 22.06.1938* (LSE, MALINOWSKI/29/5).

Leighton, Alexander H. 1939. *Letter to Bronisław Malinowski, 17.03.1939* (LSE, MALINOWSKI/36/32).

Malinowski, Bronisław. 1932. *Letter to Wilhelm Reich, 19.08.1932* (LSE, MALINOWSKI/29/15).

———. 1933. *Letter to Wilhelm Reich, 30.05.1933* (LSE, MALINOWSKI/29/15).

———. 1934a. *Letter to Wilhelm Reich, 30.01.1934* (LSE, MALINOWSKI/36/32).

———. 1934b. *Letter to Otto Rank, 12.03.1934* (LSE, MALINOWSKI/29/15).

———. 1934c. *Letter to Wilhelm Reich, 30.10.1934* (LSE, MALINOWSKI/36/32).

———. 1936. *Letter to Wilhelm Reich, 30.10.1936* (LSE, MALINOWSKI/36/32).

———. 1938. *Letter to Anna Freud, 18.06.1938* (Yale University, MS19, Series I, Box 3, Folder 207).

———. 1939. *Letter to Alexander H. Leighton, 10.01.1939* (LSE, MALINOWSKI/36/32).

———. 1941a. *Letter to Wilhelm Reich, 21.10.1941* (LSE, MALINOWSKI/36/32).

———. 1941b. *Letter to Wilhelm Reich, 27.10.1941* (LSE, MALINOWSKI/36/32).

———. 1942. *Letter to Ilse Ollendorff–Reich, 5.01.1942* (LSE, MALINOWSKI/13/14).

Rank, Otto. 1934. *Letter to Bronisław Malinowski, 5.02.1934* (LSE, MALINOWSKI/29/15).
Reich, Wilhelm. 1931b. *Letter to Bronisław Malinowski, 4.11.1931* (LSE, MALINOWSKI/29/15).
———. 1933. *Letter to Bronisław Malinowski, 16.05.1933* (LSE, MALINOWSKI/29/15).
———. 1934a. *Letter to Bronisław Malinowski, 14.01.1934* (LSE, MALINOWSKI/29/15).
———. 1934b. *Letter to Bronisław Malinowski, 17.10.1934* (LSE, MALINOWSKI/36/32).
———. 1938a. *Letter to Bronisław Malinowski, 17.11.1938* (LSE, MALINOWSKI/36/32).
———. 1938b. *Letter to Bronisław Malinowski, 21.11.1938* (LSE, MALINOWSKI/36/32).
———. 1941. *Letter to Bronisław Malinowski, 23.10.1941* (LSE, MALINOWSKI/36/32).
———. [1942]. *Letter to Bronisław Malinowski, undated (before January 31, 1942)* (LSE, MALINOWSKI/36/32).

8 Under the Wing of the Rockefeller Foundation

On the Cooperation of Bronisław Malinowski and His Polish Student Józef Obrębski

Anna Engelking

Introduction

This chapter is a contribution to the study of the relationship between social sciences and research administration. Based on the historiographical method of source analysis on the one hand, and biographical studies approach on the other, it presents an insight into the organization and course of ethnographical fieldwork, carried out by Józef Obrębski (1905–1967),[1] a Polish doctoral student of Bronisław Malinowski at the LSE. This small fragment of the biography of Józef Obrębski (or, more precisely, the biographical and cultural context of his ethnographic research and anthropological achievements) is focused on the analysis, on the one hand, of the institutional and organizational background of his fieldwork, conducted in the community of Macedonian highlanders in the years 1932–1933, on the other hand – on the student-teacher relationship between him and Malinowski. In this case study, I strive, on the basis of archival sources, to understand the facts from the past of anthropology in their own historical context, which I understand, following Grażyna Kubica, as "a specific type of field research conducted on the past of one's own tribe" (Kubica 2020: 543). Such an ethnography of the history of the discipline is the first, necessary step, to building both its anthropologically oriented critical history and the anthropological biography of Obrębski, equivalent to a perspective "focused on a person, intimate, close to experience and diachronic" and also enabling "an insight into how scientific knowledge comes about and is produced" (Kubica 2020: 543).

Crucial for this study is the fact that Obrębski was a fellow of the Rockefeller Foundation (abbreviated in the text as RF), whose financial support enabled both his studies at the LSE, and fieldwork in Macedonia. Thanks to the analysis of the correspondence between Malinowski, Obrębski and officials from the RF, as well as some other archival sources, one gains a detailed knowledge about the institutional, organizational, financial and, last but not least, scientific context of Obrębski's Macedonian fieldwork. It is also possible to understand better a particular role of Malinowski as the Foundation's advisor (Kubica 2014: 320, 332, Labbé 2011, Linkiewicz 2020). It should also be emphasized that only now one can understand the full extent of Obrębski's contribution to the ethnology of Europe as the complete Polish edition of his Macedonian writings was published in 2022 (Obrębski 2022a, 2022b), two years after the publication of an English edition of his selected writings concerning his Macedonian research (Obrębski 2020).

Outline of the Cooperation between Malinowski and Obrębski

Ten years after the publication of *Argonauts of the Western Pacific*, Józef Obrębski (1905–1967) began his ethnographic research in the community of Christian Orthodox highlanders in the Macedonian region of Poreche. It was the first fieldwork in a European village based thoroughly on Malinowski's ethnographic field method and functional theory (Engelking 2018). Obrębski was his only student at the time to conduct fieldwork outside of the borders of the British Empire colonies. Obrębski came to London in November 1930 as a fellow of the Rockefeller Foundation, which had in the previous year opened the social sciences fellowship program in Eastern Europe (Labbé 2011). He held a master's degree from Jagiellonian University, where he studied under two prominent scholars: the ethnologist Kazimierz Moszyński and the slavist and linguist Kazimierz Nitsch,[2] who was a friend of Malinowski. He obtained the fellowship on the initiative and thanks to Malinowski, to whom the both professors from Kraków recommended their gifted student.

During the first months of his fellowship, Obrębski participated in Malinowski's seminar and lectures at the London School of Economics, which saw the emergence of a "new generation [of anthropologists] gathered under Malinowski's arbitrary but fruitful tyranny" (Barth 2005: 27). Thereafter, from July 1931 to May 1932, during Malinowski's sabbatical leave, they stayed together first in Oberbozen in Tyrol and then in Tamaris (a district of La Seyne-sur-Mer) on the French Riviera, where Malinowski worked on *Coral Gardens and their Magic*, and Obrębski helped him with analysing his Kiriwinan fieldnotes. His practical experience from the seminar and his work on the "Corpus Inscriptionum Kiriwinensium" as well as the internalization of Malinowski's ethnographical method, together with Obrębski's ethnological and linguistic knowledge and his experience of previous fieldwork in the Balkans, made up a highly efficient research toolkit for the young anthropologist to make avail of during his fieldwork in Macedonia.

In late May 1932, Obrębski came up from Tamaris to Belgrade. After a period of library research, he spent a month on a preliminary survey of the field in Macedonia, at the time a province of the Kingdom of Yugoslavia. On 15 August, he began his fieldwork in a group of villages south-west of Skopje. The "region of Poreche [...] due to its archaic character is best suited for my work",[3] as he put it in a letter to Malinowski. They exchanged letters, although Obrębski did not fulfil his teacher's wish to report to him "regularly every fortnight, or better still every week".[4] After finishing his fieldwork in early spring, Obrębski returned to London in the beginning of April 1933. On the 24th of January 1934, he obtained the title of Doctor of Philosophy in Social Anthropology from the University of

London, awarded on the basis of the thesis *Family Organization Among Slavs as Reflected in the Custom of Couvade*, written under the supervision of Malinowski.

Taking up the subject of the cooperation between Obrębski and Malinowski once again – for I have written about them already in several places (Engelking 2004, 2006, 2018, 2022) – I will focus on the London-Macedonian period of Obrębski's scientific life. It was a period of close personal cooperation of Malinowski and his student, during which Obrębski "join[ed] in a forum where [the anthropologists] could adventurously and imaginatively work to shape the new kind of anthropology" (Barth 2005: 25). The correspondence, kept in both British and Polish archives, between Obrębski and Malinowski, and between the former and the Rockefeller Foundation officers as well as other people, gives a good insight both into the context and course of Obrębski's research in the Macedonian Poreche and the personal relationship of the teacher and his student.

Between Kraków and London

Józef Obrębski and Bronisław Malinowski met in person in July 1930 during Malinowski's visit to Kraków. In the LSE archives, there are three letters from Obrębski to Malinowski from before that time regarding the scientific, organizational, and financial aspects of Obrębski's planned studies in London. The first of these letters is dated 25 November 1929. Of their meeting in Kraków, Malinowski wrote in the following way to John Van Sickle, director of the Rockefeller Foundation's office in Paris, responsible for fellowships in social sciences:

> I tested Obrebski for his knowledge of English… He understood me quite well, especially when I spoke about scientific matters, and I am certain he could follow my lectures from the very first moment… Taking his scientific qualifications, his specialization in Slavonic kinship and family and his linguistic capacity, I should like to throw in all my weight in support of his application.[5]

Malinowski, who advised the Rockefeller Foundation and therefore might be viewed as a "so-called bridge figure …, was an ardent supporter of young Polish candidates for fellowships" and at the same time "was in favor of 'native' (insider) anthropologists writing about cultures close to their cultural or ethnic background" (Linkiewicz 2020: 6).

Two weeks after Obrębski's arrival in London in another letter to Van Sickle, Malinowski designed the shape of his tutelage over his student:

> The Christmas and Easter holidays I submit he should spend in London, where I shall be able to give him some private tuition. For the Summer holidays I should like him to come somewhere to OberBotzen [sic!], where both climate and the proximity of the supervisor might be an advantage to him. I like him personally. … so far his health shows no signs of deteriorating under the London climate.[6]

Under the Wing of the Rockefeller Foundation   143

Already from these first remarks about Obrębski, one can see that Malinowski was genuinely interested in this young man. Health problems would accompany Obrębski throughout his life, including his first winter in London and the later Macedonian fieldwork. Malinowski looked after him almost like a father, taking care of his health and other matters. When Obrębski was holed up far away in Macedonian mountains, Malinowski wrote to him:

> ... you do not say anything about your health and I would like to hear that [it] is alright. ... Should you be, however in any immediate need, do not forget that my telegram address is Malinowski Poloconics London, and if necessary I will see that you get some money by telegramme.[7]

As is well known, Malinowski would often establish personal relationships with his students and invite them to his family's house in Oberbozen during the holidays. Raymond Firth described his didactic style as a "liberal interpretation of the role of a teacher" and went on to say that: "It was his capacity for friendship and sympathy, going beyond the relations of a teacher to pupil, that helped to strengthen his attraction" (quoted after: Barth 2005: 29). I cannot say if he favoured Józef Obrębski in any way (as his compatriot? graduate of the same alma mater and student of the same teachers? as a young man of exceptional intelligence and capabilities?). Let me then stick to the facts.

As can be inferred from Obrębski's letters written before he left for England, he had neither a detailed vision of his studies nor a good grasp of their organizational and formal side. In these regards, he relied on Malinowski's guidance. The decision to start a Ph.D. was made in the spring of 1931, as can be seen from Malinowski's letter to N. F. Hall of University College:

> Joseph Obrebski ... has presented me recently with the plans of his work on Slavonic Kinship, based on his field-work,[8] and on researches into original sources at the British Museum. I anticipate a real contribution to our knowledge of Slavonic Sociology. As a result of our joint conversation about a fortnight ago, I have advised this student ... to register for a Ph.D., after I had found out that he will not need to go to any other lectures except those which I prescribe for him. ... I am keeping closely in touch with him.[9]

This close touch was known and appreciated also by Józef's family in Poland. His sister, Antonina Obrębska, a linguist and assistant of Kazimierz Nitsch, reported to him: "With the Malinowski's he is, it seems, on very good terms. He recently stayed in their flat when they were away, but soon he will move again. He visits Mrs. Malinowska in the countryside...."[10] Malinowski also informed Nitsch:

> The only thing is his health. If this does not bring him down, I expect Obrębski's future to be exceptionally promising. I managed to obtain a

prolongation of the Rockef[eller Foundation] (until autumn 1932)[11] and he is set to go with me for the summer to South Tyrol and for the winter to the Riviera.

(10 June 1931, letter in Polish) (Kubica-Kłyszcz 1985: 289)

It seems Malinowski had a substantial role in Obrębski's health getting better by organizing for him further studies as his personal assistant which at the same time served as climatic treatment – for they spent the following months together, away from the London fog.

In May 1931, thanks to Malinowski's effort, the London University and the Rockefeller Foundation agreed to Obrębski spending the following academic year abroad of England, accompanying Malinowski during his sabbatical leave on the French Riviera, in the vicinity of Toulon.

> I am going to devote my Sabbatical year to the working out of my field-material – he wrote to Van Sickle – and Obrebski in remaining constantly in touch with me could learn a great deal about the handling of field-work in this method. I shall spend most of my time in southern climates... where Obrebski's health might considerably improve.[12]

Further on in the same letter, he presented his opinion of Obrębski's progress and academic capabilities:

> ... I am glad to say that I am more than satisfied with Joseph Obrebski's work and that I strongly recommend him for a continuance of the fellowship next academic year, October 1931–1932. Obrebski has been attending my lectures and seminars and these he has attended very fully. ...
>
> He is preparing now two articles, one on the Function of the Couvade among the Slavonic peoples, and one on Kinship Terminologies of the Bulgarians. Both papers, of which I have seen the draft, will be in my opinion distinct contributions to science, and I trust to see them published soon in one of our special journals. Obrebski has also undertaken an extensive piece of research which I trust will culminate in a monograph on the family and kinship organisation of the Slavonic peoples.
>
> In all his work he is adapting the methods of functional anthropology to the very extensive but somewhat inchoate material on Slavonic Sociology and Folk-lore. In doing this he will I hope fertilise the social anthropology of the Slavonic countries: he will make available for Western science the results of Slavonic sources...
>
> Personally, I have formed an extremely favourable opinion of the character, intelligence, and application of Obrebski... I am certain he will be able to take a front rank among the workers in Social Science.[13]

When Obrębski returned from his fieldwork in Macedonia, he did not take up the articles on kinship terminology and organization again. He focused instead on the

Couvade. The typescript of his 200 pages long Ph.D. thesis, based, perhaps paradoxically, to a larger extent on older ethnographic sources rather than on his own fieldwork, can be found in the LSE Archives. This is not surprising, however, since it is known that Obrębski worked vigorously on the *Couvade* already during his first six months in London – it was on this topic, certainly, that his library research in the British Museum was focused. After he returned from Poreche, he only had to augment and finish the thesis.

In Oberbozen and Tamaris

Some information about Obrębski's stay with the Malinowskis in Oberbozen (from July to October 1931) comes from his sister's letters to Nitsch. In September 1931, Antonina came to Oberbozen to visit her brother who "really wanted to see me in order to discuss some semantological issues in new Anglo-American science".[14] Earlier, due to the fact that Józef, who never was a diligent correspondent, did not reply to letters (which was usually a cause of distress or anger of his relatives), she herself corresponded with Malinowski. "Malinowski now writes (instead of Józio) to our entire family" – she told Nitsch –

> And so I got a very nice reply to my letter, and he wrote to Mother of his own accord to calm her down. He gave Józio an earful, as a result of which the prodigal son now writes grand letters and makes excuses.[15]

From Oberbozen she wrote to Nitsch: "I am slowly getting to know the Malinowskis. Józio is learning and working like a dog. He is quite pleased and has gotten audacious. ... There are a lot of linguistics books here. It is beautiful here."[16] "A lot of linguistic and sisterly tasks. Józio is also linguistics-ing... The Malinowskis are wonderful people."[17]

In October 1931, the Malinowskis relocated to Tamaris on the French Riviera, where the work on Malinowski's synthesis of ethnology and linguistics continued. They were joined by Malinowski's secretary, Agnes Drew, and by their daughters' governess, Miss Ogilvie. Obrębski is mentioned a couple of times in the letters of Elsie, Malinowski's wife, to her husband. From them, one learns for example that he taught her Polish. "Obrębski is being a wonder thinking of everything and doing a great deal... Lessons seem to be going well" (14 October 1931). "I am writing in bed where I went because I was rather tired and felt also that I should give the three young folks [Drew, Obrębski and Ogilvie] a holiday from me" (19 October 1931). "Obrębski and Miss Drew are working hard at vocabulary" (26 October 1931) (Wayne 1995, vol. 2: 160–161). At that time, Elsie was already gravely ill and the help of other residents of the house, especially during Malinowski's frequent departures, was very much needed. In a letter to Van Sickle, Malinowski wrote of his student:

> Our friend Obrebski ... has developed so quickly and is helping me so much that at times I wonder how I would be getting on without him. You

know my definition of a good teacher: the man who can learn from his pupils – and I am developing this quality in my old age to a considerable degree.[18]

It should not be forgotten that this man of 'old age' was no more than 48 years old at the time. Obrębski, younger by almost a generation, was nevertheless treated by him as an equal.

Some time later, in the "Author's Preface" to *Coral Gardens*, Malinowski will write:

> In the working out of my material I received considerable help from research assistants provided by the Rockefeller Foundation; notably Dr J. Obrebski and Miss Agnes Drew, who assisted me in eliciting the material from my field notes… Also the manuscript in its semi-final form was read at one of my seminars, a chapter by each member, criticised and discussed, and from this I, and I hope the book too, have derived considerable profit.
> (Malinowski 1966: XXII)

In January 1935, Malinowski sent Obrębski, who was then back in Warsaw, a copy of the freshly published *Coral Gardens*. His former student wrote back the following:

> It gives me great joy to think that in one of the volumes of this book there is a speck of my work as well, even though I know how inept and fragmentary it was. I was especially interested by the last chapters of the first volume, the content of which was the least known to me and which together with the appendices form a further theoretical and methodological development of the functional school. And, of course, the second volume with its ethnographic theory of language, word magic and *Corpus Inscriptionum*. I am immensely glad that this volume turned out to so admiringly well. Maybe it will finally set in motion a revolution in linguistics which is long overdue and which – by ridding it of philological acrobatics – would finally make it a real, empirical, and humanistic science.[19]

It is worthwhile to return now to the spring of 1932. In all probability, this was the period when Obrębski's idea of fieldwork in Yugoslavia took shape. In April, in a memorandum on Obrębski written in Tamaris, Malinowski told Van Sickle:

> This candidate has now collected most of the material apparently available on Southern Slavonic kinship and family organisation; the subject on which he is working. Out of his research there emerge a number of gaps in information which he is unable to supply either from his personal field-notes (he has been twice already in the Balkans) or from existing literature. It occurs to me that, if you would allow him to spend the next four or five months in the Balkans, he might be able to apply in the field the new methods which

he has acquired in working with me. Personally I should be very much interested in what he might bring back now, after he has specialised in methods of sociological field-work. He has been working a great deal with me on my own material and on the theory of social anthropology, and I am confident he would do quite well alone in the field. I would therefore recommend him going to the Balkans, more specifically to the region north-east of Nish in Serbia, provided that this is compatible with the ordinary terms of his fellowship.[20]

For the context of Obrębski's Macedonian fieldwork, it's an important information that neither the student nor the teacher thought initially of Macedonia – Nish lies in north-eastern Serbia, in the vicinity of the border with Bulgaria.

In late May (or at the beginning of June), Obrębski left for Belgrade. On 25 May, Elsie wrote to Bronisław: "Obrębski came today to say goodbye and you know how dead relationships depress me" (Wayne 1995, vol. 2: 164). In a footnote to these words Helena Wayne, the Malinowskis' youngest daughter and editor of their correspondence, remarks: "There seems to have been a falling-out between Obrębski and the Malinowskis" (Wayne 1995, vol. 2: 250). I do not know how to comment on this other than to note that the student-teacher relationship would still continue and develop.

Yugoslavia – Macedonia – Poreche

Obrębski's fieldwork in the Macedonian Poreche eventually took about eight months, from August 1932 to March 1933, instead of the planned four or five. Soon after arriving in Belgrade, Obrębski wrote to his supervisor asking for his help in getting the Rockefeller Foundation to agree to prolong his fieldwork until the end of his fellowship, that is, to the end of the calendar year 1932. Ten days later, his request was granted. Obrębski asked Malinowski to prolong his stay again at the beginning of November, in a letter sent from the village of Volche, which served as his 'headquarters' in Poreche:

> In connection with my further work I would very much like to prolong my stay in the field until mid-January. This would allow me to witness and describe two important ceremonies: Bozhikj and Bogojavlenje (Vodica). The first one is important due to the pan-procreative character of the *zadruga*,[21] the second in connection to the religious organization of the village and the character of religious beliefs.[22]

The prolonged stay was to be financed by savings from the fellowship stipend. So it was, and in the end, Obrębski's stay in Poreche lasted well beyond mid-January. Although in 1933 he was not receiving a stipend, thanks to his savings and the understanding of his supervisor and sponsors, he was able to prolong his fieldwork until early spring. 30 years later, Obrębski described the religious organization of the village, which included the ceremonies he witnessed in January 1933, in a paper called *Social Structure and Ritual in a Macedonian Village*, presented at the Annual Meeting of American Anthropological Association in Philadelphia in 1961 (Obrębski 1969, also Obrębski 2006).

It seems that both Malinowski and Obrębski were aware from the very beginning of the necessity of a longer stay in the field. They acted, however, within the conditions set by the Rockefeller Foundation. The diplomatic task of negotiating with the Foundation's officers to obtain subsequent prolongations so that Obrębski would not have to return to London before the end of 1932 was undertaken by Malinowski. Even before Obrębski left for Belgrade, his supervisor wrote to him:

> The main point is you can go out to the field as soon as you possibly can now and the reports which you send me from there and the samples of work should be such that I can lay some emphasis on the point. I would advise you to correspond as little as possible directly with the Foundation, but deal with matters through me.[23]

On the other hand, the conditions set by the Foundation were not rigid:

> the RF's ability and willingness to adapt to local and individual situations is a feature of its fellowship policy... The RF officers did not manage their fellowship program in accordance with a model, but did so through consultation and progressive adjustments to the particular situations, constraints and preferences that arose.
>
> (Labbé 2011: 5–6)

What is striking in Malinowski's correspondence with the Foundation officers, beginning with his efforts for Obrębski to be awarded the fellowship, is on the one hand Malinowski's devotion and care for Obrębski, and on the other hand the kindness and willingness shown by the RF officers.

The Macedonian Poreche field comprised a handful of villages situated in remote mountains and inhabited by a community of shepherds. Obrębski, a diligent student of *Argonauts*, was interested in 'primitive groups' that had not yet been subjected to the disintegrating influence of modernity. He looked for a field that would be ethnically homogenous and as isolated as possible, in a word – his own Trobriand Islands. Documenting the social structure and family life, the economic system, annual and family rites, healing art and magic, mythology, and religion, Obrębski gathered abundant and unique materials. He was not only the first anthropologist in this region but also the first ethnographer. He settled on Poreche because he was looking for not only an isolated – and thus archaic – field but also one that would not be already described by ethnographers. A field and a community which he could discover for himself – and for anthropology.

As a historian Freddie Foks wrote in respect of cooperation between Malinowski with his students "[A]nthropological knowledge was produced between the field and the London School of Economics seminar, linked by pedagogy, internalized discipline, gifts, and displays of obedience (and sometimes rebellion) and in writing back to Malinowski in London" (Foks 2020: 719). Obrębski had a substantial role in creating this knowledge, when it comes to discipline and obedience, however, he was insubordinate. His fieldnotes are sloppy, he did not always note down the places, dates, and names of his interlocutors. He did not add colourful annotations, as Malinowski instructed his students. He did not use charts and schemes (in his fieldnotes there are maybe three small tables altogether) – although he made quite a lot of genealogical charts, drawings, and maps, and he would also take pictures.[24] He did not send Malinowski reports of his fieldwork, despite the former's repeated requests. Obrębski also did not send his supervisor any text which would be ready for publication, even though Malinowski offered to translate it into English himself.

The reason for Obrębski's silence was undoubtedly the fact that his "pen... had always suffered from neurasthenia",[25] but even more so the difficulties with winning his interlocutors' trust and the primitive circumstances in which he lived and worked in Poreche: "for systematic work, there is neither time nor conditions. By the way, I put up [at the houses of the villagers]."[26] Poreche was a "country located beyond the peripheries of civilization" (Obrębski 2022a: 56) and the ethnographer had to face all the consequences of this fact. He lived in homes of multi-generational families, and he wrote up his fieldnotes in the night next to an oil lamp, sitting on a low stool. The closest post office was in Gostivar, "a day of arduous journey [on a donkey]" (Obrębski 2020: 11) away from Volche.[27]

Two letters written to Malinowski by Obrębski in Yugoslavia survive – from 13 June 1932, written in Belgrade, and from 4 November 1932, written in Volche. It is unknown whether he wrote to Malinowski after that date. The second of the two letters could be seen as something of a modest report – although a letter to Moszyński, written on the way back to London, on 4 April 1933, in Calais, is longer and more detailed. All three are fascinating testimonies to the struggle of an ethnographer with his field: from preliminary assumptions, through adjusting them to reality, taking up a new research subject, to creating and testing new hypotheses. They also relate the difficult process of breaking through the interlocutors' distrust and steering the fieldwork from kinship to medicine, magic, and witchcraft.

"I tried to also research magic and healing practices" – Obrębski told Malinowski –

> but obtaining the slightest piece of information takes so much time, and besides the words of the magic formulae cannot be obtained: they lose their power when told to another. I will probably give up on this subject in the future.[28]

Five months later, however, the situation was starkly different. In the letter to Moszyński, one reads: "[This] work, undertaken initially because of anger at the secrecy and distrust of Macedonian hags, has developed in quite an interesting direction." One also learns from it of Obrębski's plans:

> The result of this will be a book about Macedonian witch doctors, which – if circumstances allow – I plan to prepare in English… It will constitute a quite important contribution to the knowledge of the social-cultural structure of patriarchal society. It has a rather ample collection of photographs.[29]

Between London and Warsaw

The only letters written to Obrębski in Macedonia that survive are the two letters from Malinowski, in which he opines on his student's work. "I am glad that your work in Belgrade is progressing well and that your plans for field-work seem satisfactory"[30] – he wrote in June 1932. And in November:

> Your results so far as I can judge from the brief survey which you give me, are by no means contemptible, especially if you really succeeded in 'contextualizing' the six types of myths which you have mentioned, and documented them fully from the sociological point of view – that alone should be a sufficient result of your work with me and in the field.[31]

An analysis of the six types of myths mentioned above formed the basis of Obrębski's monograph *Mit i rzeczywistość u Słowian Południowych* [*Myth and Reality of Southern Slavs*]. He wrote parts of it in Polish and parts in English and, like most of his works on Macedonia, it remained unfinished, although he did complete substantial portions of the book (cf. Obrębski 2022b: 263–494). It is a study deconstructing common ethnological myths that orientalized southern-Slavic peasants. Among other myths, Obrębski recounted and analysed the myths of parricide, incest, and selling wives. He wrote to Moszyński that this project was

> designed not as fieldwork but as a general theoretical work about the Balkans… It consists of two parts: a theoretical polemical part, where past ethnographic mistakes are dismantled, and a constructive part, where for each of the myths the appropriate social context is provided.[32]

Only one of these analyses, a deconstructive analysis of the myth of man in labour, highlighting the sociocultural determinants of gender dichotomy, was completed, under the title *Family Organisation among Slavs as Reflected in the Custom of Couvade*. This work, as already mentioned, became Obrębski's Ph.D. thesis. Although he later worked on preparing it for publication – it was supposed to be published, like books written by other students of Malinowski, with his supervisor's foreword – he never published this monograph.

Of the period Obrębski spent in London after returning from Macedonia – from April 1933 until January 1934 – is known very little. There is no correspondence between the student and the teacher since both of them were in the same place (except for the time Malinowski went to Oberbozen). Obrębski continued his doctoral studies (the condition for taking the doctoral exam was passing two years of studies) and lived on money saved from the fellowship stipend. "Józio sent a word that he did not obtain a prolongation of the stipend" – wrote his sister to Nitsch – "but since his work is not finished, he will stay until January and move to a cheaper flat".[33] While in London, Obrębski certainly participated in Malinowski's seminar. Was it then that its participants discussed subsequent chapters of the *Coral Gardens*, or did this take place earlier, when Obrębski was in Poreche? Did he present the results of his Macedonian fieldwork? The extant sources do not mention this, but it certainly is probable. In the UMass Archives (OC), there are several drafts in English, including an almost finished article called 'Bride Wealth in Macedonia'. Could this have been his paper for the seminar?

Neither did Obrębski manage to prepare an English version of his book on Macedonian witchcraft. There are, however, outlines, in English, of this monograph. The only articles he managed to write in English were about the magic of impotence and infertility – 'Marital Maladjustment and Marriage Stability' and 'Conjugal Maladjustment' – but both were left unfinished. He worked on the topic after his return to Poland in the beginning of 1934. In 1934, he published a popular science article 'Czarna magja w Macedonii' [Black Magic in Macedonia] (Obrębski 1934). A year later, he mentioned his work on this subject in a letter sent to Malinowski after receiving a copy of the *Coral Gardens and their Magic*:

> *Witchcraft* was elaborated in the field and later, while the memories of my apprenticeship under you, Professor, were still fresh, and it stems from *Coral Garden*s both methodologically and theoretically.... So far, I have written about a half of *Witchcraft*.... It is about this work that I wanted to ask you, Professor, if it were possible for you to write a foreword to this book, that is, of course, if you deem it worthy. I would be sincerely pleased if my first ethnological book was honoured with such a distinction and this sign of school and method.[34]

Obrębski did not finish his *Czarownictwo Porecza Macedońskiego* [*The Witchcraft of Macedonian Poreche*]. A reconstruction of this monograph based on extant fragments and fieldnotes was published in the collected Macedonian works of Obrębski and takes up a couple hundred pages (Obrębski 2022b: 11–260, also Obrębski 2020: 71–87). The phenomenon of Porechian witchcraft – a domain of women – is presented by Obrębski through the prism of systemic conflicts in the extended family (*zadruga*) and disruptive tendencies in the rural community, social inequalities and relations of power and domination, and finally the socio-economic determinants of the institution of marriage. The motifs of marriage by elopement, as well as impotence and infertility, surrounded by a variety of magical rites, turned out to be the key to the organization of the social and family structure of the Porechans.

Apart from these two monographs, Obrębski was also working on a third one: *Giaurowie Macedonii. Opis magii i religii pasterzy z Porecza na tle zbiorowego życia ich wsi* [*The Giaours of Macedonia. An Account of the Magic and Religion of Shepherds in Poreche against the Background of the Collective Life of Their Village*]. It was the only one he completed. Unfortunately, the typescript ready for print was destroyed during the Warsaw Uprising in 1944. The editors of Obrębski's Macedonian writings reconstructed it based on extant fragments and fieldnotes (Obrębski 2022a). An important article written on the basis of *The Giaours of Macedonia* – 'System religijny ludu macedońskiego' [The Religious System of the Macedonian People] – was published by Obrębski in 1936 (Obrębski 1936a). In it, he analysed 'the pagan Christianity' of Porechian people and its reflections in faith and daily life. Obrębski left Poreche intending to come back, "this time to study religion – a subject that seems to me most interesting and captivating", as he wrote to Moszyński.[35] The Macedonian works of Obrębski may be seen as part of the "generation of innovative monographs" (Barth 2005: 27), which sprang from the theoretical roots of Malinowski's functionalism and the atmosphere of discussion at his seminar.

The last opinion Malinowski formed of Obrębski that I know of was addressed to Tracy Kittredge and is the following:

Obrebski, as you put it, is 'rather vague'. There is no doubt at all that he is one of the most capable young men in ethnology. He is a good worker, original, clear-minded, and efficient. He certainly has also a spark of genius. With all this, it will be touch and go whether he will really come to the fore. To my knowledge, he has in his dossier at least two MSS practically ready for publication which I am afraid will never see the light. Most perfectionism, since I suffer myself from that Slav disease (and many others). I wish you to be very charitable towards Obrebski. I still hope he will come to the fore.[36]

Kittredge answered Malinowski:

I fully agree with your judgement as to Obrebski. We will follow with much interest his future career. We hope that he will be able without any too great delay, to get a definite foothold in the University of Cracow. As soon as he accomplishes this, we may be able to be of some assistance to him enabling him to develop some of his further research projects.[37]

After obtaining his doctorate, Obrębski received a proposal of further cooperation in London from Malinowski. The details of this proposal, recalled by the Obrębski family, are unknown.[38] But, loyal to the belief that "one can study abroad, but one should work in and for Poland",[39] he didn't accept Malinowski's offer and returned to his home country. Had Obrębski stayed in London and continued to cooperate with Malinowski, perhaps his perfectionism would have been better controlled and the *Couvade*, as well as later monographs, would have seen the light of day.

In everything connected with anthropology, Obrębski was definitely a good student of Malinowski. Like other students of his, he "would simultaneously embody the ethnographer, the theorist, and the data gatherer – bridging the divide between the 'armchair' and the 'field'" (Foks 2020: 726), of which his monographs on

Poreche, following the example of Malinowski's Trobriand volumes, are a great example.

Morgane Labbé, a researcher of the Polish fellows of the Rockefeller Foundation, writes that

> the goal for the eventual integration of former RF fellows in their native country led the RF to select young scholars they viewed as the future successors of their professors.... By contrast, the fellows returning to Poland who lacked institutional integration and support faced a precarious situation.
>
> (Labbé 2011: 5)

Regarding Józef Obrębski both of these statements are, paradoxically, true. When he returned to Poland in late January 1934, his former assistant lecturer position at the Jagiellonian University in Kraków was already taken by someone else. Moszyński could only recommend him for ephemeral research projects emerging at the intersection of science, expert activity, and policy making. Obrębski found himself in the precarious situation of "an anthropologist for hire". It wasn't until nearly three years later, in the autumn of 1936, that he took up the post of deputy director of the State Institute of Village Culture, a newly created research institution with sociological inclinations.

While living and working in Warsaw, where most of his friends were sociologists, Obrębski continued to be a student of Malinowski. He implemented Malinowski's theory and method in the fieldwork he conducted in the Polesie region[40] and propagated his ideas and works in Poland. He translated Malinowski's works into Polish, wrote on him ('O metodzie funkcjonalnej Bronisława Malinowskiego' ['On the functional method of Bronisław Malinowski'] (1939), Obrębski 2004) and published reviews of his books (of *Coral Gardens and Their Magic*, Obrębski 1936b), also after the war (of *Freedom and Civilization*, Obrębski 1946). Three of Malinowski's works were translated by Obrębski: *The Deadly Issue* in 1936, *Law and Custom*, and *Crime and Custom in Savage Society* in 1938.[41] In his last – to the extent of my knowledge – letter to Obrębski Malinowski thanks him for translating the last two works. It was written a few days before Malinowski left Europe and is dated 22 October 1938. Let me quote it at length:

"My dear Obrebski,

I have to apologize for my long silence. As a matter of fact, I went through the sample translation together with Waligorski. I found your translation excellent and wanted to thank you very much for doing such excellent work, and improving my texts in its Polish guise. The only corrections which I suggested proved on Waligorski's verdict to be due to my having forgotten what good Polish style is.

I should be very grateful if you sent me in future any of your publications. I have read your reprints with the greatest interest and hope only that you will go on publishing, since you, like myself, have a tendency of putting manuscripts away and letting them mature in the dark.

It was a great pleasure for me to see your sister and her husband when they were in London.[42] I am afraid they may be passing here again on their way back from China at a time when I am away in the United States of America. I am sailing on October 26th. Please remember me to your wife and accept my affectionate greetings,

Yours always."[43]

Conclusion

The first Polish researcher of Obrębski's scientific path and achievements, Anna Kutrzeba-Pojnarowa, wrote in 1977:

> Józef Obrębski owed his position in Polish academia and two offers to take up a university chair in the country – after World War II – to the well-established opinion to be a student and collaborator of the famous representative of world anthropology and ethnology, Bronisław Malinowski, who established the so-called functional school. Above all, however, he owed it to the independence and originality of the new theoretical and methodological concepts he put forward in the 1930s.
>
> (Kutrzeba-Pojnarowa 1977: 111)

Knowledge about the student-teacher relationship between Obrębski and Malinowski and the influence of functionalism on Obrębski's anthropology was common in the Polish anthropological community, but the authors writing about Obrębski contented themselves only with stating these facts. More profound studies of their intellectual relationship were undertaken only in my articles (Engelking 2004, 2006, 2018, 2022).

This chapter is a next analytical step towards recognition of the influence of Malinowski's anthropology and personality on Obrębski's work as well as the external conditions of this influence. At the same time, it can be read as a case study of Malinowski's relationship with his most remarkable Polish student and the role of the Rockefeller Foundation in establishing and developing their relationship. Thanks to efficient cooperation in this triangle, which consisted of Malinowski's authority and experience, the enthusiasm and motivation of a young anthropology student from a peripheral country, and the kindness and willingness of the RF officers, the first functionalist research carried out in a European peasant community (Engelking 2018) proved to be both possible and successful. Not until one grasps the dynamics of interconnections between the personalities of the participants in this cooperation, its financial, administrative, organizational and technical conditions, and the theory and method of European anthropology that was the subject of institutionalisation at that time, could they see how scientific knowledge arises and is produced.

The relationship of Obrębski and Malinowski, evolving under the wing of the Rockefeller Foundation, was indeed something more than a student-teacher relationship. The documents presented in this chapter showed that their bond was not only intellectual. The case of Obrębski confirms Raymond Firth's remark about Malinowski's "capacity for friendship and sympathy, going beyond the relations of a teacher to pupil" (quoted after: Barth 2005: 29). It seems that Malinowski embodied for Obrębski both the figure of a father, a friend and a sage. He wasn't a teacher, he was a master. The philosopher Barbara Skarga wrote in her essay "The Master and the Magus" (Skarga 1977):

> One has usually many teachers [...]. One has only one master at any given time usually and his influence on the student's development is always decisive. The student consciously submits to this influence because the master arouses admiration in him and becomes an example.
>
> (Skarga 1977: 10)

Her words can also be applied to the relationship of Obrębski and Malinowski: "To appreciate the true greatness of the master, you must not be ignorant yourself. That is why we observe that outstanding students cluster around outstanding academic individualities" (Skarga 1977: 13–14).

The analysis presented in this case study can be read also as a confirmation of Grażyna Kubica's statement: "biography and anthropology merge together seamlessly and are hard to separate. And that in fact there is no need to split them" (Kubica 2020: 30).

Notes

1 For more on Józef Obrębski, see: Józef Obrębski website, https://jozef-obrebski.ispan.edu.pl/en/ and Engelking 2022.
2 Both Kazimierz Moszyński (1887–1959) and Kazimierz Nitsch (1874–1958) were remarkable Slavists and experienced field researchers, the former in ethnology, the latter in dialectology. They laid the foundations for the 20th-century substantive and methodological shape of ethnology and linguistics in Poland and set the path for their development for many decades.
3 J. Obrębski to B. Malinowski, 4 November 1932 (LSE, letter in Polish).
4 B. Malinowski to J. Obrębski, 24 June 1932 (LSE, letter in English). Malinowski asked this of all his students working in the field, see: (Foks 2020: 724).
5 B. Malinowski to J. van Sickle, 2 October 1930 (LSE, letter in English).
6 B. Malinowski to J. van Sickle, 1 December 1930 (LSE, letter in English).
7 B. Malinowski to J. Obrębski, 18 November 1932 (LSE, letter in English).
8 The fieldwork mentioned by Malinowski was conducted by Obrębski in 1927–1928 when for altogether five months he worked in Bulgaria and its bordering regions. He focused on material culture and also collected field material regarding family and kinship.
9 B. Malinowski to N. F. Hall, 2 April 1931 (LSE, letter in English).
10 A. Obrębska to K. Nitsch, 22 April 1931 (Skarżyński, Smułkowa, 2018, 1: 160, letter in Polish).
11 Prolonging scholarships was a common practice at the Rockefeller Foundation, cf.: (Labbé 2011: 3).
12 B. Malinowski to J. Van Sickle, 3 May 1931 (LSE, letter in English).
13 Ibid.
14 A. Obrębska to K. Nitsch, 27 June 1931 (Skarżyński, Smułkowa, 2018, 1: 185, letter in Polish).
15 A. Obrębska to K. Nitsch, 27 August 1931 (Skarżyński, Smułkowa, 2018, 1: 197–198, letter in Polish).
16 A. Obrębska to K. Nitsch, 2 September 1931 (Skarżyński, Smułkowa, 2018, 1: 198, letter in Polish).

17 A. Obrębska to K. Nitsch, 9 September 1931 (Skarżyński, Smułkowa, 2018, 1: 199, letter in Polish).
18 B. Malinowski to J. van Sickle, 11 February 1932 (LSE, letter in English).
19 J. Obrębski to B. Malinowski, 24 January 1935 (YUA, letter in Polish).
20 B. Malinowski to J. van Sickle, 25 April 1932 (LSE, letter in English).
21 The zadruga, or extended family, organized on a patrilineal basis, was a corporate group holding property in common. It was the traditional basis of rural social organization throughout the Balkans, existing into the 20th cent.
22 J. Obrębski to B. Malinowski, 4 November 1932 (LSE, letter in Polish).
23 B. Malinowski to J. Obrębski, 23 May 1932 (LSE, letter in English).
24 Freddy Foks, in an article in which he analyses the correspondence between Malinowski and his students, discusses also the methodological limits of his 'paper technology' of note-taking and schemes and in the matter of fact the failure of Malinowski's paper technologies, see: Foks 2020.
25 M. Obrębska to J. and T. Obrębski, 20 September 1951 (OC, letter in Polish).
26 J. Obrębski to B. Malinowski, 4 November 1932 (LSE, letter in Polish).
27 Obrębski's silence was worrying not only to his family, but also to Malinowski and to the Rockefeller Foundation. The RF Secretary wrote to him on 14 November 1932: "As we were becoming a little anxious about you on account of your long silence we wrote to a former Fellow of the Foundation, Mr. Ralph Brown, who is now living in Belgrade to ask him if he could give us any news of you. He has replied saying that he has discovered that you are working upon some outlying villages and that you are well" (LSE, letter in English).
28 J. Obrębski to B. Malinowski, 4 November 1932 (LSE, letter in Polish).
29 J. Obrębski to Moszyński, 4 April 1933 (IAiEKUJ, letter in Polish).
30 B. Malinowski to J. Obrębski, 24 June 1932 (LSE, letter in English).
31 B. Malinowski to J. Obrębski, 18 November 1932 (LSE, letter in English).
32 J. Obrębski to K. Moszyński, 4 April 1933 (IEiAKUJ, letter in Polish).
33 A. Obrębska to K. Nitsch, 18 July 1933 (Skarżyński, Smułkowa, 2018, 1: 212, letter in Polish).
34 J. Obrębski to B. Malinowski, 24 January 1935 (YUA, letter in Polish).
35 J. Obrębski to K. Moszyński, 4 April 1933 (IEiAKUJ, letter in Polish).
36 B. Malinowski to T. Kittredge, 22 October 1933 (LSE, letter in English).
37 T. Kittredge to B. Malinowski, 31 October 1933 (LSE, letter in English).
38 I was told of this proposal (in conversation in 1994) by Józef's sister, Antonina Obrębska-Jabłońska.
39 M. Obrębska to J. Obrębski, 27 April 1957 (OC, letter in Polish).
40 Polesie, today in Belarus and Ukraine, was an eastern region of the prewar Polish state, densely inhabited by East-Slavic national minorities and Jews. Obrębski conducted his fieldwork there in 1934–1937 among Orthodox, Belarusian- and Ukrainian-speaking peasants.
41 These translations had a number of reprints before and after WWII; they were also included in the Polish edition of Malinowski's collected works (*Dzieła*, Warszawa 1980–2003).
42 In the beginning of 1937 Józef's sister, together with her husband, a sinologist Witold Jabłoński, stayed in London on their way to a research scholarship in China.
43 B. Malinowski to J. Obrębski, 22 October 1938 (YUA, letter in English).

References

Barth, Fredrik. 2005. "Britain and the Commonwealth". In *One Discipline, Four Ways: British, German, French, and American Anthropology*, edited by Fredrik Barth et al., 3–57. Chicago, IL–London: University of Chicago Press.

Engelking, Anna. 2004. "Obrębski o Malinowskim. Z dziejów recepcji funkcjonalizmu w Polsce", *Studia Socjologiczne* 173(2): 17–34. https://www.studiasocjologiczne.pl/img_upl/studia_socjologiczne_2004_nr2_s.17_34.pdf

Engelking, Anna. 2006. "'Nowy Malinowski', czyli o związkach Józefa Obrębskiego z europejską i pozaeuropejską antropologią społeczną". In *Klasyczna socjologia polska i jej współczesna recepcja*, edited by Janusz Mucha, and Włodzimierz Wincławski, 199–223. Toruń: Uniwersytet Mikołaja Kopernika.

Engelking, Anna. 2018. "Macedońskie Trobriandy. Józef Obrębski i pierwsze badania wsi europejskiej w paradygmacie funkcjonalizmu", *Lud* 102: 1–23. https://doi.org/10.12775/lud102.2018.06

Engelking, Anna. 2022. "From Archaic to Colonial Peasantries: An Intellectual Biography of Józef Obrębski, the (Forgotten) Polish Disciple of Malinowski". In *BEROSE International Encyclopaedia of the Histories of Anthropology*. Paris. URL Bérose: article2599. html

Foks, Freddy. 2020. "Constructing the Field in Interwar Social Anthropology: Power, Personae, and Paper Technology". *Isis* 111(4): 717–739. https://www.journals.uchicago.edu/doi/10.1086/712138

Kubica-Klyszcz, Grażyna. 1985. "Listy Bronisława Malinowskiego". In *Antropologia społeczna Bronisława Malinowskiego*, edited by Mariola Flis, and Andrzej K. Paluch, 253–300. Warszawa: PWN.

Kubica, Grażyna. 2014. "'The Survey of the Ghetto' in the Time of Anti-Semitism: Feliks Gross and His Unfinished Fieldwork on the Jewish Quarters of Krakow and Vilna, 1938–1940". *East European Politics and Societies and Cultures* 28(2): 318–340. https://doi.org/10.1177/0888325413511662

Kubica, Grażyna. 2020. *Gender, Shamanism, Race. An Anthropological Biography*, "Critical Studies in the History of Anthropology Series", The University of Nebraska Press, Lincoln 2020.

Kutrzeba-Pojnarowa, Anna. 1977. "Józef Obrębski". In eadem, *Kultura ludowa i jej badacze. Mit i rzeczywistość*, 111–120. Warszawa: Ludowa Spółdzielnia Wydawnicza.

Labbé, Morgane. 2011. *The Rockefeller Foundation Turns to the East: Polish Social Sciences Fellows during the Interwar Period*. Rockefeller Archive Center. Retrieved 14 June 2023 from https://rockarch.issuelab.org/resource/the-rockefeller-foundation-turns-to-the-east-polish-social-sciences-fellows-during-the-interwar-period.html

Linkiewicz, Olga. 2020. *Polish Experts and American Internationalists in the Field of Social Science*. Rockefeller Archive Center. Retrieved 14 June 2023 from https://rockarch.issuelab.org/resource/polish-experts-and-american-internationalists-in-the-field-of-social-science.html

Malinowski, Bronisław. 1980–2003. *Dzieła*, vol. 1–13. Warszawa: PWN.

Obrębski, Józef. 1934. "Czarna magia w Macedonii". *Kuryer Literacko-Naukowy* 111: 6–8.

Obrębski, Józef. 1936a. "System religijny ludu macedońskiego". *Kuryer Literacko-Naukowy* 24: 13–14, 26: 11–12, 28: 11–13, 29: 11–12, 30: 13.

Obrębski, Józef. 1936b. "Społeczeństwo pierwotne". *Przegląd Socjologiczny* 4 (1–2): 224–229.

Obrębski, Józef. 1946. "Wolność i cywilizacja". *Nowa Polska* 6 (9–10): 593–604.

Obrebski, Joseph. 1969. *Ritual and Social Structure in a Macedonian Village*. Boston, MA: American Association for the Advancement of Slavic Studies.

Obrębski, Józef. 2004. "O metodzie funkcjonalnej Bronisława Malinowskiego". *Studia Socjologiczne* 173 (2): 35–63. https://www.studiasocjologiczne.pl/img_upl/studia_socjologiczne_2004_nr2_s.35_63.pdf

Obrębski, Józef. 2006. "Social Structure and Ritual in a Macedonian Village". *Sprawy Narodowościowe* 29: 286–295. https://jozef-obrebski.ispan.edu.pl/wp-content/uploads/social-structure-and-ritual-in-a-macedonian-village.pdf

Obrębski, Józef. 2020. *The Giaours of Macedonia. Selected writings*, edited by Anna Engelking, translated by Helena Teleżyńska. Warszawa: Oficyna Naukowa. https://jozef-obrebski.ispan.edu.pl/wp-content/uploads/macedonia-en.pdf

Obrębski, Józef. 2022a. *Macedonia 1. Giaurowie Macedonii. Opis magii i religii pasterzy z Porecza na tle zbiorowego życia ich wsi*, edited by Anna Engelking, Joanna Rękas, and Ilija Upalevski. Warszawa: Oficyna Naukowa. https://jozef-obrebski.ispan.edu.pl/wp-content/uploads/macedonia-1.pdf

Obrębski, Józef. 2022b. *Macedonia 2. Czarownictwo Porecza Macedońskiego. Mit i rzeczywistość u Słowian Południowych. [Rozproszone teksty epickie i liryczne. Zapisy terenowe]. Struktura społeczna i rytuał we wsi macedońskiej*, edited by Anna Engelking, Joanna Rękas, and Ilija Upalevski. Warszawa: Oficyna Naukowa. https://jozef-obrebski.ispan.edu.pl/wp-content/uploads/macedonia-2.pdf

Skarga, Barbara. 1977. "Mistrz i mag". *Teksty: teoria literatury, krytyka, interpretacja* 1(31): 7–20.

Skarżyński, Mirosław, and Elżbieta Smułkowa, eds. 2018. *Materiały do dziejów polskiego językoznawstwa 3. Korespondencja Antoniny Obrębskiej-Jabłońskiej i Kazimierza Nitscha*, vol. 1, 2. Kraków: Księgarnia Akademicka.

Wayne, Helena, ed. 1995. *The story of a marriage. The letters of Bronislaw Malinowski and Elsie Masson*. London, New York: Routledge.

Internet Sources

Józef Obrębski website, https://jozef-obrebski.ispan.edu.pl/en/

Archival Sources

IEiAKUJ: Institute of Ethnology and Cultural Anthropology of the Jagiellonian University Archives, materials of Kazimierz Moszyński.

LSE: London School of Economics and Political Science Archives, correspondence of Bronisław Malinowski.

OC: Obrebski Collection, Special Collections and University Archives, University of Massachusetts, Amherst, legacy of Józef Obrębski http://scua.library.umass.edu/umarmot/obrebski-jozef/

YUA: Yale University Archives, correspondence of Bronisław Malinowski.

Part IV
Reconsiderations of Interpretive Frameworks

Illustration 5 Bronisław Malinowski and a group of Trobrianders, 1916–1918.

9 Bronisław Malinowski

An Icon of a Body-centric Anthropology?

Andreas Lipowsky

A Hidden Trajectory for the Theory of Embodiment in Anthropology

The dichotomy of body and mind is a conceptual cornerstone of the European philosophical tradition. Having already been well established in ancient Greece and exerting its influence throughout medieval theology, this dualism's Cartesian rendition is widely considered the foundation of modern Western epistemology. By establishing the thinking subject as separated from body, Descartes (1993 [1641]) introduced the notion of rationality as one located on the outside of while also being superior to nature, the latter being conceived in mechanical terms, or, in a word: objectified. Only in the second half of the 20th century did the hegemony of said notion dissolve. Poststructuralist thought became an intellectual hotbed for this development. In this regard, the rediscovery of Friedrich Nietzsche across philosophy departments in the 1960s and 1970s was of particular relevance as it greatly influenced prominent embodiment thinkers of this era, such as Michel Foucault with his notion of biopower (1973 [1963], 1977 [1975]), Gilles Deleuze and Félix Guattari with their contribution to affect theory (1987 [1980]), or Judith Butler's momentous reevaluation of essentialist concepts of gender via the notion of the performative (1990).

Anthropology followed suit. Embodiment theory virtually exploded throughout the anglophone discipline in the 1980s, remaining an influential intellectual current ever since. It variously brings into focus the emotions (Lutz and White 1986), the senses (Stoller 1989; Howes 1991, 2003; Serementakis 1994), or affect (Stuart 2007). Furthermore, phenomenology, existentialism, as well as the habitus concept have proven to be equally productive starting points for anthropology (Jackson 1989; Csordas 1990; also cf. Desjarlais and Throop 2011), while positional epistemologies in feminist and post-colonial anthropology probably break most radically with enlightenment rationality (Harrison 2010 [1991]; Behar and Gordon 1995; Smith 1999; also cf.: Haraway 1988).

It may come as a surprise that Malinowski is a prominent figure in this subsection of anthropological thought. In 1989, for example, Paul Stoller calls for a "return to the senses" and has pursued this trajectory for more than a decade afterwards. His monograph *The Taste of Ethnographic Things* seeks to move beyond what Stoller perceives as an overemphasis on vision within anthropological discourse; an overemphasis which, as he demonstrates, is deeply intertwined with the Western philosophical tradition and gravely distorts anthropological conceptions of culture. However, the emblematic historical figure whom Stoller credits with providing a trajectory for this program happens to be Malinowski. According to Stoller, Malinowski's ethnography sought "to write a document that gives the reader a *sense* of what it is like to live in the lands of others" (Stoller 1989: 8; italics adapted from original source).

In turn, in his preface to *Existential Anthropology* (2005), Michael Jackson claims that Malinowski's *Argonauts of the Western Pacific* was the first anthropology book he ever bought. However, it is not Malinowski's vision of the Kula as a non-Western economy, but his closing remarks that led to Jackson crediting this book as an influential source to his thinking. On the last pages of the *Argonauts*, Malinowski understands the journey of the ethnographer as one in which he seeks to overcome the "narrow confinements of the customs, beliefs and prejudices into which every man is born." (Malinowski 1922a: 518) Jackson was 65 when *Existential Anthropology* was published and he references Malinowski to, in his own words, describe his professional career as "a form of a search for oneself." (Jackson 2005: x) To Jackson, ethnography is an enterprise that explores life's existential dimensions, seeking "those forms of human life – transitive, ambiguous, penumbral, elusive […] that are existentially most imperative to us, and are at stake in the critical moments that define our lives, notably love, mutual recognition, respect, dignity, wellbeing." (Jackson 2005: xxix) Again, it is the *Argonauts*' Malinowski who is referred to as that iconic anthropologist who provided the blueprint for this endeavour.

Anna Grimshaw provides yet a third programmatic reading of Malinowski, which also happens to be the most unorthodox of the approaches discussed in this paper. Her monograph, now considered a classical contribution to visual anthropology, essentially redefines Malinowski's ethnographic methodology as a "way of seeing." She draws comparisons to the visual arts and media to elaborate on his historic methodology

> His [Malinowski's; AL] notion of ethnographic understanding was an essentially mystical one… The process of ethnographic understanding was secret, personal and embodied. Malinowski's approach was predicated on the distinction between *exploration* and *revelation*… For…the Malinowskian ethnographer was expected to be alone in the field. She or he must be exposed and vulnerable, returned to a prelinguistic state akin to that of childhood, as the necessary precondition for being able to break through to a different level of understanding.
>
> (Grimshaw 2001: 54–55; italics adapted from original source)

By elaborating on Clifford Geertz's reading of Malinowski's oeuvre (1988), Grimshaw considers Malinowski's texts as being deeply informed by notions of testimony. The ethnographer bears witness to non-European practices and is therefore able to report on them. Hence, Malinowski is yet again understood as one who emphasises the embodied dimensions of ethnography and his methodology as being deeply embedded within notions of lived experience.

For many contemporary readers of anthropology, these references may be counterintuitive, as the conventional narrative primarily remembers Malinowski as the representative of a particular part of his oeuvre, if not as an icon of both a specific historical era and a tradition of thought. More generally, 'histories of anthropological thought' narrate the development of the discipline as a succession of such theoretical schools and their representatives, the canon of thinkers in the long 20th century ranges from Edward B. Tylor's evolutionism via Franz Boas' relativism to Clifford Geertz's cultural hermeneutics.[1] This approach is problematic for several reasons. It notably conceives of both the discipline as a string of white male contributors while also implying its gradual progression. Correspondingly, one single author is incorporated and reduced to a single aspect of their work. As a token within this type of framework, functionalism becomes Malinowski's contribution to the resulting canon – a selection that omits his interest in economic anthropology, linguistics, and psychoanalysis, among many others.

If canonisation bears the unfortunate side-effect of promoting reductive readings of the authors whose statuses it elevates, in Malinowski's case, this process is severely aggravated by the scandalisation surrounding the publication of the *Diary in the Strict Sense of the Term*. As Kubica (2024) notes, the English translation comprises only a fraction of Malinowski's diary which only represents the final years of his daily autobiographical practice (he started keeping a notebook in 1908, the *Diary* contains excerpts from 1914 to 1918).[2] Furthermore, according to Kubica, not only were the results of Malinowski's writing routine never meant to be published, but they must be understood in the context of a very specific autobiographical tradition exemplified in Henri-Frédéric Amiel's *Journale Intime*; a daily "examination of conscience" (ibid: 16). Thus, it is hardly possible to draw general conclusions on the writer's character from it as such writing rather constitutes a conversation with oneself.

Notwithstanding the refined knowledge we possess on the purpose and nature of the *Diary* as a historical document, it remains required reading in anthropology and related disciplines and is regularly assigned to raise questions of fieldwork ethics. In many of these instances, Malinowski again is treated as an icon, if in unfavourable terms.[3] This state of affairs precludes the possibility of a more nuanced reception of his work in some anthropological traditions. As a case in point, I was unable to find a single piece of writing by an embodiment theorist from feminist anglophone anthropology who would draw a connection from their own agenda to Malinowski in favourable terms. In light of the great interest with which feminist writers approach embodiment theory since the 1980s (Mascia-Lees 2016), that absence does speak volumes.[4] Since the late 1980s, feminist and post-colonial sub-sections of the anthropological discipline tend to treat Malinowski as a proponent of "those blatantly racist and sexist Eurocentric histories that objectify or render invisible the majority of the world's peoples, both male and female" or even the "Great Master[s]" whose literature ultimately aims to dominate the peoples they purport to study.[5]

Significantly, authors who choose to engage constructively with the debates surrounding Malinowski's *Diary* commonly discuss the issues it raises as an aspect of the embodied dimension of ethnographic fieldwork, advocating for their inclusion in published monographs. Consider Ruth Behar

> As a student I was taught to maintain the same strict boundary Malinowski had kept between his ethnography and his autobiography. But I'd reached a point where these forms of knowing were no longer so easily separated.
>
> (Behar 1996)

While certainly not a beacon of best practice, the *Diary* provoked debates on ethnographic representation and provided a reference point for an entire genre of autobiographical field reports which were deemed a "recognizable anthropological subgenre" by Mary Louise Pratt as early as in 1986 (Pratt 1986: 31). Pratt's phrasing is of particular interest, as she understands the historical 'crisis' of ethnographic representation as a conflict between the incommensurability of embodied fieldwork experience and disembodied texts.

> Personal narrative mediates this contradiction between the engagement called for in fieldwork and the self-effacement called for in formal ethnographic description, or at least mitigates some of its anguish, by inserting into the ethnographic text the authority of the personal experience out of which the ethnography is made.
>
> (Pratt 1986: 33)

Malinowski's strategy to cope with this conflict was to confine most writing that concerned his personal experience as well as the corresponding doubts, insecurities, and emotional distress to his diary. However, as Eric Gable argues, the contemporary ethnographer should consciously observe their own emotions and include them in their self-analysis:

> That emotion says something. So does that compulsion to retell the story and reexperience the emotion in front of a public. In privileging the emotions elicited by fieldwork I want to convey to my audiences that in ethnography, the anthropologist is the instrument.
>
> (Gable 2014)

This statement, written roughly 100 years after the publication of the *Argonauts*, naturally indicates a shift in etiquette and what we perceive as adequate behaviour that goes beyond the discipline. Still, it bears testament to the fact that Malinowski, if inadvertently, greatly influenced auto-ethnographic methodologies. To paraphrase him: In contemporary academia, it is sometimes 'good for the ethnographer ... to put aside camera, notebook and pencil' and open up about their feelings.

As established in this preliminary review, Malinowski figures prominently in the late 20th- and early 21st-century theory of the body. The authors analysed above reference his work – the *Argonauts* in particular – in order to anchor a diverse array of contributions within the greater anthropological tradition. This may come as a surprise to many readers, as canonical readings tend to emphasise Malinowski's alignment with the positivist tradition[6] rather than considering his contributions in terms of a theory of embodiment.[7] It is noteworthy that the authors quoted above refer to Malinowski in the most general terms while presenting their own approaches in terms of specific theoretical frameworks. It seems as if Malinowski has once again become an icon of this sub-section of anthropological thought, specifically an icon for a body-centric anthropology with which a variety of more specialised approaches – an anthropology of the senses, affect, emotions, existential anthropology, and auto-ethnography – associate themselves.

In this article, I will demonstrate that scholars of the body and embodiment such as Stoller, Jackson, Grimshaw, Behar, or Gable have very good reason to see Malinowski as a precursor to their projects. At the same time, I attempt to provide a more precise understanding of Malinowski's notion of embodiment by situating his contribution within the theory of the body and embodiment of his time. As I will demonstrate, Malinowski developed his notion of fieldwork methodology and his later functionalism on the backdrop of reading Friedrich Nietzsche's *Die Geburt der Tragödie* and Arthur Schopenhauer's *Die Welt als Wille und Vorstellung*. On the basis of this genealogy, I argue that Malinowski's account of participant observation, functionalism, as well as the methodological issues raised by the *Diary* become understandable as facets of much broader developments in European intellectual and cultural history. More precisely, Malinowski's thought constitutes a transformation of the *Lebensphilosophie* tradition, which emphasised human embodiment in response to the perceived overemphasis of rationality in Kantian Idealism. It also needs to be understood as a concept that is closely linked to popular body-centric movements, such as the *Lebensreform* and *Körperkultur* movements, which adapted these ideas to propagate a new culture of embodied practices.[8]

A Theory of Embodiment avant-la-lettre

At the turn of the 20th century, notions of the body as expressive of a life-force gained popularity in both philosophical thought and everyday culture. In large part a response to rapid urbanisation, popular movements – such as nudism, sunbathing, a diverse array of sports movements, or vegetarianism – attempted to reform the modern experience by celebrating the embodied human existence. Such practices, as well as corresponding notions of embodiment, were particularly pervasive in the German-speaking world in the periphery of which Malinowski spent his formative years.[9]

A posthumously published essay from 1912 demonstrates not only that Malinowski was exposed to *Lebensphilosophie*, the dominant tradition in the 19th-century philosophy of the body, but that he critically and extensively engaged with its core concepts. This intellectual pursuit, titled "Observations on Friedrich Nietzsche's *The Birth of Tragedy*" (Malinowski 1993a [1912]),[10] falls into a formative period in Malinowski's life (Kubica 1988; Young 2004: 192–225). Aged 28, following academic stays in Leipzig and London, he had returned to Kraków where he abstained from virtually all academic obligations for roughly a year. During this period, he devoted much of his time to intellectual work and to better understanding his personal life with the help of a psychoanalyst, to which his diary bears ample testament. This self-examination under the auspices of a psychoanalytical framework clearly had a lasting impact on his later anthropological work (Malinowski 1927, also see Lena Magone's chapter in this volume). While it may be less known throughout the anglophone world, German *Lebensphilosophie* left a mark on Malinowski's thinking that is no less significant.[11]

Malinowski begins his deliberations on Nietzsche's work (2007 [1872]) with a lengthy introduction to Arthur Schopenhauer's metaphysics, as, in his view, this "conceptual system...permeates this entire work [*The Birth of Tragedy*; AL]" (Malinowski 1993a [1912]: 67). He then summarises the metaphysical tradition in a remarkably sensualist fashion:

> This subjective, emotional character, and at the same time the origin of metaphysics is reflected most distinctly in its concepts. They always express the desire to merge with and to penetrate into the objective world, as they find it around themselves, demanding that it be more human, more suitable to our feelings...Whether the absolute is a personal God...or Schopenhauer's Will – everywhere the metaphysically conceived essence of things is a subjectivization, a humanization of reality; tuning itself to the resonance of our inner experiences and longings.
>
> (ibid.: 68)

In the ensuing argument, Malinowski is utterly sceptical with regard to Nietzsche's aesthetic theory and the reading of Greek tragedy based on its premises. He barely falls short of accusing Nietzsche of mysticism. While Malinowski rejects the perpetuation of the body-mind divide that both Nietzsche and Schopenhauer incorporate in their metaphysical deliberations, he attempts to redeem Schopenhauer by translating his postulates into a language more suitable to his own scientific inclinations. To this end, he turns to psychology:

> But like every transcendentalism... Schopenhauer's metaphysics expresses certain psychological realities.
>
> (Malinowski 1993a [1912]: 74)

Hence, while refuting the notion of 'will' as a valid description of the objective world, Malinowski considers Schopenhauer's concept as expressive of a dualism through which we apprehend the world.

However, Malinowski is not content with this attempt to bring together two of the most prominent intellectual traditions of continental Europe prior to the First World War. His reading culminates in suggesting an alternative to Nietzsche's Apollinian and Dyonisian principles in the arts. In a distinctly Nietzschean fashion,

Malinowski envisions a dualistic "psychic attitude" which humanity adopts to cope with the "horror of life" (ibid.: 80). These come as forms of self-preservation. One is called the "tragic" mode, "emphasizing the dreadful most strongly... negation confirmed by man, and thus subjectivized and *eo ipso* controlled." (Ibid.) The other, incidentally, is known as "'vitalistic' ['witalistyczny'],"a paraphrasing of Nietzsche's '*Lebensbejahung*,' the pledge to develop an affirmative stance towards life in spite of the cosmological void that awaits humanity beyond the recourse to religion. This latter attitude "tends to level out all of life's bottomless abysses" (Ibid.). Considering Malinowski's later theoretical contributions, it is of great interest that, already in 1912, he postulates that the "*function* of art" (Ibid.; italics adapted from original source) is to satisfy either the vitalistic or the tragic impulse by "tear[ing] us away from the immediate grasp of the talons of horror." (Ibid.) Hence, art is understood as a human response to cope with existential angst.

In 1912, he does not yet extend the notion of function to culture in a broader sense, but remains within the boundaries outlined by Nietzsche, a theory of the aesthetic. Readers of Malinowski's later programmatic texts will, however, surely recognise how this argument develops a core element of functionalism. Art is understood as something that responds to a basic 'need,' as Malinowski would later phrase it. In 1912, however, Malinowski elaborated this idea of a 'need' in thoroughly Nietzschean terms.[12]

With his 'Observations,' then, Malinowski develops the core mechanism of his theory of culture (Malinowski 1944 [1941]) in conjunction with an intellectual tradition that would later be cast aside. In his *Scientific Theory of Culture,* he turns to psychology, psychoanalysis, and biology to define the "needs of his [man's; sic!] organism" (Malinowski 1944 [1941]: 37). Even though existential dread – the "void of the bottomless riddle" (ibid.: 82) – is no longer suitable as a conceptual grounds to a 'scientific' theory of culture, the essay from 1912 still implies that Malinowski originally developed his notion of function while reading Nietzsche's *Birth of Tragedy.*

Consequently, this version of functionalism comes into view as a transformation of core concepts of *Lebensphilosophie* philosophy. The notion of the will, as introduced by Schopenhauer and popularised by Nietzsche, influenced the intellectuals of the time so heavily because it elevated the body to an epistemological level. This conceptual move connotes a decisive shift in the history of European thought. Certainly, Schopenhauer was not the only thinker who sought to mitigate the status of embodiment in the early 19th century in a response to what they perceived as an overemphasis on the rational in Kantian idealism (Kozljanic 2004). However, his version of the *Lebensphilosophie* tradition places a unique emphasis on embodiment, insofar as his notion of the 'will' is perceptible to human understanding only *through their sense of their own bodies.* According to Schopenhauer, we can only perceive the will – an all-penetrating life-force – through introspection. It is a "knowledge of its very own kind" (Schopenhauer 1986 [1818]: 154, my translation).

Malinowski draws on this notion as part of another crucial aspect of his work.[13] With his famous recommendation to embark on "plunges into the lives of the natives" (Malinowski 1922a: 22), Malinowski grounds his approach to ethnographic fieldwork methodology on the epistemological status of the body in Schopenhauer's philosophy. "Actual life," according to Malinowski's seminal deliberations, cannot be fully grasped through questionnaires or "computing documents" (ibid.: 18). Instead of relying on such methods of observation, "it is good for the ethnographer sometimes to put aside camera, notebook and pencil, and to join in himself in what is going on" (ibid.: 22). It is through the embodied experience of cultural practices that these become "more transparent and easily understandable" (ibid.). In other words, the ethnographer may greatly benefit from participation because the body possesses a 'knowledge of its very own kind' (Schopenhauer, see above).

Ethics, Embodied Experience and the 'science of your fellow human being'

As I have argued in the introduction to this article, the ethical issues raised by the publication of the *Diary* are part and parcel of Malinowski's body-centric legacy in anthropology. This raises the question how the alignment of Malinowski's thought on embodiment with Nietzsche and Schopenhauer reflects on these issues. Ivan Strenski (1982) argued that Malinowski's early ethnographic work should be understood as one that is based on a theoretical position independent from his later functionalist writing, a so-called "second romanticism." While it remains unclear as to what extent Strenski was familiar with the popular body-centric notions and practices that became popular across Europe at the turn of the 19th century, movements such as the *Lebensreform*, *Wandervogel*, or nudism can, to a significant degree, indeed be understood as part of a neo-romantic ideology. They do exhibit essential characteristics of romantic thought, such as an emphasis on humanity's vital relationship with its natural environment as well as the corresponding antipathy towards modernity which ranges from scepticism towards technical innovation to an outright rejection of industrial modes of production.

At the time of Malinowski's 1912 essay, consequently, notions of the body were closely tied to a *Weltanschauung* that exhibited a decidedly countercultural streak. By no means does this make him an anti-hegemonial author in our contemporary understanding of the term. Nevertheless, what he does share with these latter theoretical currents is a heightened awareness of humanity's embodied existence and a critical stance towards the overemphasis on rationality in Western modernity and its purported achievements. Counterintuitively, this critical stance *includes* scientific method. Given the reductive notions of Malinowski as a proponent of positivism, the following self-reflecting remarks are of particular interest. In 1930, Malinowski writes:

> Science is the worst nuisance and the greatest calamity of our days. It has made us into robots, into standardized interchangeable parts of an enormous mechanism; it pushes us with a relentless persistence and a terrible acceleration towards new forms of existence; it changes the world around us; it transforms our inner selves with an uncannily thoroughgoing penetration.

> ... And now, after twenty years of anthropological work, I find myself, to my disgust, attempting to make the science of man into as bad and dehumanizing an agency to man as physics, chemistry, and biology have been for the last century or so denaturalizing to nature. In short, I am attempting to make anthropology into a real science.
>
> (Malinowski 1930: 405)[14]

In 1930, then, Malinowski publicly announced that he was performing a scientistic defection from an earlier way of conducting anthropology. Admittedly, in the ensuing argument, he introduces notions of cultural evolutionism into his ethnographic endeavour while also employing racialised tropes and terms throughout his early publications, features that make his benevolent reception in those sections of contemporary anthropology concerned with social justice rather unlikely. Nonetheless, Malinowski's early alignment with vitalism arguably alters the relationship between an ethnographer, who was retrospectively made a founding father of a discipline, and some of the discipline's harshest critics. Harrison, for instance, in the already mentioned *Decolonizing Anthropology*, issues the following statement: "A genuine science of humankind based upon premises of freedom and equality cannot emerge until the anthropology born of the rationalist and liberal intellectual tradition is destroyed." (Harrison 2010 [1991]) Harrison's notion of such a 'decolonised' anthropology, as demonstrated by her lifelong dedication to that program, first and foremost concerns the power relations between the ethnographer and their informants as well as marginalised groups' access to and equity in relation to the discipline's resources. Nevertheless, there is a certain irony in the way Harrison phrases her agenda. As I have demonstrated in this article, the most influential articulation of ethnographic fieldwork methodology was arguably not born out of the 'liberal and rational intellectual tradition,' but out of an intellectual countermovement to that very tradition.[15]

Malinowski, too, articulates a vision of 'a genuine science of humankind' (Harrison), though it is even further removed from his official publications than the posthumously published essay I discussed earlier. In a letter from 1918, written in the field to his fiancé Elsie Masson, Malinowski reflects on the nature and ethics of humanistic education, namely the notion that education should be based on the acquisition of the Greek and Latin languages as well as on the study of ancient Mediterranean cultures. These are his deliberations:

> Construct a New Humanism, giving all that the Human Heart and Humanistic turn of mind require, on the basis of living human societies [...] This New Humanism ... would have to pivot on Philosophy – a science of how to take life, how to spin your thoughts round the subject of life and on Sociology or the science of your fellow human beings, which science again would have to take its inspiration from ethnography mainly, or the study of living societies, and not from archeology, history or the dust and death.
>
> (Malinowski to Masson, 2 April 21, 1918; in Wayne 1995: 135)

When reading this passage in juxtaposition to his 1912 essay, the outlines of this 'science of your fellow human being' seem to differ significantly from the 'real science' he envisions 12 years later. As this New Humanism refers to an educational maxim, Malinowski essentially frames ethnography as a means of '*Herzensbildung*,'[16] the neo-romantic pedagogy that assumes that feelings and emotions need to be acquired and therefore education cannot merely consist in training a child's, or any person's, rational faculties.[17]

It remains unclear whether ethnography should be taught or practiced in the scope of this new type of Humanism. In terms of the reformist movements of his time, however, Malinowski's letter suggests that, in order to fully develop one's cognitive capacities, it is necessary to experience humankind in the full actuality of its difference and diversity. To experience it, in a word, through the practice of an ethnography that emphasises embodied experience.

Concluding Remarks

Some of the most renowned scholarship on the history of ethnographic fieldwork methodology has gone at great lengths to demonstrate that, overall, Malinowski's contribution has not been quite as revolutionary as the conventional narrative may have us believe. Stocking (1992, 1995) has shown the extent to which British anthropology's methods and practices of intensive fieldwork have preceded Malinowski's contribution. More recently, Rosa et al. (2022) expanded upon this line of inquiry and demonstrated the pervasiveness of intensive fieldwork across European national traditions in the 50 years prior to the publication of the *Argonauts*. As the centenary of the *Argonauts* has given rise to new debates about the precise nature of Malinowski's contribution, the reading of the 1912 essay here developed, answers this question with regard to fieldwork methodology. His contribution consists of a specific conceptual approach. Thinking through the epistemological dimension of Schopenhauer's metaphysics, Malinowski arrives at a programmatic language that would define the notion of a participatory approach to fieldwork for generations of ethnographers to come. Even in the light of fieldwork practices of earlier researchers, then, Malinowski can still rightfully be considered the inventor of *the notion* of 'participant observation.'[18]

A similar conclusion can be drawn with regard to Malinowski's notion of functionalism. As early as 1935, Alfred Reginald Radcliffe-Brown noted that functionalism could not be understood as a coherent school, but that the term was used quite differently by individual scholars. The most famous of these differences concerns the use of the term by Malinowski and by Radcliffe-Brown himself. Whereas the latter understood functionalism as the study of the ways in which interlocking social institutions form the coherent whole that is society, Malinowski's term sought to conceptualise the ways in which cultural practices respond to the needs of the biological organism. Furthermore, both terms draw heavily on ideas of the body, albeit in very different ways: Whereas Radcliffe-Brown builds on Durkheim (1938 [1895]) and thus conceives of social institutions as interacting in the same way as the organs of a biological organism, Malinowski understands culture as interacting with humanity's physically embodied existence (i.e., basic need: health – cultural response: hygiene; cf. Malinowski 1944 [1941]: 91).

The 1912 essay explains this very difference. Malinowski's notion of function seems to be tied much more closely to his reading of Nietzsche than to his earlier reflections on Ernst Mach and Richard Avenarius.[19] In his later work *A Scientific Theory of Culture*, functions respond to embodied needs, just as art responds to psychological needs in his essay from 1912. While the functionalist tradition is regularly traced back to Comte and understood in positivist terms, Malinowski's reading of Nietzsche suggests a different genealogy: The Malinowskian notion of function is clearly reminiscent of the Aristotelian notion of 'catharsis,' a notion developed in Aristotle's *Poetics* while discussing tragedy which also became an important reference for Nietzsche's thought in *Die Geburt der Tragödie*. If, according to Aristotle, tragedy serves to "purge"[20] the audience of their pity and fear, Malinkowski would term this the 'function' of tragedy, i.e., tragedy responds to an embodied need in a culturally specific way. Malinowski's functionalism thus takes up the idea of catharsis as mediated by Nietzsche and extends it to serve as the basis for his theory of culture.

Functionalism has arguably not stood the test of time. Whereas theoretical currents seem rather short-lived in the history of anthropology, the ethnographic method remains at the heart of the discipline. Despite the variations and adaptations that fieldwork methodology has undergone over the course of the last century, Malinowski's account in *Argonauts* emphasises the immersive quality of fieldwork like few others. At the same time, the *Diary* and the minor works cited above demonstrate that a research method based on human experience necessarily implies an ethical dimension. As I have argued throughout this article, all these articulations are deeply embedded in the tradition of *Lebensphilosophie*, the dominant mode of thinking about embodiment in Malinowski's lifetime. One could say that, as a reader of Schopenhauer and Nietzsche, Malinowski infiltrated the core of the anthropological discipline with a "Trojan horse" of vitalist philosophy. Thus, embodiment theory has always been part of the anthropological discipline, albeit clandestinely. As the body-centric contributions cited at the beginning of this article demonstrate, since the end of the 20th century, the stowaways of this conceptual infiltration have broken free.

Acknowledgements

Thanks to Max Kaplan for his help with the language of this article.

Notes

1 For versions of this canon, cf. Barrett (1996), Bates und Fratkin (1999), Erickson und Murphy (2013) or Haines (2017).
2 For the full Polish text, cf. Malinowski 2002.
3 It would be difficult to quantify this phenomenon. Personally, I witnessed the pedagogical use of Malinowski's autobiographical writings on several occasions, ranging from nuanced historical discussion to outright condemnation.

4 Annette Weiner's (1976) critique of Malinowski's work on the Trobriands was among the earliest feminist revisions of a canonical anthropologist, a factor that may also have contributed to Malinowski's marginality within feminist circles.
5 For the first declaration, cf. Harrison (2010 [1991]: 237), the second quote is from Minh-ha (1989: 57). Both Harrison and Trịnh-Thị-Minh-Hà, foundational texts of decolonial and feminist anthropology, explicitly refer to Malinowski with these statements.
6 Paluch 1981; Brozi 1992; cf. also Flis 1988; also cf. endnote 18.
7 Kubica 2023 provides a rare exception by reading Malinowski's Zakophane diaries in the context of contemporary phenomenological theory.
8 There is a vast amount of literature on these phenomena and their synergies. Among the most notable contributions, cf. Krabbe (1974, 1989) and Buchholz (2001).
9 In the late 18th century, the Polish-Lithuanian Commonwealth was successively eliminated through partition by its neighbouring powers Austria, Prussia and Russia. The Austro-Hungarian Empire first acquired Polish territory, including Zakophane, in 1772 and again in 1792, this time including Kraków. Poland only regained national independence with the foundation of the Second Polish Republic after the First World War.
10 I use Ludwik Krzyzanowski's translation published in Thornton and Skalnik (1993). The editors erroneously date this essay to 1904/05. I follow Grażyna Kubica who establishes its date through references in Malinowski's 1912 diary (cf. Malinowski 2002). Also cf. Malinowski 2002: 675–694 for the unabridged Polish original.
11 Malinowski's involvement with the 'Young Poland' movement ('Młoda Polska') is well established. An avantgardist intellectual current closely associated with the movement for Polish national and cultural independence, it would have been rather astonishing if Malinowski had not come into contact with popular body-centric discourses and practices in this context. If it is any indication, the movement's literary journal was called Życie, literally translating to 'life' (cf. Young 2004: 68). I was unable to find research on the 'Młoda Polska' that explores connections between the group, vitalism, and Malinowski's anthropology.
12 Thornton and Skalnik (1993), the editors of the volume that first made available the 'Observations' in English, offer a different version of the argument developed in this paragraph. Building on their contribution, I seek to elaborate on the implications of Malinowski's alignment with Schopenhauer and Nietzsche for the history of embodiment theory in anthropology as well as for ethnographic fieldwork methodology. Also, Thornton and Skalnik seem unaware of the much broader cultural history of body-centric thought and practices in the context of which these contributions need to be understood.
13 For an in-depth version of this argument, cf. Lipowsky (2020).
14 As I have argued in an earlier publication (Lipowsky 2020), a closer look at the language developed in the 1930 article reveals an in-depth knowledge of the tropes employed within the popular vitalist literature.
15 Ernest Gellner provided a radical take on this issue with his famous claim that societies disrupted by modernisation are torn between the two ideological poles of *Gemeinschaft* and *Gesellschaft* and that Malinowski's intellectual achievement consists in providing British social anthropology with the ultimate synthesis (Gellner 1998). Unfortunately, as Malinowski's minor writings discussed here reveal, in his own eyes Malinowski seems to have seen his professional achievements not so much as a synthesis as a betrayal of the Romantic intellectual current.
16 Cf. Sigg (2018) for both historical analysis and contemporary appraisal.
17 As Young notes (2004: 550), Malinowski's reflections on a New Humanism are "starkly at odds" with passages in his diary and letters that "betray a blatant racism." In a later article, Malinowski (1922b) expands on his vision to reform humanistic scholarship, arguing for the value of ethnographic knowledge in mitigating the mistreatment of indigenous populations by colonial administrations.

18 Notwithstanding that his methodology was only retrospectively appropriated under this term, cf. DeWalt and DeWalt (2002).
19 Many commentators understand Malinowski's functionalism in the tradition of empirio-criticism (Paluch 1981, Brozi 1992, cf. also Flis 1988). While it is true that Malinowski employs the term "function" while discussing Richard Avenarius and Ernst Mach in his dissertation (Malinowski 1993b [1906]), the attributes and implications of this term differ greatly from its later usage (Malinowski 1944 [1941]). Malinowski's deflection from the positivist tradition by way of the *Lebensphilosophie* constitutes a fascinating chapter in the history of empiricism and should be explored further.
20 'Purgation' is S. H. Butcher's translation of the Greek term catharsis; cf. Aristotle 2008: 8.

References

Amiel, Henri-Frédéric. 1922 [1883]. *Fragments d'un journal intime*. Volume 1. Paris: Cres et Cie.
Aristotle. 2008. *Poetics*. Translated by S. H. Butcher. Urbana, IL: Project Gutenberg. 12 September 2023, from www.gutenberg.org/ebooks/1974.
Barrett, Stanley R. 1996. *Anthropology: A student's guide to theory and method*. Toronto: University of Toronto Press.
Bates, Daniel G., and Elliot M. Fratkin, eds. 1999. *Cultural anthropology*. Boston, MA: Allyn and Bacon.
Behar, Ruth. 1996. *The vulnerable observer. Anthropology that breaks your heart*. Boston, MA: Beacon Press.
Behar, Ruth, and Deborah A. Gordon. 1995. *Women writing culture*. Berkeley: University of California Press.
Brozi, Krzysztof. 1992. "Philosophical premises of functional anthropology." *Philosophy of the Social Sciences* 22 (3): 357–369.
Buchholz, Kai, ed. 2001. *Die Lebensreform. Entwürfe zur Neugestaltung von Leben und Kunst um 1900*. Darmstadt: Häusser.
Butler, Judith. 1990. *Gender trouble: Feminism and the subversion of identity*. London: Routledge.
Csordas, Thomas. 1990. "Embodiment as a paradigm for anthropology." *Ethos* 18 (1): 5–47.
Deleuze, Gilles and Félix Guattari. 1987 [1980]. *A thousand plateaus*. Translated by Brian Massumi. Minneapolis: University of Minnesota Press.
Descartes, Réne. 1993 [1641]. *Rene Descartes' meditations on first philosophy in focus*. Edited by Stanley Tweyman. London: Routledge.
Desjarlais, Robert, and C. Jason Throop. 2011. "Phenomenological approaches in anthropology." *Annual Review of Anthropology* 40: 87–102.
DeWalt, Kathleen Musante, and Billie R. DeWalt. 2002. *Participant observation: A guide for fieldworkers*. Lanham, MD: AltaMira Press.
Durkheim, Émile. 1938 [1895]. *The rules of sociological method*. Chicago: Chicago University Press.
Erickson, Paul A. und Liam D. Murphy, eds. 2013. *A history of anthropological theory*. Toronto: University of Toronto Press.
Flis, Andrzej. 1988. "Cracow philosophy of the beginning of the twentieth century and the rise of Malinowski's scientific ideas." In *Malinowski between two worlds: The Polish roots of an anthropological tradition*, edited by Roy Ellen, 105–127. Cambridge: Cambridge University Press.

Foucault, Michel. 1973 [1963]. *The birth of the clinic.* New York: Vintage.
———. 1977 [1975]. *Discipline and punish.* New York: Vintage.
Gable, Eric. 2014. "The anthropology of guilt and rapport. Moral mutuality in ethnographic fieldwork." *HAU: Journal for Ethnographic Theory* 4 (1): 237–258.
Geertz, Clifford. 1988. *Works and lives. The anthropologist as author.* Stanford: Stanford University Press.
Gellner, Ernest. 1998. *Language and Solitude. Wittgenstein, Malinowski and the Habsburg Dilemma.* Cambridge: Cambridge University Press.
Grimshaw, Anna. 2001. *The ethnographer's eye: Ways of seeing in anthropology.* Cambridge: Cambridge University Press.
Haines, David W. 2017. *An introduction to sociocultural anthropology. Adaptations, structures, meanings.* Denver: University Press of Colorado.
Haraway, Donna. 1988. "Situated knowledges: The science question in feminism and the privilege of partial perspective." *Feminist Studies* 14 (3): 575–599.
Harrison, Faye. 2010 [1991]. *Decolonizing anthropology: Moving further toward an anthropology for liberation.* Arlington, VA: Association of Black Anthropologists.
Howes, David, ed. 1991. *The varieties of sensory experience. A sourcebook in the anthropology of the senses.* Toronto: University of Toronto Press.
———. 2003. *Sensual relations. Engaging the senses in culture and social theory.* Ann Arbor: The University of Michigan Press.
Jackson, Michael. 1989. *Paths toward a clearing: Radical empiricism and ethnographic inquiry.* Bloomington and Indianapolis: Indiana University Press.
———. 2005. *Existential anthropology. Events, exigencies, and effects.* New York: Berghahn Books.
Kozljanic, R. J. 2004. *Lebensphilosophie: Eine Einführung.* Stuttgart: Kohlhammer.
Krabbe, Wolfgang R. 1974. *Gesellschaftsveränderung durch Lebensreform: Strukturmerkmale einer sozialreformerischen Bewegung im Deutschland der Industrialisierungsperiode.* Göttingen: Vandenhoeck und Ruprecht.
———. 1989. "Die Weltanschauung der Deutschen Lebensreform-Bewegung ist der Nationalsozialismus." *Archiv für Kulturgeschichte* 71 (2): 431–462.
Kubica, Grażyna. 1988. "Malinowski's years in Poland." In *Malinowski between two worlds: The Polish roots of an anthropological tradition*, edited by Roy Ellen, Ernest Gellner, Grażyna Kubica and Janusz Mucha. 88–104. Cambridge: Cambridge University Press.
———. 2023. "The two worlds of Bronislaw Malinowski's Polish youth in his own writings: The anthropologist's historical autoethnography." Unpublished Manuscript.
———. 2024. "A Notorious Diarist – Bronisław Malinowski, and His Sinful Publics. Polish Editor's Remarks." In: Aleksandar Bošković and David Shankland eds., *Argonauts of the Western Pacific and The Andaman Islanders: A Centenary Study in Social Anthropology.* Canon Pyon: Sean Kingston Publishing. [forthcoming]
Lipowsky, Andreas. 2020. "*Lebensphilosophie* and the revolution in anthropology: Uncovering the original 'turn to life'" *HAU. Journal of Ethnographic Theory* 10 (3): 800–812.
Lutz, Catherine, and Geoffrey M. White. 1986. "The anthropology of emotions." *Annual Review of Anthropology* 15: 405–436.
Malinowski, Bronisław. 1922a. *Argonauts of the Western Pacific.* London: Routledge.
———. 1922b. "Ethnology and the study of society." *Economia* 6: 208–219.
———. 1927. *Sex and repression in savage society.* London: Routledge.
———. 1930. "The rationalization of anthropology and administration." *Journal of the International African Institute* 3 (4): 405–430.
———. 1960 [1941]. "A scientific theory of culture." In *A scientific theory of culture and other essays*, 1–144. New York: Oxford University Press.

———. 1967. *A diary in the strict sense of the term*. Translated by Nobert Guterman. London: Routledge.

———. 1993a [1912]. "Observations on Friedrich Nietzsche's 'The birth of tragedy'." Translated by Ludwik Krzyzanowski. In *Malinowski's early writings*, edited by Robert Thornton and Peter Skalnik, 67–89. Cambridge: Cambridge University Press.

———. 1993b [1906]. "On the principle of economic thought." Translated by Ludwik Krzyzanowski. In *Malinowski's early writings*, edited by Robert Thornton and Peter Skalnik, 89–117. Cambridge: Cambridge University Press.

———. 2002. *Dziennik w ścisłym znaczeniu tego wyrazu*, edited by Grażyna Kubica. Kraków: Wydawnictwo Literackie.

Mascia-Lees, Frances E. 2016. "The body and embodiment in the history of feminist anthropology. An idiosyncratic excursion through binaries." In *Mapping feminist anthropology in the twenty-first century*, edited by Ellen Lewin and Leni M. Silverstein, 146–167. New Brunswick: Rutgers University Press.

Nietzsche, Friedrich. 2007 [1872]. *Die Geburt der Tragödie aus dem Geiste der Musik*. Frankfurt am Main: Reclam.

Paluch, Andrzey K. 1981. "The polish background to Malinowski's work." *Man New Series* 16 (2): 276–285.

Pratt, Mary Louise. 1986. "Fieldwork in common places." In *Writing Culture*, edited by James Clifford and George Marcus, 27–50. Berkeley: University of California Press.

Radclife-Brown, Alfred. 1935. "On the concept of function in social science." *American Anthropologist* 35 (3): 394–402.

Rosa, Frederico Delgado and Han F. Vermeulen. 2022. *Ethnographers before Malinowski. Pioneers of anthropological fieldwork, 1870–1922*. New York: Berghan Books.

Schopenhauer, Arthur. 1986 [1818]. *Die Welt als Wille und Vorstellung*. Frankfurt am Main: Suhrkamp.

Serementakis, Nadia C, ed. 1994. *The senses still: Perception and memory as material culture in modernity*. Boulder: Westview Press.

Sigg, Gabriele Maria and Andreas Zimmermann. 2018. *Emotionale Bildung: die vergessene Seite der Bildungsdebatte*. Hamburg: Verlag Dr. Kovač.

Smith, Linda Tuhiwai. 1999. *Decolonizing methodologies: Research and Indigenous Peoples*. London: Zed Books.

Stocking, George. 1992. *The ethnographer's magic and other essays in the history of anthropology*. Madison: University of Wisconsin Press.

———. 1995. *After Tylor: British social anthropology 1888–1951*. Madison: University of Wisconsin Press.

Stoller, Paul. 1989. *The taste of ethnographic things: The senses in anthropology*. Philadelphia: University of Pennsylvania Press.

Strenski, Ivan. 1982. "Malinowski: Second positivism, second romanticism." *Man New Series* 17 (4): 766–771.

Stuart, Kathleen. 2007. *Ordinary affects*. Durham: Duke University Press.

Thornton, Robert and Peter Skalnik, eds. 1993. *The early writings of Bronisław Malinowski*. Cambridge: Cambridge University Press.

Trịnh-Thị-Minh-Hà. 1989. *Woman native other*. Bloomington and Indianapolis: Indiana University Press.

Wayne, Helen, ed. 1995. *The story of a marriage: The letters of Bronisław Malinowski and Elsie Masson*. Vol. 2. London: Routledge.

Weiner, Annette. 1976. *Women of value, men of renown: New perspectives in Trobriand exchange*. Houston: University of Texas Press.

Young, Michael W. 2004. *Malinowski: Odyssey of an anthropologist, 1884–1920*. New Haven, CT: Yale University Press.

10 'The Gardens Are, in a Way, a Work of Art'

Bronisław Malinowski's Social Anthropology as Anthropology of Art

Andrzej Kisielewski

This text presents an art historian's perspective on Malinowski's monographs and at the same time, it is a first attempt to treat them as anthropological ekphrases on Trobriand art. Its purpose is also to position them in the context of art history, as well as against the background of the art anthropology. It is also a proposal to expand the repertoire of examples of Trobriand art – usually associated with crafts, dance, music, and singing – to include coral gardens and their cultivation. It may seem inappropriate to view Bronisław Malinowski's social anthropology as anthropology of art, since he does not focus on art as a distinct cultural institution. Moreover, his portrayal of the Trobriand Islanders implies that they did not have a 'concept' of art in the Western sense. My reflections on Malinowski's works and the reality of the Trobriand Inslanders he describes are mediated by the Western perception and definition of art. Yet, this evaluative, interpretive, and universalizing category of art proves to be highly beneficial. It enables us to view Malinowski's work in a fresh light and gain a novel understanding of the Trobriand Islanders' reality then.

The Trobriand monographs offer a wealth of insights into art from the anthropological perspective. Many fragments can be interpreted as a unique art description known as *ekphrasis*. This literary technique showcases the visual impact of language and how it can convey images. Malinowski's anthropological ekphrases focus on the indigenous art of the Trobriand villagers and its profound significance within their cultural practices. Various passages are devoted to the work of the Trobriand artists, as well as their cultural and social position. Through an examination of Malinowski's monographs within the context of art discourse, it is possible to recognize him as one of the pioneers of anthropology of art, alongside, among others, Franz Boas, the author of the first book on indigenous art (Boas 1955 [1927]).

Additionally, Malinowski's work can be compared to that of Aby Warburg, who is considered the founder of the "second" history of art – an approach that focuses on analysing the cultural sources and contexts of artworks. Warburg proposed to study the art treating it as area of imagesand not only works of art, as the representatives of the formalist history of art did at the time. Warburg was interested in the cultural context of the work and looking for evidence of elementary human passions and emotions (Didi-Huberman 2017). Art – he stated, writing about Hopi Indian dances – served as a tool in the fight for existence (Warburg 1939: 281). He was the initiator of those methods of art research that are used today in anthropology. The difference in Warburg's and Malinowski's methods of studying art was that the former was interested in images, whose carriers were materially existing works of art and which were connected by many threads with various fields of culture, while the latter was mainly occupied with the results of craft-work treated as aesthetic objects and their functioning in a socio-cultural context. Malinowski's interest in the Trobriand Islanders went beyond art. He aimed to write a comprehensive work entitled *Kiriwina*, consisting of eight parts. The final part of the book was intended to focus on art. Unfortunately, the book was never completed. A draft of its structure can be found in the archives of the London School of Economics (Young 2004: 467–470). Although work on the monograph was abandoned, the anthropologist used it as material to write several other books, primarily *Argonauts of the Western Pacific*.

The key to any consideration of art in Malinowski's works is a sketch discovered by Michael Young in 2003 in the anthropologist's archive at the London School of Economics, entitled *Art Notices and Suggestions* (Young and Beran 2016). This text is a testimony to Malinowski's thinking about art as an object of field research – there is a description in these notes of art research methods, a classification of tribal works of art and, above all, an interpretation of the way art is understood by the anthropologist. He believed that art exists in every type of culture, that its role would be to meet the aesthetic needs of man, and that it would also be an expression of human emotions. Malinowski primarily emphasized the aesthetic function of art, i.e. the influence of a work of art through its formal layer – the layout and nature of forms and colours – while its reference to reality, the symbolism or religious or magical content encoded in it, were, in his opinion, secondary. The anthropologist perceived aesthetic needs in biological terms – as the need to experience sensual pleasures. He wrote:

> [...] in all human races and communities there is a phenomenon of strong emotional reaction to combinations of sounds, colours, lines and forms. Some combinations of sense impressions strike us as distinctly pleasurable and we speak of sweet melodies, rich harmonies, well-blended colour schemes. Others strike us as meaningless and unpleasant. This direct appeal of sense impressions must be considered as the foundation of the aesthetic *par excellence*. Not only is it a general rule that all human beings react with pleasurable or averse emotions to combinations of sounds, forms and colours, but in all human societies definite means of producing such combinations have been devised. Art corresponds to a deep human need and this need is specific and different from intellectual, moral or practical requirements.
> (Malinowski 2016: 19)

What is noticeable in Malinowski's works is not only numerous mentions of the artistic values of Trobriand craftsmanship but also references to European art, which proves that he was wellversed in these issues. It seems that this was something natural in the intellectual environment of early 20th-century Kraków, where the anthropologist grew up with Stanisław Ignacy Witkiewicz and Leon Chwistek, future outstanding artists and co-founders of the first strictly avant-garde artistic group – Polish Formists, as his friends.[1] Malinowski's passion for artistic craftsmanship is evident in his Trobriand diaries, where he even considered introducing into Trobriand art a new art style (Malinowski 1967:123).[2]

In the following paragraphs, I will delve into three instances of Trobriand's artistic culture documented by Malinowski. These include the valuables exchanged during the *kula* rite, *masawa* canoes that made this exchange possible, and the cultivation of coral gardens. However, I will precede remarks concerning these examples with placing the anthropologist's works in the context of the formalistically oriented history and theory of art at the turn of the centuries and the anthropology of art that was crystallizing at the time. The aforementioned Franz Boas was one of its most important representatives.

Formalist Theory of Art and Bronisław Malinowski's Anthropology of Art

In fact, the formalist history and theory of art, whose most influential representatives were Heinrich Wölfflin and Alois Riegl, underpinned the perception of the material culture of non-European traditional communities as examples of art – which only took hold at the turn of the 19th and 20th centuries. The formalist theory of art was an apologia of form, and indeed beauty, and therefore the question about the function of art as a cultural institution can be treated as a question about beauty – about the way it was understood, but also about the role it played in the cultural space, especially the cultural reality of indigenous communities we are interested in here (Meyers 2006). The concepts of the Viennese art historians mentioned here, especially Riegl, influenced, among others, the views of Franz Boas, the author of the first academic book devoted to what he called "primitive art" (Boas 1955 [1927]). The book focused on the works of art of non-European indigenous communities residing in North America, Africa, Siberia, Australia, and the Pacific Islands. Boas emphasized the decorative nature of "primitive art" and how the designs were primarily based on observations of surrounding fauna. He concluded his book by stating that even the poorest indigenous communities devoted considerable effort to creating "works of beauty", implying that the need for beauty is one of the most significant sources of "primitive art". In his work, Boas was inspired by Riegl's concept of *die Kunstwollen* when examining the art of non-European indigenous peoples. According to the Viennese art historian, the creative will – which he never defined – was the engine behind the development of artistic forms. It can be understood as a kind of drive that conditioned the progress in art expressed in successive stylistic changes (Elsner 2006). Boas observed that various art forms, such as the songs of Siberian indigenous peoples, African dances, New Zealanders' stone carvings, Melanesian carved reliefs, and the sculptures of the Tlingit people of Alaska, satisfied the human desire for beauty. Boas emphasized that these works of art, whether realistic or ornamental, in the form of dance, music, or poetry, carried meaning and were not created solely for aesthetic pleasure. He concluded that artistic expression is an universal human desire linked to the desire for beauty, which he saw as a revelation of the *sacrum*. From his reflections emerges the concept of "primitive art" as capturing meaning in a form characterized by beauty.

Boas approached indigenous non-European art from a formalist perspective, focusing on describing its form and acknowledging the representation of reality it conveys. His book lacks a thorough exploration of the relationship between "primitive art" and social life, religious beliefs, tribal mythology, or other ways of conceptualizing reality. Similarly, Malinowski's assessment of Trobriand's art suggests a formalist outlook and a contemplative attitude in the Kantian sense of the term. He highlighted the indigenous peoples' contemplative approach to their artistic creations. One example of Malinowski drawing attention to the contemplative attitude of the natives towards their own activities may be the following remark from the *Coral Gardens*:

> Finally, among other apparently extrinsic elements, we find a surprising care for the aesthetics of gardening. The gardens of the community are not merely a means to food; they are a source of pride and the main object of collective ambition. Care is lavished upon effects of beauty, pleasing to the eye and the heart of the Trobriander, upon the finish of the work, the perfection of various contrivances and the show of food.
>
> (Malinowski 1935:56)

However, Malinowski goes beyond formalism by exploring the connections between Trobriand art and cultural institutions such as religion, magic, myth, totemism, law, economic life, family, kinship ties, and sex life. This was a consequence of the assumptions of his functional anthropology, focused on the study of the functions of individual cultural institutions and their interrelations.

Malinowski's research on art anthropology has influenced many subsequent researchers in the field, who have expanded upon his work. Since the 1950s, the art of the Papua New Guinea region has been extensively studied and Malinowski's name is consistently mentioned in these studies. Notable researchers who have followed in his footsteps include Edmund R. Leach (1983), Patrick Glass (1978), Giancarlo M.G. Scoditti (1990), and Shirley F. Campbell (2002), Gunter Senft (1992, 2016).

Malinowski's work has played a significant role in popularizing the art of the Trobriand Islands. It became the subject of collector's efforts and can now be found in numerous ethnographic museums worldwide and on the art market. However, Trobriand art is often thought of only in terms of physical objects, such as carved boards used to decorate the canoes, ceremonial ornaments, musical instruments like flutes and drums, wooden vessels, spoons, spatulas, masks, and shields used in rites. While considered Trobriand art, carved figures are not traditionally a part of the Trobriand culture and are created with tourists in mind (Senft 1992: 71; Campbell 2002: 45–48). It is important to note that studying Trobriand art should encompass more than just material art. It should also include body adornments, ritual dances and songs, and coral gardens. Given the challenges involved in describing, documenting, collecting, and exhibiting these art forms, they remain relatively underrepresented in Western art discourse, despite their cultural importance.

The *Kula* Valuables

The *soulava* necklaces and *mvali* armshells, which Malinowski referred to as valuables, were central elements of the ritual *kula* exchange. They were highly coveted throughout New Guinea and beyond and were only worn by the most dignified members of the community during the most prominent ceremonies attended by representatives of many villages (Malinowski 1922: 86). They were not used as everyday ornaments due to their high value and often unusual size. Malinowski compared their status with European passing cups and royal insignia, i.e. objects of little usefulness, which, nevertheless, were synonymous with value, wealth, and a high position in the social hierarchy. In the case of the *kula* valuables, however, it was not so much about the material value in the strict sense, but more about, if I can put it that way, artistic value. The latter was determined by the size of the object, the uniqueness of the material, the diligence of the workmanship and thus the aesthetics, which made a great impression on the locals. Unlike European insignia, *kula* valuables were not privately owned, but circulated from hand to hand, passed on by partners forming a circle of exchange. Malinowski did not describe the *kula* valuables in detail but wanted to illustrate what they meant to the natives. Apart from *soulava* necklaces and *mwali* armshells, Malinowski also mentioned other valuable ritual and ceremonial objects that were exchanged, such as weapons, carved stone tools, beautifully ornamented household items, and more. These objects were often richly decorated and impractical to use, made from expensive materials, and required extensive labour to create. They ceased to be used in everyday life and became essential components of magical and religious rites. For instance, during the ceremonial *so'i* feasts, when pigs and mango seedlings were brought into the village, women would use polished axes with well-carved handles and move in rhythmic steps to the beat of drums while holding them. Similarly, sorcerers used richly decorated axes to strike the *kamkokola* garden fence during garden rites.

In *Argonauts of the Western Pacific,* Malinowski drew a picture of a vast network of connections involving thousands of people joined together in a shared passion for exchange, the basis of which was, among others, a sense of beauty. The objects exchanged were, in our contemporary understanding, artistic artefacts. Therefore, it can be argued here that art was also one of the important elements of the *kula* exchange ritual. Malinowski greatly admired the craftsmanship of the Trobrianders and often highlighted the beauty of their products. He noted that their creations were functional and aesthetically pleasing thanks to the personal talent and imagination of the artisans. In the *Argonauts*, Malinowski praised the craftsmen who made lime pots that were used for betel chewing: "The highly artistic designs, burnt into the lime pots, are the specialty of these villagers" (Malinowski1922: 67). And further, he wrote:

> They do not work under the spur of necessity or to gain their living but on the impulse of talent and fancy, with a high sense and enjoyment of their art, which they often conceive as the result of magical inspiration.
> (Malinowski 1922: 172)

Malinowski admired the Trobriand craftsmen for their talent, meticulous attention to detail, careful treatment of unique materials, and technical skill in creating unique and beautiful pieces. It is worth noting that he brought a vast collection of Trobriand crafts to Britain. Among these were *soulava* necklaces, *mwali* armshells, decorative bows, stern boards of canoes, wooden taro beaters adorned with carved and coloured ornamentation, decoratively engraved and coloured panels used to embellish Trobriand buildings, ornate wooden bowls, decorated scoops for scooping water from the bottom of canoes, decorated wooden axe handles and their carefully smoothed stone axe blades, hip bands, decorative breastplates, woven baskets, ornately carved wooden lime spatulas, wooden musical instruments, ritual shields, and so on. Today, Malinowski's collection of 584 items is housed in the British Museum in London.[3]

Masawa Canoes

The high seas *masawa* canoes used in the *kula* rite are among the most remarkable examples of the Trobriand Islands artistic culture. Malinowski marvelled at the impressive and intricate design of the boats, which consisted of ornate sculptures and painted decorations in addition to the recognizable shape of the sail:

> To the native, his cumbersome, sprawling canoe is a marvellous, almost miraculous achievement and a thing of beauty (see Plates XXI, XXIII, XL, XLVII, LV). He has spun a tradition around it and adorns it with his best carvings; he colors and decorates it. It is to him a powerful contrivance for the mastery of Nature, which allows him to cross dangerous seas to distant places.
>
> (Malinowski 1922: 106)

It is worth noting that the canoe was decorated with *kauri* shells at its bow, which added to its aesthetic appeal and produced audible effects when the wind blew, or the waves moved it. In the *Argonauts*, Malinowski provides a detailed description of the process for crafting a *masawa* canoe. He emphasized that constructing a canoe was not a simple task – it was intertwined with religious beliefs and magic, as evidenced by the belief in tree-dwelling sprites and the use of magic to persuade them. Although building the canoe was a team effort, it was primarily handled by a highly skilled specialist. Known as the *tokabitam*, he possessed the knowledge of canoe building and the magic necessary for its construction. He carved boards that adorned its bow and stern that cut the waves by reducing the impact of hitting the water. It was believed that his expertise in magic greatly influenced the utility of the canoe, making it faster and more stable, which was of great importance during high-sea sailing. Thus, in the Trobriand Islands, the arts were combined with crafts, myths, beliefs, and magic, and undoubtedly were of great importance in everyday life – among other things, they influenced the safety of sailors. The *tokabitam* held a special status in the village community, but he enjoyed his special status only when he received an order and during its execution. On other occasions, he performed everyday tasks such as cultivating the garden, repairing his household, fishing, and hunting. The *tokabitam* also prepared the boards placed on the fronts of the *bwayma* storehouses and decorated them with carves and paint, which required a lot of time and care. He:

> would sit over them for days and weeks with his wooden hammer and chisel made of wallaby bone. He would finish them off with his mounted shark's tooth and finally paint them in black, red, and white, with red ochre, charcoal, and calcareous earth.
>
> (Malinowski 1935: 244–245)

Malinowski observed that the *bwayma* storehouses and the *masawa* canoes shared similar construction terminology and both required the use of the same magical rites and incantations. This suggests that the Trobriand Islanders had a cohesive visual system encompassing various aspects of their culture, including architectural ornamentation, everyday objects, ceremonial body art, and women's clothing. The forms used in this system were inspired by nature and held a consistent meaning based on shared myths and an understanding of reality.

Malinowski's description of the process of creating a *masawa* canoe was later expanded upon by Shirley Campbell, who studied the artistic culture surrounding the *kula* exchange on Vakuta Island during her eight-month stay in 1974 (Cambpell 2002).[4] She viewed the Islanders' art as a text. Using Roland Barthes' semiological theory as a theoretical framework (Barthes 1989 [1964]), Campbell analysed the relationship between the canoes' carved decorations, painted designs, and other artistic expressions on the island. She showed art as a tool in the process of increasing the personal fame of the canoe owners and their makers, as well as their importance in the *kula* ritual. The beauty of the boats had a seductive and at the same time magical power to influence exchange partners. It made it possible to effectively seduce them in order to build lasting relationships with them and at the same time induce them to part with valuables. Campbell showed the art of *kula* as an integral part of a complex communication network reflecting the way of understanding and at the same time experiencing reality by the inhabitants of the island of Vakuta.

The Trobriand canoes spurred the imagination of many researchers. One of them was the aforementioned Giancarlo M.G. Scoditti, who, following in Malinowski's footsteps, analysed the boards decorating the prows and sterns of the *masawa* boats (Scoditti 1990). He conducted his research on the island of Kitawa in 1973–1974 and 1976, focusing primarily on the aesthetics of boards, their iconographic layer and symbolic expression. In his analyses, the researcher relied on the theories of the Danish linguist Louis T. Hjelmslev regarding the structure of a sign. This allowed him to combine sculptural decorations placed on the prow boards with a semantic layer created by the language used to address everything that concerns the canoe. The symbolic expression of the boards was closely related to the myths underpinning the *kula* ritual. One of them, called *tabuya* by the locals, was to cut the waves – "open" them – thus reducing the force of the canoe's collision with the water. In a semantic sense, it was associated with a vast field of meanings, created by words, which included, among others, cunning, vigilance, excitement, beauty, the world of darkness, moonlight, speed. The *tabuya* board formed a symbolic "nose" of the "face", which was an asymmetrical carved and painted board fixed transversely to the axis of the canoe, called *lagimu*.

Another researcher who followed in Malinowski's footsteps was Gunter Senft, who first visited the Trobriand Islands in 1982. He also analysed, among other things, the *masawa* canoes. He reconstructed the social context accompanying the canoes: described the scope of work of the specialists involved in the process of their construction, the economic conditions, so specific in a community preferring barter, the principles of canoe construction, as well as the process of their creation in detail, describing all the individual activities performed over time (Senft 2016). He also thoroughly described the process of transformation of cultural reality of the Trobriand islanders caused by the impact of Western civilization, as discussed in the last part of this work.

It turns out that the perception of the *masawa* canoes from the perspective of formalist art theory limits the understanding of their essence. Malinowski's research highlights that these canoes were not only beautiful and practical works of craftsmanship, but they were also integral to the cultural institutions of the Trobriand Islands. Additionally, they were even considered living beings with their own names and genealogy and held a unique social status as members of the village community. Each new canoe was seen as a continuation of its predecessor, with the same name passed down to the more recent version. The Trobriand islanders kept their canoes in huts that resembled residential homes but were much more prominent. These canoes were believed to possess superhuman abilities and were connected to various aspects of the islanders' daily lives. For instance, the natives believed that if a canoe slowed down during a deep-sea voyage, it was a clear indication that the wife of the owner, the *toli-waga,* was misbehaving in his absence. Canoes were seen as existing at the boundary between the perceived world and extrasensory reality and they played an essential part in the complex system of institutions that made up Trobriand culture. This included the ceremonial *kula* exchange and deep-sea trade, the social structure, family life, myths, magic, religion, ritual life, dances, songs, and crafts that were passed down from one generation to another.

In the *Argonauts*, the intricate process of crafting a canoe is depicted as the creation of a masterpiece. Malinowski portrays the Trobrianders' vivid imagination, including their beliefs about the dangers of sailing on the high seas, such as fires creeping over the ocean waves and stones shooting out from under the water and their fascinating myths and legends of flying sea witches and sea monsters that were believed to threaten those who dared to set sail. Through this account, we gain insight into the construction of a magnificent piece of art as well as the creative minds of its makers.

Coral Gardens

In his monograph *Coral Gardens and Their Magic*, Malinowski writes:

> The Trobriander is, above all, a gardener who digs with pleasure and collects with pride, to whom accumulated food gives a sense of safety and pleasure

in achievement, and to whom the rich foliage of yam-vines or taro leaves is a direct expression of beauty. As in many other matters, **the Trobriander would agree with Stendhal's definition of beauty as the promise of bliss rather than Kant's emasculated statement about disinterested contemplation as the essence of aesthetic enjoyment**. [emphasis by A.K.] To the Trobriander, all that is lovely to the eye and the heart, or – as he would put it more correctly – to the stomach, which to him is the seat of the emotions as well as of understanding, lies in things which promise to him safety, prosperity, abundance, and sensual pleasure.

(Malinowski 1935: 10)

The remark on Kant's "emasculated statement" revealed Malinowski's critique of Kant's views on art and expressed his well-defined judgments on the subject as he described the Trobriand Islanders' world (Kant 1987: 43–91). He illustrated the Trobriand gardens in the following manner:

The gardens are, in a way, a work of art. Exactly as a native will take an artist's delight in constructing a canoe or a house, perfect in shape, decoration, and finish, and the whole community will glory in such an achievement, exactly thus will he go about the laying out and developing his garden. He and his relatives and his fellow villagers as well will be proud of the splendid results of his labours.

(Malinowski 1935:80)

Even the sticks laid on the ground, which marked the gardens' boundaries, had aesthetic value. "During all the successive stages of the work, visits are exchanged, and mutual admiration and appreciation of the aesthetic qualities of the gardens are a constant feature of village life" (Malinowski 1935: 81). The fundamental goal of gardening was to create beautiful gardens and cultivate abundant crops:

The presence of food means to the natives the absence of fear, security, and confidence in the future. But it means more than that. It means the possibility of dancing and feasting, of leisure for carving and canoe-building, the opportunity for pleasant overseas expeditions, for visiting and social intercourse on a large scale. And to those natives who are pre-eminent as gardeners, chiefs, or magicians, it also means *butura* (renown) and the satisfaction of vanity.

(Malinowski 1935: 81–82)

The gardens were beautifully maintained by properly fertilizing and irrigating the plants and removing weeds. The plants were also supported by stakes and artistic wooden structures consisting of a vertical pole with diagonal sticks to support yam plants. These structures were created by the native people and added to the aesthetic appeal of the gardens.

They know empirically that tall, strong verticals are of value, but the fact that the higher and more luxuriant the taytu vine, the richer its development underground, engenders in them an aesthetic love of height and strength for their own sake, which is expressed in their careful choice of poles. Finally, I do not doubt that this aesthetic appreciation merges into a mystical feeling that the height and strength of their vertical system, and above all of the *kamkokola*, has a stimulating effect on the young plants.

(Malinowski 1935: 129)

The *kamkokola* was the structure erected on each of the four corners of every garden. These structures had both practical and magical functions as they supported the yam plant, allowing it to climb up in the future. As Malinowski wrote, the *kamkokola* "has a special aesthetic value to the natives. Its sight rejoices the heart of the Kiriwinian even as it would that of a modern Cubist" (Malinowski 1935: 123–124). The construction of *kamkokola* involved a lot of effort to achieve an impressive appearance. Strong, thick, straight poles were carefully selected to accomplish this. The erection of *kamkokola* "is a finishing off, so to speak, of the surface work in the garden; it is the last decorative touch given to the magical corner, and it artistically completes the *tula* system" (Malinowski 1935: 131).

In Malinowski's anthropological descriptions, gardening was not just a solitary activity but rather a significant part of the islanders' daily life. It held various emotional values, including fear for survival, pride in owning a particularly beautiful garden, and social communication. Gardening also allowed for contact with the land, which held a special place in the islanders' imagination and was tied closely to their myths and beliefs. The land was believed to be the origin of garden magic. It was there that the ancestral spirits called *baloma* resided (Malinowski 1929). These spirits would incarnate in women's bodies, make them pregnant, and then manifest as human beings who were reincarnations of their ancestors. Working with the land was a spiritual experience and the energy of life could be felt through the plants. Malinowski's monograph on coral gardens shows that the coral gardens cultivation process had an intrinsic poetic aspect, aligning with Martin Heidegger's philosophy of art, where poetry is a constitutive element of all art (Heidegger 1975).

Final Remarks

Bronisław Malinowski's research shows that the boundaries of art on the Trobriand Islands were not clearly defined and often blended with other cultural practices. Art was a collective experience and a practical tool for survival, used to enhance the power of magic during activities such as constructing a canoe, making *kula* valuables, and cultivating coral gardens. Art was a way to experience reality in all its aspects, including the visible and the invisible, and a testament to religious and magical beliefs. It served as a means to explain and influence reality, while also having communicative, representational, and aesthetic functions.

Malinowski's account suggests that art in the Trobriand culture followed established formal patterns and was used to express familiar themes that had been passed down through generations. It was bound by a strict framework of beliefs, religious and magical rituals, and depictions of reality. Based on Malinowski's account, it can be assumed that art was a continuation of traditional and proven formal solutions and served to express content that had been known for generations. But it isn't obvious. It is after all known that various types of contacts, caused by population migration, missionary activity of Christian Churches, trade or wars, usually led to cultural transformations, which also had to result in changes in art. For example, as Gunter Senft wrote, the activities of the missionaries on the Trobriands influenced the way indigenous islanders conceptualized reality and their understanding of magic. It must also have influenced their attitude to art. This led to slow social and moral transformations (Senft 2016: 248–251). In the 1970s, the Trobriand villagers commonly used mass-produced clothing, plastic dishes, and tools made of steel, as well as plastic boats powered by internal combustion engines, which turned out to be much more practical than heavy wooden canoes (Campbell 2002: 45–50). The lower number of canoes resulted in a decreased demand for decorative prow boards created by *tokabitam* sculpture masters. All this together led to a deterioration of sculptural art, as it was becoming increasingly difficult to reach traditional sculptural knowledge. A *tokabitam* usually had one apprentice to whom he passed on his magical knowledge and sculpting skills. In the context of civilizational changes that affected the culture of the Trobriands, such knowledge slowly lost its *raison d'être* and old sculptural skills turned out to be less and less needed. Over time, the old magic formulas and rituals associated with the creation of canoes were forgotten, which caused, among other things, changes in the language – for example, the disappearance of certain words related to old rituals. With the growth of tourism, traditional sculptures created by masters lost their value, because most tourists bought almost everything, without looking at the artistic quality of the sculptural work. The prow boards they bought became decorative artefacts deprived of their original function and old magical power and mythical content. The sale of sculptures to tourists became one of the few sources of monetary income for the natives (Senft 1992: 71–88).

Today, there is no longer any "primitive art" in the sense proposed by Franz Boas and the island community of the Trobriands has largely lost the former features of a traditional society. However, Bronisław Malinowski's monographs are one of the last testimonies to the reality that has undergone far-reaching transformations. This is also an important part of his legacy.

Transl. by Kamila Drapało and Agnieszka Dzięcioł-Pędich

Notes

1 The group, founded in Kraków in 1917, became the first avant-garde artistic group in Poland, drawing artistic inspiration from French cubism and Polish folk art. Its very interesting theoretical assumptions were developed primarily by Witkiewicz and Chwistek.
2 This is evidenced by a very brief mention, from which it can only be inferred that the anthropologist thought rather jokingly about the intention to introduce a new type of ornamentation into Trobriand art, which – as can be judged from the entries in the *Diary* – he worked out by making tortoiseshell combs of for his fiancée Elsa Masson.

3 This information can be found on the British Museum website: https://www.britishmuseum.org/collection/term/BIOG125915
4 Malinowski, who spent three weeks on Vakuta Island, acknowledged that the best canoes were made there.

References

Barthes, Roland. 1986 [1964]. *Elements of semiology*. Translated by Anette Lawers, Colin Smith. New York: Hill and Wang.

Boas, Franz. 1955 [1927]. *Primitive art*. New ed. New York: Dover Publications.

Campbell, Shirley F. 2002. *The art of Kula*. Oxford: Berg.

Clifford, James. 1996. *The predicament of culture. Twentieth-century ethnography, literature, and art*. Cambridge, MA, and London: Harvard University Press.

Didi-Huberman, Georges. 2017. *The surviving image: Phantoms of time and time of phantoms. Aby Warburg's history of art*. Translated by Harvey Mendelsohn. University Park: The Pennsylvania State University Press.

Elsner, Jas'. 2006. "From empirical evidence to the big picture: Some reflections on Riegl's concept of *Kunstwollen*."*Critical Inquiry 32* (4): 741–766.

Geertz, Clifford. 1988. *Works and lives: The anthropologist as author*. Stanford, CA: Stanford University Press.

Glass, Patrick. 1978. *The Trobriand code: an interpretation of Trobriand war shield designs with implications for the culture and traditional society*. M.Sc. Thesis. Salford: University of Salford.

Heidegger, Martin. 1975. *Poetry, language, thought*. Translated by Albert Hofstadter. New York: Harper & Bow.

Kant, Immanuel. 1987. *Critique of judgment*. Translated by Werner S. Pluhar. Indianapolis, IN: Hackett Publishing Company.

Leach, Edmund R. 1983. "The Kula: An alternative view." In *The Kula: New perspectives on Massim exchange*, edited by Jerry W. Lech, Edmund R. Leach, 529–538. Cambridge: Cambridge University Press.

Malinowski, Bronislaw. 1922. *Argonauts of the Western Pacific*. London: Routledge and Kegan Paul.

Malinowski, Bronislaw. 1929. *The sexual life of savages in North-Western Melanesia*. London: Routledge.

Malinowski, Bronislaw. 1935. *Coral Gardens and their magic vol. I: The description of gardening*. London: George Allen and Unwin Ltd.

Malinowski, Bronislaw. 1967. *A diary in the strict sense of the term*. Translated by Norbert Guterman. London: Routledge & Kegan Paul.

Malinowski, Bronislaw. 2016. "Arts notes and suggestions."*Pacific Arts. The Journal of the Pacific Arts Association 16* (1): 9–34.

Meyers, Fred. 2006. "'Primitivism,' anthropology, and the category of 'primitive art'." In *Handbook of material culture*, edited by Christopher Tilley, Webb Keane, Susan Küchler, Mike Rowlands, Patricia Spyer, 267–284. London: SAGE.

Scoditti, Giacomo M.G. 1990. *Kitawa. A linguistic and aesthetic analysis of visual art in Melanesia*. Berlin-New York: Mouton de Gruyter.

Senft, Gunter. 1992. "As time goes by…: Changes observed in Trobriand Islanders' culture and language, Milne Bay Province, Papua New Guinea." In *Culture change, language change: Case studies from Melanesia* edited by Tim Dutton, 67–89. Canberra: Pacific Linguistics.

Senft, Gunter. 2016. "'*Masawa-bogeokwasituta!*': Cultural and cognitive implications of the Trobriand Islanders'gradual loss of their knowledge of how to make a *Masawa* Canoe." In *Ethnic and cultural dimensions of knowledge,* edited by Peter Meusburger, Tim Freytag, Laura Sursana, 229–256. New York: Springer International Publishing.

Warburg, Aby. 1939. "A lecture of serpent ritual." Translated by William F. Mainland. *Journal of the Warburg Institute 2* (4): 277–292.

Young, Michael. 2004. *Malinowski: Odyssey of an anthropologist, 1884–1920*, Cambridge, MA: Harvard University Press.

Young, Michael, Harry Beran. 2016. "Introduction to Malinowski's 'Arts Notes and Suggestions'." *Pacific Arts. The Journal of the Pacific Arts Association 16* (1): 5–8.

11 Exploring the Intersection of Law, Culture, and Biology

Tensions and Unfulfilled Potential in Malinowski's Legal Thought

Mateusz Stępień

Introduction

Considerable literature has been dedicated to recognizing the pivotal contributions of Bronisław Kasper Malinowski (1884–1942) in the realm of anthropology, particularly as the founder of mature functionalism (see, e.g., Firth 1957; Mosko 2017). His work not only introduced functionalism as a distinct method of analysis but also left an indelible mark on general social theory. Moreover, Malinowski's pioneering participant observation technique revolutionized the field. Although his impact on anthropology remains indisputable, it's noteworthy that his investigations on language, religion, and culture resonate far beyond this discipline, echoing throughout the broader social sciences.

However, it is quite intriguing, given his superlative status in anthropological reflections on law (see, e.g., Seagle 1937; Hoebel 1954; Schapera 1957; Conley, O'Barr 2002; Kurczewski 2012; Ledvinka 2016), to observe the relatively limited attention in legal sciences afforded to Malinowski's forays into the domain of law. Legal scholarship, despite experiencing a flourishing period of cultural reflections on law, has seemingly relegated Malinowski's legal thoughts and his overarching jurisprudence to the periphery, with only some exceptions (see Stępień 2016a, 2016b).

While it might be tempting to argue that the relative lack of attention paid to Malinowski's legal reflections in legal science stems from his perceived disinterest in the study of (primitive) law, a closer examination reveals a more nuanced picture. Indeed, when he embarked on his fieldwork, Malinowski's primary focus lay in investigating the intricate relationships between magic, religion, and the economy, with a keen emphasis on understanding the underlying cognitive processes at play (Malinowski 1922: 5; 2002: 79). Yet, even in these early stages, Malinowski did consider the realm of primitive law. In 1914, Malinowski received a manuscript article from Edwin Hartland, which later formed the foundation for Hartland's monograph – *Primitive Law* (1924). Malinowski's correspondence with Hartland included assurances of his intent to "pay special attention" to the study of law within the communities he planned to research (cited in Young 2004: 369). This reveals an early inclination towards exploring the nuances of primitive law. Moreover, throughout his illustrious career, Malinowski authored numerous

DOI: 10.4324/9781003449768-16

works on law, with a particular focus on primitive law (1925a, 1925b, 1926b, 1934, 1936c, 1942a), culminating in his monograph on the subject (1926a). Notably, his mature theoretical works brimmed with references to law. He positioned law as one of the ten (1936a: 442) or five essential "aspects of culture" (1944/1961: 159, 167), viewing it as part of the broader systems of social control (1944/1961: 6) and a fundamental "cultural response" to intrinsic human needs (1944/1961: 175). During the later phase of his career, while residing in the United States, Malinowski actively conducted research on law (Murdock 1942). An important milestone was his seminar (held together with Underhill Moore) on primitive law and primitive jurisprudence held at Yale University in 1940–1941 (Schlegel 1980: 302–303). This seminar was a collaborative effort between the Department of Anthropology and the Yale Law School. Additionally, traces of legal threads can be discerned in his other works (e.g., 1913, 1922, 1929, 1935, 1936a, 1942b, 1944/1961).

Furthermore, it's worth acknowledging the profound influence of Malinowski's Kraków mentors during his formative years, who were lawyers affiliated with Jagiellonian University and engaged in the intersection of law and ethnography. Lothar Dargun (1853–1893) and Stanisław Estreicher (1869–1939) played pivotal roles in shaping Malinowski's early perspectives (see Kubica 1986). Dargun, renowned for his work on the application of ethnography to legal history, left an indelible impression on Malinowski (see Dudek 2016). Estreicher, the author of works like *Beginnings of Contract Law* (published in 1901) and *Legal Culture in 16th Century Poland* (published in 1932), held a position of mentorship and inspiration in Malinowski's intellectual journey (see Pałecki 2016). In the preface to Feliks Gross's book entitled: *Study on Nomadism and Its Impact on Society, Polity and Law*, Malinowski confessed: "I also have been associated with our old Jagiellonian University of Cracow. I also, like Dr Gross, have been inspired in my work by the teachings and personal interests of Professor Stanisław Estreicher" (1936b: x). In essence, even during his initial exposure to ethnography through James Frazer's *The Golden Bough*, Malinowski's intellectual odyssey was significantly influenced by extraordinary Kraków-based legal scholars who were deeply engaged in the exploration of cultural dimmention of law.

This multifaceted engagement with law, spanning his entire career, warrants a more comprehensive examination of Malinowski's jurisprudential contributions beyond the realm of anthropology. In line with this, the chapter seeks to rectify this oversight by providing a more nuanced and holistic understanding of Malinowski's inclinations on legal domain. To accomplish this goal, a thorough reconstruction is conducted, which encompasses Malinowski's thoughts on law throughout his entire career. It's important to clarify that the objective here is not to provide a comprehensive critique of "Malinowski's jurisprudence." Also, in contrast to earlier studies in anthropology on Malinowski's legal thought, this chapter does not aim to provide an extensive overview of the entire body of Malinowski's jurisprudential work. Instead, its focus is on revealing deeper tensions within his legal thought and demonstrating the various approaches to legal phenomena illuminated in Malinowski's work. Furthermore, this chapter seeks to spark a discussion regarding the connection between Malinowski's reflections on law and the prevailing positions within the broader field of law and society studies, and even within the realm of general social theory.

The chapter begins by offering a glimpse into the functional framework that determines Malinowski's general view and approach to the law. Subsequently, it discusses the main problems and tensions associated with his definitions of (primitive) law and its demarcation from other types of norms. The final part of the chapter explores the multi-dimensional approach to law, combining biological, social, and psychological dimensions. Concluding remarks draw attention to the overall character of Malinowski's legal thought in contrast to certain trends in social sciences.

A Functional Framework as a Starting Point

Malinowski did not present a neatly organized and comprehensive theory of (primitive) law. However, his overarching theoretical framework, functionalism, provides valuable insights into his understanding of law as a part of culture. A sociologist, Piotr Sztompka's analysis identified several types of functional analysis in Malinowski's works, including a straightforward, elaborated, two-tiered, and the most advanced motivational functional analysis (1971: 55–56, 78–79, 91–93, 111; see Sztompka 1974). These various modes of functional analysis reveal the depth and complexity of Malinowski's approach to understanding cultural phenomena through functional lenses.

At its core, Malinowski's functionalism posits that every aspect of culture, including the legal sector, is interconnected with other cultural elements. These elements interact to ensure the persistence and functioning of the entire cultural system. The functionality of cultural components is not isolated; they have relational aspects and serve specific functions within the broader context. Malinowski's functionalist perspective considers the consequences of these cultural functions at the macro-social level. It examines how these functions contribute to or hinder the satisfaction of individual and social needs within a given society. This approach offers a lens through which we can analyse the role of law in meeting societal requirements and expectations. Crucially, Malinowski considered culture as a relatively integrated whole, but he did not turn a blind eye to its inherent contradictions (1922). He acknowledged that culture is a dynamic and complex amalgamation of elements that do not always harmonize seamlessly and may carry inherent ambiguities and tensions. This recognition of cultural complexity becomes especially pertinent when examining the social functions of law. For example, in his analysis of the law of the Trobriand Islanders, Malinowski proposed a heuristic thesis about its functionality but refrained from assuming that the mere existence of certain legal constructs implies that they are inherently necessary or functional.

Functional analysis, in various variations, runs through Malinowski's entire body of work. Already in his doctoral dissertation, *O zasadzie ekonomii myślenia* [*On the Principle of the Economy of Thought*], he observed that each of the elements, including law, can only be described, and explained by determining the function it fulfils in the integral system of culture (1906/1980: 365). *Argonauts of the Western Pacific* (1922) concerned the function of exchange and the relations between exchange and other domains of life (magic and religion). Meanwhile, *Crime and Custom* (1926a) referred to the function of (primitive) law and its connections with other elements. The most mature work based on field research on the Trobriand Islands, *Coral Gardens and Their Magic* (1935), presented gardening as a way of satisfying specific needs through complex interactions between kinship structure, forms of ownership, and magic. In all these cases, Malinowski's analyses address the question of how and to what extent a particular social institution or cultural element contributes to the persistence of the whole and what its relationships with other elements are in this context.

In case of the general reflection on law, Malinowski's approach moved the interest from history, sources, or formal characteristics of law to its effects considered in terms of the persistence of the whole and how it functions in actual life (Malinowski 1926a: 125). Although Malinowski explicitly wrote about the functions performed by (primitive) law, his works do not contain precise and consistent considerations on this subject. In one place, he stated that the general function of law is to ensure that people fulfil their obligations (which ultimately enables the satisfaction of primary and secondary needs) (1926a). More precisely, it refers to the function of securing the continuity and adequacy of mutual services (p. 26), enabling the fulfilment of obligations by people (pp. 32, 64). Similarly, albeit much later, he indicated the function of law by "keeping the whole chain of activities running smoothly" (1944/1961: 98) or securing the smooth operation of organized activities (p. 104), or even more generally, "establishing purposeful, organized, and effective systems of human activities" (1942a: 1245). Based on this, it can be said that for Malinowski, the most general function of law is to enable cooperation without which needs cannot be satisfied. Importantly, Malinowski also pointed out social control as a function of law (1944/1961: 125). Regrettably, there is a dearth of information concerning his perspective on the relationship between these two functions. Nevertheless, it becomes apparent that this approach has limitations since numerous cultural elements, apart from the law, are involved in fulfilling these functions.

Problems with the Definition and Demarcation of Law

It's worthwhile to consider here Malinowski's attempts to formulate a definition of law and his work aimed at demarcating law from other types of social norms, bearing in mind this functional approach to the social realm. Although Malinowski emphasized the need to analyse the influence of normative tools on the persistence and functioning of other institutions or elements, he did not elaborate on their distinguishing features in a thorough and precise way. The lack of convincing definitional considerations was not in line with Malinowski's intellectual profile. The co-founder of functional analysis was under the overwhelming influence of the second positivist paradigm of scientific inquiry, to which he remained loyal throughout his career. Concurring with the Viennese second positivism, which was highly influential in Kraków during his study at Jagiellonian University (Flis 1988), he regarded definitional issues as the core of his jurisprudence. Even in a book written before his field research, he observed that "precise concepts and clear definitions are necessary" (1913: 10). The goal of a book *Crime and Custom* was to propose "a satisfactory classification of the norms and rules of a primitive community" (1926a: 15). He dedicated an entire subsection to this issue (p. 55 and onwards). In his last work solely focused on law, he emphasized once again that defining and demarcating law from "customs, ethical rules, norms of manners, and etiquette" is necessary not only for the field researcher but also for practitioners of comparative jurisprudence and sociologists (1942a: 1238).

The announcements regarding the necessity of conceptual precision, the proposal of a definition of law, and the demarcation from other normative elements (e.g., 1913: 10; 1926a: x, 15, 30) were not fulfilled (similarly: Schapera 1957: 139, 146; Conley, O'Barr 2002: 864). Malinowski failed to establish a consistent conceptual framework regarding law. Moreover, numerous inconsistencies and laxness can be traced in his definitions. He casually employed terms such as "law," "primitive law," "customary law," "native law," "savage law," "law and order," and "legal forces." Moreover, he did not provide any hints regarding the relationships between these terms. Of particular interest is the relationship between law and what Malinowski referred to as "primitive law." The term "primitive" carries various connotations, some of which are linked to evolutionary thinking, implying that such law is, in a way, "incomplete." While Malinowski often opposed the tradition of 19th-century evolutionary anthropology, he occasionally used this term without much reflection. Furthermore, Malinowski himself made distinctions between primitive law and "crystallized" law (1934: xxviii; 1942a: 1238), which could be seen as remnants of evolutionary thinking. Moreover, sometimes, he suggested that "law" is a category falling within "customs" (1926a: 54), while at other times, he assumed their distinctiveness (1936a: 442), occasionally using these terms interchangeably (1934: xxviii, xxx, xli). In his approach to applying Western jurisprudence concepts to phenomena occurring in primitive societies, Malinowski was inconsistent and lacked deeper reflection on his issue. Despite declarations about the dangers of such a procedure, in many cases, Malinowski seems to make this mistake, as seen when he explicitly wrote about "criminal law," "civil law," "property," and "inheritance." However, he occasionally prudently used the terms "quasi-criminal law" and "quasi-civil law" (1926a: 123).

Moreover, Malinowski's approach to primitive law possesses a significant crack. On the one hand, his arguments were consistent with the position that recognizes the clear separation of legal phenomena (law) from other areas of culture in pre-industrial societies. He also recognized, contrary to Émile Durkheim, that legal norms do not have a sacred character and do not constitute "religious commandments" (1926a: 31). He placed law alongside other elements of social control (1942a: 1238). Moreover, Malinowski observed that Trobriand Islanders also differentiate between different types of norms. On the other hand, in other considerations, he was closer to an approach assuming continuity between various aspects of the normative sphere, which can only be distinguished analytically. He generally wrote about the "legal aspect of norms" (1913: 16). He pointed out that religious acts and magical institutions have a "legal side" (1926a: 43, 87; for more on the relationship between magic and law in Malinowski, see: Foks 2018: 42–46). In a similar sense, he noted that "law covers the whole culture and the entire tribal constitution" (p. 49). However, at the same time, it "does not consist in any independent institutions" (p. 59). Law and customs are "organically connected and not isolated" (p. 125). It is evident that law is embedded and unified with other cultural elements. Malinowski did not recognize the inconsistency of simultaneously emphasizing the separation and inseparability of law from other norms.

The Specificity of Law – Combining Biological, Social and Psychological Factors

At the outset of his career, as he contemplated legal norms in comparison to other means of social control, offering a hint of a functional perspective, Malinowski sought the specificity of law primarily in its mode of sanctioning (1913: 11). There exist various "forces" and "tools" that render norms a tangible instrument of order. However, it is essential to clarify that this is not an attempt to define law as violence sanctioned by the state or a political organization, as it may initially appear. According to Malinowski, law is characterized by an organized, more or less regulated, and active social sanction (p. 11); "without a social system of enforcing norms, they would remain moral or customary" (p. 12). Thus, the hallmark of law lies in the operation of an external, stable, and, importantly, organized infrastructure ("the social system of enforcement") that makes norms binding. However, at this juncture, the overly general nature of the criteria distinguishing legal norms from other norms becomes apparent. For instance, if one were to apply the criteria proposed by Malinowski, even norms created within institutionalized religions would fall into the category of law. It is also easy to identify a complex set of norms recognized as customary, functioning based on an extensive "social system of enforcement."

In *Crime and Custom*, Malinowski further developed this stance. He observed that to classify norms, one needs to consider the "motives and sanctions by which they are enforced" (1926a: 50). In addition to sanctions as a social system of enforcement, a new element was introduced: the extracted and emphasized psychological factor. Malinowski explicitly underscored that different types of norms are grounded in various underlying psychological processes. Consequently, legal norms are associated with a specific mindset of people engaged in their implementation (p. 54). What distinguishes legal norms is that they are "felt and regarded as the obligations of one person and the rightful claim of another" (p. 55). This specific complex and distribution of experiences is said to account for the distinctiveness of law. One cannot ignore the alleged influence of Leon Petrażycki (1867–1931) on Malinowski's views. Petrażycki, a Polish author who proposed a psychological conception of law (see, e.g., 1955), whom Malinowski never mentioned in his works, expressed a similar understanding of law in terms of emotional experiences with a two-sided character: imperative-attributive (imposing and acknowledging) (see Motyka 1999; Kurczewski 2009, 2012).

Most likely, the two elements indicated by Malinowski, the social and the psychological, should be understood together. After all, the primary domain of law is "the social mechanism, which can be found at the bottom of all real obligations" (Malinowski 1926a: 62), rather than merely a specific psychological experience. Moreover, a few decades later, summarizing his intellectual position, Malinowski generally emphasized moving away from the one-sidedness of sociological and psychological analyses (1944/1961: 24). It can be suspected that he held such inclinations earlier. By articulating what Malinowski did not explicitly express, the mere "feeling and regarding" of certain claims, without the related factors pertaining to social organization, proves insufficient for an adequate definition of law. Similarly, the actual existence of "a social system of enforcement" would be insufficient without complementary acts of consciousness. Omitting either of these elements would hinder the description and explanation of law.

Meanwhile, later considerations shift the focus to a different level. Law is treated as one of many possible tools for satisfying human needs (1944/1961). The category of needs is crucial here (see Piddington 1957). Alongside primary needs (animal, basic, biological), Malinowski recognizes secondary needs related to human society and culture. Regarding the latter, he notes that cultural behaviours simultaneously generate new needs; they are "implications of man's [sic!] cultural responses to innate urges" (1936a: 447). In other words, the satisfaction of primary needs creates new, specific cultural needs rooted in the symbolic world (1942b: 77). This process creates an area governed by specific general scientific laws (1942a: 1241).

In this context, when we return to law, the "social system of enforcement" and reciprocal psychological experiences form a syndrome that facilitates the stable realization of specific functions viewed from the perspective of human needs. It's important to emphasize a noteworthy aspect of "Malinowski's jurisprudence," which entails comprehending law within the broader biological sphere. Initially, this might appear surprising from the typical perspective of legal science, where the connection between law and biology is not commonly recognized.

It is crucial to bear in mind, as mentioned earlier, that Malinowski's intellectual development occurred in the academic environment of Kraków, which was significantly influenced by neopositivism. A distinctive feature of this intellectual movement was naturalism (Flis 1985: 11, 1988). Despite later criticisms of this intellectual framework, Malinowski retained some neopositivist tendencies. This is evident in his vision of science, including cultural anthropology, which is grounded in empiricism, inductionism, and a nomothetic approach. According to him, science should aim to formulate general laws. Malinowski's position can be best described as "soft naturalism," even when it comes to law. This characteristic is justified, partly because Malinowski emphasized the biological foundations of social life and the role of biological factors in shaping culture. Additionally, he recognized the existence of new types of needs generated by culture itself and, to some extent, by the emergence of cultural determinism. According to Malinowski, "culture is a determinant of human behaviour, and culture, as a dynamic reality, is also subject to determinism" (1936a: 440). Culture represents a uniquely human way of adapting to the environment, enabling the satisfaction of needs. This process occurs through a "cultural artificial environment," constituting a specific "reinforcement of physiology." Thanks to culture, humans can act under conditions of order, continuity, predictability, allowing them to better address specific problems (1944/1961: 150). In this sense, culture is built upon biology, and Malinowski had no doubt that "the driving forces of all behaviour are biologically conditioned" (1942b: 77). Needs serve as the category that connects the realms of biology and culture. However, culture is not merely a passive tool for fulfilling biological imperatives, but an active modifier of them.

Given this theoretical context, it's essential to understand how Malinowski perceived the role of law. In one instance, he wrote that "most laws are the expression" of physiological factors and "important and functionally grounded cultural trends" (1934: lxvi). This fragment already hints at the dual nature of law. Firstly, it serves as a tool that facilitates the survival and satisfaction of biological imperatives (xxxii). Law "is not an end in itself, but an indispensable instrumentality for the achievement of the real, ultimately biological goals of human activities" (1942a: 1245). Secondly, in his earlier works, Malinowski wrote about law as a means of "curbing certain natural propensities," "controlling human instincts," and imposing non-spontaneous, coercive behaviours (1926a: 64). Following this line of thought, he also recognized law as a method of limiting biological imperatives (1942a: 1245).

Therefore, it is possible to discern a distinct tension in Malinowski's approach, as he alternately views law as a tool for expressing natural inclinations and as a means of limiting them. Although Malinowski does not explicitly develop this idea, it can be argued that law, as a cultural creation, enables the realization of certain biological imperatives while concurrently restraining and moderating their impact or the impact of other imperatives. The question naturally arises regarding which aspects of human nature are intended for protection and which are subject to limitation through the law, as well as the intricate relationships that unfold between these two spheres. In any case, Malinowski's perspective underscores the position of law within a broader context that encompasses the realm of biology.

Conclusion

Malinowski's approach to comprehending social phenomena is all-encompassing, integrating diverse perspectives and levels. He aimed to create a comprehensive view that considered various dimensions, including individual consciousness, the organization of human activities, and the societal consequences of these actions (in case of law see: Malinowski, 1942b: 73). Motivations and the sphere of consciousness played crucial roles in his approach, alongside "social organization". Malinowski synthesized these perspectives into a unified framework that may appear more comprehensive than the approaches of many other scholars. He avoided rigidly separating the individual level (consciousness and actions) from the systemic level (and subsystems) and refrained from reducing explanatory factors to just one of these levels.

Significantly, Malinowski's approach to understanding law was simultaneously based on interpretive analysis "from within," "through the eyes of a native," as well as on focusing on the development and persistence of social systems (see Parsons

1957). Thus, Malinowski's approach amalgamated both internal ("phenomenological") and external ("systemic") perspectives. In these lines, he scrutinized law as specific mental states intricately interwoven with other cultural elements. Notably, in his later works, Malinowski dissected law at a higher level, regarding it as a distinct response to one of the functional imperatives, essentially functioning as a tool for social control. These parallel paths involved the examination of human mental states within their social functions and the analysis of the social system itself. Although he didn't offer a conceptually clear way of integrating these two perspectives, his inclination to consider both characterizes his overarching approach to the social realm.

In the social sciences, many years later, sometimes independently of Malinowski's legacy but other times under his influence, scholars began to recognize the limitations of constructing social theories that solely focused on one level of social life. Especially with the publication of Jürgen Habermas's *Theory of Communicative Action* and the development of Jeffrey Alexander's neofunctionalism, there has been a gradual return to approaches that endeavour to encompass both the realms of consciousness and systems. Malinowski's concepts can still serve as an inspiration in this regard, while also cautioning against overly hasty inclusiveness in this aspect.

However, Malinowski's multi-dimensional ontology of law and the related epistemological view posed several challenges in Malinowski's analysis of primitive law as a tool for fulfilling human needs. While he resisted simplifying the description and explanation of the legal sector, this complexity sometimes resulted in inconsistency and incoherence in his original ideas. Yet, it's vital to recognize that Malinowski's jurisprudence was extremely pioneering at his time. The ambiguities in his formulations and structural challenges should be viewed in the context of the era and the work of other anthropologists interested in law. For instance, Roy Barton in *Ifugao Law* referred to the Ifugao tribe's law as "entirely based on custom and taboo," categorizing them as "barbarian head-hunters" with "a well-developed system of law," albeit in the early stages of development (Barton 1919: 6, 9, 16). Similarly, Edwin Hartland defined primitive law as "the whole body of customs of a tribe," and "the rules governing societies of lower culture," and "the traditional rules of a community" (Hartland 1924: 5, 8, 137). It is evident that Malinowski's concept of law was more sophisticated and possessed greater descriptive and explanatory power, despite its numerous imperfections.

It is unquestionable that Malinowski's concept of law rooted in multi-level thinking about the social world remains essential and warrants further development based on new scientific advancements. It is worth noting that for a long time, Malinowski's ethnographic works related to field research on the Trobriand Islands received more favourable reviews, whereas attempts to construct broad theories from the later period of his life were met with criticism. However, when examining constructive efforts to build syntheses that encompass multiple levels of social life, it is the middle career and latter works, particularly the posthumously published *Scientific Theory of Culture* (1944/1961; see also 1945), that appear more intriguing. This is because they represent a non-reductionist attempt to combine the domains of natural and social sciences. It must be emphasized that, according to Malinowski, law, although an element of culture, cannot be adequately described and explained without placing it on a biological basis – or acknowledging that biology constitutes one of its dimensions. This perspective should be understood in the context of the increasingly visible trend in science to build bridges between the realms of biology and culture, encompassing both natural and social sciences. In light of this context, Malinowski's path, characterized as "soft naturalism," holds great promise. From today's perspective, criticisms accusing Malinowski of biological distortion appear inaccurate (e.g., Radcliffe-Brown 1949: 320). Importantly, Malinowski avoided two fundamental errors: biological reductionism, which involves reducing culture solely to an instrumental role and explaining cultural phenomena exclusively by referencing biological factors, and cultural reductionism, which entails recognizing culture as entirely self-determined and independent, following the formula *omnis cultura ex cultura*. Malinowski's considerations, which steered clear of both reductionist approaches and instead sought to bridge the realms of nature and culture, were heading in the right direction. His efforts to build a comprehensive social theory appear to have been shaped by the constraints of his conceptual framework and his reliance on outdated constructs like "needs" (however, see Corning 2000). However, despite these limitations, his work could potentially have a more substantial influence in inspiring the formulation of unique research questions and the development of theories that seek to describe and explain the functioning of law by referring to both "cultural" and "biological" factors (see Meloni et al. 2018).

References

Barton, Roy Franklin. 1919. *Ifugao law*. Berkeley: University of California Press.
Conley, John M., and William M. O'Barr. 2002. "Back to the Trobriands: The Enduring Influence of Malinowski's Crime and Custom in Savage." *Society Law & Social Inquiry* 27(4): 847–874.
Corning, Peter. 2000. "Biological Adaptation in Human Societies: A 'Basic Needs' Approach." *Journal of Bioeconomics* 2: 41–86.
Dudek, Michał. 2016. "Not So Long Time ago before Malinowski: The Puzzle of Lotar Dargun's Influence on Bronislaw Malinowski." In *Bronislaw Malinowski's concept of law*, edited by Mateusz Stępień, 3–20. Cham: Springer.
Firth, Raymond (ed). 1957. *Man and culture: An evaluation of the work of Bronislaw Malinowski*. New York: The Humanities Press.
Flis, Andrzej. 1985. "Filozofia krakowska początku XX wieku i kształtowanie się poglądów naukowych Malinowskiego [19th Century Beginnings of the Kraków Philosophy and the Development of Malinowski's Scientific Views]." In *Antropologia społeczna Bronisława Malinowskiego [The Social Anthropology of Bronisław Malinowski]*, edited by M. Flis, A. Paluch, 11–33. Warszawa: PWN.
Flis, Andrzej. 1988. "Cracow Philosophy at the Beginning of the Twentieth Century and the Rise of Malinowski's Scientific Ideas." In *Malinowski between two worlds: The Polish roots of anthropological tradition*, edited by R. Ellen, 105–127. Cambridge: Cambridge University Press.
Foks, Freedy. 2018. "Bronislaw Malinowski, "Indirect Rule," and the Colonial Politics of Functionalist Anthropology, ca. 1925–1940." *Comparative Studies in Society and History* 60(1): 35–57.

Hartland, Edwin Sidney. 1924. *Primitive law*. London: Methuen.
Hoebel, Edward Adamson. 1954. *The law of primitive man. A study in comparative legal dynamics*. Cambridge: Harvard University Press.
Kubica, Grażyna. 1986. "Bronisław Malinowski Years in Poland." *JASO* 17(2): 140–154.
Kurczewski, Jacek. 2009. "Bronisław Malinowski Misunderstood or How Leon Petrazycki's Concept of Law Is Unwittingly Applied in Anthropology of Law." *Societas/Communitas* 1(7): 47–62.
Kurczewski, Jacek. 2012. "Petrażycki in Melanezia – Where Pospisil and Malinowski meet." In *Towards an anthropology of the legal field*, edited by Tomáš Ledvinka et al., 64–77, Prague: Karolinum Press, Charles University.
Ledvinka, Tomáš. 2016. "Bronislaw Malinowski and the Anthropology of Law." In *Bronislaw Malinowski's concept of law*, edited by Mateusz Stępień, 55–81. Cham: Springer.
Malinowski, Bronislaw. 1913. *The family among the Australian Aborigines: A sociological study*. London: University of London Press.
Malinowski, Bronislaw. 1922. *Argonauts of the Western Pacific: An account of native enterprise and adventure in the Archipelagos of Melanesian New Guinea*. London: Routledge and Kegan Paul.
Malinowski, Bronislaw. 1925a. "The Forces of Law and Order in a Primitive Community." *Proceedings of the Royal Institution of Great Britain* 24: 529–547.
Malinowski, Bronislaw. 1925b. "Review of: Primitive law, by E. Sidney Hartland." *Nature* 116: 230–235.
Malinowski, Bronislaw. 1926a. *Crime and custom in savage society*. New York: Harcourt, Brace & Co.
Malinowski, Bronislaw. 1926b. "Primitive Law and Order." *Nature* 117: 9–16.
Malinowski, Bronislaw. 1929. "Practical Anthropology." *Journal of the International African Institute* 2(1): 22–38.
Malinowski, Bronislaw. 1934. "Introduction." In *Law and order in Polynesia*, H. I. Hogbin, xvii–xxii. London: Christophers A. C.
Malinowski, Bronislaw. 1935. *Coral gardens and their magic: A study of the methods of tilling the soil and of agricultural rites in the Trobriand Islands*. London: Allen & Unwin.
Malinowski, Bronislaw. 1936a. "Anthropology." In *Encyclopedia Britannica*, vol. 1, 131–140. London, New York.
Malinowski, Bronislaw. 1936a. "Culture as a Determinant of Behavior." *The Scientific Monthly* 43(5): 440–449.
Malinowski, Bronislaw. 1936b. "Wstęp [Introduction]." In: *Koczownictwo. Studia nad nomadyzmem i nad wpływem tegoż na społeczeństwo, ustrój i prawo [Study on Nomadism and its impact on society, polity and law]*, edited by Felix Gross, xi–xiii, Warszawa: Instytut Popierania Nauki.
Malinowski, Bronislaw. 1936c. "Primitive Law." *Man* 36: 55–56.
Malinowski, Bronislaw. 1942a. "A New Instrument for the Study of Law – Especially Primitive." *The Yale Law Journal* 51(8): 1237–1254.
Malinowski, Bronislaw. 1942b. "Man's Culture and Man's Behavior." *Sigma Xi Quarterly* 29(3/4): 182–196.
Malinowski, Bronislaw. 1944/1961. *A scientific theory of culture and other essays*. London, Oxford, New York: Oxford University Press.
Malinowski, Bronislaw. 1945. *The dynamics of culture change: An inquiry into race relations in Africa*. New Haven, CT: Yale University Press.
Malinowski, Bronislaw. 2002. *Dziennik w ścisłym znaczeniu tego wyrazu [Diary in the Strict Sense of the Term]*, Kraków: Wydawnictwo Literackie.

Meloni, Maurizio et al. (eds.) 2018. *The Palgrave handbook of biology and society*. London: Palgrave Macmillan.
Mosko, Mark S. 2017. *Ways of Baloma. Rethinking magic and kinship from the Triobrand*. Chicago, IL: HAU.
Motyka, Krzysztof. 1999. "Beyond Malinowski: Petrazycki's Contribution to Legal Pluralism." In *Papers of the XIth international congress of folk law and legal pluralism: Societies in transformation*, edited by Keebet von Benda-Beckmann and Harald W. Finkler, 330–337. Moscow: Institute of Ethnology and Anthropology.
Murdock, George. 1942. "Bronislaw Malinowski." *Yale Law Journal* 51: 1235–1236.
Pałecki, Krzysztof. 2016. "Stanisław Estreicher: The Forgotten Master of Bronislaw Malinowski." In *Bronislaw Malinowski's concept of law*, edited by Mateusz Stępień, 21–36. Cham: Springer.
Parsons, Talcott. 1957. "Malinowski and the Theory of Social Systems." In *Man and culture: An evaluation of the work of Bronislaw Malinowski*, edited by Raymond Firth, 53–70. New York: The Humanities Press.
Petrazycki, Leon. 1955. *Law and morality*. Cambridge, MA: Harvard University Press.
Piddington, Ralph. 1957. "Malinowski's Theory of Needs." In *Man and culture: An evaluation of the work of Bronislaw Malinowski*, edited by Raymond Firth, 33–52. New York: The Humanities Press.
Radcliffe-Brown, Alfred Reginald. 1949. "Functionalism: A Protest." *American Anthropologist* 51(2): 320–322.
Schapera, Isaac. 1957. "Malinowski's Theories of Law." In *Man and culture: An evaluation of the work of Bronislaw Malinowski*, edited by Raymond Firth, 139–155. New York: The Humanities Press.
Schlegel, John. 1980. "American Legal Realism and Empirical Social Science: The Singular Case of Underhill Moore." *Buffalo Law Review* 29: 195–323.
Seagle, William. 1937. "Primitive Law and Professor Malinowski." *American Anthropologist* 39(2): 275–290.
Stępień, Mateusz (ed). 2016a. *Bronislaw Malinowski's concept of law*. Cham: Springer.
Stępień, Mateusz. 2016b. "Malinowski's Multidimensional Conception of Law: Beyond Common Misunderstandings." In *Bronislaw Malinowski's concept of law*, edited by Mateusz Stępień, 39–54. Cham: Springer.
Sztompka, Piotr. 1971. *Analiza funkcjonalna w socjologii i antropologii społecznej*. Kraków: Ossolineum.
Sztompka, Piotr. 1974. *System and function: Toward a theory of society*. New York: Academic Press.
Young, Michel. 2004. *Malinowski: Odyssey of an anthropologist 1884–1920*. New Haven, CT: Yale University Press.

Part V
Malinowski and Anthropology Today

Illustration 6 Bronisław Malinowski with the sons of the chief Toulouva, 1916–1918.

12 *Gimwala* and *Kula*

Malinowski's Living Ethnography

linus s. digim'Rina

Introduction

This paper focuses on the Trobriand underlying cultural notions of exchange – *Gimwala* and *Kula*. Since the publications of *Argonauts of Western Pacific* (1922) and *Crime and Custom in Savage Society* (1926), Malinowski was spot on in recognizing the essentials of a cultural framework for exchange using the indigenous concepts of *Gimwala* and *Kula*. These institutions and operations manifest what could be argued as the underlying principles of reciprocity from the Trobriand Islands. As elementary structures they have stood the test of time with only minor adjustments on details and scope of operations. Throughout, I consider both *Gimwala* and *Kula* as cultural institutions with recognized underlying principles, and as such I am inclined to use capitals for the first letters of the two words. Where their application is expressed within the realms of actual operations however, contextualized as it were, and therefore appear as activities guided by some rules and procedures, I would spell the words in small letters. The chapter tries to show that these underlying principles of reciprocity have been comfortably adapted into Trobriand modernity and are alive and well since Malinowski's fieldwork time and beyond. I use present events and activities in the Trobriands to demonstrate their meaningful uses and acceptance including their appropriation into modernity.

The chapter begins by citing a few related but often missed instances that nonetheless go to show how widespread and fundamental are the concepts of *Gimwala* and *Kula*. Although incomplete, a nomenclature list is cited for the same reason. This is followed by a further explanation on what these two terms actually mean and their contextual uses on a daily basis. A discussion on the contemporary uses of the terms follows largely focusing on instances observed within the Christian church and state-sanctioned events and activities. The conclusion at the end sums up the discussion and brings out the nub of the argument.

Suyabokheta/Bomkharimapu: Elements of Trobriand Reciprocity

Gimwala deli kula: vava, khokwava, wasi, valova, khatuyausa, ulatila, khatuvila, pepeni, govala valu, pokhala, vavivisa, khekeda, yawari, vabutu ula, lisaladabu, sagari, ninabwela, valam deli khemelu, silava, kulututu, ubuwabu, kharipoi, basi

DOI: 10.4324/9781003449768-18

and many others more, are all the nomenclature relevant and related to the *art of creating, sustaining and terminating social and/or exchange relations*. Let me begin by recounting a few of the mundane and far less known activities that hint on or symbolically express opportunities for exchange relations.

Sergio Jarillo's (2021) *Kwanebuyee Kilivila*, noted four ways of threading garlands of aromatic flowers (*Bwetia*) together with their respective cultural meanings. *Bwetia*, being an iconic representation of the aesthetics on threading and adorning of garlands of flowers is a common custom among the Trobriand children and youth. And among four known types of threading flowers is one called *Suyabokheta* (*suya-bo-kheta*: 'thread-garland-intercourse') or, *Bomkharimapu* (*Bom-kharimapu:* 'garland-opposed/polarized').[1] This specifically refers to this form of threading whereby clumps of petals are made to face each other as in opposition or polarity. When worn around the head of the bearer, the expressed meaning is clear. The bearer intends to initiate a dialogue to establish a social relationship with a potential partner usually someone from the opposite sex albeit, outside of the immediate family relations. And yet the intention is not narrowly and exclusively sexual as it extends to include all other forms of trade and exchange liaisons. During overseas *kula* voyages including, arriving men as guests and partners are typically attired with such fresh finery garlands of *suyabokheta*. The intention is expressly clear "Where is my partner, here I am, are you ready with the goods?"

Similarly, a ditty often performed by children is principally centered on two exchange items: a lagoon-based fish (*khetakheluva*, nicknamed '100 bones' and is a delicacy in itself) and a variety of yam (*lupilakum* [*Dioscorea esculenta*], yet another local preference). The cultural imagery is such that both originate from opposing ecological habitats, former being a mariner and latter, terrestrial – land resources pitched against the marine. Lyrics of the ditty go on to provocatively suggest that when a roasted *lupilakum* yam is eaten together with a freshly grilled *khetakheluva* fish, result is a real treat! Meaning, exchange of terrestrial goods with marine products is a natural fit with the potential to establish enduring relations. This exchange nexus of mainly fish for yams between the fishermen and the yam cultivators has the elementary features of *gimwala* and *kula* (i.e. exchange goods between hands) but is often referred to as *khokwava* and *vava* for barter, and/or *wasi* for delayed exchange, Kula-like. This evokes a fundamental ecological exchange construct intended to sustain the Bweyowa (Trobriand) livelihood. Malinowski (1926) captured these activities as well.

Gimwala

Malinowski did not miss the underlying cultural notion concomitant with the respective activities, actions, items, events, and the local meanings and agencies that went with them in various social contexts. Whether it was birth, marriage, death, agricultural or seasonal ritual, the underlying logic and/or principle of *kula* and *gimwala* exchange realms are drawn into the operation to provide the procedural guidance and justify the choice of action by and for the actors. In its most mundane usage *gimwala* is an ordinary word for outright purchase between any two or more people. Often, there are no subsequent issues needed such as to pursue enduring socio-economic relations unless the exchange ended on credit or loan basis (*wasi*). And yet the potential to pursue long lasting relations remain open. Since the potential to expand and continue remains exponentially open, *gimwala* implying direct purchase, and particularly for the Trobriander, must remain the common denominator or an elementary platform for establishing socio-economic relations. The above terms and phrases outlined, fundamentally denote exchanges to merely *establish, reactivate and/or terminate social exchange relations and obligations*.[2] Sadly, however, Malinowski picked up the verb in *gimwali* and stuck with it for publicity instead of the noun *gimwala*. By a good measure notwithstanding, Malinowski's oversight did not detract from the general cultural semantics; only that it did not sound grammatically accurate and thereby hinting at lack of proficiency in the treatment of the subject matter.

As an instance of exchange, *gimwala* manifests itself in a good number of contexts. Direct exchange for marine products with agricultural products, cash and in kind these days is essentially *gimwala* oft-expressed and variously as *khokwava, vava, taraboda, valova*, etc. Hawking one's ware such as marine products, modern store goods, agricultural products such as betel nuts, fruits and yam seeds is variously referred to as *gimwala, vem* or *valova*. Openly enquiring for the purchase of livestock such as pigs, chickens and even dogs is also referred to as *gimwala*. Strategically soliciting and persuading in one's favor with prized gifts of fish, animals, betelnuts and food for rights to land use, ownership including residential is technically referred to as *pokhala* but is essentially, *gimwala* but can evolve into Kula contexts due to its potential for continued negotiations. Returning marital gifts (*pepeni* and *khatuvila/vilakuri*) of food as one's share (*khaula*) with valuables (*takola*) to the giver of food is essentially *gimwala* between two hands (sources). And yet since, it is intended to ultimately establish a long term relationship between two groups, clans or lineages, it is kula. Even gifts of acknowledgement (*yolova*) to supporters of one's ritual clearance of death-related interdictions (*khemelu, yawari, ninabwela* and *kulututu*) are all predicated upon the fundamental directions of the invisible hands of *gimwala*. This extends to include church tithes (*semakhai, ebwaya daita, boubou*), gifts to sexual partners (*buwa-*) in the form of betelnuts, mutual lunches and dinners, dress fineries and most notoriously cash. So, all these various expressions of exchange between the parties involved are indeed manifestations of the underlying cultural notion and/or principles of *gimwala*. This is the nub of the argument.

Kula

The famous *Kula* trade laboriously described in the *Argonauts of the Western Pacific* (1922), is indeed an extension of the *gimwala modus operandi*. Again, Malinowski did not completely miss the underlying framework, so to speak, only that he and a few others that followed most probably got carried away with the *scale and details* of *kula* operations as a cultural institution. As a term, and on an isolated instance, *kula* was sadly and casually misinterpreted by Annette Weiner (1976) as 'you go'. This is an unrelated meaning of the word *kula* as a verb and should never have been part of the discourse on exchange matters. This seemingly innocuous mistake is quite similar to Malinowski's *gimwali*, and like any English speaker that cares much about the subtleties and competence with grammatical rules, it is similarly irksome to the Bweyowa speakers, Trobriand Islanders, with regard to misapplication of terms. *Kula,* as described by Malinowski (1922), is basically the art of wooing, initiating and sustaining the relationship with partners by persistently placing the partner in a credit-based and competitive relationship – the art of outwitting the other 'hoodwinking' (*wabuwabu*) including. That relationship has the potential to grow exponentially and/or terminated largely due to positive actions and/or negative inactions. *Kula* activities characteristically but not exclusively, cover wider areas including across the seas. Aside from the rituals involved that tend to arrest or manage the various emotions emanating from *kula* involvement, *kula* is basically *gimwala* – give and take. What sets it apart from the elementary dictates is again the scale of operation and the details involved. *Kula* is variously labelled as *Kun, Kune, Une* and the like from the neighboring language groups within the Massim cultural area[3] (Fortune 1932, Young 1971, 1983a & 1985, Damon 1983, Macintyre 1983a, 1983b, Lepowsky 1993, Kuehling 2005, to name a few). It is fundamentally the same form of operation including the seemingly isolated Rossel Island *Ndap* system (Liep 1983).

The much appreciated sizeable *corpus* on *Kula* exchange within the Massim literature amassed thus far seemed to have generally impressed us that there is a co-existing or parallel structural *internal and external system of Kula*. I do not necessarily share such a view as I am fully aware that *gimwala* and *kula* are the one and same operation guided by the same principles of exchange, within or without the person or group, internal or external. What differed is, and again, the scale and details of the exchange operations. The variety of exchange approaches that avail themselves are merely options for the actors to choose from in order to *initiate and justify their intentions to create, sustain and/or terminate social relations*. As indeed, any form of exchange of goods and services manifest these intentions between various individuals and groups. Opposites and even complementarities as potential partners *attract, stick and part* as may be needed. *Gimwala* and *Kula* provide the rationale and space for all three possible conditions.

Gimwala and *Kula* in the Contemporary Condition: Cultural Appropriation by Christian Churches and State Institutions

Sitting around the ambience of his feet, the chief's aura of authority, and under his rather untidy front porch with his other relatives and his senior wife in December 2021 and in May 2022, Paramount Chief Pulayasi Daniel (*GuyolaKilivila – Chief of Kilivila*) and I reflected and pondered over the various changes that have unfolded before us, besetting the Trobriand culture. Malinowski's time and his world renowned documentation in the Trobriands became the benchmark period, including works of fellow anthropologists that followed further augmented the discussion. We noted on one hand, the changing and somewhat slipping circumstances surrounding the power, authority and aura of Tabalu chiefs,[4] their henchmen the sorcerers from afar, and on the other, the emerging opportunities with leadership roles for the young Western-educated non-Tabalu Trobriand men and women along the platforms of Christian churches and Papua New Guinea's (PNG) modern state agencies. Among and within the various strands of changes, there was this apparent appropriation of *Gimwala* and *Kula* principles and their manifestations as opportunities for growth in social status. This view is shared by a few educated elites in urban areas of PNG, and a few notable elders back home too. 'A few' because not all contemporary elite, and village elders including are particularly adept in realizing and articulating such observations. And this is not unique to the Trobriand Islands people, surely.

As the world has come to learn over the years from, among others, Malinowski's works that the Paramount chief of the Trobriand Islands (i.e. *GuyolaKilivila*), has a culturally sanctioned office that has an unrivalled monopoly in maneuvering the islands' resources to itself, and principally through marriage. The strategy ultimately sustains the political office of the paramount chief. Affines or in-laws, as in-marrying production units, are immediately turned into annual suppliers of yam food to the chief's domain. In return, the chief guarantees political protection and related perks and privileges for the in-laws. The exchange relationship between the chief's domain and his in-laws is fundamentally premised upon the principles of *gimwala*: give and take. There is nothing odd about it only that the ritual details involved and the scale of operations are typically ceremonious and extravagant.

Gifts to Heaven[5]: *Gimwala and Kula*

Chief Pulayasi and I both agreed that the traditional strategic nexus of exchange between the chief and his in-laws and subjects has since shifted towards the church domain: the ministers of church, pastors, deacons and 'elders' behaving like chiefs of old. Typically, contemporary church leaders and elders are men and women that dropped out of the state-sanctioned schooling system at various stages between grades 6, 8, 10, 12 and various tertiary levels of skills training. Many of them are literate in English and culturally adept, which qualifies them to claim leadership in the church hierarchy. Since the Christian Bible verses, aside from interpretations, are generally easy to grasp, a lot of these young leaders very quickly gain ascendancy in status within the church hierarchy by demonstrating proficiency with the biblical verses; far more than their application in real life, one dare say.

Church[6] leaders have a direct relationship with members of their congregation that ensures direct control and authority over their lives. Like the state, the congregation is taxed in what is loosely referred to as 'tithes to God', *semakhai*. Tithes come in the form of food crops, animals, labour and cash. Tithes prestation has quickly embedded itself within the hierarchical structure and status of the community such that lineage and residential groups and individuals compete in outdoing each other. After a month or more of fundraising, groups generate as much as K30,000 (about $10,000 USD) which is often way above their own ability to even sustain their own households. Congregation member's weekly family schedule is even heavily appropriated by the churches whereby 3–5 days of an average person's week is taken up by church fellowship rituals and pastoral activities. This appears burdensome enough and must have impact on the states of prosperity and/ or lack of it for most of the congregation families.

Given the *dialectics of the relationship between the church leaders on one hand, and the ordinary congregation members*, on the other, it is not surprising that annually and even monthly too, church leaders are feasted with the best and most foods during synod meetings, built with the best modernized and biggest shelters, issued with vehicles, motor powered boats, bicycles and untaxed and unaccounted for emoluments. At the end of each synod meeting or tithe prestation ceremonies, church leaders are lavishly gifted with animals and prestigious food crops even invoking the cultural contexts of gifting such as *pemkwala*.[7] In the Trobriand parlance, the church leaders have become the *guyau* (chiefs) on earth while serving the Christian God. Using the higher position of being a leader in the church, they would orchestrate the time and resources of the congregation in order to receive prized material gifts including cash. In return, the church leaders do not of course assure the congregation a place in heaven rather promote the good name of the congregation as great servants of the church and therefore serving the will of Christian God. Yet another ingenious instance of playing *gimwala* and *kula* within the Christian religious contexts. This, I argue is an observed dimensional shift in Christian church adaptation to sustain its activities not by individual faith along the church beliefs rather by strategically and deliberately appropriating cultural notions and contexts. In here, it is *Gimwala* and *Kula* yet again, providing the space and rationale for the socio-economic exchange dialogue between Christian church leaders and their congregation members. These are conspicuously observed during lavish feasting occasioned by the opening (*ulemwa*) and/or anointment (*bulami*) of a new or renovated chapel, farewell and welcome feasts for new church ministers and pastors to parish. Admittedly, cultural appropriation of *Gimwala* and *Kula* concepts subtly manifest themselves in a variety of ways amongst United Church, Catholic, Seventh Day Adventist and the evangelist-oriented Pentecostal church congregations that exist on the islands. To further lend support to the observations, local politicians are often the principal sponsors of such lavish feasting, followed by urban-based Trobriand Islanders staking themselves as emerging young leaders with communal roles and responsibilities.

National General Elections: Gimwala and Kula Again[8]

What has been described above can be similarly observed in the features of a good number of modern state institutions as well. Particularly in the way leaders as bureaucrats and politicians behave towards the masses in their respective communities and villages. Most palpably however has to do with the politicians and no more than during the general elections. Regardless on the level of elections conducted, starting from the wards through to the national level, the polarized behavior of the candidates as intending leaders, and the voters on the other remain the same.

Papua New Guinea's national general election seasons are a coveted platform growing with much popularity among young aspiring leaders. By far, most of such candidates are adequately educated and skilled professionals in various trades. These are teachers, office managers, medical doctors, lawyers, accountants, entrepreneurs, academics and church clergymen of today. Aside from rural-based business entrepreneurs, very few are village-based traditional leaders. A particular candidate for instance was a policeman but hails from the chiefly clan and has had three attempts so far in three separate elections but alas without success.

The national and district elections occur once in every five years and the election system adopted is said to be democratic insofar as it is predicated on the *number game*. Victory is assured for one with the greater following (voters), and therefore greater score among other candidates. In other words, majority has voted for the leader and is therefore democratic. In this instance, each voter has three choices for a seat placed in the order of preferences. And that candidates are vaguely allowed a few weeks of 'awareness' or, general introduction to the voters prior to the issue of writs. This is followed by some four weeks of campaign. In the previous year's (2022) general election for the Kiriwina-Goodenough electorate, and involving the Trobriand voters, only five of the 18 candidates that contested actively campaigned and generated awareness on election related issues. The rest including the incumbent just did not see the need to openly campaign and seemingly 'waste meagre resources' when one could quietly dish out cash (*gimwala*) at critical moments particularly during the voting and counting periods. The campaigns typically involved feasting, dishing out packaged store goods such as rice and sugar, cash, providing school fee subsidy and medical transportation assistance to potential voters that bothered to ask for help (i.e. *Kula*). Most audaciously, and like other seasoned and incumbent members in other seats elsewhere in the country, some strategically used or abused their office positions to handpick provincial government officers as election managers and officials to take charge of (and manipulate) the final lap of the election – counting and tallying of votes and the authority to declare winners in the face of losses. In so doing, favors were exchanged between leaders and election managers much to the disgust of most voters. This is a combination of *gimwala* and *kula* behavioral characteristics at work.

Voters even explicitly declared that they were only 'playing games'. "*Khadokhesala mamwasawasi!*" ('We think we are just having fun!') The game is about gambling (*gimwala* and *kula*) one's opportunities. Thus, 'if you want my vote well, you might as well pay for it'. On the other hand, candidates go into great lengths promising voters with goods and services well beyond their own abilities to procure. Typically, this turns out as blatant hollow lies. This, I argue is a typical wooing *kula* strategy called *wabuwabu* or *wabu*, which is merely lying to persuade and/or dissuade one's mind. Moral considerations are usually out of the question hence, such lies may be deemed heroic for having the ability to outdo a rival, for instance. It is therefore not necessarily unethical to do so, and again much to the disgust of those on the losing end. This is *kula* in the contemporary world of general elections in Papua New Guinea.

Over time therefore, candidates and leaders have become very much aware of this elementary requirement within the state-sanctioned election process and consequently aim to *purchase, stock up and protect these numbers* – the coveted ballot votes. It is the numbers that matter, and the protection of ballot papers, therefore. The methods of purchasing, stocking up and protecting these numbers vary but all agree at the point on *exchanging goods, services and cash for votes*. This is essentially *gimwala* and *kula* in the full sense of the words. Because the election system is predicated on the *number game*, it became only logical and easy for the Trobriand candidate to purchase votes by invoking the *gimwala* and *kula modus operandi*. In other words, if the principles of *gimwala* and *kula* are premised upon the principles of reciprocity, then they have essentially redefined the aims and goals of Papua New Guinea's Preferential Election voting process which nonetheless is said to be based on the protection and promotion of individual rights and choices – the essence of democracy. Election candidates, through the appeal of *gimwala* and *kula* principles, have redefined and reframed perhaps the intended meaning on the basic rights of individual voters by entering into a dialogical socio-economic exchange relationship. Arguably, the intended meaning of freedom of choice meant to be exercised in the state-sanctioned Preferential Voting process has been blatantly appropriated and undermined on one hand, but somewhat enriched on the other, by the *gimwala* and *kula* cultural constructs. It is therefore of little wonder that both the candidates, as modern leaders, and the voters, as ordinary Trobrianders have no hesitation in invoking the principles of *gimwala* and *kula* in order to enrich and enhance economic opportunities and in turn grow social relations. The received notion of democracy for individual rights is apparently undermined and set aside by the overwhelming and mutative presence of *gimwala* and *kula*.

Conclusion

Unlike the time of Nicholas Miklouho-Maclay (1871–1883) among the Bongu and Gorendu villagers of Rai coast, Madang,[9] although in another part of Papua New Guinea, Malinowski's (1915–1918) time of fieldwork in the Trobriands had the presence of seemingly marooned capitalist traders, Christian missionaries and the colonial government authority effectively in place. These arms of authority co-existed alongside of the traditional Bweyowa chiefly (*Gweguya*) system of power and authority. *Gimwala* and *Kula* have been well embedded in the customary practices of the Trobriand people as principles of exchange and customarily manifest themselves in various cultural contexts: births, marriages, deaths and related exchange ceremonies and rituals.

A century later, the principles and rationale of *Gimwala* and *Kula* as described by Malinowski are palpably alive and well. Just as before, they persistently remain the most efficient and effective, and audaciously gaining popularity with telling ascendancy by defining approaches in negotiating contemporary leadership roles, management and disbursement of resources. Viewed across time, there is an observed shift in dimension mainly in relation to methods used and details involved. Overall, however their application has remained viably and meaningfully active.

Although a non-Trobriander and yet a renowned ethnographer, Malinowski may be commended for recognizing the cultural meanings of *Gimwala* and *Kula* as vital cultural constructs enabling socio-economic relationships that have stood the test of time. He would certainly stand tall among the few Kula greats that are known within the many cycles of exchange in the Massim cultural area. Malinowski has shown that he understood the essentials of *Gimwala* and *Kula*, and their appropriate uses in the various cultural contexts. And the fact that they are adaptable into today's world of exchanges is a further vindication of Malinowski's ability to recognize the essential cultural constructs of the Bweyowa people. *Gimwala* and *Kula* are indeed the common denominators of Massim reciprocity.

Notes

1. Jarillo (2021: 70) named Bomkarimapu but not Suyabokheta perhaps because he was not aware of the latter name. Both are however of the same style only named differently.
2. Lepani (2012) discusses the various contexts in which Trobriand sexuality is expressed and through exchanges of gifts and the risks involved amidst rising health issues posed by HIV, for instance.
3. Massim Cultural Area geographically refers to the eastern tip region of Papua New Guinea. This roughly represents the Kula trade region as depicted on maps produced since Malinowski's time. Aside from the Kula trade, the people themselves share much cultural affinity including languages, although there are about 50 different languages that have been recognized to have been spoken in the area (see Young 1983b). Politically, the same cultural area is referred to as the Milne Bay Province within the modern day state of Papua New Guinea.
4. Trobriand Islands, as Malinowski (1922) is socially a hierarchical society made of some ruling groups at the top usually referred to as chiefs or of chiefly status (*guyau* as singular, and *gumgweguya* as a class/social category). The current, and since Malinowski's time, ruling group is named Tabalu (see also Mosko 2017).
5. Gregory (1980, 1982) and among a few others more have shown much on the way Melanesians exploit man-God relations through gifts of exchange. And Mosko (2017) similarly demonstrated how Trobrianders maintain kinship relations with the spirits (Baloma) of the deceased kin through magic and other rituals.
6. There are four main Christian church denominations that coexist in the Trobriand Islands. The United Church, initially named as the Wesleyan, which arrived in the 1890s, followed by the Catholic church that arrived in the 1930s, the Seventh Day Adventists that came after the World War II, and the various sects of the Pentecostal groups that only proliferated in the 2000s. By far, the United church has the greater following although the Catholic which appeared to be more progressive in providing a well-structured educational support, closely follows.
7. As in Kula, *pemkwala* gifts in effect challenges the recipient to reciprocate in the near feature. The gifts are usually of prized long yams and/or whole pigs. It is observed however, that the church recipients consistently fail to reciprocate despite the clear invocation of the term during presentation by congregation members. It is likely that the giver intends to create an exchange relationship whereas the recipient sees such cultural uses as inappropriate overtones to church beliefs and practices; and yet ironically pick up the gifts of food and walk off nonchalantly.
8. digim'Rina (2010) provides a fairly comprehensive discussion on the way national elections were conducted based on his 2007 candidature experience. *Gimwala* and *kula* contexts and tactics were clearly displayed then.
9. See Mikloucho-Maclay, Nikolai Nikolaevich. 1975. *New Guinea diaries 1871–1883*. Translated by C. L. Sentinella, Madang, PNG: Kristen Press for instance.

References

Damon, Frederick. 1983. "What moves the Kula: Opening and closing gifts on Woodlark Island." In J.W. Leach and E. Leach (eds.), *The Kula: New perspectives on Massim Exchange*, pp. 309–342. Cambridge: Cambridge University Press.

digim'Rina, linus silipolaKhapulapola. 2010. An electoral miscarriage: Limited Preferential Voting and cultural interpretations in Papua New Guinea. The DEPTH project (2015 issue). University of California, Sacramento.

Fortune, Reo. 1932. *Sorcerers of Dobu: The social anthropology of Dobu Islanders of the Western Pacific.* London: Routledge.
Gregory, Chris. 1980. "Gifts to men and gifts to God: gift exchange and capital accumulation in contemporary Papua." *Man* 15: 626–652.
———. 1982. *Gifts and commodities.* London: Academic Press.
Jarillo, Sergio. (ed.) 2021. *Trobriand Tales, Kwanebuyee Kilivila: Folktales and mythical stories from the Trobriand Islands of Papua New Guinea, collected by Jerry W. Leach and held at the National Anthropological Archives, Smithsonian Institution.* Washington, DC: Smithsonian Institution Scholarly Press.
Kuehling, Susanne. 2005. *Dobu: Ethics of exchange on a Massim Island, Papua New Guinea.* Honolulu: University of Hawaii Press.
Leach, Jerry. 1983. "Trobriand territorial categories and the problem of who is not in the *kula*." In J.W. Leach and E. Leach (eds.), *The Kula: New perspectives in Massim Exchange,* pp. 121–146. Cambridge. Cambridge University Press.
Lepani, Katherine. 2012. *Islands of love, islands of risk: Culture and HIV in the Trobriand Islands.* Nashville: Vanderbilt University Press.
Lepowsky, Maria. 1993. *Fruit of the motherland: Gender in an egalitarian society.* New York: Columbia University Press.
Liep, John. 1983. "Ranked exchange on Rossel Island." In J.W. Leach and E. Leach (eds.), *The Kula: New perspectives on Massim Exchange,* pp. 503–525. Cambridge: Cambridge University Press.
Macintyre, Martha. 1983a. Changing paths: An historical ethnography of the traders of Tubetube. PhD thesis. Canberra: Australian National University.
———. 1983b. "Kune on Tubetube and in the Bwanabwana region of the southern Massim." In J.W. Leach and E. Leach (eds.), *The Kula: New perspectives in Massim Exchange,* pp. 369–379. Cambridge: Cambridge University Press.
Malinowski, Bronisław. 1922. *Argonauts of the Western Pacific. An account of native enterprise and adventure in the Archipelagoes of Melanesian New Guinea.* London: Routledge & Kegan Paul.
———. 1926. *Crime and custom in savage society.* London: Routledge.
Mikloucho-Maclay, Nikolai Nikolaevich. 1975. *New Guinea diaries 1871–1883.* Translated by C. L. Sentinella, Madang, PNG: Kristen Press.
Mosko, Mark. 2017. *Ways of Baloma: Rethinking magic and kinship from the Trobriands.* Chicago, IL: HAU Books.
Weiner, Annette. 1976. *Women of value, men of renown: New perspectives on Trobriand exchange.* Austin: University of Texas Press.
———. 1983. "'A world of made is not a world of born.": Doing Kula in Kiriwina.' In J.W. Leach and E. Leach (eds.), *The Kula: New perspectives on Massim Exchange*, pp. 147–170. Cambridge: Cambridge University Press.
Young, Michael. 1971. *Fighting with food: Leadership, values and social control in a Massim society.* Cambridge: Cambridge University Press.
———. 1983a. *Magicians of Manumanua: Living myth in Kalauna.* Berkeley: University of California Press.
———. 1983b. "The Massim: An introduction." *The Journal of Pacific History* 18(2): 74–95.
———. 1985. "On refusing gifts: aspects of ceremonial exchange in Kalauna." In D. Barwick, J. Beckett and M. Reay (eds.), *Metaphors of interpretation,* pp. 95–112. Rushcutters Bay: Australian National University.

13 What If We Had Followed Malinowski Instead of Staying on the Trobriand Islands? Notes on the Anthropological Multiverse

Marta Songin-Mokrzan

The many-worlds interpretation of quantum mechanics, proposed by Hugh Everett III, posits that everything that could potentially happen is actually happening in separate branches of reality. In this view, the universe continuously splits into alternate histories, giving rise to a multitude of parallel worlds, rather than a single one. The branching occurs as a fundamental consequence of quantum superposition, where particles that exist in multiple states simultaneously give rise to distinct realities, each unfolding with its unique outcome (Greene 2011).

In this perspective, the world we inhabit is just one among numerous potential realms. The totality of these potentialities finds expression across an infinite number of parallel branches in the universe. Consequently, within this framework, one can envision the existence of myriad worlds where the very definition of anthropology takes distinct forms, contingent upon the choices we, as individuals and societies, make. Consider, for a moment, that in some alternate realms, anthropology may unfold with entirely dissimilar principles and aims, shaping its identity and purpose uniquely. In stark contrast, there could even exist a world where the discipline of anthropology has yet to emerge, or where the endeavour to study humanity in this particular manner has not materialized. Whether one views the multiverse theory as plausible or considers it a domain of science fiction, it helps to highlight the fact that the essence of anthropology, as we know it, is fundamentally a result of specific choices and decisions undertaken by its practitioners throughout its history. It is a product of the intellectual and methodological paths we follow, the questions we pose and find important, and the themes we explore.

In the chapter, I draw a parallel between the concept of the many-worlds theory and the anthropological identity practices, which consists of construction and navigation of multiple disciplinary accounts of what anthropology is, could or ought to be. These narratives, which encompass making sense of the past, interpreting the present, and envisioning future, play a significant role in shaping the perception of the anthropological realm. They are interpretations that weave together diverse events into coherent narratives, and when embraced by the interpretative community, they become pathways for conceptualizing anthropology and what it means to be an anthropologist.

To delve into the topic, I focus on the way Bronisław Malinowski, who is considered along with Radcliffe-Brown, a father of modern social anthropology

DOI: 10.4324/9781003449768-19

is portrayed and remembered within the discipline and how this image is incorporated within the broader narrative of anthropological history and scholarship. Through an analysis of the case of Malinowski, I aim to reflect on certain tendencies that exist in the processes of knowledge production and acquisition within the discipline. My focus will solely be on written forms, excluding other modes of teaching and learning experience. I believe that these written forms, such as textbooks provide valuable guidance on what is eventually remembered and integrated into the imaginative landscape of the discipline's identity.

Identity Practices within Anthropology

My primary focus is on what I term "core anthropological identity." This concept pertains to the fundamental body of knowledge widely embraced and shared within the global community of professional anthropologists. It serves as the cornerstone of our discipline and is particularly prominently featured in textbooks that outline the fundamental aspects and development of anthropology, encompassing critical ideas, research methodologies, theoretical frameworks, and its history. It is important to emphasize that possessing this core understanding does not automatically confer professional status. Instead, it signifies that those aspiring to be recognized as anthropologists must establish a solid foundation in this knowledge. Therefore, while not everyone with this background may choose to pursue a career as an anthropologist, the absence of it undeniably disqualifies one from attaining that recognition.

In the chapter, I refrain from presenting an exhaustive list of the specific components that comprise the canon of anthropological knowledge. However, even without an in-depth examination, it is challenging to dispute that the recognition of the development of anthropological theory from evolutionism through functionalism and structuralism to postmodernism, as well as concepts like otherness and relativism, or ideas such as "the gift" by Marcel Mauss, to name just a few, are not crucial building blocks. It would also be particularly difficult to imagine a professional anthropologist who is not aware of Bronisław Malinowski's research on the Trobriand Islands or the significance of the method of participant observation.

As mentioned earlier, my primary concern is not to pinpoint the precise elements that constitute the foundational identity of contemporary anthropologists. Instead, my focus is on exploring the mechanics of how this identity is constructed. The canon of anthropology is not static; it undergoes reconstruction over time in response to the ever-changing landscape of our field and the broader world. For instance, the perception of anthropology today significantly differs from that in the early 20th century. However, the mechanisms for organizing and presenting it as the fundamental underpinning of anthropology remain consistent. This consistency is mainly due to the institutionalization of anthropology as an academic discipline, which comes with specific ways of acquiring and disseminating knowledge within the academic realm. As a result, my explorations serve as an invitation to investigate how, as an interpretational community, we shape our core anthropological identity. Taking the work of Bronisław Malinowski as an example, my focus is not on defining the constituents of this knowledge, but rather on understanding the methods by which it is constructed and functions.

Before delving into this topic, however, there is a crucial dimension that deserves further consideration. Specifically, it is essential to delve into how anthropologists expand their core knowledge and construct their individual professional identities in greater detail.

As previously mentioned, proficiency in the anthropological canon does not inherently confer professional status upon someone within the field of anthropology. It serves as a foundation for further exploration and the continual voyage of individuals who aspire to make contributions to the field. Therefore, beyond the fundamental grasp that establishes the shared core of anthropological identity, individuals engage in a dynamic process of expanding their understanding of the discipline and its specificity as they progress in their anthropological journey. This continuous learning experience contributes to the development of their professional selves, which is an ongoing endeavour involving the absorption of various types of information to varying degrees, as well as the refinement of their analytical and methodological skills. It is worth highlighting that the learning experience is always selective, and the knowledge we accumulate depends on the choices we make, the topics we prioritize, and the sources we engage with. As anthropologists navigate through the intricate web of available information, they shape their unique professional identities, each influenced by personal backgrounds, interests, research experiences, and academic trajectories.

The anthropological quest of each individual also represents one of the many potential realities that materialize through various experiences and situations we encounter. It forms a complex network of intersections, both opening opportunities for the development of certain skills and knowledge and simultaneously closing off other paths. The course of unfolding in each individual's academic journey relies on multiple decisions and choices, including their research directions, methodological approaches, and the themes they wish to explore throughout their professional careers.

The country in which one has the prospects to study, along with its unique historical and political context that influences and shapes local anthropology, and the department's distinct schools and traditions,[1] collectively play a pivotal role in shaping the possibilities encountered. Additionally, both lecturers and students serve as catalysts for further exploration of specific topics, the relegation of others, the acceptance or rejection of various ideas, and the adoption or dismissal of methodological frameworks. Therefore, every anthropologist's journey represents a unique realization of numerous potential outcomes, influenced by various elements, including the individual's upbringing and predispositions, the characteristics of local anthropological traditions, the mentors and fellow students they interact with, the books they study and those they overlook, and even unexpected encounters (such as forming connections with colleagues at a conference that lead to collaborative research). Each distinctive trajectory shapes a unique anthropological path within the multiverse of potential unfoldings, contributing to the formation of an individual's identity, which is not static but in constant flux.

This diversity within the anthropological field results in each of us bringing our unique blend of knowledge and expertise to the table.[2] Furthermore, the distinctive trajectories of local anthropological schools significantly shape our expertise. Consequently, researchers in different countries may have varying levels of understanding when it comes to specific themes or threads within anthropology. For instance, the importance and scope of the decolonization theme might differ between British and Polish anthropologists due to the distinct political contexts and historical circumstances in which these traditions have evolved.

To reiterate, each anthropologist brings their unique set of skills and expertise to the field, contributing to a collective pool of knowledge within the research community. Researchers also share some areas of expertise with their colleagues to varying degrees. As previously mentioned, we also possess a base of information, typically acquired during our early education, which forms the core of our anthropological identity. Understanding the formation and development of this knowledge, which can serve as a heuristic model, providing insights into the development of other anthropological identities characterized by different levels of generality, such as national traditions, academic departments, schools of thought, specializations, and more, is the principal focus of the forthcoming sections of this chapter.

The Trobriand Islands: A Cornerstone of Anthropological Imaginary

Without delving into the details of the theories, concepts, and historical events that populate our core anthropological imaginary, it is undeniable that one of its cornerstones for multiple generations of researchers is Bronisław Malinowski's work on the Trobriand Islands, popularized with the publication of *Argonauts of the Western Pacific* (2002 [1922]), which, by referring to multiverse theory, can be recognized as one of the critical junctures in the field. This transformative book reshaped the identity of anthropology by shifting the discipline from a speculative and armchair evolutionary approach to an empirical endeavour with meticulous methodology, setting it apart from mere travel narratives. The book itself, along with the research model it presented, served as a blueprint for aspiring anthropologists eager not only to follow in Malinowski's footsteps but, more importantly, to develop into professionals in the acquisition of knowledge about indigenous societies. It became a guiding framework for understanding what it truly means to be an anthropologist. And although functionalist interpretation has been subject to scrutiny over time, the model of empirical research that emphasizes the anthropologist's presence in the field has remained the cornerstone of anthropological identity.

It can even be stated that our anthropological identity revolves around the idea of participant observation.[3] It is fieldwork that makes anthropology a distinct discipline, setting it apart from other academic pursuits and travel accounts. And although Malinowski neither invented it nor was its only practitioner, it is his image sitting among the natives that remains iconic and serves as a point of reference for all kinds of research endeavours undertaken within the discipline. The name of Malinowski stands as a synecdoche for fieldwork, and although his academic exploration extends far beyond his Trobriand journey, it remains deeply ingrained within the majority of the anthropological community as his enduring legacy. This is not to suggest that many anthropologists do not explore other facets of his work; however, these aspects do not form the core of anthropological knowledge.

There are numerous accounts explaining why Melanesian research gained such popularity. George W. Stocking suggests, for instance, that it was partly coincidental (1992: 28) and partly due to his entrepreneurial skills, institutional circumstances, and the ability of Malinowski to transform "a research strategy into a methodological myth" (1992: 32). Stocking, in his detailed account dedicated to the establishment of ethnographic fieldwork as a method of social anthropology in Great Britain, describes a large group of scholars who were engaged in conducting this type of research before the outbreak of World War I.[4] However, most of them faced various challenges and difficulties during their expeditions, which impacted their academic success. Some encountered personal issues, while others took up positions outside academia or in different countries. Consequently, despite their contributions to anthropology, only a few, such as Alfred Radcliffe-Brown and Bronisław Malinowski, managed to establish themselves in British academic life (1992: 28) and eventually within the collective imaginary of the anthropological community.

Stocking emphasizes that Malinowski effectively appropriated shared experiences and transformed them into concrete narratives, validating not only his own fieldwork but also contributing to the validation of modern anthropology. It was his ambition and entrepreneurial talent, as well as his charisma, that made him "a spokesman for a methodological revolution" in both anthropology and non-anthropological academic and intellectual circles. What is more, the success of his research model also stems from the fact that many future social anthropologists in the British sphere served as apprentices under Malinowski. Although some of them later found their theoretical inspiration in Radcliffe-Brown, "they continued to regard Malinowski as the archetypical fieldworker" (1992: 57–58).

It is important to note that while this empirical approach was embraced by the majority of researchers, from the standpoint of multiverse theory, it was just one of the possible directions in the discipline's development. As highlighted by Stocking, it was due to a combination of various circumstances that fieldwork, particularly in the form of "own, direct observation" proposed by Malinowski, became the bedrock of ethnographic practice. As the journey through the anthropological multiverse continues, the recognition emerges that at these numerous juncture points, there exist other potential paths for both personal and disciplinary development, and that the dominance of Malinowski in our collective imagination as an intrepid explorer of the Trobriand Islands was just one of these possibilities.

It is also worth to emphasize, that our core anthropological knowledge is fragmented, containing only the essence of what we consider constitutive of our identity as anthropologists. Consequently, it omits certain fragments from anthropological history that may seem redundant in this context. This selectivity means that it does not encompass all facts but includes only what we deem vital for shaping our identities. This is a primary reason why every anthropologist is familiar with *Argonauts of the Western Pacific* but may not be as well-versed in *Baloma*.

We have chosen ethnographic fieldwork as the pillar of modern anthropology and Bronisław Malinowski's work has provided the most convincing narrative that has captivated the anthropological imagination and, most importantly, paved the way for the true professionalization of anthropology, firmly anchoring the discipline in the academic realm. However, framing Malinowski predominantly within the context of his Melanesian research carries notable implications. It moulds our anthropological perspective and can guide our interpretation of his contributions, crafting a distinct portrayal of his achievements. This depiction may not offer a comprehensive or entirely accurate representation unless we complement it with Malinowski's other works and accomplishments.

My Personal Journey: An Unexpected Encounter

The success of the Trobriand research has caused Bronisław Malinowski to occupy a prominent position in the majority of publications conveying anthropological knowledge, particularly regarding its history, methodological development, and foundational concepts. He is recognized as one of the key figures in the establishment of social anthropology as a modern discipline. It is commonly emphasized that his contributions include pioneering participant observation, advocating for extensive fieldwork research, and fervently promoting functionalism. This enduring image of Malinowski, steadfastly passed down from one generation to another, prevails in the collective memory of the anthropological community.

The perception of this portrayal persisted so vividly in my mind during my years as a student that when I began working on my doctoral thesis, which focused on the concept of engagement in anthropology, I was very much surprised to discover that Malinowski, whom I had previously regarded as a rather traditional, modernist anthropologist, had left a substantial body of writings where he expounded on practical anthropology and the responsibilities of social researchers.

As I argued elsewhere (2017), affects can serve as valuable cognitive tools and guide us towards a deeper understanding of cultural assumptions. They often manifest as subjects' reactions to the disruption of social consensus, the violation or questioning of norms, and non-standard behaviours that deviate from the prevailing values, or principles within a given community (as also discussed by Malinowski in the introduction to *Argonauts*). In this instance, the puzzlement connected to the discovery of Malinowski's writings condemning war and supporting practical anthropology also served as an alarming indication of the way my individual anthropological trajectory was shaped during my formative years as a student. And it did not diverge much from the path followed by my colleagues at that time. In the debates that took place in Poland in the first years of the 21st century, which were dominated by discussions around the crisis of authority and representation, in accordance with the interpretation that we collectively referred to as postmodernist, he was portrayed as a classic anthropologist, representing a realist mode of writing. He was seen as a researcher who contributed to reinforcing the image of natives as radical others, living in coherent groups, isolated from the influence of the outside world, and considered ahistorical.

The discovery of Malinowski's dedication to practical anthropology was a revelatory moment that prompted me to reflect more deeply on the construction of knowledge and anthropological identity in our discipline on many different levels. It highlighted the tendency to selectively accumulate and remember certain fragments of our anthropological heritage, which then form the core of anthropological common sense and are often resistant to revision (until circumstances change, than we are less hesitant to review and redefine the past). While there are experts who diligently explore overlooked writings, their work, for the most part, exists as a parallel discourse that does not disrupt the prevailing imaginary of discipline's core identity. Occasionally, we may unearth forgotten passages from the works of long-gone predecessors that anticipate and address problems that only gained urgency decades later (as is the case with Malinowski's writings).[5] However, these revelations tend to be short-lived anomalies that pose no significant threat to the overarching body of knowledge shared by anthropologists. If we take, for example, Derek Freeman's work (1983) and consider to what extent it challenged the prevailing image of Samoans created by Margaret Mead (1928), we discover that the anthropological discussion around this publication is primarily centred on the controversy surrounding the undermining of Mead's authority and Freeman's questionable behaviour, rather than on the Samoans themselves (Stocking 2010: 160–163).

"The unmaking of anthropological myth" proves to be not an easy task because within the realm of anthropology, certain narratives hold stronger position than others and often escape critical scrutiny. These narratives, treated as black-boxed patches of knowledge, are widely accepted as factual and form the core or imaginary of every anthropologist's perspective and sense of identity. Despite the long-standing recognition of the power of interpretation in shaping our worldviews, there remains a tendency to consider them as indisputable realities.

Beyond the Trobriand Legacy: Reevaluating Malinowski's Contribution to Anthropology

As mentioned earlier, the common portrayal of Bronisław Malinowski's legacy focuses on the groundbreaking status of his Trobriand research. It is often highlighted that the meticulous observations and vivid accounts, presented in several of his monographs following fieldwork have paved the way for a new era of anthropological inquiry. With an emphasis on the significance of participant observation, ethnography, and a holistic understanding of social and cultural phenomena, Malinowski's approach is regarded as one that has profoundly influenced the very foundations of modern anthropology. And it is thanks to the resounding success of *Argonauts of the Western Pacific* that he has primarily been remembered through the prism of his research on the Trobriand Islands.

The textbook image of Malinowski as a functionalist and the inventor of the method of participant observation is further reinforced in numerous publications. It can be argued that the vast majority of anthropological texts dedicated to Malinowski explore his Melanesian research from various angles, clearly showing which aspects of his work are the most vital for the anthropological community. However, as mentioned earlier, this prevailing perception has also had certain consequences. This exclusive emphasis on his Melanesian research can have certain implications and may limit the perspective of his overall contributions, potentially leading to a less nuanced understanding of the full scope of his scholarly endeavours.

In the introductory chapter to the book *Anthropological Locations*, dedicated to the idea of fieldwork in anthropology, Akhil Gupta and James Ferguson argue that the research model introduced by Malinowski contributed to "an active forgetting of conquest and colonialism" and reinforced the belief that the work of an anthropologist does not rely merely on the reconstruction of "the natural state of the primitive" (Gupta, Ferguson 1997: 7) but on direct observation. They claim that it was precisely due to "the Malinowskian dominant orthodoxy" (1997: 19) or "Malinowskian dogma" (1997: 24) that social anthropology became defined as the study of remote societies, portraying them as cohesive, ahistorical units frozen in time. It was not only the model of fieldwork that contributed to perpetuating this but also the functionalist framework with its definition of culture as a well-integrated functioning whole, which appeared particularly apt for studying small communities in geographically limited areas. Gupta and Ferguson also emphasize that the Malinowskian model of ethnography solidified and sanctioned the "radical other" as a subject of anthropological research, specifically "those most Other and most isolated from 'ourselves'" (1997: 8), thereby, for a long time, excluding from the scope of anthropological interest, for example, "Native Americans working in towns" or "Aborigines employed on ranches" (1997: 7).

In my view, this interpretation of Malinowski's contribution to establishing modern anthropology should, however, be accompanied by a certain reservation. Namely, while he undoubtedly played a crucial role in laying the foundation for it, it was not Malinowski himself but rather the interpretational community of anthropologists that reproduced this model of research without significant alterations. This community accepted his approach with minimal hesitation or amendments, solidifying his legacy as a pioneer of participant observation and ethnographic fieldwork. It is noteworthy that Malinowski, in his later work, diverged from this model and delved into entirely different themes and approaches, engaging in discussions that stand in stark contrast to the concerns raised by Gupta and Ferguson. Therefore, as I demonstrate below, there is a certain paradox that must be taken into account: Malinowski himself was not so much a Malinowskian orthodox.

The above, quite popular interpretation of Malinowski's contribution proves valid, only when we narrow our focus to the Melanesian research. However, when we consider the studies he conducted in Africa (1945) or his reflections on war, democracy, justice, and liberty (1944), this image no longer aligns with the previously proposed perception of his legacy. In his later writings, he addressed the transforming world and acknowledged the significance of these changes as factors that would compel anthropologists to reconceptualize their research methods, problems, and the application of anthropological knowledge. Even when reflecting on his earlier journey to Melanesia, he expressed this sentiment in the article *The Rationalization of Anthropology and Administration* from 1930:

> Anthropology, to me at least, was a romantic escape from our overstandardized culture. On the islands of the Pacific, though I was pursued by the products of the Standard Oil Company, weekly editions, cotton goods, cheap detective stories, and the internal combustion engine in the ubiquitous motor launch, I was still able with but little effort to relive and reconstruct a type of human life moulded by the implements of a stone age, pervaded with crude beliefs and surrounded by a wide, uncontaminated, open stretch of nature.
> (1930: 406)

His account of the natives was, therefore, as he admits, not so much an attempt to directly reflect reality but rather an effort to reconstruct the radical other based on ethnographic experience. In my view, during his initial research, Malinowski was primarily guided by the disciplinary expectations. Anthropology was by default a study of "primitive societies." Therefore it was not solely his own choice to concentrate on the Trobrianders, but rather a reflection of the demands imposed by the discipline. In his later writings, Malinowski repeatedly emphasized the importance of anthropologists acknowledging the transforming world. As he aptly points out:

> "Scientific observation can only be directed at what is; and not on what might have been or has been, even if this had vanished but yesterday" (1938a: XI). And also: "The anthropologist is becoming increasingly aware that the study of culture change must become one of his main tasks in field work and theory. The figment of the 'uncontaminated' Native has to be dropped from research in field and study. The cogent reason for this is that the 'uncontaminated' Native does not exist anywhere"
> (1945: 2).

In my view, Malinowski was primarily dedicated to reconstructing anthropology as a truly scientific endeavour, which I will discuss further in the remainder of the chapter. And this can be clearly recognized in the above-quoted sentences. What is particularly noteworthy is that he exhibited a profound receptiveness to the realities of fieldwork. His exceptional openness and sensitivity to the intricacies of the research compelled him to expand the horizons of the methodological framework beyond the confines of the Trobriand Islands. The empirical approach he pursued demanded viewing the world as it was experienced directly, revealing that there were no untouched indigenous communities unaffected by external influences anywhere. His statements also indicate that while his contemporaries were still mastering the model of anthropological research presented in *Argonauts of the Western Pacific*, he had already embarked on a different intellectual journey.

Further Journey

As mentioned earlier, there is an overwhelming tendency to remember the work of Bronisław Malinowski quite selectively, with a primary focus on his research in Melanesia. When we examine the analyses of Malinowski's legacy, both critical and laudatory, presented by highly recognizable scholars, they predominantly centre around various aspects and intricacies of *Argonauts of the Western Pacific*, while his other contributions, such as *Dynamics of Cultural Change*, are often not taken into account[6] (Gupta, Ferguson 1997, Stocking 1992, Geertz 1988, Clifford 1988, Young 1979). This raises the question of what might have transpired if his later work had received the same level of recognition as his expedition to the Trobriand Islands. Would our discipline have taken a different trajectory? How would this affect our anthropological selves? Exploring these questions can provide valuable insights into the anthropological multiverse, which refers to the ways in which the interpretative community constructs the core anthropological identity.

Upon returning to Europe after his long expedition to Melanesia, Malinowski primarily focused on education and writing. In 1921, he resumed teaching at the LSE and immersed himself in academic work. During this period, he published the outcomes of his Trobriand research, notably the monograph *Argonauts of the Western Pacific* which, as widely acknowledged, received significant attention. It is also noteworthy to highlight George Stocking's suggestion that the popularity of Malinowski's research was not solely attributed to the validity of the methodology itself but, as mentioned earlier, also to his entrepreneurial skills and his adeptness in effectively disseminating it among his students (1992: 58). Malinowski taught an entire generation of prominent British anthropologists, including Raymond Firth, Edward Evans-Pritchard, Hortense Powdermaker, Audrey Richards, Isaac Schapera, Meyer Fortes, Edmund Leach, and Siegfried F. Nadel, who played a crucial role in popularizing the new model of ethnographic research.

What is also worth emphasizing is that Malinowski himself did not revisit the Trobriand Islands, either physically or metaphorically. Unlike his extensive fieldwork among the Trobrianders, he did not replicate the same level of engagement with native societies in his later explorations. Although he did return to the field on several occasions to study various indigenous groups, including the Hopi in the United States and the Bemba, Kikuyu, Maragoli, Maasai, and Swazi people in Africa, his subsequent endeavours did not attract the same level of attention as his Melanesian research. As a result, these later explorations remain relatively unknown to the larger anthropological audience.

I will refrain from speculating extensively on the reasons why the interpretative community showed less interest in Malinowski's other works. There could be several factors contributing to this. For instance, he did not publish a monograph that could captivate readers' attention and inspire young ethnographers in the same manner as *Argonauts* and the field monographs written by his students. Additionally, as his research subjects shifted, he was less inclined to replicate the methodology he employed in studying the Trobrianders, as it didn't fully align with the outcomes of his subsequent investigations. Furthermore, the applied anthropology he advocated for failed to achieve success in light of the changing political landscape.

It is not uncommon for the interpretative community to omit certain information about researchers and their publications from what is considered shared knowledge. However, when it comes to constructing anthropological core identity, this mechanism is often overlooked, and delving into its intricacies reveals informative aspects of the processes of knowledge production. In the remainder of the chapter, I offer an alternative perspective on Malinowski's legacy that places less emphasis on his contributions to fieldwork methods and instead highlights some of his later endeavours and intellectual findings. As mentioned earlier, this viewpoint is just one of many possible approaches within the anthropological multiverse, utilizing similar mechanisms as other interpretations. Namely, it places emphasis on certain aspects of Bronisław Malinowski's work while downplaying others.

Within the alternate narrative I am offering here, the central theme running through Malinowski's work is not his commitment to ethnographic research but rather his unwavering dedication to transforming anthropology into a legitimate science. This approach made him particularly receptive to the fieldwork. He demonstrated a remarkable openness and sensitivity towards the actualities of the field, and this attitude forced him to go beyond his research in the Trobriand Islands as it did not correspond with his later experience. In his research in Africa, he did not simply replicate the Trobriand model but instead adopted a more comprehensive methodology, which he described as a bird's-eye view (this approach, although employed for different purposes, was also evident in the work of Marcel Griaule, who studied the African Dogons).

Malinowski summarizes it in a remarkable excerpt from *The Dynamics of Culture Change: An Inquiry into Race Relations in Africa*, he writes: "(…) let us glance at what Africa looks like today. A passenger flying over the inland route of the Imperial Airways can obtain what is almost literally a bird's eye view of the cultural situation" (1945: 9). Later, in this 1.5-page passage, he describes three distinct stages in the development of African communities. As he soars through the air, he observes the transforming cultural landscape: from the humble huts of tribal societies, through the spaces of cultural diffusion, to the Westernized world of Nairobi.

The account is not however merely a picturesque narrative, but a metaphor that later aids Malinowski in introducing the analytical tool he develops in order to explore the process of cultural change. This study refutes the accusations made by contemporary interpreters that Malinowski overlooked the transformative nature of the world as a vital factor in anthropological analysis (see Gupta, Ferguson 1997: 20). It may also pose a challenge to anthropologists who, in their education, were taught to view diffusionism and functionalism as contrasting approaches. Moreover, it is worth highlighting the distinct difference between the all-encompassing gaze he presents in his exploration of African contexts and the participant observation approach he employed in his Melanesian studies. And even though his

Trobriand research model gained significant acclaim during that period, Malinowski emphasized the importance of anthropologists directing their attention not only towards more "radical others" but also, in an innovative manner, expanding the scope of ethnographic interest to encompass other actors present in the field.

"All of them together form as it were a tribe, enlarged and somewhat complicated, but yet sufficiently well integrated for the time being to be studied by the old methods of fieldwork" As he further points out: "the 'detribalized' native must become as much the subject of scientific study as the one who walks about in cowhide or leopard skin; **and that even the white settler, missionary, or administrator is as essentially a part of the modern cultural problem** as the most deeply pigmented African. The anthropologist is now faced with the tragic situation which has often been bewailed in lecture-rooms and in print, even by the present writer. Just as we have reached a certain academic status and developed our methods and theories, our subject-matter threatens to disappear. In some parts of the world it has been wiped out—as in Tasmania, the eastern states of America, and certain islands of the Pacific. **Instead, however, of lamenting the inevitable, we must face the new, more complex and difficult task which history has set before us, the task that is of building new methods and new principles of research in order to reclaim the 'anthropological no-man's-land' and take up the 'new branch of anthropology… the anthropology of the changing native**. This was but a pious wish when expressed by the present writer a few years ago"

(1938a: XIII – emphasis added).

Most likely, due to the resounding success of *Argonauts*, which established a new model for practicing anthropology that every aspiring anthropologist had to adopt, these words from Bronisław Malinowski went largely unnoticed.

Malinowski's studies on cultural change, where he proposed a new perspective and methodology, also prompted him to contemplate the practical value of knowledge and advocate for applied science. Simultaneously, he remained steadfast in his lifelong mission of supporting anthropology as a discipline and striving to enhance its standing in academia and the public domain.

Already in the introduction to *Argonauts of the Western Pacific*, it was of great importance for Malinowski to demonstrate that the method of direct observation is a truly scientific approach for collecting ethnographic data and should be acknowledged as such by the audience. Throughout the chapter, it becomes evident that his underlying goal was to persuade a reader that direct observation, is a legitimate scientific pursuit. For Malinowski science was a point of reference and an esteemed institution within Western society, and he remained fully committed to presenting anthropology as a discipline which on par with such domains as chemistry or biology, relies on firsthand experience rather than speculative considerations.

This commitment to empirical methods and scientific principles also informed his exploration of the changing landscape of Africa. It is from this dedication to empiricism and the pursuit of scientific knowledge that he advocated for the recognition of the importance of anthropology in understanding the transformations experienced by native societies. Likewise, Malinowski's emphasis on the practical application of knowledge serves a similar objective, as it enables the validation of anthropology's scientific worth and the substantiation of anthropological claims and theories.

British applied anthropology advocated by Malinowski was widely criticized in later decades and condemned as a form of collaboration with colonial powers (Willis 1972; Feuchtwang 1975; Onoge 1979; Polgar 1979; Bennett 1996).[7] Under this approach, anthropological knowledge was intended to assist administrators in their interactions with colonized populations. However, I believe that Malinowski's perspective can be compared to contemporary arguments advocating for anthropologists to engage in projects focused on underdeveloped societies. In this context, their role would involve understanding the cultural needs and behaviours of these societies to effectively carry out projects supported by Western agencies. Malinowski directly experienced the realities of imperialism[8] on a daily basis (see James 1975) and did not actively contest it, much like how many individuals today do not protest the polarization of our world.

He viewed the calls for applied anthropology as a response to the shortcomings of colonial policies that disregarded local conditions and the needs of indigenous populations, and this deeply concerned him. He believed that a lack of understanding of the native communities resulted in detrimental impacts on their lives, leading him to advocate for the involvement of anthropologists in assisting colonial governors.

> It is equally true that most of the blunders of the administration are due to lack of knowledge, which made a determined constructive policy and a sound administration impossible. This weakness led to chaos in the benevolent attempts at too rapid in-dividualization of land holding, or else allowed white land-grabbers to annex territories indispensable to natives. It created discontent and disorder and was responsible for half the troubles in Africa.
> (1930: 415–416)

At times, his concern seems to focus less on the fate of the local communities and more on the errors attributed to the colonial administration due to insufficient knowledge, competence, and training.[9] He recognized the potential of anthropological expertise and was frustrated by the dismissive attitude towards it. This presented yet another opportunity to demonstrate the value of anthropology and bolster its position in academia and society. He aimed for anthropology to be acknowledged as a science, and substantiating its theories through practical application would enhance its cultural significance. He argued:

> "a new method and a new theory, the functional school, is rapidly crystallizing, and that this, if it receives the cooperation of the men in the colonial field, will undoubtedly play the same part in constructive policy as physics

and geology have played in engineering" (1930: 408). And as he stated earlier: "I am attempting to make anthropology into a real science"

(1930: 406)

This argument resurfaces in his later studies focused on war. In his book titled *Freedom and Civilisation*, initially published in 1944, he wrote:

"A call was made there for intellectual vigilance and for a mobilization of scientific thought and academic activities on the urgent issues of the day. Among other deficiencies of our unpreparedness, we have also failed to mobilize spiritually. There is no doubt that all around us we hear the slogans of 'Fight for freedom', 'The struggle of democracies against slavery', "The need of establishing justice and decency in the world". Yet when one of us raises his voice to affirm such values as 'freedom', 'justice', and 'democracy', he does it at the risk of being accused of the academically unpardonable sin of 'value judgments' or 'suffering from a moral purpose'. There are many who condemn value judgments in the vested interests of academic futility, laziness, and irrelevancy. **The best remedy here is to recognize that the soundest test of an adequate theory is always to be found in practical applications**. The student of society and of human culture has, under present circumstances, the duty to draw practical conclusions, to commit himself to views and decisions referring to problems of planning and to translate his conclusions into definite propositions of statesmanship"

(2015: 19 – emphasis added)

Malinowski was deeply disturbed by the rise of totalitarianism and the outbreak of World War II. He expressed his concerns through numerous lectures and essays written before his death while residing in the United States. These texts were composed during a time of uncertainty, making it challenging to predict the future. In his attempts to comprehend the nature of war and its underlying causes, he stressed the importance of objective examination.[10] Malinowski strongly felt a sense of duty and a deep necessity to contribute to the ongoing struggle, utilizing the means available to him – writing, analysis, and contemplation – to delve into topics such as war, freedom, justice, and democracy. He posited that genuine freedom is the essential condition for the flourishing of culture and the unleashing of creative forces (2015: 20).

Malinowski put forth the argument that the practical application of anthropological knowledge serves as the ultimate validation of its truth. He held a strong belief in the power of science and desired for anthropology to be recognized as a genuine scientific discipline. These aspirations are evident throughout his body of work, spanning from *Argonauts of the Western Pacific* to *Dynamics of Cultural Change* and *Freedom and Civilization*. I perceive this as an unwavering and tireless endeavour to enhance the cultural capital of anthropology, with the aim of fortifying the discipline and establishing its significance. It is my interpretation that he held the conviction that anthropology, when regarded as a true science on par with fields like chemistry and biology, would earn the rightful respect both within academia and in the public sphere.

I believe that this attitude also allowed him to envision concepts and ideas that would only be fully recognized and appreciated decades later. One such example is his advocacy for the practice of anthropology within one's own society, which was a pioneering notion that would be acknowledged as a legitimate approach to the field much later on.Początek formularDół formularza In one of his essays entitled *A Nation-Wide Intelligence Service*, published in 1938, in quite innovative way he advocates anthropology at home,[11] and emphasizes that

> "From the start of my own field-work, it has been my deepest and strongest conviction that we must finish by studying ourselves through the same methods and with the same mental attitude with which we approach exotic tribes". And later he adds: "Had I written the book on mythology ten years later than I did, I might have (...) shown that any powerful social movement today requires as much mysticism, magic and mythology as does a primitive clan"
>
> (1938b: 104)

These are not the words one would typically expect to come across in Malinowski's writings. And this is attributed to the fact that, as I previously argued, he is primarily recognized through the lens of his research in Melanesia. Upon delving into his works, it becomes apparent that his perspective on field research undergoes a gradual transformation. Initially, his focus lies on exploring the customs and traditions of traditional societies. Subsequently, he underscores the significance of acknowledging the presence of previously overlooked actors within the field, including missionaries, traders, and others. Ultimately, he recognizes that the forthcoming task involves utilizing anthropological tools to examine our own society.

Last Take on Identity Practices in Anthropology

Anthropology as a discipline has been constructed through a variety of means, including institutional and research practices, public debates, and narratives passed down to future generations. These narratives not only recount history but also impart a fundamental understanding of what anthropology encompasses. What is more, within the time the discipline has emerged and developed as a separate field of inquiry, each new wave of anthropologists faces the urgent task of re-examining the essence of anthropology and defining it anew. Every now and again, the fundamental questions of what anthropology truly entails and how it should be practised have been raised, and the answers to them contribute to the continual formation of the core anthropological identity, which is always in a state of development and never fully realized, remaining perpetually under construction. These moments can be considered as branching points where the trajectory of anthropological thought diverges and new perspectives and paradigms emerge.

The development of our professional identities in anthropology is deeply entrenched within academic context. Anthropology's institutionalization brings extensive implications to our professional realm, setting forth a structured framework encompassing standardized educational programs, curricula, and academic institutions. Within these educational settings, individuals are introduced to the foundational principles, methods, and theories of anthropology, which collectively contribute to shaping of their professional identity.

As I have emphasized, each anthropologist shares foundational knowledge with their peers, which develops and diversifies as we navigate our unique academic journeys. This core understanding acts as the bedrock of the anthropological imaginary, taking on a distinct character. Moreover, as I attempted to demonstrate through reflecting on how Bronisław Malinowski's work is integrated into the canon, the core identity shared among researchers worldwide, regardless of their backgrounds and specializations, adopts the characteristic of what can be referred to as the "textbook form of knowledge." This doesn't necessarily imply exclusive delivery through textbooks; rather, it is structured in a manner aligning with the format commonly offered by primary academic resources. What characterizes this type of knowledge?

Every academic genre,[12] through which knowledge is disseminated represents a linear mode of expression with inherent constraints, such as time, length, and the medium's capabilities, resulting in selective knowledge delivery. It highlights specific aspects of a subject while inevitably omitting others, constructing a tailored perspective that resonates with its particular audience. Textbook knowledge comprises of narratives that are often transmitted from one publication to another, and have a profound impact on our anthropological imaginary. It consists of common, factual information about the history of anthropology, methodologies applied by previous generations of researchers and most significant theories and concepts that we recognize as fundamental in our discipline.

This particular body of information is often presented in a standardized, structured way. It is also simplified and typically offers an overview of key concepts and ideas within a particular field or subject, and is intended to provide a basic understanding of a topic. Although textbook form of knowledge relies on primary research and scholarship, it is often distilled into a more easily digestible format and presented in a linear, sequential way. Therefore, it is often limited, and by definition incomplete. Furthermore, its mundane and factual nature inhibits our vigilance and typically fails to foster critical thinking or promote questioning and challenging of established imaginaries unless due to its significance in a researcher's work, one recognizes a necessity for an in-depth analysis of the subject at hand.

It can be also argued that the core anthropological knowledge, is to a large extent based on generalizations, and it therefore takes condensed form as found in textbooks. Generalizations are indispensable in the sense that, due to the linear nature of our communication, we are incapable of conveying every detailed facet of the phenomena under scrutiny. Although we may focus on specific aspects of the researched issue, we cannot avoid the necessity of simplifying some of the peripheral themes or concepts, particularly those that contextualize the discussed problem but are not crucial for its understanding. We also possess only a general overview of some anthropological topics because acquiring knowledge requires time, which is a limited resource. Our primary focus is usually on deepening our respective research fields and areas of expertise. Consequently, we often lack the time to explore additional subjects and delve deeper into various aspects of the discipline, and as a result, without any critical scrutiny, we consider those pieces of information that have already been widely accepted as unquestionable.

What is also characteristic of the textbook form of knowledge is that it includes only certain anthropological facts that the interpretational community finds crucial for understanding what it means to be an anthropologist. It contains only a selection of basic information, thus contributing to the construction of a distinct collective imaginary. These blackboxed narratives, often rely on generalizations passed from one publication to another, and even when subjected to scrutiny, they exhibit resistance to change. This resistance, as mentioned earlier, is rooted in the constraints of our individual paths; we cannot exhaustively explore every element of anthropological intricacies. Instead, our academic journeys guide us towards specific realms of knowledge in alignment with our unique interests.

Nonetheless, this dynamic has specific consequences. Namely, a portion of our knowledge materializes, as once phrased by Malinowski, in the guise of a "fanciful dummy creature" (2002: 46) – a contrived representation that falls short of capturing the intricate nuances of human behaviour and motivation. These "dummy creatures" are often operational concepts within the social sciences and anthropology, and we all serve as their repositories due to the nature of knowledge acquisition and dissemination. However, these concepts are not entirely detached from the empirical domain or the realm of experience, nor are they purely speculative. Instead, they represent interpretations that tend to emphasize specific aspects of phenomena while overlooking others, considering them insignificant or less relevant. In this way, they shape our understanding of the subject matter and influence how we perceive and study it.

As I attempted to illustrate, although Bronisław Malinowski's journey is far more complex, only select fragments of his legacy have contributed to the collective imaginary of anthropologists. This portrayal of Bronisław Malinowski has played a significant role in shaping anthropological identity, defining our understanding of what anthropology is and what it means to be an anthropologist. However, when this imaginary is situated within the broader context of his achievements, the concept of "Malinowskian dogma" proves not to be applicable to Malinowski himself.

When we delve into his later writings, it becomes apparent that he transcended the confines of the research model he developed in the Trobriand Islands. He displayed a willingness to venture beyond his earlier studies and actively pursued new avenues of reflection. His later work in Africa showcased his recognition that anthropology should encompass a much broader scope, acknowledging the presence of other social actors in the field. Moreover, he recognized the potential to apply anthropological tools and methods in the study of Western societies. Additionally, towards the end of his life, he dedicated himself to studying peasants in Mexico, further illustrating his versatility and refusal to be limited to studying only "radical others," as he is often portrayed.

In my view, his openness to various methods and perspectives stemmed from his primary dedication to a scientific approach, which allowed him to explore new avenues rather than rigidly adhering to the established models of research. Regardless of the topic he explored or the stance he adopted, Malinowski demonstrated a steadfast commitment to advancing anthropology as a genuine science. By consistently striving to uphold the principles of scientific inquiry and empirical evidence, Malinowski sought to elevate anthropology to the status of a respected and valued field of study both within academia and in the broader public sphere.

Bronisław Malinowski's work holds significant importance in the context of shaping anthropological identity. By examining which segments of his legacy have become integral components of our anthropological imaginary, we can uncover the mechanisms of knowledge production and acquisition within the academic realm. This exploration provides insights into the choices we make during our academic journeys, both at the individual and collective levels, regarding the paths we are determined to follow. Moreover, delving into Malinowski's impact on the construction of anthropological identity allows us to gain a deeper understanding of how particular narratives and interpretations are solidified within the field. These narratives often become ingrained in our academic practices and shape our perception of what it means to be an anthropologist. Ultimately, we can also uncover that the interpretational multiverse encompasses numerous potential alternative anthropological stories.

Notes

1 It is also worth underscoring that the processes of constructing national and departmental anthropological traditions are similar to the formation of anthropological identities at other levels of generality. These, too, are shaped by certain circumstances and choices made by practitioners, creating a diverse array of anthropological paths.
2 For example, one anthropologist may excel in the field of economy but might not possess the same level of expertise when it comes to the topic of religion. Similarly, we may have a comprehensive understanding of posthumanism but might not delve as deeply into structuralism. We could be well-versed in the intricacies of Amazonian hunter-gatherer societies but lack the same depth of knowledge regarding the pastoral Tuaregs of North Africa. Our familiarity with activist research may be extensive, while our grasp of cognitive methodology remains less developed.
3 As pointed by Grazyna Kubica (2023, unpublished manuscript), it is important to highlight that while Malinowski is often credited as a leading advocate of participant observation, he did not explicitly utilize this term in his work. Instead, he stressed the significance of the ethnographer's personal, direct observation (Malinowski 2002: 12). That particular insight serves as one among several instances showcasing the construction of core anthropological knowledge through generalizations and shortcuts. Within the widespread landscape of anthropological imagination, Malinowski's name has become virtually synonymous with the concept of participant observation.
4 And as he points out Malinowski was "in fact the last of them actually to get into the field" (Stocking 1992: 28).
5 This is a common practice in times when anthropologists engage in the reconstruction of the discipline's identity. When the paradigm undergoes certain changes, such as reevaluating the subject of research, methods, and theoretical frameworks, and introducing new standards of practising anthropology, there is a tendency to reassess the works of anthropologists whose contributions were not previously appreciated or recognized. It is

often after revolutionary changes that we realize alternative ways of doing anthropology were already present but went unnoticed until a paradigm shift occurred. For instance, the works of Zora Neale Hurston or Hortense Powdermaker, who herself was a student of Malinowski, were only noticed decades later.
6 It is also worth emphasizing that his earlier writings did not receive the same level of recognition. For example, his monograph *The Natives of Mailu* published in 1915, which was based on his earlier expedition, also did not garner as much attention.
7 This is the most common context in which his research in Africa is referenced. It is also worth emphasizing that, the process of decolonization had a profound impact on the development of the entire discipline, it was particularly vital to those anthropological communities who were directly involved in it.
8 The entrenchment of this reality in the lives of people is exemplified in the previously mentioned paragraph from *The Dynamics of Culture Change* where Malinowski recounts his travel with Imperial Airways. He was positioned as a researcher within a colonizing state and could not simply disassociate himself from it. Metaphorically, this would imply jumping out of the plane.
9 Although in his later work he wrote: "There is a moral obligation to every calling, even to that of a scientific specialist. The duty of the anthropologist is to be a fair and true interpreter of the Native (…) He ought to be able to make clear to traders, missionaries, and exploiters what the Natives really need and where they suffer most under the pressure of European interference. There is no doubt that the destiny of indigenous races has been tragic in the process of contact with European invasion (…) Shall we, therefore, mix politics with science? In one way, decidedly 'yes' (…)" (1945: 3–4).
10 However, some of his essays also reflected his personal beliefs regarding the geopolitical situation at the time. For instance, he regarded even a democratic sovereign state as "the worst enemy." He passionately advocated for ideas that promoted the establishment of international institutions like the League of Nations, which could contribute to conflict resolution and prevention. He firmly believed that states should relinquish a portion of their sovereignty to a federation or union of nations, equipped with an international military force dedicated to upholding peace.
11 The article was written at the invitation of Mass Observation – a pioneering social research organization established in the late 1930s to document everyday life in Britain. Malinowski's endorsement of this organization's concept inspired him to approach anthropology in a novel way and present ideas that became popular a few decades later (see also Kubica 2014: 333).
12 Including textbooks, articles, monographs, documentary films, debates, lectures, conferences, seminars, research projects, etc.

References

Bennett, John W. (1996). Applied and Action Anthropology: Ideological and Conceptual Aspects. *"Current Anthropology"*, vol. 37, no. 1, pp. 23–53.
Clifford, James. (1988). *The Predicament of Culture: Twentieth-Century Ethnography, Literature, and Art*. Cambridge, MA: Harvard University Press.
Eriksen, Thomas Hylland. (2012). *A History of Anthropology*. London: Pluto Press.
Feuchtwang, Stephen. (1975). The Colonial Formation of British Social Anthropology. In Talal Asad (Ed.) *Anthropology and the Colonial Encounter*. London: Ithaca Press, pp. 71–102.
Freeman, Derek. (1983). *Margaret Mead and Samoa: The Making and Unmaking of an Anthropological Myth*. Cambridge, MA: Harvard University Press.
Geertz, Clifford. (1988). *Works and Lives: The Anthropologist as Author*. Stanford, CA: Stanford University Press.

Greene, Brian. (2011). *The Hidden Reality: Parallel Universes and the Deep Laws of the Cosmos*. New York: Alfred A. Knopf.
Gupta, Akhil, James Ferguson. (1997). Discipline and Practice: "The Field" as Site, Method, and Location in Anthropology. In Akhil Gupta, James Ferguson (Eds.) *Anthropological Locations: Boundaries and Grounds of a Field Science*. Berkeley: University of California Press, pp. 1–46.
James, Wendy. (1975). Anthropologist as Reluctant Imperialist. In Talal Asad (Ed.) *Anthropology and the Colonial Encounter*. London: Ithaca Press, pp. 41–70.
Kubica, Grazyna. (2014). The Survey of the Ghetto: In the Time of Anti-Semitism: Feliks Gross and His Unfinished Fieldwork on the Jewish Quarters of Krakow and Vilna, 1938–1940. "*East European Politics and Societies and Cultures*", vol. 28, no. 2, pp. 318–340.
———. (2023). *The two worlds of Bronisław Malinowski's Polish youth in his own writings: the anthropologist's historical autoethnography* (unpublished manuscript).
Malinowski, Bronislaw. (1930). The Rationalization of Anthropology and Administration. "*Africa*", vol. 3, no. 4, pp. 405–430.
Malinowski, Bronislaw. (1938a). Introductory Essay on the Anthropology of Changing African Cultures. In Lucy P. Mair (Ed.), *Methods of Study of Culture Contact in Africa*. London: Oxford University Press, pp. VII–XXXVIII.
Malinowski, Bronislaw. (1938b). A Nation-Wide Intelligence Service. In Charles Madge, Tom Harrison (Eds.), *First Year's Work: 1937/1938 by Mass-Observation*. London: Lindsay Drummond, pp. 83–121.
Malinowski, Bronislaw. (1945). *The Dynamics of Culture Change: An Inquiry into Race Relations in Africa*. New Haven, CT: Yale University Press.
Malinowski, Bronislaw. (2002 [1922]). *Argonauts of the Western Pacific: An Account of Native Enterprise and Adventure in the Archipelagoes of Melanesian New Guinea*. London: Routledge.
Malinowski, Bronislaw. (2015 [1944]). *Freedom and Civilization*. New York: Routledge.
Mead, Margaret. (1928). *Coming of Age in Samoa: A Psychological Study of Primitive Youth for Western Civilisation*. New York: Morrow.Onoge, Omafume F. (1979). The Counterrevolutionary Tradition in African Studies: The Case of Applied Anthropology. In Gerrit Huizer, Bruce Mannheim (Eds.) *The Politics of Anthropology from Colonialism and Sexism toward a View from below*. The Hague: Mouton Publisherspp. 45–66.
Polgar, Steven. (1979). From Applied to Committed Anthropology: Disengaging from our Colonialist Heritage. In Gerrit Huizer, Bruce Manheim (Eds.) *The Politics of Anthropology from Colonialism and Sexism toward a View from below*. The Hague: Mouton Publisherspp. 259–268.
Songin-Mokrzan, Marta. (2017). Rola autoetnografii w procesie wytwarzania wiedzy antropologicznej, „*Kultura i Społeczeństwo*", vol. 61. no. 3, pp. 53–66.
Stocking, George W. Jr. (1992). *The Ethnographer's Magic and Other Essays in the History of Anthropology*. Madison: University of Wisconsin Press.
Stocking, George W. Jr. (2010). *Glimpses into My Own Black Box: An Exercise in Self-Deconstruction*. Madison: University of Wisconsin Press.
Willis, Jr., William S. (1972). Skeletons in Anthropological Closet. In Dell Hymes (Ed.) *Reinventing Anthropology*. New York: Random House, pp. 121–152.
Young, Michael W., ed. (1979). *The Ethnography of Malinowski: The Trobriand Islands, 1915–1918*. London: Routledge & Kegan Paul.

14 Bronisław Malinowski and the Anthropology of Nostalgia

Dariusz Brzeziński

Introduction

The relationship between anthropology and nostalgia is ambiguous. On the one hand, nostalgia was one of the foundation stones of anthropology as a discipline. As David Berliner explained: "For anthropologists, (…) nostalgia for disappearing worlds constitutes a foundational trope, lying at the very heart of the major anthropological traditions" (2014: 373). While anthropologists' motivations have been changing significantly over time, the sense of "losing culture" (Berliner 2020) has remained a distinctive feature of their research. What is more, anthropologists have proposed concepts and theories that are of special importance for the development of contemporary studies on nostalgia. Such formative ideas notably include "armchair nostalgia" by Arjun Appadurai (1996), "structural nostalgia" by Michael Herzfeld (2005 [1996]), and "imperial nostalgia" by Renato Rosaldo (1989). All of them have been widely applied in theoretical and empirical studies (e.g., Salmose 2019; Jacobsen 2020, 2021). On the other hand, nostalgia itself has not been frequently addressed by anthropologists. A few years ago, Olivia Angé and David Berliner admitted that "fine-grained ethnographies of nostalgia and loss are still scarce" (2014: 1). Very similar observations were made by Amber R. Reed in her monograph on nostalgia for apartheid published in 2020, where she noted that such analyses were few and far between in contemporary anthropology (Reed 2020). However, the increasing interest in the study of nostalgia perceivable in the social sciences and humanities in recent years – and sometimes referred to as the "nostalgic turn" (Jacobsen 2020) – has exerted influence on anthropological investigations as well (Bissel 2014; Herzfeld 2021). Recent anthropological publications include works on the nostalgia for the lost empires (e.g., Hann 2014; Walton 2019), the role of nostalgia in postcolonial societies (e.g., Nsele 2016; Reed 2020), and the relationship between nostalgia and the climate crisis (e.g., Angé and Berliner 2020).

In my view, research should also be launched to analyse the existing anthropological literature from the perspective of theories and concepts that have lately emerged within "nostalgia studies." There are several reasons why this approach is relevant. Firstly, the sense of loss is one of the most frequently mentioned emotions in the context of field research (Davies and Spencer 2010). It refers both to the absence of family, friends, or fellow academics during the fieldwork and to a kind of mourning – called "disciplinary melancholy" by Holly High (2011) – following the return from the field.[1] Contemporary explorations of nostalgia in psychology and cultural studies (e.g., Sedikides et al. 2015; Wilson 2015; Routledge 2016) provide a valuable perspective to comprehensively examine this emotion. Secondly, the classical anthropologists were convinced, as Bronisław Malinowski put it, that "the material of [their] study melts away with hopeless rapidity" (1922: xv). In this sense, nostalgia for cultures that they believed were on the brink of extinction – which is a form of "anticipatory nostalgia"[2] (Batcho 2020) – was a crucial motivation for them to undertake field research. Contemporary theories and concepts of nostalgia can be helpful in exploring this phenomenon, as well as in examining how this motivation went on to evolve (Berliner 2020). Thirdly, the discourse on the role and function of nostalgia has been vigorously developing in recent years (e.g., Wilson 2015; Routledge 2016; Batcho 2020; Wildschut and Sedikides 2020). I believe that anthropologists' autoethnographic testimonies of yearning for the past may shed some important light on this multilayered phenomenon.

In this chapter, I apply the research perspectives outlined above to analyze Malinowski's anthropology and his personal reflections.[3] I explore the meanings, roles, and functions of nostalgia he experienced during his fieldwork, as well as the significance of this emotion for the way he perceived the tasks of anthropology. In my investigation, I draw on the concepts of "endonostalgia" and "exonostalgia," propounded by Berliner (Berliner 2014, 2020). The former conveys a longing for what an individual has personally lost, or what is currently unavailable to them, and the latter refers to the awareness of the loss of something independent of one's personal experience. Endonostalgia features very prominently in Malinowski's diaries, both in the *Diary in the Strict Sense of the Term* (Malinowski 1989 [1967]) and in his other diaries, as of now only available in Polish (Malinowski 2002). In these personal notes, Malinowski portrayed a varied range of emotions experienced during his fieldwork and related to his longing for his family, friends, and beloved women, as well as the customs practiced in Poland and Britain. These resources perfectly exemplify the multifaceted and ambiguous status of longing for the past, while allowing some generalizations about nostalgia associated with fieldwork. For its part, exonostalgia is expressed in Malinowski's conviction, dating from the time of his fieldwork in the Trobriand Islands, that the culture there was then vanishing under the impact of Western civilization. In his later research, however (e.g., Malinowski 1945), he reconsidered his stance on cultural change, and that reassessment had serious implications for the way he thought of the tasks of anthropology.

My argument in this article has a tripartite structure. In the first part, I present the main positions in the debate on the roles, meanings, and dimensions of nostalgia in anthropology and beyond. In part two, I scrutinize Malinowski's diaries for the different dimensions of his nostalgia as rendered in them and for the various implications of nostalgia for his fieldwork. In part three, I look into the relationship between Malinowski's exonostalgia and his changing vision of the tasks of anthropology. In conclusion, I bring together the issues examined in the article and highlight their relevance to the development of anthropological theory. Importantly, although some scholars have pointed out the significance of nostalgia in Malinowski's works, particularly in his *Diary in the Strict Sense of the Term* (see e.g., Geertz 1967; Harris 1967; Young 2004; Nazaruk 2014; Kubica 2002; 2015), this issue has never been exhaustively studied. Moreover, the available research usually does not reference psychological and cultural studies on nostalgia or theories and concepts emerging as part of the "nostalgic turn." All this contributes to the novelty of the perspective I adopt in this chapter.

Theorizing Nostalgia

Although reflection on longing for the past can be retraced to very early stages in the history of humanity, as famously borne out, for example, by Psalm 137 and Homer's *Odyssey*, the concept of nostalgia only came into being in the late 17th century. The term was coined by the Swiss medical student Johannes Hofer in his *Dissertatio Medica de Nostalgia. oder Heimwehe* [*Medical Dissertation on Nostalgia*] to depict the health of his compatriots who fought as mercenaries for European monarchs. Hofer described their condition in terms of disease, as an affliction characterized by sadness, insomnia, a loss of appetite, heart disorders, and impaired concentration. To name their malady, he combined two Greek words: *nóstos*, meaning "homecoming," and *álgos*, that is, "suffering." He argued that nostalgia was "the sad mood originating from the desire for the return to one's native land" (Hofer 1934 [1688]: 381). This and similar understandings of "nostalgia" persisted over the following centuries (Illbruck 2012; Dodman 2018). A major evolution in defining this concept only began in the 20th century, gaining momentum in its last decades (Davis 1979; Boym 2001; Sedikides et al. 2015; Wilson 2015; Routledge 2016). These changes were marked, above all, by, first, a shift from discussing nostalgia in medical discourse to psychological and, later, sociological discourse; second, moving away from defining nostalgia in spatial terms alone, as induced by distance from the home country, and adding a temporal aspect, specifically pleasant memories of the past, to it; thirdly, abandoning the exclusively negative associations of nostalgia with destructive feelings and putting a spotlight on its multiple dimensions and functions. I analyse these transformations below, with a particular focus on their relevance to ethnographic theory.

It is perhaps best to begin the examination of the first above-mentioned issue by highlighting that for decades after Hofer's dissertation, attempts were made to identify either biological or environmental causes of nostalgia (Boym 2001: 2–18). When these efforts ultimately proved unsuccessful, and, additionally, nostalgia turned out to be much more widespread and much more complex than its discoverers had thought, medical scholars abandoned the study of it as a disease. From there, the issue was picked up by psychologists, who started to analyse nostalgia in the early 20th century (Sedikides et al. 2015: 3–6). However, this disciplinary shift did not change the belief in the pathological nature of nostalgia. In Clay Routledge's account: "Psychologists were (…) continuing the tradition of viewing nostalgia as an ailment. They did not believe that nostalgia was necessarily a disease of the body. Instead, it was a disorder of the mind" (2016: 5). For most of the 20th century, nostalgia was defined as a psychiatric or psychosomatic disorder. This attitude was fundamentally revised at the end of the 20th century and persisted in the altered form into the 21st century, when more in-depth psychological studies on nostalgia were conducted, using either qualitative interviews or experimental methods. Ever since, research has focused on capturing the complex and multi-dimensional nature of nostalgia and on pinpointing its various causes and consequences (Routledge 2016; Batcho 2020; Wildschut and Sedikides 2020).

Since the second half of the 20th century, social scientists and culture scholars have also studied nostalgia. A landmark work of this research was penned by Fred Davis, a representative of the Chicago school of symbolic interactionism, in 1979. Titled *Yearning for Yesterday: A Sociology of Nostalgia* (Davis 1979), the book argued that nostalgia could be metaphorically thought of as "a kind of telephoto lens on life which, while it magnifies and prettifies some segments of our past, simultaneously blurs and grays other segments, typically those closer to us in time" (31). In Davis's view, social analyses of nostalgia should involve a multifaceted inquiry into the causes, manifestations, and consequences of various ways of idealizing the past. The path paved by Davis was soon followed by other social- and cultural-sciences scholars, and the number of articles and books on nostalgia has grown exponentially ever since (see Jacobsen 2020: 3–6). These publications either investigate specific expressions of nostalgia, for example, in popular culture (e.g., Cross 2015; Mills 2019), media (e.g., Niemeyer 2014; Pallister 2019), and politics (e.g., Bonnett 2010; Porter 2020), or attempt to characterize the nature of nostalgia more generally (e.g., Boym 2001; Wilson 2005; Bauman 2017). On both these levels, works produced by anthropologists are of great importance (Stewart 1988; Rosaldo 1989; Appadurai 1996; Bissel 2005, 2014; Herzfeld 2005 [1996], 2021; High 2011; Angé and Berliner 2014, 2020; Hann 2014; Nsele 2016; Reed 2016, 2020; Berliner 2020).

The analyses are a good introduction to the second focal issue of this part of the article, namely, the change in the semantic field of the term "nostalgia." This field was slowly expanding, as a result of which the notion of *nóstos* acquired very different, and increasingly metaphorical, meanings. In the most important of these transformations, the spatial dimension of nostalgia was supplemented with a temporal dimension, meaning that the process of the idealization of the past came to concern time as much as place. Janelle L. Wilson elucidates: "Nostalgia is more than 'homesickness.' Nostalgia refers to the desire for a time and place that may be subjective (e.g., 'remember when I felt secure, confident?') or physical ('remember the house we grew up in?' or, 'remember the college campus where we were students?'). 'Home' itself could very well need a redefinition" (1999: 302). Importantly, the past idealized by an individual or a society can be something they really experienced, but it can also only be known to them through the mediation of ideology or cultural productions. The latter type of yearning for the past has been described by Christina Goulding (2002) as "vicarious nostalgia" and by Arjun Appadurai (1996) as "armchair nostalgia." This form of longing is more and more common today as a result of the increasing commercialization, consumerization, and mediatization of nostalgia (e.g., Niemeyer 2014; Cross 2015; Lizardi 2015; Mills 2019).

Contemporary anthropological research abounds with excellent examples of the mythologization of historical periods which were often very difficult for the communities concerned. One such example is nostalgia for the Soviet domination in today's post-communist countries of Central and Eastern Europe (e.g., Nadkarni and Shevchenko 2014). In Svetlana Boym's typology (2001), most of these nostalgic longings can be classified not really as "restorative," that is, aimed at reinstating the old order, but as "reflective," that is, oriented toward a decontextualized celebration of selected practices and objects characteristic of the communist era. Another example is brought into relief in anthropological studies of nostalgia for the colonial period in African countries (Bissel 2005) and for the Apartheid in South Africa (Nsele 2016; Reed 2016, 2020). This research reveals that the dissatisfaction with the social, economic, political, and cultural processes characteristic of the contemporary world can spawn and cause the proliferation of idealized visions of the old regimes. Regarding all these varieties of nostalgia, Michael Herzfeld has warned:

> Whether in respect of colonial rule, control by a Soviet-directed dictatorship, the harshness of an apartheid or other racist regime, or the rigid exclusions of class and caste, [nostalgia] expresses regret for conditions that from the outside appear to range from the unbearable to the unspeakable. This type of nostalgia calls for careful attention if we are not to assume that people want what we think they ought to want (or what we imagine we would want in their place).
>
> (2021: 135)[4]

Interestingly, exonostalgia, as defined in the introduction to this article, is also rooted in mythologization. In this form of longing for the past, an idealized image of the societies anthropologists study is coupled with the conviction that they are doomed to destruction as an effect of globalization (Berliner 2014, 2020). I will discuss this issue in detail in relation to Malinowski's work later in this article.

The third issue examined in this part of my argument concerns changes in problematizing both emotions related to nostalgia and its roles and functions for individuals and societies. Of particular importance is the fact that contemporary research by no means confirms that suffering, foregrounded in Hofer's coinage by the Greek word *álgos*, is the constitutive, let alone the sole, feature of nostalgia. Rather, yearning for the past is defined as a "bittersweet emotion" today (see Wilson 2015; Batcho 2020; Wildschut and Sedikides 2020). For example, Krystine Batcho emphasizes: "Nostalgia entails pleasant feelings of happiness and comfort along with feelings of sadness, longing, and loss. Nostalgia poses the puzzle of how one can be happy and sad simultaneously" (2020: 31). Research results are inconclusive, and different studies not infrequently differ as to whether nostalgia should be considered an overwhelmingly positive or negative emotion. Malinowski's diaries (Malinowski 2002), which I analyse in the next section, provide valuable arguments for the debate between the proponents of both positions.

Besides ambivalence, multifunctionality is another facet of nostalgia underscored in today's discourse. Psychological research shows that nostalgia can both strengthen a sense of identity coherence and contribute to the rupture of identity.

Similarly, it can both consolidate agency and deprive individuals of it. The way a longing for the past affects people depends on a variety of factors that are thoroughly investigated by scholars today (Iver and Jetten 2011; Sedikides et al. 2015; Batcho 2018; Newman et al. 2020). Social scientists also infer very different conclusions about the role of nostalgia in social, cultural, political, and economic life. For example, some of them follow Davis and stress that nostalgia does not hinder social change, but fosters a sense of community, which is necessary for the preservation of cultural identity amidst the ongoing transformations (Davis 1979). Others, such as Zygmunt Bauman in his posthumously published *Retrotopia*, argue that the development of nostalgia inspires people to search for solutions to the problems at hand in the past practices and institutions, which makes it impossible to deal with them effectively (Bauman 2017). The discourse on the role of nostalgia in social life is developing rapidly, and every year brings numerous new publications on the subject (e.g., Leggatt 2018; Kurlinkus 2019; Porter 2020; Jacobsen 2021; Bartmański 2022).

Nostalgia scholars often cite the title of Simone Signoret's memoirs – *La nostalgie n'est plus ce qu'elle était est* [*Nostalgia Isn't What It Used to Be* (1978 [1975]). The phrase very aptly expresses the fact that nostalgia is an emotion subject to constant metamorphoses, which unfold along with socio-cultural changes. Thus, new theorizations and empirical studies of nostalgia are still needed. In my view, the study of individual testimonies of nostalgia plays a major role in this regard. In this way, we can gain very valuable knowledge of the various ways in which nostalgia manifests itself and obtain precious insights into its nature and functions. In the next two parts of this article, I analyse Malinowski's work from this perspective.

Nostalgia in Malinowski's *Diaries*

Prior analyses of Bronisław Malinowski's diaries to some extent addressed the experience of nostalgia illuminated in them. For example, in a review of *A Diary in the Strict Sense of the Term*, Clifford Geertz (1967) listed Malinowski's aspiration to overcome the nagging feeling of nostalgia through practicing anthropological work in the manner of Protestant ethics among the main themes of the text (Geertz 1967; see Weber 1930 [1905]). In another review published the same year, Marvin Harris described Malinowski's work as a "melancholy fragment" consisting "almost entirely of expressions of the inner psychological turmoil that lay beneath the brilliantly posed exterior of this supreme field worker" (1967: 74). Malinowski's longing for the past was granted a far more central place in the subsequent in-depth analyses of his diaries by Grażyna Kubica and Michal Young. Kubica, the editor of the only complete edition of Malinowski's diaries to date,[5] wrote extensively about his nostalgia for people and places that had been close to him when growing up in and around Kraków and Zakopane (e.g., Kubica 2015, 2024 forthcoming). Various dimensions of nostalgia experienced by Malinowski and their impact on his field research were also discussed in Young's biography of Malinowski titled *Malinowski: Odyssey of an Anthropologist, 1884–1920* (2004). However, none of the works published so far has examined Malinowski's nostalgia from the perspective of the theories and concepts developed in historical and contemporary studies on nostalgia. To redress this gap is my goal in this part of my article.

To start with, the manner in which Malinowski writes about his nostalgia in his diaries is entirely in line with the way this concept was understood in the early 20th century. First, he considered nostalgia in terms of a psychological, rather than medical, condition; he realized that nostalgia arose from an emotional background. For example, in his diary entry dated 20 January 1915, he wrote: "When I feel fairly well physically, when I have something to do, when I am not demoralized, I do not experience a constant state of nostalgia."[6] Second, a literal rather than metaphorical understanding of *nóstos* prevails in Malinowski's diaries. He linked this notion to his home country (e.g., 27 September 1914; 20 January 1915), to some places in Great Britain (e.g., 21 October 1914), or in general to "civilization" (16 February 1918). Also, many entries in Malinowski's diaries concern nostalgia for people to whom he was attached. For example, on 19 December 1914, he wrote:

> Overcome by sadness, I bellowed out themes from *Tristan and Isolde*. 'Homesickness.' I summoned up various figures from the past, T. S., Zenia. I thought of Mother – Mother is the only person I care for really and am truly worried about.

Third, as these quotations reveal, nostalgia was understood by Malinowski as destructive for the individual. He associated it with notions such as, for example, "suffering" (27 September 1914), "sadness" (19 December 1914), "torments" (16 February 2018), and "irritation" (21 February 1918). As a matter of fact, the entry dated 23 January 1915, explicitly contrasts nostalgia with positive emotions: "I sat withdrawn, not thinking much, but without homesickness; felt a dull pleasure in soullessly letting myself dissolve in the landscape."

Although, as emphasized in the previous section, nostalgia is understood today as a "bittersweet experience," its "bitter" component is by no means lost sight of. For example, Aarti Iyer and Jolanda Jetten (2011) found in their research that the way nostalgia is experienced depends on whether or not individuals maintain identity continuity between the past and the present. When that continuity is interrupted, nostalgia can have detrimental effects on individuals' well-being and their ability to cope with the current challenges. What is more, a study by Morton Beiser (2004) showed that in nostalgia, a very strong attachment to the world left behind might generate depressive disorders. That and similar research provides a useful perspective for analyzing the "bitter" dimension of nostalgia experienced by Malinowski. The fits of despondency he repeatedly describes in his diaries are often related to the feelings of alienation on his fieldwork trips and to a vast discrepancy between his life in Europe and in North-Western Melanesia. For example, on 21 September 1914, he wrote

> Fits of dejection. For instance, when reading Candler about India and his return to London, I was overcome with a longing for London, for *N*., how I lived there the first year in Saville St. and later in Upper Marylebone St. (…).

I also keep remembering the later times after I came back from Cracow. (…) Beautiful moonlit nights on the veranda at Mr. and Mrs. McGrath's – I am filled with dislike for these ordinary people who are incapable of finding a glimmer of poetry in certain things which fill me with exaltation.

This passage vividly illuminates that the sense of incommensurability experienced by Malinowski during his fieldwork sparked multiple difficult emotions and often interfered with his fieldwork. Combined with the superiority he felt to the community he was studying, these emotions have provoked numerous controversies in the reception of Malinowski's diaries (Kubica 2024, forthcoming).

In his diary, Malinowski also described the various ways of dealing with the "bitter" facet of nostalgia, or "managing" nostalgia, as I propose calling this strategy, following Arlie Russell Hochschild (1983). One of these strategies, which Malinowski practiced from the very beginning of his field research (21 September 1914), was to "escape" into the Western world through its culture and art. Malinowski referenced many novels he read when in the field. He mentioned newspapers that brought him closer to the reality of Western culture too, although, as Young notes, they were "fodder for his nostalgia" at the same time (Young 2004: 522). Malinowski was also able to cope with the damaging effects of nostalgia through contacts with Westerners he encountered during his research expeditions. Notable among them were French-speaking Levantine Jews, Raphael Brudo and his wife, pearl traders from the Trobriand Islands, who befriended him. Malinowski eulogized Raphael in his diary on 2 March 1918: "I have the impression that he is the only man whose company *would bring me in contact with civilization*" (italics original). In a letter to Elsie Masson dated 10 April 1918, Malinowski related: "The Raffaels … insisted on my coming there every night pour *diner*, and I find them really nice and their company enjoyable and in a way they have changed the perspective of the Trobriands as a 'home' can change…" (Malinowski in Wayne 1995: 124). Finally, Malinowski's writing about his fieldwork experiences and the emotions involved, both in his letters and in diaries, was a salient nostalgia-relieving act. For example, in an entry dated 31 December 1917, he admitted that through writing to Elsie Masson, the intensity of his longing for civilization "vanished," replaced by nostalgia for his beloved (31 December 1917). Eight days later, he wrote in his diary: "This morning (1.6.18) it occurred to me that the purpose in keeping a diary and trying to control one's life and thoughts at every moment must be to consolidate life, to integrate one's thinking, to avoid fragmenting themes."

These realizations provide a perfect introduction to reflections on the "sweet" dimension of nostalgia. Importantly, since the publication of Davis's *Yearning for Yesterday: A Sociology of Nostalgia* (1979), this function of nostalgia has been increasingly appreciated and at the same time more thoroughly analysed (Routledge 2016). Numerous subsequent studies have confirmed the instrumentality of nostalgia in overcoming loneliness (e.g., Zhou et al. 2008), affirming the meaning of life (e.g., Routledge et al. 2013), and feeling socially supported (e.g., Wildschut and Sedikides 2020). It is noteworthy that the studies on nostalgia conducted during the COVID-19 pandemic showed the dominant positive role of longing for the past in coping with the challenges of physical isolation and in maintaining the sense of ontological security (Zhou et al. 2022; Cho et al. 2023). Another important observation arising from research on nostalgia is its reciprocal relationship with feelings of loneliness. If loneliness generates a yearning for the past, this yearning contributes to relieving loneliness (Zhou et al. 2008). This correlation is evident in Malinowski's diaries. According to Maja Nazaruk

> Malinowski's "homesickness that causes physical pinning and a wistful regret of the past" (Dickens 1979) was a reaction to the possibility of identity dissolution. By reaffirming his ties he was escaping disorientation, acquiring coordinates but also accessing the possibility of new perspectives. It was in a sense a submergence in a period of scrutiny for central values and axioms, leading to self-understanding, reflection, and behavioral evaluation.
> (2014: 628)

It is worthwhile to illustrate these statements with examples from the diaries.

Malinowski's diaries – both those written during his research expeditions to Melanesia and the earlier ones, chronicling his perception of himself and others while living in Kraków, Zakopane, Leipzig, the Canary Islands, and the U.K. (Malinowski 2002) – contain a great many paragraphs devoted to the women he loved and the various emotions that separation from them generated. In the last diary, his attention mainly centred around Elsie Masson. On the one hand, longing for her was a very difficult experience for him, epitomizing the "bitter" dimension of nostalgia. On the other hand, it gave him a sense of embeddedness, stability, and ontological security. For example, Malinowski's diary entry of 17 April 1918, begins by spelling out the emotional difficulties occasioned by his research work, before concluding: "About Elsie I think constantly, and I feel *settled down*" (italics original). More than two months earlier, on 5 February 1918, he stated: "Through all this strong, unexpressed longing for E. R. M. now I really can say she is the only woman for me." This assertion is one example of how the endonostalgia that Malinowski experienced during his field research fostered profound self-reflection and reevaluation of his life goals, which helped him to make the most important decisions about his private life.[7]

These decisions also concerned his career ambitions. For example, in an entry dated 21 December 1917, Malinowski drew a very clear connection between the nostalgia he felt when doing his field research and the development of his career plans. He recounted: "All that day I was longing for civilization. I thought about friends in Melbourne. At night in the *dinghy*, pleasantly ambitious thought: I'll surely be 'an eminent Polish scholar.'" This statement is an excellent illustration of how nostalgia can have a part not only in sustaining the sense of identity continuity but also in setting plans for the future, as well as enhancing creativity and agency. These issues are now the subject of intensive research in robustly expanding nostalgia studies (e.g., Routledge 2016; Batcho 2020; Wildschut and Sedikides 2020). In the context of my argument, it is crucial that Malinowski's longing for Elsie Masson, while often a source of his heartache and suffering, came to bolster his enthusiasm for fieldwork at certain points of his stay in the Trobriand Islands. For example, on 19 February 1918, he wrote in his diary: "thought about E. R. M. [Elsie Rosaline Masson] and the need to work intensively if I am to keep my *self-respect*" (italics original). On 1 April 1918, he confessed: "*I feel that if E. R. M. were here, I would develop it to her and feel stimulated, and then I begin to write it to her*" (italics original). This suggests that the repeatedly emphasized importance of Elsie Masson in the development of Malinowski's work (e.g., Wayne 1995; Young 2004; Salvucci et al. 2019) dated back to his field research in the Trobriand Islands, rather than commencing after his return from there.

To conclude this part of my argument, let me restate that Malinowski's endonostalgia during his fieldwork in the Trobriand Islands had very diverse dimensions to it and affected him in various ways. He frequently felt overwhelmed by the incommensurability of his current condition and his earlier experiences. The juxtaposition of these frames – or, as Svetlana Boym metaphorically put it, "double exposure, or a superimposition of two images" (Boym 2001: xiii–xiv) – generated the feeling of "emptiness and unhappiness" (3 December 1917). This sentiment often came unexpectedly, independent of his will or consciousness (e.g., 21 September 1914). Over time, however, Malinowski found various strategies to alleviate his misery, and reading novels and writing letters and a diary had a significant part in this process. At the same time, his desire to return to people and places that were important to him gave him a sense of stability and provided ontological security. Multiple passages in his diaries imply that nostalgia constructively contributed to the intensification of his fieldwork and the anticipations of his future career. Importantly, although Malinowski understood "nostalgia" first and foremost as a destructive phenomenon, he became aware of the upsides of yearning for the past, and even made a conscious effort to develop it. Read in this way, Malinowski's diaries partly confirm Batcho's belief that "seeking nostalgia is different from feeling nostalgic. Deliberately reflecting on nostalgic moments may be beneficial, but involuntary nostalgia evoked by situational cues may be predominantly negative" (Batcho 2020: 39). My only reservation about Batcho's conclusion is related to the fact that it is sometimes challenging to distinguish between "seeking nostalgia" and "feeling nostalgic" in Malinowski's diaries. Yet, this difficulty only further confirms the ambivalent status of longing for the past.

Finally, descriptions of nostalgia in Malinowski's diaries are frequently considered typical of emotions of anthropologists during fieldwork. In the introduction to the second English edition of *A Diary in the Strict Sense of the Term*, Raymond Firth paints an evocative portrayal of the intrinsically nostalgic position of anthropological field researcher:

> The feeling of confinement, the obsessional longing to be back even if for the briefest while in one's own cultural surroundings, the dejection and doubts about the validity of what one is doing, the desire to escape into a fantasy world of novels or daydreams, the moral compulsion to drag oneself back to the task of field observation – many sensitive fieldworkers have experienced

these feelings on occasion, and they have rarely been better expressed than in this diary.

(1989 [1966]: xv–xvi)

Young adds: "Few have documented better than Malinowski this shock of the new and the bewildered mind's response of detachment" (2004: 334–335). Given this, I believe that examining the various dimensions of yearning for the past in Malinowski's diaries can be relevant not only to the study of his life and work, or the current attempts to re-theorize nostalgia, but also to research on the emotions anthropologists experience during fieldwork (Davies and Spencer 2010). This should be one of the directions for the anthropology of nostalgia to take in its development.

Exonostalgia and Beyond

In an article published in 2016, Krystine Batcho and Sumran Shikh defined the concept of "anticipatory nostalgia" (Batcho and Shikh 2020).[8] According to them, while nostalgia is typically founded on a longing for the past from the perspective of the present, anticipatory nostalgia involves looking with apprehension at the present from the perspective of future predictions. This anxiety stems from the fear of losing what is valuable in the world as it is now. One example of anticipatory nostalgia is "solastalgia," that is, anxiety caused by environmental change in the age of the Anthropocene. The etymology of "nostalgia" indicates that solastalgia is suffering (*álgos*) resulting from a longing for the Earth (*nóstos*) in the face of changes that may lead to its further degradation (Galway et al. 2019).[9] Another example of anticipatory nostalgia is "exonostalgia," an already mentioned notion proposed by Berliner (2014, 2020), who linked its primary meaning to the belief that the cultures studied by the early anthropologists were passing away. As elucidated by Berliner,

> in the works of Malinowski, Boas, or Marcel Griaule, the position of the anthropologist in the narrative is that of a powerless observer, the herald of impending cultural disaster. While these peoples were perceived as the last survivors of a bygone age, the anthropologist became the last witness to these paradises being led inexorably toward their doom.
>
> (2020: 72)[10]

In this section, I analyse exonostalgia in Malinowski's anthropology and retrace its evolution over time.

Malinowski's *Argonauts of the Western Pacific* is furnished with a compositional frame made up of explicitly exonostalgic statements. The book begins with the claim that:

> Ethnology is in the sadly ludicrous, not to say tragic, position, that at the very moment when it begins to put its workshop in order, to forge its proper tools,

to start ready for work on its appointed task, the material of its study melts away with hopeless rapidity.

(Malinowski 1922: xv)

Its last sentence reads: "Alas! The time is short for Ethnology, and will this truth of its real meaning and importance dawn before it is too late?" (Malinowski 1922: 518). Between these two insights, *Argonauts of the Western Pacific* offers an analysis of a culture whose existence Malinowski believed was about to come to an irrevocable end.[11] Taking this into account, the book could share the title with a novella by Gabriel Garcia Marquez and be called a "chronicle of a death foretold" (Marquez 1983 [1981]). It is worth asking the question about the premises on which Malinowski based his conviction of the imminent demise of the Trobriand culture? And more generally, what reassured him that anthropology would soon lose its object of study.

The exonostalgia of the early ethnographers, including Malinowski, was related to the theory of culture they espoused. It is widely known that despite the differences between the most important schools of anthropology at the time, they all understood culture as a fairly coherent whole, all the elements of which were closely interrelated. For example, Malinowski claimed in "A Scientific Theory of Culture" that culture was "the integral whole consisting of implements and consumers' goods, of constitutional charters for the various social groupings, of human ideas and crafts, beliefs and customs" (1944b: 36; see; Richards 1957). Similarly, Ruth Benedict concluded in *Patterns of Culture*: "A culture, like an individual, is a more or less consistent pattern of thought and action" (1960 [1934]: 53). Such an understanding of culture led to the conclusion that it could only be sustained if changes within it were slow enough to gradually integrate new cultural components into the existing whole. On this model, more thorough and more rapid transformations – such as those described in the famous words of a chief of the Digger Indians that open the second chapter of *Patterns of Culture* (Benedict 1960 [1934]: 33–34) – must unavoidably lead to the "breakdown" or destruction of cultures.

This "achronic," to use Michael Carrithers's term (1992), theory of culture endorsed by the early anthropologists is perfectly exemplified by Malinowski's diary entry dated 13 November 1914:

Despite everything there is a great deal of primitive man in this, going back to the age of polished stone. I also thought about the extreme rigidity of habit. These people cling to certain specific forms of dance and melody – a certain rigid combination of buffoonery and poetry. I have the impression that changes occur only slowly and gradually.

Accordingly, the dominant influence of Western culture could not, in Malinowski's view, lead to the evolution of the Trobriand culture, but only to its annihilation. In this sense, the anthropologist was becoming both a researcher and chronicler of a world that was gradually passing away.

This understanding of culture remained rather common in anthropology for decades to come (e.g., Kuper 2000; Eriksen, Nielsen 2001; Erickson, Murphy 2021). Major changes in the conceptualization of culture were triggered by debates in the late 20th century (e.g., Clifford and Marcus 1986; Clifford 1988; Fox 1991; Carrithers 1992). Specifically, the belief that cultures were vanishing morphed into an idea that there were continuous, uninterrupted, and dynamic changes in cultures. In studying these transformations, anthropologists began to take into account both the active role of individuals and exogenous influences. Furthermore, they also rejected the vision of the fully coherent, integral nature of cultural reality. For example, concluding his analyses in *Europe and the People without History*, Eric Wolf argued: "A culture is thus better seen as a series of processes that construct, reconstruct, and dismantle cultural materials, in response to identifiable determinants" (2010 [1982]: 387). Likewise, Roy D'Andrade famously stated that researching culture "is like attempting to study the physics of moving bodies while living in the middle of an avalanche" (1984: 111). Of course, the belief in incessant cultural variability has had a major impact on exonostalgia (Berliner 2020).

This process is well illustrated by the work of Malinowski, who, a dozen years after his research in the Trobriand Islands, revised his way of theorizing culture (e.g. Malinowski 1938, 1939, 1945). This transformation was primarily influenced by his field research in Central Africa. Importantly, some of these reflections – much less frequently examined by other scholars than his theory of culture in the vein of classical functionalism – can be seen as a harbinger of the changes that have taken place in subsequent years in anthropology.

In his introduction to the edited collection *Methods of Study of Culture Contact in Africa* (1938), Malinowski referred to the despondent insights previously voiced in *Argonauts of the Western Pacific* (1922: xv). Yet, this time, his earlier exonostalgic conclusions were replaced with a particular appeal:

> Instead, however, of lamenting the inevitable, we must face the new, more complex and more difficult task which history has set before us, the task that is of building new methods and new principles of research in order to reclaim the 'anthropological no-man's-land and take up the 'new branch of anthropology ... the anthropology of the changing native'.
>
> (Malinowski 1938: xii)

This passage encapsulates the significant transformation that was taking place both in Malinowski's theory of culture and in the methodology of its study at the time. Having come to regard "an untouched native culture" as a fiction, he argued that all cultures were embedded in the global economic and political system. Accordingly, he wrote in 1939 in the journal *Africa*: "Culture under conditions of change, of more or less rapid assimilation, is the only actuality open to observation" (Malinowski 1939: 27). Crucially, this by no means meant that Malinowski abandoned his functionalist tenets. Rather, he modified them to insist that anthropology should focus on the study of how indigenous institutions coexisted with those of exogenous influences and with new institutions formed as a result of ongoing cultural contacts. In his view, anthropologists should explore the interrelationships between elements of different cultures and the dynamic changes in them.

Common to Malinowski's theory of culture and his methodology from the time of his field research in the Trobriand Islands and in Africa was his dismissal of the assumptions of the historical school in anthropology, which he ironically depicted as "antiquarian and romantic" (Malinowski 1945: 6; see Gellner 1988: 127–137). Closely related to functionalist theory, this position was buttressed at the time he researched cultural change by an awareness of the mythologizing properties of nostalgia. Malinowski insightfully observed:

> The memories of your old informants, especially trustworthy in all matters of tribal lore, depict the Old Times as the Golden Age of human existence. The natural bias of every ethnographer leads him also to regard the untainted Native culture not merely as the *terminus ab quo* but as the *terminus ad quem* of normalcy, as the only legitimate standard of comparison between the pathology of change and the healthy condition of tribalism.
>
> (1945: 27)

Malinowski stressed that while this research approach might seem enticing, it was in fact based on the illusion of human memory, imbued with a longing for the past. This conclusion was fully in line with the contemporary research on the nature of nostalgia (Sedikides et al. 2015; Routledge 2016). What is more, Malinowski reasoned, those that benefitted from the social, cultural, and political transformations painted the past in completely different colours. Rejecting a preoccupation with the past, he recommended focusing on the "psychological reality of today." Only by doing so, he argued, would anthropology be able to properly perform the tasks of both describing cultural reality and helping to bolster necessary social and cultural changes.

All this does not mean, however, that Malinowski's shift to reflection on social change made him relinquish his exonostalgic orientation. What it accomplished was rather an alteration of his sentiments. Referring to the title of Signoret's memoirs (1978) mentioned in the first part of this article, Berliner claims: "Exonostalgia is not what it used to be" (2014: 381). In his view, the classical form of exonostalgia remains on the margins of anthropological interest today. Nonetheless, the pre-apocalyptic tone characteristic of this form of longing for the past – resounding in Malinowski's *Argonauts of the Western Pacific* – continues to be used and heard in many anthropological writings today. Explaining its persistence, Berliner notes

> in these times of never-ending crisis, the effects of globalization, the development of neoliberalism, and the increase in social insecurity, wars, and global warming are all new, often deadly threats for groups and individuals. Nowadays, the anthropologist's fragile other is less the endangered cultural savage, the powerless colonized figure (although this is still the case in certain regions of the world); no, today, it is more likely to be the poor, the

weak, the suffering, the powerless facing social instability, urban poverty, economic migration, war, and political marginalization.

(2020: 80)

The themes detailed by Berliner were often analysed by Malinowski in his late work. For example, in *Freedom and Civilization* (Malinowski 1944a), he addressed war, totalitarianism, and social inequality. He also presented his own stance on the foundations of the democratic society. His work from that time was very important in the development of applied anthropology.[12] In the perspective adopted in this chapter, it is worth emphasizing that Malinowski wanted to give these exonostalgic recognitions a performative dimension. This is a perfect exemplification of Berliner's final observation on exonostalgia: "Hope is never far from nostalgia" (2020: 80).

Conclusion

In this article, I have analysed the work of Malinowski from the perspective of contemporary discourses on nostalgia. Having outlined the most important theories and concepts of this phenomenon, I examined Malinowski's diaries, letters, and research publications in the context of two forms of longing distinguished by Berliner: endonostalgia and exonostalgia. Regarding the former, I have highlighted a very diverse range of longings felt by Malinowski during his field research in the Trobriand Islands. While he understood nostalgia in the manner characteristic of his time, that is, as suffering (*álgos*) arising from physical remoteness from home (*nóstos*), that is Western civilization, as well as family and friends, his diaries are replete with different expressions of nostalgia as well. Some of them illustrate that nostalgia can be an important source of agency. In terms of exonostalgia, I have illuminated the fact that while doing fieldwork in the Trobriand Islands, Malinowski deeply believed that the culture of the local community would completely pass away in the near future. This was consistent with the theory of culture he upheld then, which was characteristic of that stage in the historical development of anthropology. Over time, however, the way Malinowski conceptualized both culture and social change transformed. In both of these areas, he was in the vanguard of the development of anthropology and blazed the trail for new dimensions of exonostalgia too.

My findings support general conclusions about the theorization of nostalgia in anthropology and other social sciences and humanities. Firstly, I have identified very different manifestations of nostalgia and various functions that it can perform. For example, I have shown that it can be linked to both suffering and hope, that it can inhibit and promote agency, and that it can concern the relationship between the present and the past, as well as between the present and the future, etc. Secondly, I have referred to the methodology of nostalgia research. My reading of Malinowski's work demonstrates that the experience of nostalgia can considerably vary, depending on how it is triggered. Thirdly, I have highlighted that anthropologists' intimate diaries can be important resources for the study of longing and other emotions accompanying fieldwork. In my view, it would be worthwhile to study such diaries comparatively as autoethnographic testimonies of endonostalgia. Fourthly, I have elucidated the significant – indeed, fundamental – role of exonostalgia in the history of anthropology. At the same time, I have also used Malinowski's work as an illustration of the persistence of this attitude, which has transmuted rather than disappeared. Fifthly and finally, I have brought into relief the salience of inquiry into the various forms and functions of nostalgia for the development of anthropology. I fully share Amber Reed's belief, that: "Ironically, studies of nostalgia may be the future of anthropology" (Reed 2020: 147).

Acknowledgements

This research was funded by the National Science Centre in Poland from the SONATA grant (No DEC-2021/43/D/HS2/03321).

Notes

1. For example, in a letter to Elsie Masson dated 17 March 1919, Malinowski, then residing on Sanaroa Island, located south of the Trobriand Islands, wrote the following about his nostalgia for Kirivina: "I am feeling a bit homesick after Kiriwina and ethnological work and Kiriwina is assuming a little bit of its old glamour ... a glamour which it had completely lost, in fact the pendulum had swung far out the other way" (Malinowski in Wayne 1995: 116).
2. I discuss the concept of "anticipatory nostalgia" in detail in the third part of the article.
3. Malinowski's views on the study of the past in anthropology are well known (see e.g. Gellner 1988: 127–137). In this article, I explore other aspects of the relationship between the present, the past and the future in his work.
4. It is also worth noting that nostalgia for totalitarianism, colonialism, and the Apartheid is very much present among the young generation (e.g., Reed 2020). It is, therefore, an example of "vicarious" nostalgia.
5. Only Malinowski's diaries from his fieldwork at Mailu Island and his second research expedition to the Trobriand Islands are available in English (Malinowski 1989 [1967]). In Polish, a complete collection of Malinowski's diaries, annotated and prefaced by Grażyna Kubica in 2002, also includes his earlier notes from 1908 to 1915 (Malinowski 2002).
6. For practical reasons, I give the daily dates of the entries instead of page numbers in the English or Polish edition of his diaries.
7. The issue discussed here is also well evident in Malinowski's letters to Elsie Masson (Wayne 1995).
8. Recent psychological literature distinguishes between 'anticipatory nostalgia' and 'anticipated nostalgia'. Cheung Wing-Yee and colleagues wrote on this issue as follows: "In the future-oriented emotions literature, anticipated emotions are what individuals expect to experience in the future in light of the possible occurrence of a certain event (e.g. anticipated pride), whereas anticipatory emotions are what individuals experience now based on their future projection (...). Hence, when we refer to anticipated nostalgia, we refer to what Davis (1979) described as the process whereby one expects nostalgia to arise in the future when looking back on life events. In contrast, anticipatory nostalgia entails that one experiences nostalgia in the present when looking ahead to life events (specifically, future losses)" (Wing-Yee et al. 2020: 512, 513). This distinction is

important because, as empirical research shows, 'anticipated nostalgia' tends to imply positive emotions, in contrast to 'anticipatory nostalgia'.
9 Glenn Albrecht and colleagues clarify that "solastalgia refers to the pain or distress caused by the loss of, or inability to derive, solace connected to the negatively perceived state of one's home environment. Solastalgia exists when there is the lived experience of the physical desolation of home" (Albrecht et al. 2007: 96).
10 William Cunningham Bissell wrote on this subject as follows: "This tragic consciousness of change was critical in the development of anthropology as a form of scientific rationality premised on encountering and encompassing lifeworlds of authentic, aboriginal, and primitive experience – worlds that were seen as disappearing or dissolving in the face of the very forces of colonial modernity that made anthropology possible in the first place" (2005: 223–224).
11 Malinowski's exonostalgia, like that of many of his contemporary anthropologists, went hand in hand with his ambition to explore the areas of the earth that had not been studied in ethnographic fieldwork before. This syndrome is evident in his diaries. For example, on 1 December 1917, he wrote about the Amphlett Islands: "Feeling of ownership: It is I who will describe them or create them." His later description of Gumasila Island, penned on 26 March 1918, was accompanied by the following comment: "Joyful feeling of recognition. This island, though not 'discovered' by me, is for the first time experienced artistically and mastered intellectually." Malinowski's joy, resulting from the intellectual "appropriation" of these territories, blended with his grief ensuing from the conviction that they were being irreversibly transformed. The uniqueness of his position stemmed from the fact that, as he believed, he could be both the first and the last explorer of these lands in their original form.
12 See Marta Songin-Mokrzan's chapter in this volume.

References

Albrecht, Glenn et al. 2007. "Solastalgia: The Distress Caused by Environmental Change." *Australasian Psychiatry* 15 (1): 95–98.

Angé, Olivia, and David Berliner, eds. 2014. *Anthropology and Nostalgia*. New York: Berghahn.

Angé, Olivia, and David Berliner, eds. 2020. *Ecological Nostalgias: Memory, Affect and Creativity in Times of Ecological Upheavals*. New York: Berghahn.

Appadurai, Arjun. 1996. *Modernity at Large: Cultural Dimensions of Globalization*. Minneapolis and London: University of Minnesota Press.

Bartmański, Dominik. 2022. "Post-Revolutionary Nostalgia." In *Matters of Revolution. Urban Spaces and Symbolic Politics in Berlin and Warsaw After 1989*, by Dominik Bartmanski, 86–124. London: Routledge.

Batcho, Krystine Irene. 2020. "Nostalgia: The Paradoxical Bittersweet Emotion." In *Nostalgia Now: Cross-Disciplinary Perspectives on the Past in the Present*, edited by Michael Hviid Jacobsen, 31–46. Abingdon and New York: Routledge.

Batcho, Krystine Irene, and Simran Shikh. 2020. "Anticipatory Nostalgia: Missing the Present before It's Gone." *Personality and Individual Differences* 98: 75–84.

Bauman, Zygmunt. 2017. *Retrotopia*. Cambridge: Polity Press.

Beiser, Morton. 2004. "Trauma, Time and Mental Health: A Study of Temporal Reintegration and Depressive Disorder among Southeast Asian Refugees." *Psychological Medicine* 34: 899–910.

Benedict, Ruth. 1960 [1934]. *Patterns of Culture*. New York: Mentor Books.

Berliner, David. 2014. "On Exonostalgia." *Anthropological Theory* 14 (4): 373–386.

Berliner, David. 2020. *Losing Culture: Nostalgia, Heritage, and Our Accelerated Times*. Translated by Dominic Horsfall. New Brunswick, Camden: Rutgers University Press.
Bissel, William Cunningham. 2005. "Engaging Colonial Nostalgia." *Cultural Anthropology* 20 (2): 215–248.
Bissel, William Cunningham. 2014. "Afterword: On Anthropology's Nostalgia – Looking Back/Seeing ahead." In *Anthropology and Nostalgia*, edited by Olivia Angé and David Berliner, 213–223. Oxford: Berghahn.
Bonnett, Alastair. 2010. *Left in the Past: Radicalism and the Politics of Nostalgia*. New York: Bloomsbury.
Boym, Svetlana. 2001. *The Future of Nostalgia*. New York: Basic Books.
Carrithers, Michael. 1992. *Why Humans Have Cultures: Explaining Anthropology and Social Diversity*. Oxford: Oxford University Press.
Clifford, James. 1988. *The Predicament of Culture: Twentieth-Century Ethnography, Literature, and Art*. Cambridge, MA: Harvard University Press.
Clifford, James, and George E. Marcus. 1986. *Writing Culture: The Poetics and Politics of Ethnography*. Berkeley: University of California Press.
Cross, Gary. 2015. *Consumed Nostalgia: Memory in the Age of Fast Capitalism*. New York: Columbia University Press.
D'Andrade Roy. 1984. "Cultural Meaning Systems." In *Culture Theory: Essays on Mind, Self and Emotion* edited by Richard Schweder and Robert A. LeVine, 88–119. Cambridge: Cambridge University Press.
Davies, James, and Dimitrina Spencer, eds. 2010. *Emotions in the Field: The Psychology and Anthropology of Fieldwork Experience*. Stanford: Stanford University Press.
Davis, Fred. 1979. *Yearning for Yesterday: A Sociology of Nostalgia*. New York: Free Press.
Dickens, Charles. 1979 [1857]. *Little Dorrit*. Oxford: Clarendon.
Dodman, Thomas. 2018. *What Nostalgia Was? War, Empire and the Time of a Deadly Emotion*. Chicago: University of Chicago Press.
Erickson, Paul A. and Liam D. Murphy. 2021. *A History of Anthropological Theory*. Toronto: University of Toronto Press.
Eriksen, Thomas Hylland, and Finn Silvert Nielsen. 2001. *A History of Anthropology*. London: Pluto Press.
Firth, Raymond. 1989 [1966]. "Introduction." In *Diary in the Strict Sense of the Term*, edited by Bronisław Malinowski, xi–xix. London: Athlone Press.
Fox, Richard G. ed. 1991. *Recapturing Anthropology: Working in the Present*. Santa Fe: School of American Research Press.
Galway, Lindsay P. et al. 2019. "Mapping the Solastalgia Literature: A Scoping Review Study." *International Journal of Environmental Research and Public Health* 16 (15): 1–24.
Geertz, Clifford. 1967. "Under the Mosquito Net." *The New York Review* 9 (4): 12–13.
Gellner, Ernest. 1988. *Language and Solitude: Wittgenstein, Malinowski and the Habsburg Dilemma*. Cambridge: Cambridge University Press.
Goulding, Christina. 2002. "An Exploratory Study of Age Related Vicarious Nostalgia and Aesthetic Consumption." *Advances in Consumer Research* 29: 542–546.
Hann, Chris. 2014. "Why Post-Imperial Trumps Post-Socialist: Crying Back the National Past in Hungary." In *Anthropology and Nostalgia*, edited by Olivia Angé and David Berliner, 96–122. Oxford: Berghahn.
Harris, Marvin. 1967. "Diary of an Anthropologist." *Natural History* 76: 72–74.
Herzfeld, Michael. 2005 [1996]. "Structural Nostalgia: Time and the Oath in the Mountain Villages of Crete." In *Cultural Intimacy: Social Poetics in the Nation-State*, by Michael Herzfeld, 147–182. New York: Routledge.

Herzfeld, Michael. 2021. "Anthropology and Nostalgia: Between Hegemonic and Emancipatory Projections of the Past." In *Intimations of Nostalgia: Multidisciplinary Explorations of an Enduring Emotion*, edited by Michael Hviid Jacobsen, 129–150. Bristol: Bristol University Press.
High, Holly. 2011. "Melancholia and Anthropology." *American Ethnologist* 38 (2): 217–233.
Hochschild, Arlie Russel. 1983. *The Managed Heart. Commercialization of Human Feeling.* Berkeley: The University of California Press.
Hofer, Johannes. 1934 [1688]. "Medical Dissertation on Nostalgia." *Bulletin of the History of Medicine* 2: 376–391.
Illbruck, Helmut. 2012. *Nostalgia: Origins and Ends of an Unenlightened Disease.* Evanston, IL: Northwestern University Press.
Iyer, Aarti, and Jolanda Jetten. 2011. "What's Left behind: Identity Continuity Moderates the Effect of Nostalgia on Well-being and Life Choices." *Journal of Personality and Social Psychology* 101 (1): 94–108.
Jacobsen, Michael Hviid, ed. 2020. *Nostalgia Now: Cross-Disciplinary Perspectives on the Past in the Present.* Abingdon and New York: Routledge.
Jacobsen, Michael Hviid, ed. 2021. *Intimations of Nostalgia: Multidisciplinary Explorations of an Enduring Emotion.* Bristol: Bristol University Press.
Kubica, Grażyna. 2002. "Wstęp." In Bronisław Malinowski, *Dziennik w ścisłym znaczeniu tego wyrazu*, annotated and prefaced by Grażyna Kubica, 5–36. Kraków: Wydawnictwo Literackie.
Kubica, Grażyna. 2015. "A Flâneur and Ethnographer in Their Home City: The Krakow of Bronisław Malinowski and Feliks Gross. Remarks of a Historian of Anthropology." In *Rytíř z Komárova. K 70. narozeninám Petra Skalníka / Knight from Komárov: To Petr Skalník for his 70th birthday*, edited by Adam Bedřich, Tomáš Retka, 71–82. Praha: AntropoWeb.
Kubica, Grażyna. 2024 (forthcoming). "A Notorious Diarist – Bronisław Malinowski, and His Sinful Publics. Polish Editor's Remarks." In *Andaman Islanders and Argonauts after a Hundred Years*, edited by Aleksandar Bošković and David Shankland. Canon Pyon: Sean Kingston Publishing.
Kuper, Adam. 2000. *Culture: The Anthropologist's Account.* Cambridge, MA: Harvard University Press.
Kurlinkus, William. C. 2019, *Nostalgic Design: Rhetoric, Memory, and Democratizing Technology.* Pittsburgh, PA: University of Pittsburgh Press.
Leggatt, Matthew. 2018. *Cultural and Political Nostalgia in the Age of Terror: The Melancholic Sublime.* London and New York: Routledge.
Lizardi, Ryan. 2015. *Mediated Nostalgia: Individual Memory and Contemporary Mass Media.* Lanham, MD: Lexington Books.
Malinowski, Bronisław. 1922. *Argonauts of the Western Pacific: An Account of Native Enterprise and Adventure in the Archipelagoes of Melanesian New Guinea.* London: Routledge & Kegan Paul Ltd.
Malinowski, Bronisław. 1938. "Introductory Essay on the Anthropology of Changing African Cultures." In *Methods of Study of Culture Contact in Africa*, edited by Lucy Mair, vii–xxxviii. London: Oxford University Press.
Malinowski, Bronisław. 1939. "The Present State of Studies in Culture Contact: Some Comments on an American Approach." *Africa: Journal of the International African Institute* 12 (1): 27–48.
Malinowski Bronisław. 1944a. *Freedom and Civilization.* London: George Allen & Unwin.
Malinowski, Bronisław. 1944b. *A Scientific Theory of Culture and Other Essays.* Chapel Hill: University of North Carolina Press.

Malinowski, Bronisław. 1945. *The Dynamics of Culture Change: An Inquiry into Race Relations in Africa*, edited by Phyllis M. Kaberry. New Haven, CT: Yale University Press.

Malinowski, Bronisław. 1989 [1967]. *Diary in the Strict Sense of the Term*. London: Athlone Press.

Malinowski, Bronisław. 2002. *Dziennik w ścisłym znaczeniu tego wyrazu*, annotated and prefaced by Grażyna Kubica. Kraków: Wydawnictwo Literackie.

Marquez, Gabriel Garcia. 1983 [1981]. *Chronicle of a Death Foretold*. Translated by Gregory Rabassa. New York: Alfred A. Knopf.

Mills, Richard. 2019. *The Beatles and Fandom: Sex, Death and Progressive Nostalgia*. New York: Routledge.

Nadkarni, Maya, and Olga Shevchenko. 2014. "The Politics of Nostalgia in the Aftermath of Socialism's Collapse: A Case for Comparative Analysis." In *Anthropology and Nostalgia*, edited by Olivia Angé and David Berliner, 61–95. Oxford: Berghahn.

Nazaruk, Maja. 2014. "'Fifty Islands That I Have Never Seen and Never Set Foot on': On the Importance of Bronislaw Malinowski for Comparative Literature." *Anthropos* 109 (2): 626–633.

Newman, Davis B. et al. 2020. "Nostalgia and Well-Being in Daily Life: An Ecological Validity Perspective." *Journal of Personality and Social Psychology* 118 (2): 325–347.

Niemeyer, Katharina, ed. 2014. *Media and Nostalgia: Yearning for the Past, Present and Future*. Basingstoke: Palgrave Macmillan.

Nsele, Zamansele. 2016. "Post-Apartheid Nostalgia and the Sadomasochistic Pleasures of Archival Art." *South African Literary History Project. Special Issue: Nostalgia* 43 (3): 95–116.

Pallister, Kathryn, ed. 2019. *Netflix Nostalgia: Streaming the Past on Demand*. Lanham, MD: Lexington Books.

Porter, Patrick. 2020. *The False Promise of Liberal Order: Nostalgia, Delusion and the Rise of Trump*. Cambridge: Polity Press.

Reed, Amber. 2016. "Nostalgia in the Post-Apartheid State." *Anthropology Southern Africa* 39 (2): 97–109.

Reed, Amber. 2020. *Nostalgia after Apartheid: Disillusionment, Youth, and Democracy in South Africa*. Notre Dame, IN: University of Notre Dame Press.

Richards, Audrey I. 1957. "The Concept of Culture in Malinowski's Work." In *Man and Culture. An Evaluation of the Work of Bronislaw Malinowski*, edited by Raymond Firth, 15–31. London: Routledge & Kegan Paul.

Rosaldo, Renato. 1989. "Imperialist Nostalgia." *Representations* 26 (April): 107–122.

Routledge, Clay. 2016. *Nostalgia: A Psychological Resource*. New York: Routledge.

Routledge, Clay et al. 2013. "Nostalgia as a Source for Psychological Health and Well-being." *Social and Personal Psychology Compass* 7 (11): 808–818.

Salmose, Niklas, ed. 2019. *Contemporary Nostalgia*. Basel: Mdpi AG.

Salvucci, Daniela, Elisabeth Tauber, and Dorothy L. Zinn, 2019. "The Malinowskis in South Tyrol: A Relational Biography of People, Places and Works." In *Bérose – Encyclopédie internationale des histoires de l'anthropologie*. Paris: Berose.

Sedikides, Constantine, et al. 2015. "To Nostalgize: Mixing Memory with Affect and Desire." *Advances in Experimental Social Psychology*, edited by Mark Zanna and James Olson, vol. 52: 189–273. Burlington: Academic Press.

Signoret, Simone. 1978 [1975]. *Nostalgia Isn't What It Used to Be*. London: Weidenfeld and Nicolson.

Stewart, Kathleen. 1988. "Nostalgia: A Polemic." *Cultural Anthropology* 3: 227–241.

Walton, Jeremy F. 2019. „Introduction: Textured Historicity and the Ambivalence of Imperial Legacies." *History and Anthropology* 30 (4): 353–365.

Weber, Max. 1930 [1905]. *The Protestant Ethic and the Spirit of Capitalism*. Translated by Talcott Parsons. London: Unwin University Books.

Wayne, Helena, ed. 1995. *The Story of Marriage: The Letters of Bronislaw Malinowski and Elsie Masson*, Vol. I–II. London: Routledge.

Wildschut, Tim, and Constantine Sedikides. 2020. "The Psychology of Nostalgia: Delineating the Emotion's Nature and Functions." In *Now: Cross-Disciplinary Perspectives on the Past in the Present*, edited by Michael Hviid Jacobsen, 47–65. Abingdon and New York: Routledge.

Wilson, Janelle L. 1999. "Remember When. A Consideration of the Concept of Nostalgia." *ETC.: A Review of General Semantics* 56 (3): 296–304.

Wilson, Janelle L. 2015. *Nostalgia: Sanctuary of Meaning*. Minneapolis: University of Minnesota Publishing.

Wing-Yee Cheung, Erica G. Hepper, Chelsea A. Reid, Jeffrey D. Green, Tim Wildschut & Constantine Sedikides 2020. "Anticipated Nostalgia: Looking forward to Looking Back." *Cognition and Emotion* 34 (3): 511–525.

Wolf, Eric. 1982. *Europe and the People without History*. Berkeley: University of California Press.

Young, Michael. 2004. *Malinowski: Odyssey of an Anthropologist, 1884–1920*. New Haven, CT: Yale University Press.

Zhou, Xinyue et al. 2008. "Counteracting Loneliness: On the Restorative Function of Nostalgia." *Psychological Science* 19 (10): 1023–1029.

Afterword

Malinowski in Context

Aleksandar Bošković

Introduction

How does one evaluate a scholar? Based on her/his ideas, what was written or published, or based on what a scholar did in her/his life? Or the combination of the three? Furthermore, when it comes to ideas – how does one draw a line between what was the intention of the author at the time of the writing, what was the prevailing climate in the scholarly world at the time, and how these ideas are perceived today? Some of these issues were debated in the history of science, either through the change of paradigms (Kuhn 2012), or the actual cultural settings in which most influential theories were developed or accepted (Feyerabend 1993, 1995, 2010) – to name just some most famous examples since the early 1960s. Anthropology is in a particularly interesting situation, given its broad scope and aim, that sometimes bring about interesting misunderstandings. The present volume explores these issues, with the focus on Bronisław Malinowski, and on the centenary of the publication of his most influential work, *Argonauts of the Western Pacific*.

Of course, the work and legacy of one of anthropology's most influential scholars has been debated at least since the volume edited by Sir Raymond Firth (1957). Further interest was aroused after the publication of the *Diary in the Strict Sense of the Term* (1967), and again in the 1980s, as well as in the most recent debates that concern "decolonizing anthropology" (Lewis 2014, 2022; Gupta and Stoolman 2022; Bashkow 2023; Bošković 2023a, 2023b). Polish edition of the complete *Diary* (Malinowski 2002) still has to reach a larger audience. The contributions presented here highlight several different perspectives on Malinowski's work, corresponding to phases of his intellectual development, putting them in perspective of the prevailing political and social climate of the time – as well as pointing to the extent that these debates sometimes speak more about the interpreters, than about the actual topics they were discussing. As a matter of fact, the complexity of Malinowski's work and the extent of his influence span across different disciplines, and the essays here are an important marker of his lasting importance.

Making of a Myth

One of the foremost authorities on Malinowski, Grażyna Kubica, presents a fascinating story about the construction of his ethnic identity – with all the ambiguities

DOI: 10.4324/9781003449768-21

connected to the time when he lived. It is fitting that she also refers in her chapter to Ladislav Holý (1933–1997), another great anthropologist who, as she nicely put it "came from our region, the Central Europe." Holý is not only relevant for his concepts about identity (Holy 1995) but also as an example of another nomad, whose work made great impact on anthropology, especially through his studies of the Berti of Sudan (1991). Kubica points to different important aspects of Malinowski's "Polishness," referring in her conclusion to Rapport's idea of "passing" of individuals through different social identities. Peter Burke adds a perspective based on the family accounts and often conflicting debates. He is the son of Malinowski's youngest daughter, Helena Wayne (1925–2018), the only one from the family who actually wrote about her father (Wayne 1984, 1995), and the relationship that he had with her mother, as well as with their three daughters. Just like a presentation on which it was based (Burke 2022), this essay compares her account with other stories and different family recollections. Some research of the Malinowski family histories have been published recently by the scholars based at Bolzano (Salvucci et al. 2019).

Situating Malinowski and explaining the sources of his interests is present in several other papers. While Peter Skalník looks at the first three decades and some formative influences in Malinowski's intellectual development, Adam Kuper presents him as a product and a representative of a particular moment of Western intellectual and artistic development – modernism. This is a very important aspect of situating Malinowski both culturally and historically, and modernism is explored, especially in regard with his intellectual development and his studies in Leipzig, in the contribution by Krzysztof Łukasiewicz.

Of course, considering Kuper's contribution, there are also questions about the originality of the method – "from the native's point of view" was a perspective already described by Boas in his report of the 1886 research among the Igulik Eskimos (Boas 1888). As Boas' work was well-known in the United States (he was the first Professor of Anthropology, after all), this might explain why some of his students (in practice, almost all first-generation American anthropologists) were less bedazzled by Malinowski than his peers in the United Kingdom and Europe. Was Malinowski aware of all the previous research? Or was it simply the fact, as put by Kuper in the last version of his history of British social anthropology (2015), that he did all that, but that he was simply better than his predecessors?

All these aspects make for an important reading of Malinowski's role for anthropologists (cf. Bošković 2021: 135 ff) – frequently criticized, while at the same time revered as a mythical ancestor. It also makes for an intriguing story of how our discipline was developed, and where it is going.

The Diary and Its Limits

Natalija Jakubova focuses on Malinowski's important relationship with Polish artist Stanisław Ignacy Witkiewicz (1885–1939), starting from the data published in different versions of his diaries. Witkiewicz is also mentioned as inspiring Malinowski's early interest in psychoanalysis in the chapter written by Lena Magnone. The publication of the English translation of a version Malinowski's *Diary* in 1967 created a considerable stir in anthropology. On the one hand, the projected (or imagined) image of the pure, innocent, and objective figure that an anthropologist was supposed to be, looking dispassionately and objectively into the world around him/her, and duly noting all the facts with exemplary accuracy, was shattered. This was also an important moment in the global development, when the world was still recovering from the Second World War, and decolonization was rapidly changing political and social image of the world. Social sciences and humanities were not an exception, and this is also a period that some anthropologists have called the beginning of the "reflexive turn" in the discipline. This publication of the *Diary* presented an image of an anthropologist as a solitary and insecure figure, frequently angry and sometimes even condescending with the people where he lived. A lengthy critical review article was published by Clifford Geertz in September 1967, and there were immediate angry responses by two of Malinowski's former students, Hortense Powdermaker and Sir Ashley Montague, in the issue of 9 November (Montagu 1967; Powdermaker 1967). Geertz would repeat some of his points – in a more general context, and in a much more conciliatory tone, as also noted by Kubica in her paper referred to above – in his later chapter in *Works and Lives* (1988). In Geertz's words:

> For this man of "lively powers of personal contact," everything local and immediate in the South Seas seems to have been emotionally offstage, a profitable object of observation or a petty source of irritation. For more than three years, this "diary" suggests, Malinowski worked, with enormous industry, in one world, and lived, with intense passion, in another.

Should the *Diary* have been published at all? It was clear that it was never intended for publication. The Introduction written by one of his former students and friends, Raymond Firth was immediately recognized as an exercise in "damage control" (Geertz 1967), and anthropologists like Fredrik Barth or (another former participant in Malinowski's seminars) Sir Edmund Leach were very critical of publication of something that was clearly not intended for the wider audience.

In her unpublished paper, "Notorius Diarist," Grażyna Kubica (2023) presents a lengthy and very detailed discussion about the reactions to the publication of the *Diary*. She traces different readings and interpretations, problems (real or imagined with translation), as well as how different decades (1960s, 1970, 1980s…) meant shifts in the approaches to this work. She is also uniquely positioned for this type of analysis, as she prepared and edited the full version of his *Diaries*, which were published in Polish, in 2002. Unfortunately, the text of this book remains for the most part unknown to non-Polish readers, with the exception of passages quoted by Young in his biography (2004: 107–120).

It seems that much more useful observations could be based on the actual ethnographic notes, as remarked by Firth, several decades after the publications of the "first" book:

> To trace out just what cognitive and emotional elements have been involved in an anthropologist's interpretation of a particular event or situation is

probably impossible. Even with all the evidence of the "Diary", and our increasing knowledge of Malinowski's family circumstances and Polish background it is still a matter of speculation just how and indeed if such personal factors entered into his assessment of the role of the "paramount" Tabalu chief To'uluwa in the Trobriands in 1915-18, or of the meaning of the magical spells he collected.

(Firth N.d.: 11)

Finally, the whole debate about the personality of Malinowski (as "revealed" in the *Diary*) and the role of anthropologists in general is probably best seen in the whole context of the "reflexive" (perhaps today one would use the term "decentring" or "decolonizing") narrative, with the risk that the interpretations form worlds that are very different from the ones that are actually described by the scholars whose works are analysed (in this case, Malinowski). This was already noted by Leach when he criticized Geertz's book (1989), and is explained in much more detail by Kubica in her chapter.

The importance of the *Diary*, its characterization, and impact on scholarship are all discussed in the contributions by Jakubova, Kuper, Lipowsky and Brzeziński – so it is an aspect of Malinowski's legacy very much present in this volume.

Genealogies and Influences

Anthropologists – not unlike other people – tend to construct genealogies, with appropriate mythical ancestors. Malinowski is an important ancestor of a line of research in British social anthropology, but his influence can also be traced in alternative genealogies of the study of myth by anthropologists, or by another line, tracing individualism, from Boas, through Malinowski, to Firth, Barth, and Rapport. In another aspect, when it comes to methodology and meaning of anthropology as a discipline, at least two of the participants in the present volume (Kubica, Kuper) are Malinowski's descendants.

Anna Engelking presents a story of Malinowski's relationship with Józef Obrębski (1905–1967), his former doctoral student, and another – although considerably less known – brilliant Polish anthropologist. This is part of the excellent research that she has been doing for quite some time and includes excellent examples of presenting the ways of "how institutions think" (in this case, the Rockfeller Foundation). As many contributions are in communication with each other, Obrębski is also mentioned in Kubica's chapter.

Andreas Lipowsky's contribution looks at different sets of influences from the ones presented by Skalník: the ones that deal with "contemporary theories of the body," and this again opens a possible genealogy. The genealogy presented here is the one from Malinowski's reading of Nietzche in 1912, through to Stoller, Jackson, and Grimshaw. Another possible genealogy, the one that focuses on representations of art and different objects in Malinowski's work, is presented in the chapter by Andrzej Kisielewski, and it includes Boas and Warburg. More specifically,

Kisielewski looks at "the valuables exchanged during the *kula* rite, *masawa* canoes that made this exchange possible, and the cultivation of coral gardens" as art.

The influence that Malinowski had in the area of law (especially "primitive law," as it was called at the time) is explored by Mateusz Stępień. The author points to the curious lack of interest of scholars (especially legal scholars) in Malinowski's extensive writings on this topic, as well as its implications. Stępień also situates Malinowski in the context where he studied and lived, with the important philosophical influences, like the Vienna Circle.

The paper by linus s. digim'Rina deals with the two crucial concepts that explain exchange in the Trobriand Islands, *gimwala* and *kula*. In this small but insightful ethnographic study, digim'Rina manages not only to explain the meaning of these key terms for the Trobrianders' ideas about reciprocity, but to also point to their contemporary meaning and relevance in the local political arena.

Marta Songin-Mokrzan's contribution takes what she sees as a "core anthropological identity," and looks at the *Argonauts* as one of the key components in the construction of contemporary anthropological imaginary. However, she also points at the different aspects that inform a view of Malinowski as someone very much engaged in the world where he lived, as can be seen from his writings about democracy and freedom, among others. This is also connected to some aspects of what Dariusz Brzeziński calls Malinowski's "anthropology of nostalgia." Brzeziński presents a historical context that helps readers situate Malinowski in particular space and time, while also claiming, provocatively, that "nostalgia might be the future of anthropology."

Concluding Remarks

Contributors to this volume open numerous important questions that go across the disciplines. The century of presence of Malinowski as a crucial part of anthropology's past and present also speaks volumes about the discipline's internal struggles and developments. From the initial success, then being overshadowed by Radcliffe-Brown and new approaches, then criticized by many of his former students, Malinowski rose again into prominence in the 1960s, only to be harshly criticized after the publication of his personal notes and feelings. But he was resurrected again, as new archives become available, and more sources tell us about the importance and the influence that he and his students had. To refer to the review article by Leach, even as we speak about Malinowski, we actually speak about ourselves (Leach 1989: 140–141).

Just as Malinowski was attempting "to enter into a soul of the savage," his goal was to understand the world in its entirety.

> In the roamings over human history, and over the surface of the earth, it is the possibility of seeing life and the world from various angles, peculiar to each culture, that has always charmed me the most, and inspired me with real desire to penetrate other cultures, to understand other types of life.
> (Malinowski 1961: 517)

This is compatible with his idea that anthropology "insists (…) upon the principle that in every type of civilisation, every custom, material object, idea and belief fulfils some vital function, has some task to accomplish, represents an indispensable part within a working whole" (Malinowski 1926: 133). This makes him very much our contemporary, and, together with the methodological aspects of his work (the first professionally trained anthropologist to do the type of research that he did), crucial for understanding the history of our discipline (Peirano 1995: 37–41). At the same time, this makes him, in a peculiar way, also a participant (sometimes hardly visible) in many future projects – hence Brzeziński's claim at the conclusion of his essay.

Even with all of his criticism directed at Malinowski and his disciples, Geertz at the same time referred to *Diary* as "that backstage masterpiece of anthropology" (1988: 75) – perhaps recognizing that he was also, as a theorist, one of "Malinowski's children" that he was writing his chapter about. Perhaps we all are.

References

Bashkow, Ira. 2023. "There's more to anthropology's past than most of us know." *American Anthropologist* 125: 177–180. https://doi.org/10.1111/aman.13820

Boas, Franz. 1888. "The Central Eskimo," in the *6th Annual Report, Bureau of American Ethnology*, pp. 399–669. Washington, DC: Smithsonian Institution.

Bošković, Aleksandar. 2021. *Antropologija – od kamenog doba do kompjutera.* [Anthropology – From the Stone Age to Computers.] Belgrade: Evoluta.

———. 2023a. "William Robertson Smith e os primórdios da antropologia social." Aula Inaugural, Universidade Federal de Pernambuco, Recife, Brazil, 15 August.

———. 2023b. "Imagined histories: Why do you say 'colonial' and think of 'anthropology'?" *Antropologija* [forthcoming].

Burke, Patrick. 2022. "Making sense of Malinowski as an ancestor." Paper presented at the conference *The Legacy of Bronislaw Malinowski in Present-Day Social Sciences and Humanities*, Jagiellonian University, Cracow, 27 September.

Eriksen, Thomas Hylland. 2005. *Engaging Anthropology: The Case for a Public Presence.* Oxford: Berg.

Feyerabend, Paul. 1993. *Farewell to Reason.* 2nd ed. London and New York: Verso.

———. 1995. *Killing Time: The Autobiography of Paul Feyerabend.* Chicago, IL: University of Chicago Press.

———. 2010 [1975]. *Against Method: Outline of an Anarchistic Theory of Knowledge.* 4th ed. London and New York: Verso.

Firth, Raymond. N.d. "Reflections of a centenarian anthropologist." Unpublished MS in possession of the author.

Firth, Raymond. (ed.) 1957. *Man and Culture: An Evaluation of the Work of Bronislaw Malinowski.* London: Routledge & Kegan Paul.

Geertz, Clifford. 1967. "Under the Mosquito Net." *New York Review of Books*, Vol. 9, No. 4, 14 September 1967. https://www.nybooks.com/articles/1967/09/14/under-the-mosquito-net/

———. 1988. "I-Witnessing: Malinowski's Children." In: C. Geertz (ed.), *Works and Lives: The Anthropologist as Author*, pp. 73–101. Stanford: Stanford University Press.

Gupta, Akhil, and Jessie Stoolman. 2022. "Decolonizing US Anthropology." *American Anthropologist* 124(4): 778–799.

Holy, Ladislav. 1991. *Religion and Custom in a Muslim Society: The Berti of Sudan.* Cambridge: Cambridge University Press.

———. 1995. *The Little Czech and the Great Czech Nation: National Identity and the Post-Communist Social Transformation*. Cambridge: Cambridge University Press.

Kubica, Grażyna. 2023. "A Notorious Diarist – Bronisław Malinowski, and His Sinful Publics. Polish Editor's Remarks." In: Aleksandar Bošković and David Shankland (eds.), *Argonauts of the Western Pacific and the Andaman Islanders: A Centenary Study in Social Anthropology*. London: Peter Lang. [forthcoming]

Kuhn, Thomas S. 2012. [1962] *The Structure of Scientific Revolutions*. Chicago: University of Chicago Press.

Kuper, Adam. 2015. *Anthropology and Anthropologists: The British School in the Twentieth Century*. 4th ed. London: Routledge.

Leach, Edmund. 1989. "Writing Anthropology." *American Ethnologist* 16(1): 137–141.

Lewis, Herbert S. 2014. *In Defense of Anthropology: An Investigation of the Critique of Anthropology*. New Brunswick, NJ: Transaction Publishers.

———. 2022. "American Anthropology and Colonialism: A Factual Account." In *Bérose – Encyclopédie internationale des histoires de l'anthropologie*, Paris. URL Bérose : article2684.html

Malinowski, Bronislaw. 1926. "Anthropology." In *Encyclopaedia Britannica*, 13th ed., Supplement.

———. 1961 [1922]. *Argonauts of the Western Pacific. An Account of Native Enterprise and Adventure in the Archipelagoes of Melanesian New Guinea*. New York: E. P. Dutton & Co.

———. 1967. *A Diary in the Strict Sense of the Term*. Preface by Valetta Malinowska, introduction by Raymond Firth. Translated by Norbert Guterman. New York: Harcourt, Brace & World, Inc.

———. 2002. *Dziennik w ścisłym znaczeniu tego wyrazu*. Kraków: Wydawnictwo Literackie.

Montagu, Ashley. 1967. "An Agreeable Man." *New York Times Book Review*. November 9. https://www.nybooks.com/articles/1967/11/09/an-agreeable-man-2/

Peirano, Mariza G. S. 1995. *A favor da etnografia*. Rio de Janeiro : Relume-Dumará.

Powdermaker, Hortense. 1967. "An Agreeable Man." *New York Times Book Review* November 9. https://www.nybooks.com/articles/1967/11/09/an-agreeable-man-2/

Salvucci, Daniela, Elisabeth Tauber, and Dorothy L. Zinn. 2019. "The Malinowskis in South Tyrol: A Relational Biography of People, Places and Works," in *Bérose – Encyclopédie international des histoires de l'anthropologie*, Paris. URL Bérose : article1754.html

Wayne, Helena. 1984. "Bronisław Malinowski: The influence of various women on his life and works." *Journal of the Anthropological Society of Oxford* 15(3): 189–203.

———. (ed.) 1995. *The Story of a Marriage: The Letters of Bronisław Malinowski and Elsie Masson 1916–1920*. Vol. I. London: Routledge.

Young, Michael W. 2004. *Malinowski: Odyssey of an Anthropologist, 1884–1920*. New Haven, CT: Yale University Press.

———. 2015. "Malinowski, Bronislaw (1884–1942)." In: James Wright (ed.), *International Encyclopedia of the Social & Behavioral Sciences*, pp. 453–456. 2nd ed. New York and Amsterdam: Elsevier.

Index

622 Downfalls of Bungo or a Demonic Woman by Stanisław Ignacy Witkiewicz 7, 9, 95, 107, 109, 122

Abel, Theodore 31, 35–36, 39, 43
Aborigines Australian 5, 41, 63, 70–72, 74, 220
Adorno, Theodore 134
Africa 1, 4, 6–7, 24, 36, 63–64, 68, 94, 96, 130, 178, 220, 222–225, 229–230, 237, 240, 245
agency 169, 238, 241, 247
Albrecht, Glenn 249
Amiel, HenriFrédéric 163
Angé, Olivia 233, 236
Anthropocene 243
anthropology 1, 6, 8–13, 32, 38, 48, 56, 61–63, 66, 69, 71, 74, 82, 84–89, 94, 96–97, 99–100, 103, 125–126, 128–129, 135, 140–142, 144, 147–148, 125, 154–156, 161–163, 165, 167–169, 171–172, 176–179, 189–190, 193, 195, 213–221, 223–231, 233–234, 243–249, 254–259; anthropological community 154, 217–218, 220; anthropological imaginary 216, 228, 230, 258; anthropology of art 11; applied anthropology 1, 12, 223, 225, 247; cultural anthropology 62, 158, 195; social anthropology 6, 8, 11
Appadurai, Arjun 233, 236
Argonauts of the Western Pacific: An Account of Native Enterprise and Adventure in the Archipelagoes of Melanesian New Guinea by Bronisław Malinowski 1–4, 6, 9, 11, 13, 24, 41, 63, 69, 82–83, 86–89, 92, 95–98, 100, 125, 141, 148, 162, 164–165, 170–171, 177, 180–181, 183, 191, 203, 205, 216, 218, 219, 221, 222, 224, 226, 243–246, 254, 258

Aristotle 171, 173
art 176–186, 204, 206, 240, 257–258; indigenous art 176; *primitive* art 28, 96, 178–179, 186
Asad, Talal 4, 62
Astacio, Patricia A. 47, 51
Auerbach, Nina 113–114
Australia 5, 9, 22, 24, 26, 32, 42, 63, 70–73, 95, 101, 178
Austria-Hungary 23
Avenarius, Richard 4, 32, 65
Azoulay, Ariella 12

Baker, Stuart 115, 121
Barth, Fredrik 19, 141–143, 152, 154, 256, 257
Barthes, Roland 182
Bartmański, Dominik 1, 238
Barton, Roy F. 197
Bashkow, Ira 254
Batcho, Krystine I. 234, 236–238, 241–243
Bates, Daniel. G. 171
Bator, Joanna 28
Baudouin de Courtenay Ehrenkreutz Jędrzejewiczowa, Cezaria 37
Bauman, Zygmunt 236, 238
Behar, Ruth 161, 164–165
Beiser, Morton 239
belief 5, 30, 32, 63, 67–68, 72–73, 87, 93, 98, 101, 147, 162, 179, 181, 183, 185, 208, 211, 221, 231, 244
Bennett, John W. 96, 225, 244
Beran, Harry 177
Berent, Wacław 114, 122
Bergman, Martin S. 134
Berliner, David 233–234, 236–237, 243, 245–247
Bernhard, Thomas 10
biology 11, 167, 169, 195–198, 224, 227
Bissel, William C. 233, 236–237

Blackmore, John T. 86
Boas, Franz 96, 99, 103, 163, 176, 178–179, 186, 243, 255, 257
Bonaparte, Marie 136
Bonnett, Alastair 236
Borkowska, Grażyna 21
Bošković, Aleksandar 254, 255
Boym, Svetlana 235–236, 242
Breton, André 96
Bronte, Charlotte 113
Bryan, Douglas. 128
Brzeziński, Dariusz xvii, 5–6, 12, 42, 257–259
Brzeziński, Stanisław 43
Bubak, Józef 78
Bücher, Karl 86, 88
Buchholz, Kai 172
Burke, Patrick ix, 6, 8, 255
Butler, Judith 161
Bystroń, Jan Stanisław 81

Campbell, Shirley F. 179, 182, 186
canoe 181–185
Carrithers, Michael 10, 245
Cell, John W. 94
ceremony 39, 54
Chałasiński, Józef 37
chemistry 4, 6, 62, 80, 84–86, 93, 99, 110, 169, 224, 227
Chickering, Roger 86–87
childhood 25, 28, 50, 53, 55–56, 162
Christianity 95, 152
Chwistek, Leon 178
civilisation (civilization) 1, 7, 13, 23, 39, 41, 50, 64, 76, 94, 126, 149, 153, 183, 226, 234, 239, 240–241, 247
Clifford, James 1, 222, 245
Cohen, Anthony 19, 30
colonialism 1, 21, 220, 248
Conley, John M. 189, 193
Conrad, Joseph 41, 113
cooperation 10, 34, 38, 86
coral garden 176, 178–179, 183, 185, 258
Coral Gardens and Their Magic: A Study of the Methods of Tilling the Soil and of Agricultural Rites in the Trobriand Islands 1, 6, 11, 88, 94–95, 141, 146, 151, 153, 179, 183, 192
Corning, Peter 198
cosmopolitanism (cosmopolitan) 8, 20, 23, 62, 63, 86, 103
Costa, André O. ii
Crawley, Alfred E. 73

Cross, Gary 181, 236
Csordas, Thomas 161
cultural studies i, 1, 9, 234, 235
culture 1, 2, 9, 11, 19–20, 22, 24, 27, 31, 34–37, 40–41, 62, 67, 79, 81–83, 86, 88, 99–101, 113, 118, 126–129, 131, 153, 155, 165, 167, 170–171, 177, 178–179, 181–183, 185–186, 189, 191, 193–194, 195–198, 220–221, 226, 233–234, 236, 240, 244–247
Czaplicka, Maria 26, 42
Czekanowski, Jan 82, 85
Czerwijowska, Helena 122

D'Andrade, Roy 245
Dąbrowska, Maria 25–26
Dagen, Philippe 96
Damon, Frederick 206
Dargun, Lotar 190
Davies, James 233, 243
Davis, Fred 235–236, 238, 248
Dawid, Jan Władysław 80
decolonization 216, 231, 256
Deleuze, Gilles 161
Deliège, Robert 1
Dembowska, Zofia 122
democracy 12, 29, 40, 42, 210, 220, 226, 258
Descartes, René 161
Desjarlais, Robert 161
Dessoir, Max 80
determinism 65, 126, 195
A Diary in the Strict Sense of the Term (and *Dziennik w ścisłym znaczeniu tego wyrazu*) by Bronisław Malinowski 1, 4, 7, 9, 12, 24, 30, 31, 35, 39, 42–43, 48, 51, 53, 56, 78, 87–88, 93, 99, 102, 107–109, 112–114, 118, 121–122, 124, 135, 163–164, 166, 172, 238, 239, 240–244, 255–256
Dias, Durate 87
Dickens, Charles 241
Didi-Huberman, Georges 176
Digim'Rina, Linus S. 5, 12, 211, 258
Djohari, Natalie 1
Dobrowolski Kazimierz 37
Dodman, Thomas 235
Domanalus, Anna 35
Drapało, Kamila 186
Drew, Agnes 145–146
Dubiński, Krzysztof 119, 120, 122
Dudek, Michał 190
Dulczewski, Zygmunt 34–35

Durkheim, Émile 69, 73, 74, 87, 170, 193
Dynamics of Culture Change. An Inquiry into Race Relations in Africa by Bronisław Malinowski 7, 61, 222–223, 226, 231
Dzięcioł-Pędich, Agnieszka 186
Dziuban, Agata xvii

economy 4, 15, 24, 32, 62–65, 74, 162, 189, 191, 230
ekphrasis 3, 11, 176
Eliot Thomas S. 92, 94
Ellen, Roy 1
Elsner, John R. 178
embodiment 11, 40, 161, 163, 165, 167–168, 171–172
emigration 26, 30, 129, 133
emotions 93, 161, 164–165, 172, 174, 176–177, 184, 206, 233–234, 237, 239–243, 247, 248–249
empiriocriticism 85, 86
energeticism 86, 87
Engelking, Anna 6, 10, 37, 141–142, 154–155, 257
England 24, 26, 29, 34, 49, 53, 95, 101, 131, 143–144
epistemic virtues 9, 79, 87, 89
Erickson, Paul A. 171, 245
Eriksen, Thomas H. 1, 245
Espagne, Michel 86, 124
Estreicher, Stanisław 32, 38, 43, 190
ethnographer 3, 9–10, 24, 81–82, 94, 98–103, 148–149, 152, 162, 164, 168–169, 210, 246
European Union 40
evolutionism 67, 87, 163, 169, 214
exogamy 5, 66, 69, 73–74

fascism 30, 64, 130
Ferguson, James 220, 222–223
Feuchtwang, Stephen 225
Feuerhahn, Wolf 87
Feyerabend, Paul 254
fieldwork 3, 5, 30, 32, 36, 48, 51, 53, 62–64, 70, 72, 74, 94, 97–98, 125, 140–141, 143–147, 149–151, 153, 155, 163–165, 168–172, 189, 203, 210, 216–224, 233–234, 239–240, 242–243, 247–249
Firth, Raymond 1, 6, 17, 27, 41–42, 62, 71, 94, 143, 189, 222, 242, 254, 256–257
Flis, Andrzej 32, 65, 172–173, 192, 195
Flis, Maria xvii, 157, 198

Foks, Freddy 1, 148–149, 152, 155–157, 194
Fortune, Reo 206
Fox, Richard.G. 245
Fratkin, Elliot M. 173
Frazer, Jame 66–69, 74–75, 92, 95, 97, 100
freedom 1, 40, 42, 62, 131, 169, 210, 226, 258
Freedom and Civilisation by Bronisław Malinowski 39, 41, 50, 64, 153, 226, 247
Freeman, Derek 219
Freud, Sigmund 9, 33, 125–131, 135–136
functionalism i, 10–11, 61–62, 67, 74, 82, 92–94, 152, 154, 163, 165, 167, 171–173, 189, 191, 214, 218, 223, 245

Gable, Eric 164–165
Gadowska, Kaja xvii
Galicia 4, 64
Galway, Lindsay. P. 243
Geertz, Clifford 1, 56, 222, 231, 235, 238, 256, 259
Gellner, Ernest 1, 8, 22, 23, 32, 40, 62, 69, 172, 246, 248
Germany 29, 35, 78, 80, 131
Gerould, Daniel 110–111, 119–120
Gęsikowska, Kamila 79
Gimwala 12, 203–211, 258
Glass, Patrick 179
Głębicka, Ewa 26
Golden Bough by James George Frazer 66, 92, 95, 97, 190
Goulding, Christina 236
Greene, Brian 213
Griaule, Marcel 243
Grimshaw, Anna 162, 165, 257
Gross, Feliks 6, 19, 27–32, 35, 37–39, 41–43
Gupta, Akhil 220, 222–223, 254
Guterman, Norbert 1, 113, 118

Habsburg Empire 22–23, 32
Haggard, Rider 96
Hahn, HansPeter 88
Hale, Nathan G. 134
Hall, Northrop F. 143
Handelsman, Marceli 36, 43
Hann, Chris 233, 236
Haraway, Donna 161
Harris, Marvin 235, 238
Harrison, Faye 161, 169, 172
Hartland, Sidney 189, 197

Harvard University 6
Hatfield, Gary 79
Heidegger, Martin 185
Herczyńska, Grażyna 124
hermeneutics 163
Herzfeld, Michael 233, 236–237
Hewitson, Mark 86
Higgings, Mary 133
High, Holly 234, 236
Hirsch, Marianne 8
history xvii, 1, 3–4, 9, 11, 21, 40, 51, 73, 80, 83–89, 92–95, 127, 135, 140, 165, 167, 169–173, 176, 178, 190, 192, 213–214, 217–218, 224, 227–228, 235, 245, 248, 254–255, 258–259
Hochschild, Arlie R. 240
Hofer, Johannes 235, 237
Holy, Ladislav 20, 41, 255
homesickness 236, 239, 241
Hopi 176, 222
Howes, David 161
Hurston, Zora N. 231

identity 2, 8–9, 19–22, 25, 27, 40–41, 49, 213–217, 219, 223, 227–230; identity coherence 237; identity continuity 239, 241; national identity 20
Illbruck, Helmut 235
interpretation 11, 126, 143, 177, 213, 216, 218–220, 226, 256
Iyer, Aarti 239

Jabłoński, Witold 30, 156
Jackson, Michael 161–162, 165, 257
Jacobsen, Michael H. 233, 236, 238
Jagiellonian University 4, 6, 30–32, 38, 42–43, 59, 63–64, 78, 83–84, 101, 141, 153, 158, 190, 192
Jakubova, Natalija 5, 7, 9, 255, 257
James, Clifford 1, 225
James, Wendy 1
James, William 87
Jamin, Jean 96
Jarillo, Sergio 211
Jerschina, Jan 32
Jetten, Jolanda 239
Jones, Ernest 9, 125–126, 128, 130–131, 135–136

Kaberry, Phyllis M. 7
Kant, Immanuel 184
Kaschuba, Wolfgang 88
Katzen-Ellenbogen Edwin W. 80

kinship 40, 70–72, 98, 142–144, 146, 149, 155, 179, 192, 211
Kipling, Rudyard 113
Kisielewski, Andrzej 3, 11, 42, 257–258
Kister, Roman 39
Kittredge, Tracy 152, 156
Klautke, Egbert 88
Kobyłecki, Stanisław 80
Kołaczkowski, Stefan 81
Kopczyńska, Ewa xvii
Koppers, Wilhelm 23
Korsbaek, Leif 61, 64
Kozljanic, Robert J. 167
Krabbe, Wolfgang. G. 172
Kraków xvii, 4–5, 8, 22–23, 25, 28, 30–34, 37–38, 42–44, 59, 63–65, 70, 72, 74, 85, 87, 99, 101, 125, 141–142, 153, 166, 172, 177, 186, 190, 192, 195, 238, 241
Kubica (Kubica-Klyszcz), Grażyna xvii, 1–8, 20–21, 32, 41, 56, 102, 110, 122, 140, 143–144, 155, 163, 166, 172, 190, 231, 235, 238, 240, 248, 254–257, 260
Kuehling, Susanne 206
Kuhn, Thomas 254
Kuklick, Henrika 1
Kula 12, 96–97, 102, 162, 178, 180–185, 203–211, 258
Kuper, Adam 1, 4, 9, 42, 62, 257
Kurczewski, Jacek 189, 194
Kurlinkus, William C. 238
Kurlinkus, William C. 238
Kuryłowicz, Jerzy 30, 37
Kutrzeba, Stanisław 34
Kutrzeba-Pojnarowa, Anna 154

Labbé, Morgane 140–141, 148, 153
laboratory 79–80, 85, 87–89
language 2, 21, 26, 31, 32, 34, 37, 42, 88, 93, 100–101, 107–108, 122, 146, 166, 170–172, 176, 182, 186, 189, 206
law xvii, 4, 11, 24, 32, 81, 84, 93, 126, 128, 153, 179, 183, 189, 193–198, 258
Leach Jerry W. 211
Leach, Edmund R. 6, 179, 256–258, 211, 222
Lebensphilosophie 11, 85, 165–167, 171, 173
Ledvinka, Tomáš 189
Leggat, Matthew 238
Leighton, Alexander H. 133
Leipzig 5, 9, 36, 64, 74, 78–83, 85–89, 93, 101, 112, 166, 241, 255

Leipzig School 78, 86–88
Lepani, Katherine 211
Lepowsky, Maria 206
Leuba, John 130
Lewis, Herbert S. 254
Liep, John 206
Linkiewicz, Olga 142
Linton, Ralph 19
Lipowsky, Andreas 5, 11, 12, 85, 172, 257
literature 4, 9, 29, 31, 42, 63, 74, 81, 83, 92, 95, 107, 112–114, 122, 146, 163, 172, 189, 206, 233, 248
Lizardi, Ryan 236
London 5, 7, 22, 24–26, 28–31, 33–34, 37–41, 49, 64, 66, 70–72, 74, 85, 100–101, 103, 130–132, 136, 141–145, 148–153, 156, 158, 166, 239
loneliness 240–241
Lowie, Robert H. 86
LSE (London School of Economics and Political Science) 5–7, 10–11, 26, 32, 63–64, 71, 130, 141, 149, 177, 181
Lubaś, Marcin xvii, 19
Łukasiewicz, Krzysztof 4, 5, 9, 28, 43, 255
Łukasiewicz, Sławomir 28
Łuniewski, Witold 124
Lutz, Catherine 161

Macedonia 140–141, 144, 147, 150–152
Mach, Ernst 4, 32, 65, 85–86, 99, 171, 173
Macintyre, Martha 206
magic 1, 3, 6, 11, 25–26, 48, 51, 63, 66, 68, 88, 94, 97–98, 146–149, 151, 153, 179, 181, 183, 185–186, 189, 192, 194, 211, 227
Magnone, Lena 9, 41, 124–125, 255
Mailu Island 248
Malinowska (Masson), Elsie 6, 42, 47, 52, 98, 169, 186, 240–242, 248
Malinowska (Swann) Valetta 6, 39
Malinowska Józefa 25
Manganaro, Marc 97
Mańkowski Bolesław 80
Marett, Robert R. 99
Marquez, Gabriel G. 244
Masawa 178, 181–183, 258
Mascia-Lees, Frances E. 163
Massim 206, 210–211
Massonimus, Marian 80
mathematics 4, 32, 62, 64, 74, 110
Mauss, Marcel 96, 214
Mead, Margaret 219
melancholy 25, 235, 238

Melanesia 63–64, 68, 74, 94, 221–222, 227, 239, 241
Melbourne 6, 22, 101, 241
Meloni, Maurizio 198
metamorphosis 108, 115
methodology 1, 12, 24, 80, 83, 86, 162–163, 165, 168–173, 216, 222–224, 230, 245–247, 257
methods 3, 67, 69, 86, 89, 97, 99, 124, 132, 144, 146–147, 168, 170, 177, 209–210, 215, 220, 223–224, 227–230, 236, 245
Mexico xvii, 1, 6, 49, 229
Michalski, Stanisław 43
Micińska, Anna 122
MiklouchoMaclay, Nikolai N. 211
Mills, David 1
Mills, Richard 236
Młynarski, Feliks 84
modernism 9, 92–93, 95–96, 255
Molik, Witold 78
Mond, Robert 5, 64
monism 8, 87
Montemora, Tina 56
Morstin, Ludwik H. 80
Mosko, Mark 189, 200, 211
Moszyński, Kazimierz 33, 141, 149, 150, 152–153, 155–156, 158
Motyka, Krzysztof 194, 198
movement 9, 22, 29, 32, 36, 40, 62, 82, 96, 102, 116–117, 120, 124–128, 130–131, 135, 172, 195, 227
Mucha, Janusz 42, 62
multiverse 12, 213, 215–217, 222–223, 230
Murdock, George 190
Murphy, Liam D. 245
mwali 180–181
Mylik, Mirosław 84

Nadkarni, Maya 237
national socialism 64
nationalism 8, 23, 40
Nawroczyński, Bogdan 79, 80, 84
Nazaruk, Maja 235, 241
New Guinea 5, 7, 9, 32, 42, 64, 68, 70, 95, 97–98, 101, 125, 179, 180, 209–211
New Haven 6, 39, 54, 134
New York City 7, 31, 35, 38–39, 42–44, 54, 56, 135
Newman, Davis B. 238
Nielsen, Finn S. 1, 245
Niemeyer, Katharina 236
Nietzsche, Friedrich 10, 85, 114, 121–122, 161, 166–168, 171–172

266   Index

Nitsch, Kazimierz 30, 33, 43, 141, 143, 145, 151, 155
North, Michael 95
nostalgia 8, 12, 25, 42, 233–243, 246–249, 258; nostalgia studies 12, 233, 241
notebook 112, 163–164, 168
Notes and Queries on Anthropology 9, 97, 98, 99
Nowak, Jacek xvii
Nowakowski, Stefan 37
Nsele, Zamansele 233, 236–237

Oberbozen (Soprabolzano) 17, 49, 52–53, 55, 64, 141, 143, 145, 151
Obrębska (Obrębska-Jabłońska), Antonina 30, 43, 143, 155–156
Obrębska, Maria 156
Obrębski, Józef 6, 10, 19, 20–21, 30–31, 36–38, 41, 83, 140–156, 257
Oceania 68, 70, 94, 96
Ochorowicz, Julian 79
Ochorowicz, Julian 79
Olderogge, Dmitri A. 61
Omarakana 5
Onoge, Omafume F. 225
ontological security 241–242
ontology 197
ornamentation 181–182, 186
Ossowska, Maria 37
Ostwald, Wilhelm 80, 85–87
Oxford 42, 96

Pacific Islands 178
Pałecki, Krzysztof 190
Pałecki, Krzysztof 190
Pallister, Kathryn 236
Paluch, Andrzej 32, 62, 172–173
Parin, Paul 134
Parsons, Talcott 196
participant observation 97, 165, 170, 189, 241, 216, 218–220, 223, 230
Paskauskas, Andrews R. 136
Pawlicki, Stefan 84, 87
Peirano, Mariza G. 259
Pels, Peter 87
Petrażycki, Leon 194
philosophy 4, 32–33, 61–62, 64–65, 74, 79, 80–85, 87, 95, 97, 99, 133, 141, 161, 165, 167–169, 171, 185
physics 4, 62, 64, 80, 85, 93, 95, 99, 103, 169, 225, 245
Piddington, Ralph 195
Pieter, Józef 7, 28, 31, 37, 42, 46

Piotrowski, Jerzy 81
Polgar, Steven 225
Polish Academy of Arts and Sciences (Kraków) 33–34, 38–39, 42
Polish Institute of Arts and Sciences (New York) 7, 37–39, 42–44
Polish Sociological Institute 82
Poniatowski, Stanisław 37
Poreche (Macedonia) 141–142, 145, 147–149, 151–153
Porter, Patrick 236, 238
positivism 67, 88, 168, 192
postmodernism 214
Pound, Ezra 92
Powdermaker, Hortense 222, 231, 256
Poznań 34–38, 43, 81
Poznań University 34, 35
Pratt, Mary L. 164
Price, Sally 96
primitive societies 128, 193, 221
psychoanalysis 5, 10, 95, 124–130, 134–135, 163, 167, 255
psychology 63–64, 71, 74, 79–81, 83–88, 93, 99, 125–126, 130, 135, 166–167, 234
Pudłocki, Tomasz 25, 43–44
Pulman, Bertrand 124, 136

Rabinbach, Anson 87
Radcliffe-Brown, Alfred R. 92, 96, 170, 198, 217, 258
Rank, Beata 137
Rank, Otto 9, 125, 127–129, 130, 135, 139
Raphael, Chester M. 133
Rapport, Nigel 1, 41, 56, 257
Reed, Amber 233, 236–237, 248
Reich, Wilhelm 10, 130–136, 138
relativism 163, 214
Retingerowa, Otolia 41
revolution 29, 84, 120–121, 127, 131, 146, 217
Richards, Audrey 6, 53, 222, 244
Riegl, Alois 178
Riegl, Alois 80
rite 178, 181, 258
ritual 148, 179, 180–183
Rivers, Wiliam H. R. 94, 96, 99, 100, 124, 135
Riviere, Georges H. 96
Robinson, Paul A. 130
Rockefeller Foundation 10, 30, 37, 132, 140–142, 144, 146–148, 153–156
Róheim, Géza 131–132

Romaniszyn, Krystyna xvii
Rosa, Frederico Delgado 53, 99, 170
Rosaldo, Renato 233, 236
Ross, Dorothy 92–93
Roudinesco, Élisabeth 130
Routledge, Clay 234–236, 240, 241, 246
Royal Anthropological Institute 97, 126
Rubczyński, Witold 80
Rudniański, Stefan 80
Russia 63, 117–120, 125, 172
Russian Revolution 120
Rzepa, Teresa 80

Salmose, Niklas 233
Salvucci, Daniela 242, 255
Schaffer, Simon 103
Schapera, Isaac 189, 193
Schlegel, John 190
Schopenhauer, Arthur 166–168, 171–172
A Scientific Theory of Culture and Other Essays by Bronisław Malinowski 7, 83, 88, 171, 244
Scoditti, Giancarlo M. G. 179, 182
Seagle, William 189
Sedikides, Constantine 234–238, 240–241, 246
Seligman, Charles G. 5, 22, 24, 42, 64, 74, 124, 126, 128
Senft, Gunter 1, 179, 183, 186
Senis, Angela 1
Serementakis, Nadia 161
The Sexual Life of Savages in North-Western Melanesia: An Ethnographic Account of Courtship, Marriage, and Family Life Among the Natives of the Trobriand Islands, British New Guinea by Bronisław Malinowski 1, 6, 37–38, 72, 83, 131–132
Shankland, David 70
Shevchenko, Olga 237
Shore, Marci 23
Sickle, John 142, 144–146, 155–156
Sigg, Gabriele M. 172
Signoret, Simone 238, 246
Simmel, Georg 80
Skalník, Petr 4, 8, 27, 32, 42, 62, 99, 122, 172, 255, 257
Skarga, Barbara 155
Skarżyński, Mirosław 43, 46, 155–156, 158
Słomczanka, Maria 31
Smith, Linda D. 161
Smith, Woodruff. D. 61, 86
Smoleński, Jerzy 38

Smoluchowska, Zofia 42
Smułkowa, Elżbieta 43, 155–156
Smuts, Jan C. 61
social change 94, 238, 246–247
social inequality 131, 247
sociology i, 1, 5, 24, 30, 32, 35, 37–38, 43, 61–62, 64, 66, 70–71, 74, 81–85, 126, 135, 143–144, 169, 236, 240
Songin-Mokrzan, Marta 6, 12, 249, 258
soulava 180–181
Soviet Union 61
Spencer, Walter B. 73, 233, 243, 61
Spiro, Melford. E. 136
Spittler, Gerd. 88
Staff, Leopold 122
state institutions 206, 208
Stepansky, Paul E. 127
Stępień, Mateusz 4, 11, 189, 258
Stewart, Kathleen 236
Stirling, Nina 113
Stocking, George W. Jr. 1, 135, 170, 217, 219, 222, 230
Stoller, Paul 161–162, 165, 257
Straszewski, Maurycy 84
Strenski, Ivan 168
structuralism 214, 230
structures 130, 184–185
Stuart, David 43, 48–50
Stuart, Kathleen 161
Stuart, Rebecca M. 47–53, 55–57
Stuart, Sebastian 49–52
Stuart, Zachary 47–48, 50, 53–54
Suyabokheta/Bomkharimapu 203–204, 211
Świętochowski, Aleksander 79
Sztompka, Piotr 1, 191

Taine, Hyppolite 88
Tamaris (a district of La SeynesurMer) 141, 145–146
Tarnawski, Władysław 29, 31
Tarnowski, Adam 29
Tatarkiewicz, Władysław 84
Tatra Mountains 5, 108
Tauber, Elisabeth 1, 64
theatre xvii, 95, 107, 114, 119–121
theory of art 178
theory of culture 1, 62, 167, 171, 244–247
Thomson, Christina 42, 97
Thomson, Kelly 47–53
Thornton, Robert 32, 99, 122, 172
Thurnwald, Richard 74
Tokabitam 181–182, 186
totalitarianism 30, 63, 226, 247–248

totemism 63, 66–69, 72–75, 179
Trąbka, Agnieszka xvii
tradition 11, 66, 68, 117, 126–127, 161–162, 165–167, 169, 171, 173, 181, 193, 235
Turner, Victor 40
Twardowski, Kazimierz 80

Ulrich, Lucy 47, 49, 56
Üner, Elfriede 86
University of Leipzig 5, 101
University of Melbourne 6
University of Warsaw 36–37, 84
USA 35, 62

Vermeulen, Han F. 99
Vienna 23, 30, 42, 85–86, 101, 126, 128–129, 133
Vienna Circle 99, 258
vitalism 169, 172

Waligórski, Andrzej 6, 29, 31, 37–48, 85–86, 153
Wallis, Wilson D. 100
Walton, Jeremy F. 233
Warburg, Aby 176, 257
Warsaw 21, 36–38, 42–43, 84, 122, 146, 150, 152–153
Wax, Murray 1
Wayne, Helena 6, 21–27, 29, 31, 33–34, 42–43, 47–48, 53–55, 97–98, 101–102, 128, 134, 136, 145, 147, 169, 240, 242, 248, 255
Weber, Max 88, 238
Weiner, Annette 3, 205
Weltanschauung 168
Weston, Gavin 1
White, Geoffrey M. 161

Wildschut, Tim 234, 236–237, 240–241
Willis, William S. Jr. 225
Wilson, Janelle L. 234–237
Wing-Yee Cheung, Erica G. 248
witchcraft 149, 151
Witkiewicz (Witkacy) Stanisław Ignacy 9, 42, 107–112, 116–117, 121, 255
Witwicki, Władysław 80
Wojnowska, Bożena 122
Wolf de, Jan J. 87
Wolf, Eric 245
Wolfradt, Uwe 87
World War I 5, 13, 217
World War II 6, 25, 35, 38, 40, 154, 211, 226
Wundt, Wilhelm 5, 79–81, 86–88, 93, 98

Yale University 6–7, 38, 42, 136, 138, 158, 190
Young Poland Movement 32, 62, 101, 116–117, 120, 172
Young, Michael W. 1, 21, 32, 42, 54–55, 62–63, 72, 78, 88–89, 94–95, 99, 101–102, 166, 172, 177, 189, 206, 211, 222, 235, 238, 240, 242–243, 248
Yugoslavia 141, 146–147, 149

Zagórska, Aniela 42
Zakopane 5, 26, 28, 43, 64, 101, 105, 108–109, 112, 124, 238, 241
Zapotec 6, 96
Zhou, Xinyue 240
Zinn, Dorothy L. 1, 64
Znamierowski, Czesław 36, 43, 81–83
Znaniecki, Florian 34–35, 37–38, 40–41, 43, 82–84
Żuławski, Zygmunt 28
Zweig, Stefan 23, 240–241

Printed in the United States
by Baker & Taylor Publisher Services